Joining Places

The John Hope Franklin Series in African American History and Culture

Waldo E. Martin Jr. and Patricia Sullivan, editors

Anthony E. Kaye

Joining Places

Slave Neighborhoods in the Old South

The University of North Carolina Press   Chapel Hill

Designed by Jacquline Johnson
Set in Janson
by Keystone Typesetting, Inc.

This book was published with the assistance of the John Hope
Franklin Fund of the University of North Carolina Press.

Parts of this book originally appeared in "Neighbourhoods and Solidarity
in the Natchez District of Mississippi: Rethinking the Antebellum Slave
Community," *Slavery and Abolition* 23 (April 2002): 1–24, reprinted in
revised form by permission of Routledge; and "Slaves, Emancipation, and
the Powers of War: Views from the Natchez District of Mississippi," in
The War Was You and Me: Civilians in the American Civil War, edited by
Joan E. Cashin, 60–84 (Princeton: Princeton University Press, 2002).

The paper in this book meets the guidelines for permanence and
durability of the Committee on Production Guidelines for Book
Longevity of the Council on Library Resources.

Library of Congress Cataloging-in-Publication Data
Kaye, Anthony E.
Joining places : slave neighborhoods in the old South / Anthony E. Kaye.
p. cm. — (The John Hope Franklin series in African American history and
culture)
Includes bibliographical references and index.
ISBN 978-0-8078-3103-8 (cloth: alk. paper)
ISBN 978-0-8078-6179-0 (pbk. : alk. paper)
1. Slaves — Mississippi — Natchez (District) — Social life and customs.
2. Slaves — Mississippi — Natchez (District) — Social conditions.
3. Community life — Mississippi — Natchez (District) — History.
4. Neighborhood — Mississippi — Natchez (District) — History. 5. African
American neighborhoods — Mississippi — Natchez (District) — History.
6. Natchez (Miss.: District) — Social life and customs. 7. Natchez (Miss.:
District) — Social conditions. 8. Slaves — Southern States — Social life and
customs — Case studies. 9. Slaves — Southern States — Social conditions —
Case studies. 10. Community life — Southern States — Case studies.
I. Title.
E445.M6K29 2007
307.3'36208996073076226 — dc22   2007003201

cloth 11 10 09 08 07 5 4 3 2 1
paper 13 12 11 10 09 5 4 3 2 1

To Melissa

Contents

Maps

Acknowledgments

This book has benefited from the help of many people, and it is a pleasure, at long last, to thank them in print. Several archivists went beyond the call of duty. Gordon Cotton kindly put me up during a research visit to the Old Courthouse Museum in Vicksburg, Mississippi. Anne Lipscomb Webster answered queries for years after my work at the Mississippi Department of Archives and History. Mimi Miller of the Historic Natchez Foundation afforded me the rare pleasure of working all night in the archives.

I received financial support from several institutions. Primary research got off the ground during fellowships at the National Museum of American History. The Princeton University Committee on Research in the Humanities and Social Sciences provided a grant for work in the Natchez Trace Collection. Time for sustained work on revisions was provided by a semester leave courtesy of the Pennsylvania State University College of Liberal Arts and by a course release funded by the Institute for the Arts and Humanities and the Richards Civil War Era Center.

Several people at these and other institutions took me under wing and contributed to this book in their own singular ways. Pete Daniel, famous for his boon companionship, is also a gifted teacher who taught me what I needed to know about the South but did not know to ask and would never have read in books. Dale Tomich initiated me into the Caribbean history of slavery. John M. Murrin showed me what historical problem solving looked like and what a comparative approach to American history could accomplish. Leslie S. Rowland and Steven F. Miller of the Freedmen and Southern Society Project at the University of Maryland, College Park, renewed my engagement with the history of emancipation and Reconstruction. Nan E. Woodruff brought me to Penn State, a kindness for which I repaid her by—I kid you not—buying the house next door. That she responded by making our neighborhood the warmest place I have ever lived will surprise no one who knows her. William A. Blair has made collaborating with the Richards Center a provocative endeavor in institution and community building. I first met Michael Rudolph West in graduate school at Columbia University, and he has been a constant source of strength ever since. Eric Foner has been an abiding source of encouragement and good counsel. Barbara Fields, who directed my dissertation work, has brought her uncommon grace and generosity to many roles — teacher, adviser, mentor, and friend.

Many people have contributed their time and intelligence to this book. Anne Y. Brinton, James M. Lewis III, and Nancy Worth were conscientious researchers. Ariela J. Gross and Christopher Morris generously shared research. Stephen D. Weaver of Penn State's Gould Center for Geography Education did the maps. Joan E. Cashin, Gad Heuman, and James Walvin improved this book by editing two previously published pieces. I am grateful for the comments and suggestions of those who read the manuscript in various forms: Elizabeth Blackmar, Bill Blair, Kerry Candaele, Nancy Cohen, Pete Daniel, Drew Gilpin Faust, Barbara Fields, Eric Foner, Katherine M. Franke, Ariela Gross, Ellen Kaye, Peter Kolchin, Christopher Morris, Edwin S. Redkey, Adam Rome, Marie J. Schwartz, Carey Shulman, Dale Tomich, Michael Wayne, and Michael West. Michael P. Johnson and Walter Johnson gave astute advice as reviewers for the University of North Carolina Press. At UNC Press, Lewis Bateman saw the potential of this book, and Charles Grench saw it into production with his usual finesse.

Friends and family who sustained me in this work are too numerous to mention, but a few people require notice here. The manuscript proved to be one of the last books my father, Robert Kaye, read before he died. I will be forever grateful for his characteristically generous evaluation of this portrait of slave society: "I can see it." It has not been lost on my five-year-old daughter, Vivian, that I have been working on this book all her days, and her relationship to it has taken on some of the intensity and ambivalence of a sibling rivalry. I hope when she finally gets to read these words her father's preoccupations will finally make some sense. This book needed someone who believed in it without reservation and without fail, and it is dedicated to my wife, Melissa Kaye, because you were the one.

Introduction

John Wade, a slave on the Terry plantation in Jefferson County, Mississippi, could claim many friends in his vicinity. Wade knew Aaron Barefield and his people on Poplar Hill well enough to take note when Barefield's son went to Natchez during the Civil War in the wake of a Union raid into the hinterland. And Barefield the younger knew his father's friend well enough to brighten at the mention of Wade's name years later: "I knew John Wade during the war and know him yet, too; in fact I knew him before the war; we lived on joining places."[1] Wade also had other contacts on Poplar Hill. "I have known Harriet Pierce all my life," he recalled; "we lived in the same neighborhood."[2] "Neighborhood," this seemingly prosaic term, opens a window with a panoramic view of antebellum slave society.

Slave neighborhoods cut across Jefferson County, up and down the Natchez District in Mississippi, and throughout the South. They prevailed from the Chesapeake to the trans-Mississippi West and virtually everywhere in between in the Upper South and the Old Southwest. This is where Frederick Douglass grew up, Nat Turner launched his inspired revolt, men and women struggled in obscurity all their days. In some locales, neighborhoods marked the field of discipline or the terrain of marriage and family life, the dominion where a coterie of old folks held sway. In others, this was the circuit worked by slave preachers, where seekers repaired to their praying grounds and convened for religious meetings. In some precincts, neighborhoods were the quarters of every kind of fraternizing. The geography of kinship, work, sociability, and struggle overlapped with neighborhoods in different ways in different regions. Neighborhoods might encompass some of these social relations or all of them and more. Everywhere neighborhoods covered different geographic areas. In short, they were pervasive but not uniform. Neighborhoods in the Natchez District, then, were similar but not identical to those migrants had left in the Upper South.

The slave neighborhoods in the Natchez District were, in their physical geography, in the works for thousands of years. The Mississippi River collected soil during the last ice age from an area encompassing two-fifths of what

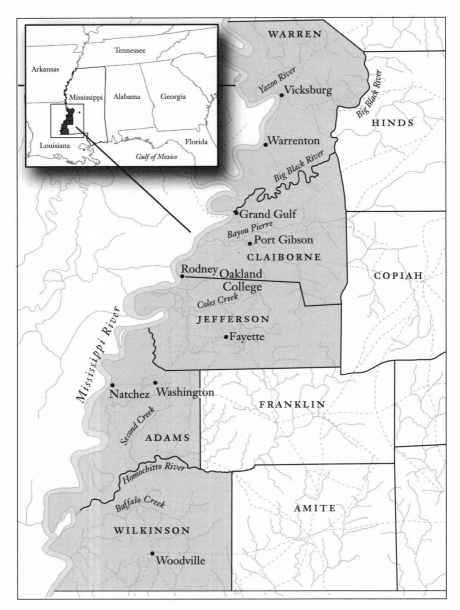

Map 1. Natchez District of Mississippi

is now the United States. The Father of Waters sifted the riches of the soil, congealed them into a claylike alluvium, and deposited it along the riverbank in a narrow strip, with a crest of bluffs. Winds whipped up the fine silt of the Far West and spread it over the hillsides and a swath of land to the east, where it laid up in a deep, brown loam.[3]

Planters began turning this fertile soil during the eighteenth century, when the region was still a modest prize traded in diplomatic settlements among the French, English, and Spanish, who named it the Natchez District. Southwest Mississippi was an anchor in the Jeffersonian vision of a commercial farming republic during the 1790s. The Louisiana Purchase finally guaranteed American sovereignty over the length of the Mississippi and an outlet for exports from the cotton frontier. By then, Congress had already decided the slaves in the district would be mostly American born. The act organizing the Mississippi Territory in 1798 prohibited importing slaves from Africa or anywhere else abroad and authorized slaveholders to bring their chattels from anywhere in the United States. Many of those slaves had come from Africa by the trans-Atlantic trade before undertaking their second middle passage to Mississippi. Even after the United States dropped out of the international slave trade, Americans smuggled an untold number of Africans into the Deep South, Mississippi included.[4]

Slaves were essential to local planters' hopes for the region. One coterie declared in a petition to Congress that without slavery, their farms would be merely "waste land."[5] From their vantage point, the district still extended beyond the territory to include lands along the west bank of the Mississippi. The district also persisted as a regional identity among the planters, many of whom presided over plantations in Louisiana or Mississippi from a town seat in Natchez. By the time Mississippi joined the Union in 1817, settlers had already organized the district into five counties: Wilkinson, Adams, Jefferson, Claiborne, and Warren.[6] (See map 1.)

Here slaves carved out neighborhoods in one of the most princely domains in the Cotton Kingdom. Many arrived from the Upper South in a forced march accompanying owners, and most had been acquired via the slave trade. Throughout the antebellum period, most slaves were only a generation or two removed from the Upper South.[7] Slaves outnumbered the rest of the population by a ratio of two to one in 1830 and three to one at the end of the antebellum period.[8] By 1840, the Natchez District also included the three Mississippi counties that produced the most cotton in the state, which was now ensconced among the first rank of the United States producing the staple.[9] Wear and tear from all these strivings was already starting to show on the land, most dramatically where the soil collapsed into deep ravines.[10] The district was home to only two of the state's five most productive counties in 1849, none ten years later.[11] Yet these planters still had few peers for riches. Wilkinson, Jefferson, and Claiborne numbered among the dozen wealthiest counties in the country in 1860.[12] The size of slaveholdings in the district, though smaller than those in the Louisiana sugar country and the rice kingdom in the low country, were three times those of the South as a whole, on a par with the South Carolina Sea Islands.[13]

In the Natchez District, slaves defined neighborhoods precisely, as adjoining plantations, because this was the domain of all the bonds that constituted their daily routine. Slaves worked and went visiting on adjoining plantations and attended dances, Christmas celebrations, and other big times there — weddings, religious services, and prayer meetings, too. Slaves courted, married, and formed families across plantation lines. Here slaves told their stories, conversed, gossiped, conspired, and collected intelligence about intimate relations, parties, and other affairs; about the staple, the livestock, and other goods; about newcomers to the neighborhood, drivers, overseers, and brutal owners; about harsh words, whippings, and other run-ins. Adjoining plantations were also where slaves lay out, purloined food, and otherwise contended with the powers that be. Neighborhoods encompassed the bonds of kinship, the practice of Christianity, the geography of sociability, the field of labor and discipline, the grounds of solidarity, the terrain of struggle. For slaves, neighborhoods served as the locus of all the bonds that shaped the contours of their society.

Neighborhoods were dynamic places. To endure, they could not be otherwise. Making places is always a process.[14] Making places under the exactions of slavery and slave trading, which enabled owners to unmake neighborhood ties as readily as slaves made them, was a perpetual struggle. Slaves were continually sent out of the Natchez District after their forced migration from the Upper South. They were sold as punishment, mortgaged for debt, bequeathed to heirs, and pressed into caravans by owners migrating to distant parts along the rolling southern frontier. The planters' exchanges of human property reproduced the plantation household across generations, further into the Deep South, and created a steady traffic in and out of slave neighborhoods in the district. Slaves were forever giving up their neighbors and incorporating folks new to the place. This is not to say that individual people could be replaced exactly; rather, the social relations they had forged, broken by their departure, had to carry on. Men and women still had to keep up all the ties — intimate relations, work, trade, struggles, links to adjoining plantations — that bound neighborhoods together. Slave neighborhoods were in a constant state of making, remaking, and becoming.

Neighborhoods hemmed in and laminated variegated physical and social landscapes. Every neighborhood was a place of kinship as well as discipline, of both work and amusement, of collaboration and strife, of spiritual sojournings and brutal exploitation, of loves and hatreds, of contempt and fellowship, of admiration and indifference, each in myriad forms. The topography had its own sharp contrasts. As assiduously as planters courted King Cotton, most land in the district remained unimproved on the eve of the Civil War. Amid the fields of corn along with the cotton, the countryside was cross-cut with rivers, bayous, creeks; dense with woods; and broken by swamps and hollows, among other wild places. Different places had different uses and hence different meanings. The fields and the great house were places of work and struggle. The wild places were good for worship and for running away. The watercourses were places of transit, between places of work, between work and leisure, between plantations in the neighborhood. The meaning of any given place could change depending on the occasion, the circumstances, the time, or the person doing the comprehending. The quarters, for instance, were places of both rest and work, especially for women, who did the bulk of the washing, the cooking, and all the other reproductive family labor. Certain people and places were more important than others, too. As much as men and women extended ties across plantation lines, the bonds of work and kinship overlapped most among slaves on the same plantation. So the lines of solidarity were strongest there, and the divisions ran deepest as well.

As much as neighborhoods were inseparable from the physical geography, they were also a state of mind. The terrain, stretching out over bottomlands, rolling over hills and up into bluffs, did not shape up neatly into grids, even after slaveholders divvied it up with property lines and laid it out in plantation spaces. What gave the landscape order for slaves was their own sense of place. That slaves in the Natchez District were only a generation or so removed from distant parts only underscores how thoroughly fabricated and socially constructed this sense of place was. Neighborhoods were a mode of understanding society, which slaves mapped along lines of adjoining plantations. The natural geography lent permanence to the social milieu neighbors inscribed on it. And the milieu slaves imagined became deeply embedded in their social consciousness. The neighborhood was a place; the arena for activities of every type; a set of people, bonds, and solidarities; a collective identity. Just as neighborhood, like all collective identities, implied a certain solidarity, so a particular antagonism defined the terrain.

The boundaries of neighborhood founded divisions as well as alliances and led thereby to political boundaries. From the standpoint of neighborhood, slaves, like all people living within social boundaries, were Janus-faced. Neighbors simultaneously looked inward and outward, established conditions for collaboration and imposed conditions on collaboration too, came alive to foes along with allies. Neighborhoods had little meaning apart from notions of insiders and outsiders. Slaves both divided and united along neighborhood lines, deemed some folks neighbors and others strangers. The politics of neighborhood obliged rebels to cross those lines, to forge alliances both within and between neighborhoods. As rebels navigated divisions among slaves, they had to confront owners' formidable presence to boot.

Slaveholders were inextricable figures in slave neighborhoods. The planters had their own neighborhoods, too, bigger than those of the slaves. From the slaves' standpoint, their neighborhood was enclosed within the slaveholders' neighborhood and surrounded by it. Slaves in the Natchez District and elsewhere in the South mounted fewer revolts than their peers elsewhere in the Americas not because they loved master more but because they knew where power was located.

What is most remarkable about neighborhoods is not how little slaves achieved in struggle on these grounds but how much. They used the neighborhood to monitor intimate relations and gain recognition for permanent unions between men and women unrecognized by law. The slaves established the neighborhood as a field where runaways could find respite from increasingly exacting regimes of labor and discipline. The slaves' critical achievement, though, was the neighborhood itself. Despite planters' attempts to control mobility — by the whip, the law, the slave patrol, and the pass system — slaves forged enduring bonds to adjoining plantations. Men and women multiplied the possibilities of courtship, worship, amusement, struggle, and collective identity, of love, faith, pleasure, and solidarity; extended networks of kinfolk, friends, collaborators, and Christians; gave permanence to their neighborhoods by creating and re-creating the bonds that held them together, even as slaveholders constantly sold people in and out of the place. By pressing social ties across plantation lines, in short, slaves attenuated the power relations of slavery and cleared some ground for themselves to stand on.

The boundaries of neighborhood were by no means impenetrable. They marked the horizons of slaves' everyday lives but not their collective experience. People in every neighborhood cultivated family ties beyond adjoining plantations, went visiting, to church, or to work abroad. The powers bolstering slavery, though they converged on neighborhoods, emanated from county seats and the state capital at Jackson, where laws were made and adjudicated and an extensive police apparatus was organized and headquartered. Slaves who navigated paths outside the neighborhood learned a thing or two about law, elections, and the ways of state power. Only during the war did the bonds of neighborhood loosen for the vast majority of slaves, and the bonds of slavery broke soon thereafter.

Slaves transformed the neighborhoods amid the crisis of civil war. The first order of business, to reckon what the fighting was all about, was neighborhood business, too, and slaves enlarged the place in the process. Mobile slaves provided indispensable contacts between neighborhoods. As these men brought home intelligence about the war, folks circulated it from plantation to plantation, neighborhood to neighborhood. In wartime, lines between neighborhoods became more or less as readily crossed as those between plantations. As slaves breached and extended neighborhood boundaries from within, powerful forces penetrated from without. First Confederate authorities, then the Union army proved in tests of will with neighborhood planters that slaveholders were no longer their own masters. Slaves were duly impressed by these new powers abroad in the land — Confederate officers determined to requisition slave labor, to discipline planters sympathetic to the Union, to police compliance with regulations pertaining to King Cotton; Union squads recruiting men for the Federal army, hiring men and women, appropriating plantation property at will. Under Union occupation, men filled the ranks of U.S. Colored Troops and toiled as military laborers, women went to work in camps, and just about anyone could go back and forth to Union lines. Under the blows of wartime emancipation, neighborhood boundaries fell away, at least for a time.

This portrait of neighborhoods reformulates debates that have shaped thirty years of revisionist scholarship on antebellum slavery. It invites historians to think anew about intimate relations, independent production, resistance, and, most broadly, the slave community.

Neighborhoods brought remarkable ingenuity to monitoring a variety of intimate relations. Since Herbert Gutman's pioneering research on the durability of the nuclear family, recent work has emphasized the diversity of slave families.[15] Intimate relations in the Natchez District illuminate the range of unions undergirding this pluralistic structure of slave kinship. Men and women not only married but lived together, "took up," and "sweethearted." Slaves would have puzzled over the scholarly tendency to equate cohabitation with marriage, for they saw the two as having subtle yet important differences.[16] Placing these bonds in their neighborhood context, furthermore, reveals how much couples relied on other slaves to secure even the most intimate bonds. Neighbors assumed responsibility for defining these relationships, articulating them as norms, and enforcing their claims on owners as well as other slaves. The campaign to safeguard bonds between women and men, in turn, was one of the strongest ties binding neighborhoods together.

Neighborhoods also offer a new perspective on the problem of resistance. That framework has enabled historians to order seemingly random acts from absconding and breaking tools to murder and rebellion along a spectrum from accommodation to resistance. Recent work on "everyday resistance" upends this mechanistic structure, giving due weight to the power of rumor, clandestine socializing, and other forms of supposedly accommodationist transgressions.[17] This book shifts analysis from resistance to terrains of struggle and points away from an abstract spectrum of actions to three-dimensional places: neighborhoods. Struggles on this terrain were pervasive and ran in unexpected directions. Slaves made alliances with planters in the neighborhood as well as with other slaves. By the same token, they battled not only owners and their agents but other slaves as well, especially runaways from outside the neighborhood. Slaves turned all the ties between plantations — work, intimate relations, and neighborhood space itself — into sites of contention. Mapping the terrain of struggle reformulates the problem of resistance with the sense of limitations and possibility with which slaves themselves approached it.

At work, the most active site on the terrain of struggle, relations of power between slaves and owners were much the same in staple and independent production. An impressive body of scholarship has shown that slaves across the South produced, owned, and exchanged a diverse mix of crops and handicrafts. Historians of this independent production regard the work slaves performed on their own account as fundamentally different from that performed on owners' crops.[18] Yet the terms of staple production were the key to those of independent production. In the cotton fields, planters defined rules, left direct supervision to overseers and drivers, and monitored results from time to time. Planters intervened likewise in their people's work and trade on their own account. Masters presumed to dictate what slaves could make, to keep tabs on how their crops progressed and on their work for other owners in the neighborhood, to buy most of what they produced, and thus to fix the parameters of the whole enterprise. If planters' control here was imperfect at best, so was their control over staple production. The similarity between the power relations in the gardens and in the fields suggests few aspects of the slaves' economy were truly independent. An offshoot of the staple economy, it is best understood as auxiliary production.

Most of all, neighborhoods cast the slave community in a new light. Community has served as the touchstone of scholarly discourse on antebellum slavery since John W. Blassingame and George P. Rawick introduced the concept to the field in 1972. Historians have subsequently traced the sinews of the slave community in the extended family, a brisk trade in the fruits of independent production, a distinctly African American culture, and resistance across the spectrum. Community, like any productive thesis, has corollaries that further shape debate. Scholars defined the slave community in terms of a universal solidarity that reconciled conflicting interests between slaves, closed fissures of privilege between field hands and house servants, and laid a foundation for autonomy. Autonomy, in turn, enabled the social ties, loyalties, and culture of enslaved people to burgeon unfettered by owners.[19] The common practice of analyzing slaves without reference to slaveholders makes little sense outside this framework. Some scholars, expressing the notion of autonomy in spatial terms, write of "social space," "cultural space," "economic . . . space," the "internal economy," the "underside of slavery"—a veritable underworld where all manner of underground activities took place and subterranean metaphors prevail.[20]

Autonomy's conceptual lock on the historiography is especially striking in the work of scholars who have their doubts about community. Eugene D. Genovese, often criticized by scholars of the slave community, also conceptualizes slave resistance in terms of autonomy. At the crux of the conflict between masters and slaves, he argues, was the master's struggle to make the slave an extension of his will and the slaves' struggle "to assert themselves as autonomous human beings."[21] More recently, scholars have denied claims of autonomy in one context only to affirm them in another.[22] Some cast doubt on claims of universal solidarity yet take autonomy as axiomatic, or vice versa.[23] Still others problematize community and its corollaries, skillfully charting divisions of African nationality or between town and country, only to argue autonomy was slaves' ultimate achievement in a new racial identity.[24]

The community paradigm, abandoned some time ago by social historians in most fields of American history, leaves the historiography of antebellum slavery ensconced in an anachronistic liberal framework.[25] Autonomy, after all, has been the definitive concept of liberalism since its classical origins in the Enlightenment. Philosophers and theorists have posited autonomy as a necessary condition for the exercise of reason; for self-legislating individuals who can make moral choices, calculate their own interests, and keep promises; for a public sphere where citizens competent to form their own judgments engage in rational discourse and fairly adjudicate claims on the individual and the community. Diverse schools of liberal thought posit autonomy as a prerequisite for the rational individual, for political justice, for liberal society itself.[26] If liberal conceptions of freedom seem far afield from the historiography of slavery, consider an arresting formulation that took the autonomy of the slave community to its logical conclusion, "the paradox of the 'free slave.' "[27]

A paradox indeed. Slaves did not conceive of themselves in terms of the autonomous individual predominant in the liberal imagination, which was virtually inconceivable in the neighborhoods of the Old South. Slaves' determination to control their intimate relations, work, trade, and religious practice will not be gainsaid in these pages. These struggles, however, were waged on the grounds of another battle for control over social space, a terrain that slaves were compelled to share with owners. Women and men made secret romantic unions, ran away, bought and sold goods on the sly, made clandestine visits in the neighborhood, and otherwise acted apart from and navigated around owners. Men and women also solicited owners' permission to marry and their attendance at weddings, enlisted them in contentions with overseers, engaged them in trade, asked them for passes, and otherwise contended for slaveholders' cooperation to fasten and sanction neighborhood ties. The scholars of the slave community have changed how Americans think about slavery forever and for the better. Yet slave society cannot be explained in simple terms of autonomy and universal solidarity because it was not monolithic but plural, comprised not a single community but many neighborhoods.

This study builds on the work of other scholars who have challenged the concept of community and its corollaries. Historians of women and gender have recently contributed to a reconsideration of the slave community by consistently registering objections to its corollaries. Brenda E. Stevenson's work on women and families identifies gender as a pervasive fault line in the slave community.[28] Nell Irvin Painter and other scholars have called autonomy into question by examining the profound ramifications of sexual exploitation on slaves' psychology and culture, of the exactions of labor on mothering, of slaveholders' notions of soundness on slave doctoring.[29] Historians of women, gender, and slaveholding households have also broken ground on space as a critical domain of conflict in the Old South between planters and yeomen as well as planters and slaves.[30] Revisionist adherents to the paternalism thesis, particularly Eugene Genovese and Elizabeth Fox-Genovese, have issued the most far-reaching challenge to claims of autonomy. Paternalism forged inextricable bonds between slaves and masters. It made both parties members of a single household where owners routinely intervened in the slave community and slaves lacked the material resources to wrest control over their internal affairs from a resident planter class.[31]

The paternalism thesis, however, requires modifications to make it serviceable in the Natchez District, where a little paternalism went a long way. Owners, by their lights, owed all their people the creature comforts — neat cabins, two changes of clothes in summer and winter, regular rations, conscientious attendance in case of illness, firm but reasonable discipline. Beyond that, it sufficed for planter men and women to display their benevolence regularly on a few important occasions to most of master's people and to confine regular personal attention to just a few slave families, mostly those inherited from the white family's own kin. Owners saw these "family servants" daily, kept up with them and their people, had notions of their personality and character. They appreciated these folks, liked, and in some ways respected them when not frustrated, disappointed, or otherwise infuriated with them. Outside this small circle, owners were not terribly well acquainted with their slaves.

From the slaves' perspective, the psychology of paternalism was not much in evidence in Mississippi.[32] A regime where forbearance and kindness were reserved for a few appeared to the many as something less than the benevolent, orderly mastery the planters thought it was. Slaveholders flattered themselves in thinking they imposed order and regularity on their unruly inferiors. But their exercise of power was more capricious — at once more remote and more volatile — than paternalist doctrine suggested. Owners had different rules for different slaves, and these rules could change from one day to the next. Worked, traded, and punished with caprice, slaves were inclined to think, if their society was to have any order at all, it would have to come mostly from them. Most bondpeople were strangers to the dialectic of the master-slave relation insofar as its intertwining of thought and feeling was concerned.

As these modifications to the paternalism thesis imply, the concept of hegemony obscures more than it reveals about slave neighborhoods. Planters surely exercised hegemony to the extent that it means ruling classes rule, and planters ruled the South. Advocates of hegemony may conclude slave neighborhoods contributed to it, and they would be right, as far as that goes, too. But hegemony is plain wrong to the extent it entails an ideological accord between slaves and owners because paternalism was the planters' ideology, not the slaves'. Yet according to Genovese, paternalism was critical to planters' hegemony because the ideology humanized slaveholders, legitimized their mastery, and forestalled slaves' challenges to masters' ultimate rule. Genovese famously insists slaves were not "political men" because he delimits politics to struggles to overthrow the slaveholders' regime and consigns everything short of that to culture.[33] Hegemony thus obscures the political character of slave neighborhoods. I have, like other scholars, adopted instead a relatively open-ended definition of politics as struggles that carried weight in the balance of power.[34] Creating and re-creating neighborhoods was, among other things, a way for slaves to recalibrate the balance of power in their society. Neighborhoods, then, were a place, a political institution, and a political idea.

This book also joins the work of historians in many fields who are presently taking up questions about space. There is even talk, more hopeful than descriptive just now, of "a spatial turn." In southern history, of course, place is a long-standing, perhaps definitive, theme. Since the 1920s, scholars have elaborated how continuities of place and attachments to place distinguished the South and its history.[35] Historians of slavery, extending a distinguished literature of local studies on the colonial era into the antebellum period, are illuminating how the peculiar institution differed across space and over time.[36] Others are examining how yeomen, planters, and slaves, among other parties, employed space in class rivalries.[37] This study contributes to this literature by exploring how slaves made and thought about social spaces. It plumbs how slaves fashioned places in intimate relations, work, and leisure, in narratives about themselves and their neighbors, in struggles with owners and other slaves.

Exploring slave neighborhoods has required a few departures from the usual procedures in theory and method. This account makes ample use of familiar primary sources on slavery: Works Progress Administration interviews with ex-slaves, plantation journals, newspapers, county court cases, travelers' diaries, and the records of the Southern Claims Commission.[38] It is also based on an important new source, the files of the U.S. Pension Bureau.[39] This work also employs a notion of agency culled from Anthony Giddens's theory of structuration.[40]

Historians have much to learn from his project to reinsert the dimension of space into the human sciences. The problem Giddens means to solve is how power is exercised at a distance, projected across space, throughout society. His solution does away with the dichotomy between individual and society in favor of what he calls the "duality of structure." The individual's relationship to social rules and institutions is, he argues, reflexive. Rules (laws, customs, expectations) and institutions (resources held by the state, corporations, households) both constrain and enable individual action. Nor are rules and institutions simply imposed on individuals, who also create and re-create rules by following them, create and re-create institutions by interacting with them. Laws prevent one thing, permit another. Ordinary people create the rule of law by doing what law permits in the way law requires.

Giddens's duality of structure invites historians to think differently about agency. Scholars in many disciplines think about the impact of action on society from the standpoint of individual intention. Yet many powerful actions make a mark in their unintended consequences. People do not follow laws to contribute to the rule of law as much as avoid penalties. Unintended consequences only increase in the case of informal rules and collective actions. Our part in making an informal rule is all the more unintentional to the degree we act, interpret, and hence reproduce it unconsciously. We often do our part in "reflexive monitoring": routine encounters seemingly unrelated to rule making, casual conversation, carrying out responsibilities at home or work. As repetition gives a pattern to our actions' unintended consequences, rules and institutions are replicated across space and gain a place in society.

Giddens's formulation of agency reveals much about how slaves made neighborhoods. Slaves fashioned ties across plantation lines, the very ligature of neighborhoods, in what he might call reflexive monitoring. The distinctions slaves drew between different types of intimate relations were, in Giddens's terms, informal rules about how men and women established unions and what partners owed one another. Slaves articulated these rules and enforced them at weddings, in gossip, in myriad routine encounters. Bondpeople elaborated their terms of labor in protests against relentless drivers and in the pace of their movements through the crop rows; terms of struggle in hushed conversations about how to get rid of the overseer or whether to help a runaway; the rules of their society in stories, preaching, tales, and all the talk that took place in all sorts of more or less serious socializing.

Furthermore a neighborhood was very much the slaves' creation, even though they did not set out to make it. Slaves worked on adjoining plantations to make money or at owners' behest, absconded there to avoid work or punishment at home, went visiting to court sweethearts or praise God. In going about their business from day to day, they made neighborhoods. Every neighborhood, like every place people make, had boundaries and therefore imposed pressing constraints — on romance, trade, rebellion, and social space itself. Yet it also enabled men and women to find lovers, to work on their own account, and to run away by defining a proper field for these and other activities. Readers have heard the last in these pages of the abstruse terminology of structuration, duality of structure, reflexive monitoring, but Giddens's ideas inform the discussion to follow and bear keeping in mind.

Testimony before the federal Pension Bureau, which figures prominently in this volume, raises problems of method that warrant discussion in some detail. Scholars have used the pension records to illuminate the history of the American welfare state, health, mortality, and employment as well as freedpeople's intimate relations, kinship, and struggles for citizenship.[41] Yet historians of slavery have yet to submit testimony in the pension files to sustained analysis.[42] Pension claims are a far larger source of postbellum testimony, much of it dating back to the 1870s, than the Works Progress Administration interviews, conducted during the 1930s.[43]

Between 1862 and 1866, Congress adopted several measures providing pensions to Union soldiers, including black troops, and their surviving family members.[44] Pensioners increased from 5 percent of all veterans in 1870 to 31 percent in 1890, thanks to revised qualifications after Reconstruction.[45] The Arrears Act of 1879 qualified men suffering from recent disabilities related to military service and repealed a five-year limit on the time petitioners had to press their claims. A rule giving widows only sixteen months to apply for a lump-sum payment of arrears back to the date of the soldier's injury was repealed in 1888. Subsequent laws transformed a system of provision for injured soldiers and their dependents into a broad program to support the elderly and disabled. The number of pensioners doubled in just one year after the Dependent Pension Act of 1890 provided stipends to veterans for disabilities unrelated to military service. After 1904, all veterans became eligible for pensions upon turning sixty-two.[46]

Evolving qualifications for pensions generated extensive testimony about slavery. Widows' claims were the most revealing. Because slave marriages were not recognized by law, freedwomen could not produce marriage licenses to establish their bona fides as soldiers' wives. The bureau made it standard procedure for "special examiners" to collect oral testimony in freedwomen's claims. In addition to testimony about intimate relations, provisions increasing a widow's pension for each child under sixteen obliged witnesses to describe relationships between parents and children. To prove they had turned sixty-two, veterans recounted events in their youth, thereby revealing intriguing methods of keeping time. Veterans told war stories to relate recent ailments to military service or simply to prove they had served. Elderly veterans supplied new details about wartime marriages in reply to questionnaires sent out by the bureau in anticipation of claims from eligible widows.[47]

Freedwomen and -men keenly portrayed virtually every aspect of slavery in testimony to the Pension Bureau. Widows recounted their intimate relations with their men, and former slaves called in to confirm the widows' accounts explained how they came to know so much about other couples' personal affairs. Witnesses described the work they did in slavery times; relations with spouses, children, and other kin, drivers, overseers, and owners, with friends and neighbors; conversations, weddings, hangings, holidays — episodes of every kind. These accounts glean the entire landscape of slave society. They offer up, glimpse by glimpse, vivid, concrete details about slaves' lived experiences, their intimate relations, their work, their struggles, their neighborhoods.

The pension files demand careful handling, though, because testimony can be deceiving. First, witnesses testified after the fact. Their testimony is less problematic than the Works Progress Administration narratives in important respects. To the bureau, witnesses of all ages testified about adulthood in slavery relatively soon after emancipation — often within a decade. Still, much had changed in the intervening years, and recollections were undoubtedly distorted by witnesses' present circumstances. Second, their testimony, like any document, is a collaboration. Some words attributed to witnesses were not strictly their own. Attorneys, agents, investigators, to name a few, put words in witnesses' mouths. Witnesses, for their part, shoehorned messy lives to fit the bureau's tidy categories.

Third, cases of outright fraud also occurred. Between 1866 and 1912, the average pensioner received $135 annually.[48] The Arrears Act mandated a windfall (the accumulated monthly pension from the date of the soldier's discharge or death to the date the bureau admitted the claim) amounting on average to $950 for disabled soldiers in 1881.[49] A large apparatus produced false testimony to the Pension Bureau in bulk. Pension attorneys, taking statutory limits on fees as incentive to press as many claims as possible, retained local agents to match up deceased veterans with widows — and not necessarily the right woman in every case.[50] Agents, in turn, hired old soldiers to do the legwork.[51] Other veterans set themselves up as professional witnesses.[52] The bureau often condemned attorneys, agents, and old soldiers for cheating the federal government and claimants, too. Claimants paid witnesses, sometimes to attest to false claims. Attorneys pressed the claims, legitimate or not, and skimmed off the top of payments to widows.[53]

Claimants regarded some of these practices as legitimate charges for services rendered. Agents and old soldiers helped fill out complicated forms, did the writing for witnesses who could not do it themselves, tracked down folks claimants had lost touch with or army comrades whom widows had never known. Professional witnesses gamely recited secondhand accounts as first-hand information they knew for a fact. Other witnesses claimed payment for taking the time to testify, which could amount to half a day or more after all was said and done — going to a plantation where the bureau man was holding court, waiting to testify, saying your piece, and getting back home. Delila Clasby generously volunteered to pay all parties concerned. "I will pay my witnesses $20–$30, apiece," she told an examiner, "and the man who brought you out there ought to have $10. You ought to get $30."[54]

Despite claimants' often kindly view of sharp practice, some testimony was corrupt, and much of it is easily avoided. Professional witnesses are easy to spot by their ubiquitous appearances in addition to examiners' complaints. After initiating an application to the bureau, claimants provided supporting affidavits from witnesses, written by attorneys, agents, old soldiers, or court clerks. So many witnesses denied statements attributed to them in these documents that affidavits will be cited sparingly.[55] This book relies mainly on testimony to the special examiners beginning in the mid-1870s — "exhibits" and "depositions" in bureau parlance. Neither type of document recorded witnesses verbatim. This was acknowledged in exhibits, where testimony was recorded in the third person. Although depositions were written in the first person, often in question-and-answer form, others appeared as a running narrative with quotation marks to underscore striking turns of phrase. Exhibits and depositions, then, paraphrased witnesses in part and omitted what examiners deemed irrelevant. Yet examiners also read exhibits and depositions back to each witness, who pointed out errors and stated whether he or she had otherwise been recorded correctly. Thus we know documents accurately represent former slaves' testimony because they said so.[56]

The most difficult testimony to evaluate is partly contrived and partly true. Take the case of Mary Ann Helam. On August 30, 1879, she made an affidavit before a chancery court clerk in Adams County in application for a pension as the widow of William Madison, a veteran of the 58th U.S. Colored Infantry.[57] Under the Arrears Act, she sought allowances above the minimum stipend of eight dollars per month on the grounds her husband had died of illnesses contracted in the service and left behind two children under sixteen years old at the time of his death. Her claim, therefore, put his health and their children's ages at issue in addition to the matter of whether she and Madison were husband and wife. The bureau left claimants hanging for years before investigating their cases, and special examiner Edwin M. Clarke finally got around to interviewing Helam on January 24, 1887.[58]

Her case was complicated even by her own account, which left much unsaid.

She knew neither her age nor her date of birth, only the place, Richmond, Kentucky. Her owner had sent her to Rodney, Mississippi, where she belonged to Margaret Logan. When Logan died, Helam said, she was sold to Latham Brown, who lived up the road about five miles from Fayette. She "took up" with Madison five years after her arrival on the Brown plantation, and she named six men and women who attended their wedding. At the time Madison enlisted, their oldest living child was already "a big man grown" with a mustache and beard, at least twenty-one years old, she thought, and their youngest, a daughter, was three years younger, or about eighteen. Since the children were over sixteen, it was apparent Helam would receive no increase for orphans by the end of her testimony, which took up nine handwritten, legal-sized pages. According to Helam, Brown was her second and last owner in Jefferson County, Madison was her only husband, and they had three children together.[59]

There was, it turned out, a good deal more to Helam's story—namely another owner, two other husbands, and three more children. Over the next several weeks, the examiner questioned sixteen of her associates, starting with former slaves mentioned in her testimony and application. Frank Humphrey was the first witness to reveal the other owner and husbands, and her friend, Rose Ballard, elaborated on these connections. When Ballard was sold by the Logan estate to the Brown place, she explained, Mary Ann was sold to another planter in Jefferson County, Isaac Jordan. On the Jordan plantation, she lived with a free black man, Buck Ace, and had two children with him. After Ace died, she lived with a fellow slave on the Jordan place, Robert Helam. In fact, although she testified under the name Mary Ann Madison, she was known as Mary Ann Helam for the duration of her marriage to Madison, Ballard noted.[60] When the examiner interrogated Helam a second time on February 18, she acknowledged her two children with Buck Ace, whom she lived with for five or six years before he died. Helam also disclosed another child, her first, born when she belonged to Margaret Logan. Yet she denied to the end ever having had a husband by the name of Helam. That, she claimed, was just a nickname dreamed up by her owner.[61]

For all Helam's deception, the testimony in her case is revealing on many points. Although she evidently feared that using a prior husband's name undermined her claim as Madison's widow, no one denied the two were married, and several witnesses confirmed Helam's account of the wedding, including Rose Ballard, who married the same day. The examiner, passing on to the bureau his report along with the testimony, took little note of the prior husbands she elided except to note a "patient and laborious investigation," and he recommended her claim be admitted.[62] The bureau awarded Helam a pension of $12 per month, including the $4 allowance for a soldier's death attributable to military service. Helam's depositions are replete with evidence about her life and Madison's, such as her parents' names (Chassy Jane Burnham and James Douglas Burnham), Madison's birthplace (in the Blue Ridge mountains of Virginia), the church where they wed (Belle Grove). She limned the circumstances of her migration to Mississippi, their marriage, and Madison's death and hinted at what she thought and felt about critical moments and relationships in her life. Sifting the details and circumstances yields further insights about her ties and experience, such as the namesakes she chose for her children, even though Helam did not call attention to these decisions.

Mary Ann Helam, despite her deceptive testimony, will appear repeatedly in the chapters to follow. In some other cases, readers will be apprised of contradictions or ambiguities in witnesses' accounts, especially where the vagaries clarify nuances of the argument. In general, though, I have elected not to clutter the text with reflections on the evidence as such. Instead I have done what historians usually do: read and reread the documents, discard some testimony and use the best available, consider various interpretations, submit them to the discipline of the evidence, report my findings, and keep most of the deliberations to myself.

The method used to sift out the best evidence in the pension files was simple — comparing testimony. Several witnesses testified in each claim — some repeatedly — to clarify conflicting testimony or to address issues raised as pensioners made new applications under the evolving law. Helam testified twice, while both Frank Humphrey and Rose Ballard spoke to Helam's prior connections. Men often enlisted in the Union army with kin and friends, so the records invite comparisons between testimony in different cases, too. Juxtaposing testimony makes it possible to confirm, reconcile, or discard many accounts; to describe particular episodes, struggles, and people, their intimate relations, families, friendships, and neighborhoods from different points of view.

This study also compares evidence from the pension files with antebellum sources.[63] Antebellum autobiographies of escaped slaves substantiate freedpeople's testimony about neighborhoods; plantation journals, planters' correspondence, newspapers, and legal records provide evidence about the terms of work and struggle. The terminology of intimate relations finds confirmation in, of all places, investigations of slave conspiracies.

Finally, the scope of this book is suggested in the subtitle's mention of the "Old South." At the core of this volume is a local study of the Natchez District. Yet the boundaries of this study, like those of neighborhoods themselves, are porous. All local history is implicitly comparative, and the pages to follow include several comparisons between the Natchez District and the Upper South, the low country, the Caribbean, and elsewhere. The Old South was a time as well as a place, a synonym for the antebellum years between 1830 and 1860. That period is the focus here, although I have overstepped those boundaries, too, especially toward the end of the book in discussions of the Civil War and Reconstruction. The "Old South" also carries resonances of an image antebellum planters crafted of a harmonious, unchanging society. The slaves' unending struggles with owners and each other to create and re-create neighborhoods provides further evidence that the image was more myth than fact. But slaves' sense of place expressed their own persistent aspirations for continuity.[64]

The chapters in this book are organized around the power relations in which slaves made neighborhoods. Chapter 1 surveys neighborhoods across the Old South. Chapter 2 explores kinship through the variety of intimate relations men and women created. Chapter 3 traces relations of labor. Chapter 4 maps the field of struggle. Chapter 5 examines slaves' ambit outside the neighborhood and the novel powers encountered there. Chapter 6 examines the Civil War and emancipation. The epilogue sketches the endurance of neighborhoods during Reconstruction and their place in freedpeople's politics.

Neighborhoods

When Nat Turner looked back on the origins and progress of his rebellion, he told his story from beginning to end as a neighborhood story. There he found confirmation for the childhood sense he possessed an intelligence beyond his years and above a chattel's station. As a boy, no one had taught Nat his letters, yet when he was handed a book to stay his tears, he spelled the objects pictured, a "wonder to all in the neighborhood." Turner never felt compelled to steal, but those who did relied on him to plan their exploits, for such was the faith in his judgment among "the negroes in the neighborhood."[1] If the conceit of all prophets is that they are born, the truth, of course, is that they are made. And by Nat Turner's account, his identity as a prophet was a neighborhood production.

Neighbors tendered the prophet's mantle early, yet he accepted it slowly and reluctantly. He cultivated the reputation of a gifted child, yet their faith in him surpassed his own, for they also believed his good sense "was perfected by Divine inspiration." Turner, demanding further signs, kept aloof from his neighbors and "wrapped myself in mystery." All the while, he fasted and prayed and reflected on the Scriptures, especially a passage from the Sermon on the Mount,[2] which struck him most powerfully. He prayed upon it daily, even at the plow, and there the "Spirit that spoke to the prophets in former days" appeared and spoke the words himself: "Seek ye the kingdom of Heaven and all things shall be added unto you." Only after two more years of prayer did the Spirit reveal himself a second time. And only then was Turner at long last convinced of what the slaves in his neighborhood had known all along: his "wisdom came from God." Now his faith surpassed theirs, for he also believed God had chosen him for "some great purpose." And Turner "now began to prepare them for my purpose."[3]

Turner was sidetracked from his appointed task for some six years because the neighborhood that exalted him soon brought him low. Around 1822, just as he began to confide intimations "something was about to happen," he came under an overseer's hand and absconded to the woods for thirty days.[4] Fellow slaves assumed Turner had followed in the footsteps of his father, who had run away years earlier, never to return. Then Turner reappeared, quoting the Spirit: "For he who knoweth his Master's will and doeth it not, shall be beaten with many stripes, and thus have I chastened you."[5] Fellow slaves rebuked him — "murmured against" him, as Turner put it, casting himself as Moses and his neighbors as the ungrateful Israelites who "murmured" for lack of food and drink when he led them out of Egypt into the wilderness.[6]

Turner, scorned by his neighborhood, began to conceive his plot in earnest just then. After this reproach — perhaps in response to it — he had the most vivid revelation yet of his future course: a battle between white spirits and black spirits eclipsed the sun; blood streamed, thunder rolled across the sky. Again Turner withdrew from other slaves to devote himself to the Spirit, and the Spirit rewarded him with further revelations. Blood dropped like dew on the corn in a field where Turner labored. He revealed this vision to "many, both white and black, in the neighborhood," but it did little to uplift his standing. A reprobate white man was the only person suitably impressed by these visions, and Turner took him down into a creek, where the Spirit baptized them and onlookers "reviled us." In May 1828, the Spirit told Turner to take up Christ's yoke and "fight against the Serpent" when the next sign appeared in the skies and to say nothing of his mission in the interim. When a solar eclipse occurred on February 12, 1831, Turner confided his purpose to four slaves: Hark Travis, who lived on the same farm as Turner; and Sam Francis, Henry Porter, and Nelson Edwards, all of whom belonged to owners nearby. These were the men, all from the neighborhood, "in whom I had the greatest confidence."[7] Nat Turner's rebellion sprang up from neighborhood soil.

The neighborhoods of the Natchez District, distinct though they were, had counterparts across the South. Slaves created them throughout the border states, along the Black Belt, across the Mississippi Valley. The prevalence of neighborhoods, moreover, points to the roots of those in the district. Neighborhoods in Mississippi, though ingenious creations, were reconfigured from those in the Upper South. Neighborhoods were pervasive in other ways, too. Fashioned in the course of visiting and storytelling and other everyday exchanges, neighborhoods were the incarnation of a sense of place that permeated slaves' consciousness and even lent a spatial dimension to their conception of time. Neighborhoods illuminate the contours of slave society in southwestern Mississippi and beyond.

By the time of Turner's rebellion, neighborhoods in Virginia had been a century in the making. The struggle to hitch social ties together across plantation lines was well under way between 1710 and 1740 in the Chesapeake. The small size of plantations made visiting essential to cultivating organic social bonds within slave society. After nightfall and on Sundays, slaves crowded the roads, waterways, and other byways on foot, in canoes, and by horseback, heading to nearby quarters to dance, drink, and otherwise carouse. On large plantations, men and women began the tender work of cultivating ties of kinship in adjoining quarters. Owners unwittingly lent a hand in breaking ground on neighborhoods. Upon the death of great planters, heirs parceled out slaves among nearby estates, where old ties facilitated extending bonds to these new locales.[8] Men and women extended family ties into new precincts wherever slaves were sold or bequeathed in the vicinity. By the 1770s and 1780s, the slave population in Tidewater Virginia had grown in size and density, and the proportion of slaves living on farms with more than ten bondpeople had increased from less than half at the beginning of the century to about two-thirds.[9] Slaves withdrew some distance away from owners to quarters, where the cabins were rampant with kinfolk. Bonds of many sorts grew apace as slaves gained the run of nearby plantations. The new field of sociability laid a new groundwork for solidarity. Many slaves harbored runaways from their neighborhood.[10]

Across the Virginia border in Person County, North Carolina, neighborhood was the terrain of struggle and discipline as well as solidarity and kinship, according to James Curry. His mother felt pulled in two directions — away from the neighborhood and back toward it — when she ran away and was captured fifteen miles gone, awaiting news about her family before pressing on. Shortly thereafter, she married her first husband, "a slave in the neighborhood," Curry noted. Slaves there felt the impact of Nat Turner's revolt in the scarcity of books. Curry had already gotten his start learning to read in a spelling book procured by his mother. Before the rebellion, slaves "in our neighborhood," he observed, could readily buy hymnals and spellers.[11]

The several plantations in the neighborhood, where slaves were likely to suffer the exactions of other slaveholders and overseers from time to time, comprised a single field of discipline. Curry and his two brothers realized they had not seen the last of their overseer the day he threatened to whip them before nightfall, even though he allowed he could not do it himself. They knew "there were men in the neighborhood he could get to help him," so Curry and his brothers ran away before the overseer made good on his threat.[12]

The stories slaves exchanged about the regimes of punishment on different farms gave "a rich slaveholder in our neighborhood," Thomas Maguhee, a perfectly dreadful reputation. "I never saw blood flow any where as I've seen it flow in that field," a fellow slave told Curry as they walked by the Maguhee place. "It flowed there like water." Curry's companion had been strong enough to carry bushels on his shoulder before he was hired out to Maguhee the previous summer; now he could scarcely lift one. "When I went there to work, I was *a man*, but now, I am *a boy*." Other stories about the notorious Maguhee made the neighborhood rounds. One man, having refused to submit to a whipping, drowned in a millpond where he fled from the dogs. Anyone who had the temerity to shed tears for the dead man got a whipping. Neighborhood defined a field of struggle where the terms of discipline differed from place to place. Many "slaves in the neighborhood," Curry surmised, would have preferred to belong to his owner, if only the man were not a slave trader.[13]

Neighborhood, as the stories told in Curry's account suggest, was the main field of the grapevine telegraph. Here slaves rapidly and extensively collected and exchanged information. Neighborhood provided fodder as well as the field for circulating every kind of news, formulated as stories in which slaves told and heard tell of each other's struggles, families, and intimate relations as well as owners' outrages and other doings, among other tendencies and prospects. During the 1836 presidential election, for example, word tore through Curry's neighborhood that Martin Van Buren would free the slaves if he won. One old man prophesied amid the general rejoicing that they, like the Israelites on the shore of the Red Sea, had merely to "stand still and see the salvation of God." If President Van Buren ultimately declined to be their Moses, slaves knew far more about politics than white people realized, Curry pointed out, because slaves "from neighboring plantations hold frequent intercourse with each other."[14]

Lewis Clarke was reluctant to tell an abolitionist meeting in Brooklyn in the fall of 1842 too much about his Kentucky neighborhood, yet he made clear it was the nexus of kinship and discipline. He had second thoughts about naming a slave who was "*all* white," for example, because the audience might then ask "whether *I* came from his neighborhood."[15] Generally speaking, though, he amply demonstrated spouses who lived in different neighborhoods had a heap of troubles. One fellow slave got whipped time and again for visiting his wife some distance away, and she begged him "to find somebody round in his neighborhood that would buy her." After she lost patience and ran away to her husband, her owners turned more cruel than ever, and thereafter she was "the most suffering creature" Clarke ever knew. Historians still have much to learn about the geography of intimate relations.[16] Marriage between spouses belonging to different owners was common in the border South. The distance between husbands and wives and all the visiting and family ties traversing it would have increased the size of neighborhoods in some regions or placed intimate relations outside the bounds of neighborhood in others. In Clarke's neighborhood, like many others, intimate relations beyond those grounds could be unhappy affairs.

Slaveholders in the neighborhood determined the outer limits of propriety in discipline, not that such limits did the slaves much good. If an owner tied a slave to the whipping post at the local market and whipped the man until his legs gave out, Clarke observed, the "neighbors all cry out, 'What a shame!'" Yet the neighbors' objections to the whipping in the marketplace, he judged, had less to do with the severity of the punishment than the indiscretion of subjecting onlookers to a screaming slave. Slaveholders might go to great lengths to discipline an owner, like one of Clarke's, who neglected to keep good order on his plantation. Yet only the most egregious departures from conventional brutality moved slaveholders to discipline one another. When Clarke was a child, his owner finally stopped pulling Clarke's hair out after "one of the neighbors" questioned her claim he was afflicted with "scald head." No matter how cruelly owners flogged slaves, "the neighbors" would never go so far as to testify about it in court.[17]

Slaves created neighborhoods all over the Upper South, from the Atlantic Seaboard to the Mississippi River. In Middle Tennessee, Elizabeth Sharp had a daughter by a white man who "slipped" off the road into her cabin. Although she did not put too fine a point on their relationship when she recounted it many years after emancipation, she scarcely knew the man, only his last name. "He didnt belong in the neighborhood," she explained.[18]

Neighborhoods lined the Chesapeake Bay in Maryland as well. In 1855 Frederick Douglass opened his autobiography in Tuckahoe, the "district, or neighborhood," on the Eastern Shore where he lived with his grandparents. Douglass apologized for describing it at length, but since he did not know when he was born, he could not situate his story in time, so he attended to the place, and "it is always a fact of some importance to know where a man is born." Douglass's grandparents "were considered old settlers in the neighborhood." His grandmother, Betsey Baily, was held in especially high regard as an able nurse, "a capital hand at making nets for catching shad and herring," and generally "born to 'good luck.'" Douglass, however, thought her good fortune had less to do with luck than thrift. "Grandmother," he observed, was "more provident than most of her neighbors."[19]

Ann Garrison extracted her mistress's assurance to "never sell any of us out of the neighborhood" outside Havre de Grace, where the Susquehanna River empties into the bay. Garrison was well aware some of her children were bound to be sold to settle her master's estate after he died, which is why she sought the promise, but her mistress was true to her word, at least for a while. She sold one of Garrison's daughters to a doctor just three miles away, but that did not prevent him from taking the girl to the Southwest two years later. One of Garrison's sons was hired out to "a tavern-keeper in the neighborhood" but was subsequently sold to a slave trader in Baltimore. Garrison and three of her children were sold to a trader there in 1841. Only intervention by friends and abolitionists gained freedom for her and the children before they were sold south.[20]

Slaves brought neighborhoods to the Natchez District from the border states whence they came. Ann Garrison's neighborhood, Elizabeth Sharp's, Lewis Clarke's, and James Curry's were all in states exporting slaves to the Deep South by the thousands. More than 240,000 slaves, on average, undertook this second middle passage every decade during the antebellum period. Its ebb and flow closely tracked the fortunes of the staple economy and peaked during the boom years of the 1830s, fell in the depression of the 1840s, and rose again on the speculations of the 1850s.[21] Most left from Maryland, Virginia, and the Carolinas. Kentucky became an exporting state during the 1820s; Tennessee did so during the 1850s.[22] Much of this traffic passed through Natchez, where the second largest entrepôt in the trade lay northeast of town at the mocking crossroads of Washington and Liberty. Franklin and Armfield, the leading speculators in the business, had offices in Natchez as well as New Orleans, the preeminent center for the trade. Even during the slow season, the market in Natchez was large enough for Franklin and Armfield to send a coffle there every summer. Planters from the district bought a great many people on offer at the Forks of the Road, as the market outside town was known.[23]

The migration tore deeply into neighborhoods in the Upper South. Its impact differed, depending on whether slaves left with their owners or with traders. From the standpoint of kinship, traders did more damage to slave society than did planters.[24] Yet the reverse is true from the perspective of neighborhoods.[25] Traders received a premium in the Deep South for slaves in the prime of life, around their peak capacity for work, after the onset of sexual maturity. About two out of three slaves caught up in the interstate trade, by the most authoritative estimate, were men and women between sixteen and thirty years old, and half were separated from husbands, wives, or children.[26] Slave families fared somewhat better in the migration with planters, who took many of their people south together and even traded folks — spouses, parents, children — with other owners to keep some families intact.[27] Still, even the most scrupulous planters left broken families in their wake somewhere in the neighborhood. Traders, moreover, plucked slaves out of neighborhoods one by one, in pairs, or in small groups, but planters wrought their havoc wholesale, carrying off slaves by the score, shredding ties throughout the neighborhood, transforming the contours of a social terrain slaves had shaped over generations. Planters and speculators together did untold damage to the fabric of neighborhoods across the border states.

Most slaves made their way to the Natchez District, like other regions of the Lower South, by way of the slave trade. By scholars' estimates, 30–50 percent of all migrants journeyed South with owners, while 50–70 percent did so with traders.[28] The soul drivers, as slaves called the traders, scattered Rachel Tilden's family to the winds along the way. She and her husband, Sam Bausley, had four children in Nashville, Tennessee, two girls and two boys, one named after their father. From the outset, she and the children were separated from Bausley when they were sold to traders without him. They managed to stay together as far as Aberdeen in eastern Mississippi, where all her children were sold off before she proceeded southwest to Natchez, where she was sold for house service in town.[29]

Some families got through the ordeal more or less intact by their own persistence in rare combination with the goodwill and good faith of owners and traders. A lesser man than Warrick Hartwell from Middle Tennessee might have been driven to despair by his owners' decision to sell his wife. Yet Hartwell, having prevailed on them to buy her from another slaveholder three years earlier, believed he could persuade his white people to keep him and his wife together. Sure enough, Hartwell convinced the owners to sell them both to a slave trader with the proviso he too would not separate them. The Hartwells listened closely to the trader's pitch to prospective buyers on the way to Mississippi for signs he might go back on his word. Many years after emancipation they recounted to associates how the trader declined several offers to buy them individually, saying he had promised not to sell them apart. The couple may have pressured him to make good on his pledge, for Hartwell also related the trader telling buyers he "would not lie" to them. Finally, he sold them together in Adams County, where they remained through the late 1880s, when they returned to Tennessee and told the story of how they had stayed together all those years.[30]

The passage from the Upper South to the Natchez District was an ordeal by any route, whether by flatboat or steamer along the inland Ohio and Mississippi Rivers; by ship under sail along the Atlantic Seaboard and the Gulf Coast; or by foot through the Appalachian, Tennessee, and Mississippi Valleys.[31] Forty-nine slaves, bought up in small groups on farms in southwestern Virginia, were on the road for two months in late 1834 on their way to Washington, a hamlet six miles outside Natchez. They trekked inexorably southwest between the Iron and Clinch Mountains, through Tennessee, then into Mississippi from the Tombigbee in the northeast, through a prairie of black soil, and across the Big Black River near Vicksburg in early December. As they walked south through the district, the trader procured goods to make them presentable for sale: hats, shirts, and other clothes; needles, thread, calico, and other cloth for the slaves to make up into shirts and dresses for themselves; whiskey to pick up their spirits around the Christmas holidays.[32]

Passage by boat, though easier on the legs, proved hard on the nerves for two dozen men, women, and children sent from the Downey place in the North Carolina piedmont in 1836. On the final leg of their journey, a storm kicked up waves on the Mississippi, and "we escaped imminent danger several times," according to their owner's agent. The wind died down by morning, "a death like stillness prevailed," and a bright sun revealed what might have become of them: "here and there a boat freighted with cotton lodged on a sand bar; or a corn boat stove against a sawyer and sunk with only its deck above the water, or a livestock boat with its 50 or 60 head of cattle and poultry innumerable, all drowned and floating."[33]

The second middle passage did indeed exact a high death toll.[34] Relatively few died in transit, yet like the first middle passage, the second also had its period of seasoning, and many did not survive. The Downey slaves' troubles were just beginning when they alighted at Natchez in late February. The sickness seemed mild at first — diarrhea that kept ten or twelve people from working for a day or two. But within the first several weeks, one man was already "writhing in all the agonies of pain imaginable," and Lucy's child was dead. Anderson eventually died, suffering "paroxism of hiccoughs continually" for days until the end.[35] The children and the elderly were the worst afflicted. Everyone seemed on the mend in mid-May, "except old Uncle Lewis," and "Old Granny" was still "quite sick" in mid-July, as were several children with "whooping cough."[36]

Several circumstances conspired with the exactions of the trade to exacerbate the illness among the Downey slaves: the heavy work of building a railroad, the neglect of rented slaves, and a "pestilence" in Natchez. Although word had it that the diseases in the vicinity were mainly common fever and ague, yellow fever was reported downriver in New Orleans, the last stop before Natchez for many slaves in the trade.[37] The Downey people were also ill-served with spoiled meat and "shanties," notwithstanding provisions in the rental contract requiring their employer on the railroad to supply them "plenty of good and wholesome meat" and "comfortable houses." The agent's inquiries into the healthfulness of the area and conditions around the railroad in particular led him to expect some casualties among the slaves: "[W]e may calculate upon loosing some of them in becoming acclimated," he wrote to their owner back in North Carolina. "All our negroes seem to be dissatisfied here," suffering from the heat by day and mosquitoes by night.[38]

Yet the agent was convinced the Downey slaves were also suffering the ravages of the trade. The stretch of track they were building was near the Forks of the Road. "The hearse has been running regularly . . . bearing dead bodies from the negroe Market to the publick Cemetery," and those slaves "died of the same diseases that ours were afflicted with." The simple change in climate was more than some slaves could bear. The weather, he pointed out, is "very warm, too warm for our hands to work all day without killing them up."[39]

Deaths after the second middle passage were not merely common but predictable. John Knight, a merchant in Natchez, expected the slaves he imported from Maryland and purchased from the traders in New Orleans to suffer bouts of illness and kept tabs on their health after they settled in at his plantation on the Red River in Louisiana.[40] "My chief anxiety now," he confided to his father-in-law after taking delivery of several dozen new people in June 1844, "is, to get them all safely acclimated." The prospects for doing so appeared good to Knight, "but I can hardly expect this, without the loss of a few." Three died that summer. William Russell dropped dead in the fields the day after his arrival, struck down with "apoplexy" (essentially a stroke brought on by heat), Knight thought. He blamed two deaths on the overseer, who put Russell and William Bennett to work too soon after their arrival. Yet even Knight's criticism of the overseer, which amounted to improper management of recent arrivals, implicitly acknowledged the rigors of seasoning.[41]

The risks of mortality were sufficiently well known to influence supply and demand in the slave trade. Buyers in the Deep South were reluctant to purchase slaves in the summer months, a potentially sickly season. Traders kept their ships in port for the season, fearing the extreme change in climate between the Upper and Lower South would kill slaves.[42]

Migrants passed through a period of emotional crisis as well as physical debility. "I consider all my N. Orleans negroes will be well acclimated after two years," Knight predicted. He alluded to the psychological dimension of migrants' struggle when he begged off a proposition to buy some people in Maryland, including an elderly man and woman. "It is much more difficult to acclimate *old* negroes than young ones; and after their removal from their old homes to new ones, they seldom, if ever, become reconciled to the change."[43]

The buying and selling did not stop after migrants reached the Natchez

District. On the contrary, perhaps twice as many slaves were sold locally as in the interstate trade in the Old South.[44] Mary Ann Helam had one owner in the Upper South and three in the Natchez District, as we have seen. When her owner in Richmond, Kentucky, sent her to his ward in Rodney, Mississippi, via a slave trader, she understood the transaction was not a sale, strictly speaking. But migration separated her from her parents nonetheless, and she marked the breach by naming her first daughter after her mother, Chassy. She and her daughter were sold together around 1833, when Helam's first owner in Jefferson County died. Mother and daughter were then sold separately in the late 1830s. Chassy's new owner sent her to Kentucky, whence her mother had come, while Helam landed on Latham Brown's plantation.[45]

Sundry exercises of the rights of ownership — the purchase of laborers to increase production, the punishment of recalcitrant slaves, the exactions of debt, bequests to children upon marriage and after death — made for a brisk trade in slaves in and out of every neighborhood. Knight was enough of a paternalist to buy kin of his recent purchases and to profess disdain for selling slaves — "All I buy I expect to retain" — but considered them perfectly fungible at times. In 1837, when yellow fever in Natchez put a scare into him, he mused on liquidating his house servants as readily as goods in trade at his store. "I should like very much to be able to get rid of my store, wind up my business as I intend, sell off our servants," who would fetch with the "furniture &c" five or six thousand dollars, he reckoned. They ultimately stayed put in Natchez along with Knight, however.[46]

Yet the uncommon wealth of planters in the district hardly gave slaves tenure in the neighborhood. Slaves were routinely bought on credit in the local trade or put up as collateral to secure owners' debts, and creditors were prepared to call in these obligations eventually.[47] Seventeen slaves on John Nevitt's place in Adams County were exiled across the river to a Louisiana plantation in 1831 to settle his accounts dating back to 1822 with three Nabobs. At least three families were separated in the transaction, which Nevitt celebrated with an oyster supper in Natchez. Ten people left on the place were put up to secure fifteen other slaves whom Nevitt purchased for his son a year later.[48] Slaves also changed hands when Henry Turner, scion of one of Nevitt's creditors, fell hopelessly into arrears ten years later. Ten men, seven women, and four children were sent from Palmyra plantation in Warren County to the Forks of the Road to cover Turner's debt to a trader there. At least twelve of these folks might have thought they had seen the last of the speculator's yard by December 1842, half a dozen years after their purchase.[49] Adams and Wilkinson Counties actually registered slight declines in slave population during the 1850s.[50]

Slaves did not sit still for transfer, even when it seemed inevitable. Men on the Nevitt place opened a new front in the struggle with their owner over the separation of their families. At least one man on Palmyra, William Smith, ran away while his return to the traders was in the offing. Slaves routinely fled while owners' estates were in probate, a legal proceeding lasting from several months to the better part of a year.[51] Inheritance was as much a part of the life cycle of slaveholding families as death itself, and folks in the quarters knew the signposts along a course that often ended with some people removed to another neighborhood. Shortly after the owner's death, some slaves might be hired out.[52] Commissioners, typically including at least one slaveholder on a plantation adjoining that of the deceased, showed up to survey land or assess the value of slaves.[53] Put on notice that people would soon be sold for debt or bequeathed to heirs, slaves might take to their heels at any point to influence, avoid, or protest the outcome. Several men belonging to the vast Benjamin Roach estate, which included more than 150 bondpeople in the district and at least twice as many in the Delta, absconded in 1855. Two were jailed in Vicksburg. John, who traveled by mule, may have gotten furthest before he was taken up in Claiborne County and brought back in handcuffs. The estate purchased two more pairs of cuffs in December, either to retrieve other fugitives or in anticipation of future departures.[54] Runaways were expected while estates were in probate.

The slave trade, interregional and local, had a formative ideological impact on slaves.[55] Migrants themselves or the children of migrants, everyone had firsthand encounters with the trade or knew people who had such experience. And experience showed, if proof were needed, slaves would not necessarily stay put after they landed in the region. Planters and speculators rent bonds between husbands and wives, tore children from the embrace of parents, pulled sisters and brothers, aunts and uncles, nephews and nieces out of the web of extended kinship, broke up friendships and Christian fellowships. These constant ruptures posed the most elemental problems of social organization as vexed questions to slaves: What bonds to one another could they establish, by what means, and for what ends? Slaves addressed these matters in intimate relations between men and women, in the work of making crops, and in extending and drawing boundaries of solidarity. In the course of these struggles, slaves were constantly fashioning and remaking neighborhoods. The constant presence of the trade reveals just how contrived slaves' profound sense of place was. Yet contrive it they did.

The Natchez District was replete with slave neighborhoods. Several lifelong friends of Lettie and Calvin Perryman situated their ties squarely on neighborhood grounds. They had all gotten to know each other during the 1850s, even before she married a fellow slave on the Wood place who died before the Civil War was out. Many years after emancipation, she told the U.S. Pension Bureau she had no other husband between the death of her first and her marriage to Perryman, and "almost any colored person in this neighborhood" could bear her out. Three freedmen confirmed her testimony, including Silas Burt, who knew all about Mrs. Perryman and both her husbands. "She never married anybody else till she married Calvin Perryman. I know this because she has lived in this neighborhood all her life and it would have been impossible for her to have had any other husband without my knowing about it." Zachariah Thomas likewise said he knew she was the only wife Perryman had ever had because "we both lived in this neighborhood until he died."[56]

Geographically speaking, slaves defined neighborhoods exactly and consistently. Just as her friends insisted they knew the history of her intimate relations because they lived in the same neighborhood, so she placed the neighborhood on adjoining plantations. The Wood place, her home, bordered the Archer plantation, where Calvin Perryman and their friends lived. "We lived on adjoining farms," she explained, "and I knew him continuously from that time. He belonged to Mr. Archer and I belonged to Robert Wood, whose farms were right together, so if Calvin had ever been previously married I am quite sure I would have known about it." Neighbors, as far as slaves were concerned, were people who lived on a plantation contiguous to their owner's. In testimony before the Pension Bureau, former slaves routinely mapped antebellum neighborhoods along lines of adjoining plantations.[57]

Slaves inscribed their neighborhoods on natural landscapes. Men and women who entered the district by overland routes crossed through the hill counties in the northeast corner of Mississippi and then a band of pinelands before reaching an arc of varied topography bounding the Natchez District in the southwest corner of the state. To the west was the Mississippi River; to the north a seventy-mile expanse, mottled with swamps, rooted in dense canebrake and wide-trunked trees, between the rivers forming the Yazoo-Mississippi Delta; to the east a belt of plantations, growing thicker decade by decade over the antebellum period.[58] The physical geography of the district, no mere backdrop, underlay definitive features of the neighborhood social terrain. The topography lent its contours to the field of struggle, set off places of work and leisure, inclined certain kinds of socializing toward particular venues.

The land rolled over hills, sloping abruptly upward near the Father of Waters. Particular soils undergirded their own complementary stands of trees.

As coffles entered from the east, men and women with an eye for the terrain noticed the pines in retreat to the ridgetops. Rivers and streams cross-cut the district, bending southwest toward the Mississippi, like branches down a tree trunk. The Yazoo formed a triangle in the northwest corner of Warren County; the Big Black, the border with Claiborne County; the Homochitto, the border between Wilkinson and Adams. The hills came up one after the next between the Big Black and Bayou Pierre at the north end of Claiborne County. At the south end, extending into Jefferson County, a broad stretch of gently undulating hills opened up ten miles wide. The hills supported plentiful oaks (black, chestnut white, and Spanish red), beech trees, and in lesser profusion some holly, basswood, sassafras, and elm. A narrow strip of magnolias meandered a course parallel to the Mississippi twelve to fifteen miles inland. Here and there islands of poplar, linn, blackjack, and hickory clustered to the exclusion of other species. Trees everywhere were tangled with grapevines and draped with moss. Where dun-colored silt piled the hills up into bluffs, honey locust, sweet gum, mulberry, and crab apple trees also flourished. The bluffs towered 180 feet at their heights along the Mississippi around Vicksburg in Warren County and Grand Gulf in Claiborne.[59]

Bondpeople new to the vicinity found it alive with a medley of colorful fauna: red fox squirrels, green turtles, and red-headed lizards, blue jays, blackbird crows, golden orioles, red-winged starlings, woodpeckers of many types and hues — red-headed, ivory-billed, yellow-bellied, and golden-winged. Frigate birds, great loons, marsh terns, white pelicans, green-winged teals, sprigtailed ducks floated on the waters. Beavers inhabited every stream. Raccoons gorged in the cornfields. Slaves hunted abundant opossums and enjoyed them as a delicacy. Less welcome were skunks and large bats with leathery wings. The landscape was a soundscape as well, loud with screech owls, turtledoves, hummingbirds, whistling plovers, and whooping cranes.[60] In the night air, mockingbirds cast out mournful riffs of imitative melodies, and whippoorwills seemed to hold forth in full sentences. Panthers retreated into the swamps during the antebellum decades; steamboats drove alligators from the navigable rivers into shallow streams and interior lakes. Bears and wolves were nowhere to be found by the 1850s. Wildcats still held their ground on the plantations, though, and were known to venture into slave cabins in Adams County.[61]

Slaves mapped neighborhoods across this countryside in necessarily irregular configurations. The geographic center of the neighborhood was invariably out of kilter with its social center. After all, the typical neighborhood was given over mostly to wild places. Less than half the acreage in the Natchez District was under cultivation as late as 1860.[62] Yet it was not simply that woodlands were likely to occupy the midpoint of any given plantation. In an arena of adjoining plantations, the social centers in every slave neighborhood — the quarters — were multiple. The built environment comprised the most consistent arrangement in the neighborhood. Slave cabins were arrayed in neat rows along a dirt street. The great houses were surrounded by their attendant outbuildings — kitchen, smokehouse, stables, barns, chicken coops, icehouses, and other storehouses.[63] Yet property lines fell less into neat squares than into complicated, inexact figures: rectangles askew at different orientations, diamonds, near-triangles, kidney shapes, T, L, and other shapes besides.[64] Power relations did not speak for themselves in the spatial arrangement of plantations, much less with one voice.[65]

Functional spaces were disparately located within these capricious boundaries. On any given place, the quarters might be in the owners' yard or set off a way, in sight of the overseer's house, or for ready access to the fields. Woodlands might separate quarters and yard, intersperse the crop fields, or join neatly at the boundary between plantations. However the home place was laid out, the course between quarters in the neighborhood was apt to be serpentine. It ran by cotton rows, past the great houses, through natural places in one order here and another there. The boundaries between plantations were irregularly placed and hard to find in many neighborhoods. The vagaries of property lines obliged planters to survey boundaries, mark them on trees, point them out to neighbors, debate the placement of fences, and occasionally resort to legal proceedings.[66] Slaves on Fairfield plantation in Adams County ambled over a boundary that changed course at four points and was marked by hickory, red oak, and poplar trees to get to places at the southern end of the neighborhood.[67]

Slaves had multifarious ways of taking neighborhood bearings from quarters, the big house, fields, and woodlands. Where planters on adjoining places situated mansions on public roads at the edges of estates and quarters were literally "back of the big house," slaves might assign owners to the periphery of the neighborhood.[68] Of course, even this orderly space was open to interpretation. Slaves might just as well have conceived owners surrounding this neighborhood as marginal to it. Sounds also carried harbingers from adjoining plantations. Former slaves from distant parts in the South recalled hearing a cacophony of sounds from a mile off or more: bells and horns calling the people out of bed and into the fields around daybreak, sticks beating and women singing on washing day, the high-pitched wail of a great wooden screw bearing down on the bales in the cotton press. Such soundings carried far enough to cross plantation lines in virtually any neighborhood in the Natchez District and cued people when neighbors were rousted out of the quarters, on their way in and out of the fields, at worship, or under the lash.[69]

Passages through the neighborhood, wherever they might cross plantation lines, were fixtures on the landscape. Watercourses, footpaths, and roads connected one plantation to another. Nature cleared these paths wherever rivers, bayous, and creeks flowed between adjoining places.[70] In Adams County, four branches of a creek spiraled through Fairfield and connected it to several adjacent plantations.[71] Slaves themselves created byways through the neighborhoods wherever they built roads and other trails between plantations. A road meandered between the fields and great houses on Mary Rowan's place and her brother's next door. Owners directed slaves to build such roads to clear a way between quarters, fields, and the mansion to facilitate work, marketing crops, and visiting between planters, not between slaves. Yet the roads served the latter purpose equally well, and slaves used these routes to beat a path through the neighborhood. Some neighbors had their pick of naturally occurring pathways or one they had made themselves. Slaves on Concorde in Adams County could make their way to every adjoining plantation along a bayou or creeks or by road.[72]

Every neighborhood also bore the unmistakable imprint of slaveholders' power, as slaves knew all too well. Owners left their mark by exercising rights of property and discipline. And slaves acknowledged the planter class cut a figure in the neighborhood when they fixed its boundaries according to owners' property lines. For analytical purposes, slave neighborhoods are hard to conceive without slaveholders and their neighborhoods.

Owners created neighborhoods from a cluster of households — surrounded by wilderness; connected by ties of kinship, sociability, and exchange; distinguished by family and wealth.[73] During the early nineteenth century, when settlers ventured into the northern reaches of the Natchez District, slaveholders constructed neighborhoods around a nucleus of one or several families who had migrated together from the seaboard states. Exchanges of labor, tools, and produce sustained households in rude circumstances and bound them together as a neighborhood. During the antebellum decades, planters identified each neighborhood with a particular family, which may have accounted for as few as one in five households in the vicinity but for a lion's share of the land and slaves. Neighborhoods were the fulcrum of democratic politics, where voters took cues regarding candidates of choice for county offices, patronage was divvied up, and decisions about public works from building bridges to caring for the poor were hashed out.[74] Boards of police organized slave patrols by neighborhood, too.[75] For planters, then, neighborhoods were the locus of kinship, politics, and slave discipline.

Planters' neighborhoods were a good deal grander than the slaves', at least in size. By 1830 slaveholders' neighborhoods in Warren County comprised between twenty and thirty square miles.[76] A single planter neighborhood encompassed several slave neighborhoods. The latter, moreover, could not be measured in miles at all. Owners' landholdings varied too capriciously for slaves to arrive at a common standard for measuring the size of their neighborhoods by distance. Planters forged neighborhoods, building roads and hammering out political alliances during the 1830s and 1840s. Warren County comprised a single slaveholder neighborhood by 1850.[77]

In addition to the differences in size, neighborhood constituted different geographies of power for slaves and slaveholders. To be sure, members of both groups assembled the place in much the same way. Ties of kinship were long the warp and woof of slave neighborhoods, yet neighborhood was merely one of several stages on which planters acted. All the social ties expanding the neighborhood's boundaries also drew slaveholders into relations of power extending far beyond neighborhood by 1830. Politics enlisted slaveholders in parties with headquarters in county seats and capitals at Jackson and Washington, D.C.[78] Neighborhoods ceased to be the nexus of exchange for owners, who traded slaves, procured supplies, and marketed crops at Natchez and Vicksburg. Ties of trade engaged owners with merchants at New Orleans and Philadelphia, among other points north, as well as Liverpool, where planters sold the cotton marketed with factors in the district.[79] Correspondence and rituals of visiting as well as financial transactions kept planters regularly in touch with kin throughout the South.[80] Slaves also had ties outside the neighborhood but tended them only irregularly if at all. Some kept track of the market price for goods they traded or even kept up with presidential elections. Yet the planters' rights over their human property prevented kinship, trade, and politics from expanding most slaves' horizons.[81] They mapped their society along lines of neighborhood because it circumscribed virtually every bond that shaped their daily routine and that they invested with meaning. Neighborhoods, in short, occupied a different place in slaves' and owners' social terrains.

For slaves, the bond of neighborhood itself was tethered to the relations of property between slaveholders. The process of creating and re-creating neighborhoods was inextricably bound to the life cycle of planter families.[82] Relations of gender within slaveholding families meant when an owner died, many slaves would stay put, but some were bound to change hands.[83] Neighborhoods remained more or less intact to the extent that planters bequeathed land and slaves together to the same heir. Historians know little as yet about how often slaves were removed from neighborhoods by local sale. Valuable work on the separation of families in the interregional slave trade has overshadowed the significance of parting slaves from land.[84] Sons generally inherited land and slaves; daughters, cash and slaves.[85] Heirs routinely exchanged slaves and sometimes sold them out of the family to round out the allotted portions of an estate. Slaves distilled the uncertainties of inheritance in their own inimitable terms. After Alice Simpson's first owner died, she, her husband, and two of their children were bequeathed to their owner's son, and they stayed on Locust Grove plantation. But her eldest son, Sandy, as she put it, "fell to one of the heirs who carried him off, to New Orleans."[86] Simpson's expression, "fell to," widely used among slaves, cogently expressed the caprice of inheritance.[87]

Planters could transform a neighborhood at any time by separately selling or buying land and slaves. When James Girault put his twelve-hundred-acre plantation in Wilkinson County up for sale in 1830, he recommended its natural amenities — six hundred acres of pasture, four hundred acres of woods, several springs, "a mile front on a beautiful clear creek with fine fish," all in a "pleasant and healthy neighborhood." As for the forty-two slaves on the place, all their ties to the neighborhood were put up for grabs with Girault's offer to sell the land "with or without the negroes, to suit purchasers."[88]

Every purchase of bondpeople posed slaves with the problem of integrating newcomers into the neighborhood. Lucy Saddler, John Smith, and Dennis Douglass were among six people bought together from a trader in Kentucky and taken to the Calvert plantation in Adams County. They were still strangers to almost everyone else on the place when Saddler married Smith, and several others took spouses. "[W]e only got there three weeks before Christmas, and we were all married about Christmas time," Saddler explained, "so that I did not know much about the colored folks."[89] The difficulties did not necessarily diminish in direct proportion to the size of the lot and could be as varied as the personalities and experiences of all parties concerned. Mary Ann Helam was relatively lucky to find even one familiar face on the Brown plantation. Rose Birch, who had also belonged to Helam's first owner in Jefferson County, could certainly ease her path into the society of the neighborhood. Yet she still had to contend with the losses of a daughter and a husband, and making certain kinds of new ties, especially family ties, remained a struggle for her over the years.[90] Slaves understood all their connections in the neighborhood hung in the balance, from start to finish, with their property relation to owners.

Slaveholders made their presence felt in the neighborhood by trying to control slaves' passage to adjoining plantations and policing the boundaries between them. Planters had conflicting interests in slaves' mobility. Moving to and fro within a neighborhood removed slaves from their owners' supervision, with unpredictable consequences for good order. On the other hand, considerations of discipline and productivity inclined owners to tolerate some mobility. It hardly served the purposes of discipline to make a contest of every instance of sociability, and planters occasionally sent slaves to work on adjoining plantations. Slaveholders, then, had their own reasons not to eliminate but to regulate their people's access to adjoining plantations. Slaves, even when at their leisure, were not at liberty to travel the neighborhood at will. The overseer on Aventine in Adams County called the roll three times on Sundays.[91] Every planter administered a pass system. State law demanded it, of course, a reflection of as well as a stimulus to the planters' aspirations to control slaves' mobility.[92] Free people could be fined for suffering a slave's presence on their premises without a pass. Slaves who violated the pass law were liable to receive up to twenty lashes.[93] Slaveholders at some times permitted crossing plantation boundaries and at other times forbid it.

Given planters' mixed motives, slaves were bound, in turn, to fashion neighborhoods in both collaboration and struggle with owners. Intimacy between slaveholding families could facilitate passage to adjoining plantations. Frequent visiting between the Stanton and Whitmore households fostered ties between slaves. Frederick Stanton, who knew Susan Alexander as a favorite of the Whitmore family, would hardly have objected to her calling at his quarters. The Stantons' people were likewise welcome at the Whitmore place, where Isaac Sloan, for example, got to know the Alexanders around 1845.[94] How did Harriet Willis, a slave in Claiborne County, explain her close friendship with Easter Wilson? Why, they "lived on neighboring plantations" and their owners were brothers.[95] Of course, neighbors often visited each other despite owners' objections,[96] even though doing so required outwitting owners, overseers, and slave patrols. Yet visiting was necessarily less frequent in neighborhoods where it occurred mainly on the sly. To choose between the pass system and clandestine visiting was a zero-sum game. Simple prudence led slaves to venture out into the neighborhood surreptitiously when they had to and get a pass when they could.

Visiting was just one mode of the everyday socializing in which slaves made neighborhoods—in conversation, in the act of worship, in "big times" of all sorts. John Wade, Harriet Pierce, the Barefields, and other neighbors on Pop-

lar Hill were fast friends because folks there and on the Terry place "were constantly visiting each other," according to Emanuel and James Genifer, Wade's
fellow Terry slaves. People on the Hamilton place regularly visited adjoining
Ball Hill in Claiborne County, even if Lewis Johnson likely exaggerated when
he claimed to have done so "[e]very Sunday night of my life."[97] Similar connections prevailed between slaves on the Alverson and Harris plantations in
Warren County. Both Curtis Lockhart and John Turner were free to pay their
respects at the Alverson quarters when they felt inclined to do so. "I was at
liberty to visit Mr. Alverson's place whenever I chose," Lockhart recollected,
noting his owners were on intimate terms with Mrs. Alverson's family. Turner
likewise said he "was permitted to visit there whenever I pleased."[98]

Balls, frolics, barbecues, candy pulls, weddings, and other affairs converged
during the busy seasons of neighborhood socializing. Neighbors filled the
respites in crop production with rounds of parties after the cotton was laid by
in July and picked out around Christmas. Owners were sometimes a party to
these festivities. Independence Day celebrations—if not on July 4th then on
the following weekend—were an annual rite during the 1830s and 1840s,
sometimes with owners.[99] Planters in the Natchez District encroached on the
lull in heavy field labor over the course of the antebellum period, yet slaves
persisted in making the season popular for weddings. Yuletide found slaves in
the Warren County neighborhood around Fonsylvania plantation occupied
with various festivities. Fonsylvania people attended a party at Kensington on
December 26 and spent the next several days procuring supplies and cooking
so they could reciprocate. The women baked pies and bread and prepared
other treats in sufficient quantities to run up a thirty-dollar tab. The party at
Fonsylvania for Kensington people went off in high spirits, with women in
neat dresses and smiles all around. The slaves, according to the hosts' owner,
claimed "much credit for their gentility on the occasion."[100]

Christmas saturnalias were one practice among many in which slaves wove
Christianity into neighborhood social life during the antebellum decades.
Evangelicals had made only a fitful beginning in the mass conversion of slaves
during the 1820s in Mississippi.[101] During the following decade, evangelical sects, hoping to overcome planters' opposition to slave missions, finally
stanched the egalitarian currents of the first Great Awakening and accommodated the Gospel to slavery. Baptists eschewed sermonizing on the equality of
believers and rituals like extending the right hand of fellowship to slaves,
harassed licensed slave preachers and separate black churches, formed committees to regulate slaves' conduct, and closed ranks against opponents of

slavery. Annual camp meetings around lay-by time were one manifestation of the reconciliation between planter and missionary.[102] For Isaac Stier, a carriage driver on the Stowers plantation in Jefferson County, this happy convergence marked his favorite time of year. "De bes' time I can 'member always come 'roun' de fourth of July."[103]

The missionaries' accord with the planters hewed sacred space to hierarchies of slavery and mastery. Baptists and Methodists alike increasingly consigned slaves and slaveholders to separate seating or services. Most important, evangelicals relocated the mission to slaves from churches to plantations, where owners could keep an eye on it.[104] John C. Jenkins retained a minister to preach to his slaves on Elgin every second or third Sunday in 1842.[105] Planters throughout the district embraced slave missions with some enthusiasm after 1845. The great sectional schisms among evangelicals, in effect, consolidated gains planters had made in decades of struggles with missionaries and slaves. When evangelicals formed the Methodist Episcopal Church, South in 1844 and the Southern Baptist Convention in 1845, planters asserted and formalized their sovereignty over the terrain of slave Christianity. Only during the 1840s did Christianity finally gain common currency among slaves.[106]

The plantation mission and all its agents and collaborators unwittingly strengthened the neighborhood moorings of slave religion. Planters had not intended to do so, if the slave code was any indication. Statutes enjoined bondpeople from going to other plantations to hear slave preachers and required them to confine their ministry to their owners' property. An 1830 law forbade slaves from preaching off their home plantations and prohibited a master from allowing "any other slaves but his own to assemble there on such occasion."[107] Such measures, however, prevented neither slave preachers from taking a hand in building the plantation mission nor neighbors from worshipping together.[108]

Slaves carved out places of worship in their neighborhoods. Slaves put praise houses, "brush arbors," or "hush harbors" in the liminal spaces around the margins between plantations, away from the quarters, the fields, and the great house — typically on unimproved acreage in the woods, secluded in the natural camouflage afforded by a stand of trees, hollows, gullies, swamps, the banks of a creek or river.[109] Former slaves from Mississippi east of the Natchez District pointed to some of these natural places of worship. "On Sundays," Emily Dixon told a Works Progress Administration interviewer, "us would git tergether in de woods." There they "could sing all de way through an' hum 'long an' shout, yo' all know, jist turn loose lak." A song recalled by Ellen King told Christians where the savior went.

Down by the river side,
Jesus will talk and walk,
Ain't going to study the world no more,
Ain't going to study the world no more,
For down by the river side,
Jesus will talk and walk.[110]

Congregations appropriated the ground for worship by laying up brush and poles and cutting rough planks for seats. They secured the meeting with an overturned kettle or pot to catch all the sounds — sounds of spirituals and hymns and prayers, sounds of teachings from Scripture, sermonizing from the preacher, testifying from the congregation — and keep owners, overseers, and patrols from breaking up the proceedings.[111] Slaves who convened from adjoining plantations for worship deepened their ties to each other as well as God and imbued the entire field of neighborhood with a sacred dimension.

When all was said and done, neighborhoods were made in no small measure from stories.[112] Neighbors told each other about where in the Upper South they had come from, how they came to the neighborhood, and other tales about their pasts.[113] They passed along rumors about who said and did what to whom.[114] They told the sagas of struggles with owners and other powers that be, of their intimate relations, their children, and other kinfolk.[115] They gossiped about other people's romances, who was courting or married to whom, about husbands and wives who quarreled, strayed, and parted.[116]

This was more than idle gossip. It elaborated the connections between neighbors. It pooled intelligence, synthesized and reformulated all the talk as common knowledge and common sense. It integrated small circles of neighbors (a family, a plow gang, folks at a prayer meeting) with folks who were new to the neighborhood, were otherwise not in the know, or had missed the main event — a wedding or birth, a run-in with an overseer or slave patrol, a vision of sin, of salvation, of God himself. In creating a lore of the neighborhood, slaves also mapped its social contours: the plantation where the meanest overseer, the cruelest owners presided; a swamp with thick ground cover to lay out in; the hollow where an inspired preacher exhorted; the woods where dancers showed their stuff; the quarters where good times were had by all. Slaves embellished the texture and particularity of the neighborhood in the narratives they crafted, turned mere space into a familiar place, endowed it with meanings, history, and symbolism that set it apart from other neighborhoods. Storytelling, in short, was integral to the creation and re-creation of neighborhoods.

Neighborhoods were more the slaves' creation than they ever intended or even realized. Slaves, after all, did not worship, tell stories, or socialize for the purpose of creating neighborhoods. Barbecues, balls, dances, storytelling, prayer meetings all had their own rewards. The revelations, epiphanies, wisdom, truisms, and manifold pleasures they afforded were more than sufficient to animate Christians, storytellers, gourmands, dancers, and revelers of every stripe. And yet in these and myriad other purposeful activities, neighbors created bonds across plantation lines; renewed, repaired, and reproduced these ties; multiplied and deepened them; transformed a space — adjoining plantations — into the place of their lived experience, a neighborhood. It was less the cause or impetus behind slaves' social relations than their result and product.

Slaves, then, did not see the neighborhood simply as their own handiwork. It was, after all, a secondary effect of their own actions. By their lights, moreover, other parties were at work in the social relations in which slaves created and re-created neighborhoods: owners, other slaveholders, even God himself. This is not to suggest slaves considered their neighborhoods master's gift or an act of divine intervention. God and planters were a presence in the neighborhood, to be sure. Yet the neighborhood did not seem any more directly attributable to those parties than to the slaves' own talk, religious practice, or other types of socializing. From slaves' point of view, a neighborhood was more than the social relations in which they created it, more than the bonds by which they fastened it together — more, put simply, than the sum of its parts.

By embedding their social relations in the natural world, slaves gave their communities, which owners made vulnerable and temporary, a semblance of the organic and permanent. Neighborhoods defined the field where slaves cultivated friendships, religious fellowship, and a common sense of how their society worked. As slaves placed these shared understandings and loyalties on neighborhood ground, they embedded it in their social terrain, rooted it in the ground beneath their feet, and imprinted it on the landscape. In the conception of neighborhood, slaves laid a foundation for their bonds and solidarities, naturalized and invested it with a sense of place that seemed to precede their own arrival and would survive when they left the scene. Men and women routinely were transferred and traded, their ties ruptured or forever broken, yet neighborhoods, with all the associations they encompassed, endured and prevailed.

Slaves' sense that the neighborhood somehow had an independent existence was a source of both power and constraint. It enabled their ties to take space in their society by placing them on neighborhood grounds. By the same token, slaves also imposed certain limitations on those ties. Every neighborhood, after all, had boundaries. And adjoining plantations, like any boundary, marked a perimeter keeping some people in and others out. Even as slaves facilitated the work of extending their ties by creating neighborhoods, they also put up borders in slave society. Creating neighborhoods also created expectations of loyalty and collaboration that defined the field of adjoining plantations, distinguished it from other terrains, and subsided beyond its edges. Slaves could and often did cross that boundary, sometimes at their peril. The constraints of neighborhood seemed all the more imposing to the extent they seemed to come with the territory.

Neighborhoods, as well defined as they were, varied widely nonetheless. Their spatial dimensions, for example, differed as arbitrarily as the economic fortunes of planters. Slaves on Adam Bingaman's 800 acres in Adams County and Benjamin Newman's adjoining 600-acre plantation lived in a neighborhood more than two miles square, for example — nearly twice the size of that comprised by Elisha Fox's 160 acres and his brother's 610-acre plantation in Warren County.[117] The boundaries of a neighborhood could also change over time as slaveholders bought or inherited, sold or bequeathed tracts of land.[118]

The boundaries and personnel differed even for slaves in the same neighborhood. Many ties prevailed between the quarters on Elgin and Forest plantations in Adams County. Their owners were in-laws. And they were in attendance when the slaves convened to celebrate the new year in 1852, although Dr. John C. Jenkins, master of Elgin, was inclined to see it as the slaves' affair, "a party . . . given by Forest negroes," as he called it in his journal.[119] Such festivities helped make Robert and Sancho Lloyd, father and son, intimates with neighbors on Forest, including Sunday Gardner. "We lived as neighbors from the time he was a child," the Lloyds recalled.[120] Elgin and Forest, of course, adjoined several other plantations: Grove, Hedges, and Cole Hill. (See map 3.) Each also bordered places that did not adjoin the other. For the Lloyds and other Elgin people, Saragossa was part of their neighborhood, but such was not the case for their neighbors on Forest. By the same token, Palatine and Brighton Woods were part of Forest's neighborhood but not Elgin's.

Slaves still made contacts on plantations outside the neighborhood, even if they did not quite adjoin and the networks were sparse. Neighborhood boundaries were always porous and blurred at the edges. While folks on Grove and Palatine, for example, were not in the same neighborhood strictly speaking, they could still enter into joint endeavors. During contentions with owners, slaves sometimes appropriated this marginal space between neighborhoods and annexed it to a terrain of struggle otherwise defined by adjoining plantations.[121]

Moreover, even for people living in the same neighborhood, the place had different focal points. Slaves invariably deemed the quarters on their owner's plantation the central locus. Here the ties of kinship, work, struggle — all the bonds slaves extended to adjoining plantations — overlapped at maximum density. Even fellow slaves on the same plantation had connections to different people and places in the neighborhood. The most beaten track ran from the quarters to the fields for most slaves, to the pens and stables for stock tenders, to the big house for domestic servants. Field hands rarely went to the house except on business, nor did servants often go to the fields except at the height of the cotton-picking season. Some slaves associated most closely with neighbors who trod similar paths at work or leisure. A particular spot in the neighborhood could also serve disparate purposes and have distinctive meanings to different people or even to one person depending on the circumstances. The woods past the edge of the fields was a place of work for men clearing new ground for cultivation, a place of worship for Christians, a safe haven for runaways. The forest could be a workplace or hunting ground by day and a dance floor, a sweethearts' rendezvous, or the hush arbor for a prayer meeting at night. The broadest difference in neighbors' sense of place prevailed between men and women. Relations of gender accorded women fewer routes than men to work or go visiting outside the neighborhood. Its boundaries, relatively permeable for men, comprised especially close quarters for women. Men, in short, had a subtly different relationship to the entire neighborhood terrain.

Neighborhood was critical to the ideology of slaves because it was not simply a place but a collective identity. To be sure, it was not their sole identity. They also conceived their place in the world in terms of the particular relations within the neighborhood ambit, especially kinship and Christianity. Slaves could take strength from their membership in families and religious fellowships, like neighborhoods, because these relations too appeared to be given rather than made. There were moments in the making of particular ties when slaves felt their kinship with family or Christians more deeply than with neighbors. And there were even times when their identification with family or God's children took the place of neighborhood. Yet neighborhood and other collective identities were neither conflicting nor synonymous but coexisting.[122]

The sense of place that took concrete form in neighborhoods lent a spatial dimension to their conception of time as well. Dates were a rare knowledge among slaves. A special examiner for the Pension Bureau vented his frustration with the inability of Lucy Waller, a freedwoman from the Mississippi Delta just north of the district, to provide dates for milestones in her marriage to a late veteran of the Union army. "[I]t is nearly impossible to get an idea from *her* as to whether a thing occurred before or after the big snow, the high overflow, or the time the levee broke, or the town burned. Before creation and after damnation are one and the same thing to her," the examiner complained. This was a picturesque exaggeration, as he conceded, and he alluded to her intricate means of keeping track of time as he rattled off what Waller ostensibly could not recall about events. "[S]he absolutely can not tell whether they occurred last year or year before — in the spring or in the fall — in Cotton hoeing time or in Cotton picking time." In fact, where an event occurred in the annual routine of cotton cultivation is precisely what Waller did know about time. Thus she told the examiner she met her husband about two years after emancipation in " 'picking cotton' time."[123] As late as the 1890s, Waller was still using the technique of marking time slaves had used before emancipation.

The slaves' folk chronology was a complex technique of mapping time by the proximity of events. Instead of keeping dates by the day, month, and year, slaves placed one event in time by juxtaposing it to another. To mark when a child was born or began to do field work, when a couple wed or were sold apart, when a man began to lose his hearing, enlisted in the army, or died — any milestone in the life of a person, family, or neighborhood — slaves plotted a convergence between that moment and another event of common knowledge. Henry Clay Bruce, formerly a slave in Virginia as well as in northern Mississippi, related how his parents, like many others, "in order to approximate the birth of a child, usually associated it with the occurrence of some important event, such, for instance, as 'the year the stars fell,' (1833), the death of some prominent man, the marriage of one of the master's children, or some notable historical event." The meteor shower of November 13, 1833, was an especially brilliant and widely used natural time marker.[124] Slaves in the Natchez District used it for years thereafter to get a rough fix on their own age or someone else's. Mary Ann Helam did not know her birthday exactly but put her age at about ten "when the stars fell."[125] Zadrick Bowie presumably did not remember his birth that day, so other slaves must have related the coincidence to him.[126] Natural wonders could fix a milestone indelibly in the collective memory of a neighborhood. Yet unique events were necessarily specialized tools for locating the time of other occurrences.

Far more handy were episodes recurring at predictable intervals. The common works of nature served admirably. It was "good peach time," for example, when Union soldiers appropriated a mule belonging to Wallace Turner's father during the Civil War.[127] According to Moses Fletcher, an army comrade's legs had given out on a march between Vicksburg and Jackson "in water melon time."[128] Slaves also made ample use of holidays as time markers. Independence Day was a common time marker for marriage.[129] Moses and Adaline Tester married in 1849, although she had an easier time recollecting the day than the year of their wedding. "I don't remember the year," she allowed, "but I know it was on the 4th day of July."[130]

Some slaves placed events in time by combining markers with rudimentary knowledge of numbers and dates. Jane Douglass confessed she could not give dates for any events prior to emancipation, but "I can Keep count of the number of years." She married her first husband two or three years before he enlisted, and they had two children in the interim. Their first, she noted, died at the age of four months, their second at just six days.[131] Patsy Clayborne, a slave in Adams County, also did not know exact dates, but she could name and count months and count years, too. So she knew her first child was taken away at one year, the second at seven months, although she could not tell in what years they were born. She left her owners during "the first July the Yankees garrisoned Natchez," which was to say 1863, three years after her second child "was taken away."[132] The Civil War figures prominently among time markers cited in testimony before the Pension Bureau, but slaves had no way of knowing they were living in the antebellum period before the war came. Until then, slaves counted forward and backward from commonplaces in their collective experience. Time markers, especially when combined with some understanding of numbers or the calendar, enabled slaves to place events in proper order.

Even a casual acquaintance with numbers or months added considerably to the flexibility and precision of keeping time by markers. Such knowledge enabled slaves to measure the distance between an event and a marker in any given year or put markers together from one year to the next and extend the field of time itself from one year to two or three years or more. Mary Williams could reckon time by her migration from South Carolina to Jefferson County, such as the two prior years she lived with her first owner's daughter in Charleston, the two years before that when she married her first husband, or the year after her arrival in the Natchez District when she married her second husband.[133] Tempting as it is to think of the difference between keeping time by date and placing events by markers as one of kind rather than degree, the distinction between the two modes blurred in practice.[134]

Still, keeping time by markers, even when supplemented by a familiarity with numbers and months, had its limitations. Slaves who kept dates by month, day, and year were mostly literate and hence a small minority. Washington Gray knew his letters well enough to transact business for his owner in New Orleans and to serve in the Union army as a sergeant in the 58th U.S. Colored

Infantry, Company A. Gray knew roughly when a fellow slave, Burl Lewis, arrived in Natchez from Virginia — "about 1857" — and would forever remember the date of his own enlistment, January 1, 1864.[135] Time markers equipped slaves to keep better track of the sequence than the duration of events. The rhythms of particular tasks in the annual routine of agricultural labor — planting, hoeing, cotton picking, to name a few — and the orderly recurrence of holidays accorded slaves a fair number of markers to situate events in the rough order of their occurrence. Much harder to track was how long events lasted because so many lapsed between markers or extended beyond them. Slaves, then, had a better notion of when, say, a neighbor arrived from the Upper South, a child was born, a couple married, or a wife was sold than of the length of time between such events or since an owner's last whipping frolic. Time markers cast a veil of ambiguity over all the affairs of a neighborhood, from family matters to struggles with owners.

For slaves, time had a way of doubling back on itself in a cycle, of encompassing them, rather like the boundaries of neighborhood itself. In their conception, time did not unfold infinitely backward and forward in linear fashion. Nor was it bound to notions of progress by any means. Yet time also was not circular, by these lights. The cycles lasted one year for most folks, several years for the numerate. Slaves, adept at putting events in sequence, did not conflate successive cycles into one but rather, to continue the spatial metaphor, placed them next to each other. For slaves, time was a series of cycles stretching back to the horizons of a collective memory, such as it was, forged by the neighborhood.[136]

The Natchez District was one of many locales where migrants to the Old Southwest broke ground on new neighborhoods. Slaves also carved neighborhoods out of the swamps and canebrake to the north in the Mississippi Delta, mainly along the Yazoo River. Slave population in the several counties of the Delta was growing exponentially, although it exceeded that of Adams County alone only around 1850. By then, slaves outnumbered white people by more than fourteen to one in one county, where the average slaveholding topped eighty.[137] Where settlement was so recent and thickly clustered, slave neighborhoods might encompass just a single plantation or stretch to adjoining places.[138] There were also neighborhoods below the district in the sugar country of southern Louisiana, where Dick Richards began to buy livestock during the 1840s and accumulated a small herd over the next twenty years. In the spring of 1866, his wife's former owner seized them, supposedly as compensation for her departure during the Civil War at Richards's behest. When he and a friend hunted up twenty head of cattle and five horses with Richards's brand, they went looking on a prairie behind the former owner's plantation "and in the neighborhood."[139]

In Middle Tennessee, where Israel Campbell migrated with his owners from the Vicksburg hinterlands in 1837, neighborhood comprised the terrain of slave religion. Campbell had long been anxious "to make my peace with God" but could never accomplish the work in Mississippi, "that wicked place." Although he succeeded less than a year after his arrival in Tennessee, it seemed a long time coming by Campbell's reckoning, after a weeklong camp meeting, a moment of conversion, and an agonizing season of doubt. He heard the call to the ministry in 1839 and began preaching that summer at "meetings around the neighborhood." This evidently encompassed a large area, perhaps as far as ten miles around, for he claimed to have walked that distance on many Sundays when he went preaching. Within those bounds lay virtually every landmark of his Christian life — the "praying-ground" where he first sought conversion in earnest; the several farms where he met with other slaves to sing and pray well into the night, exhorted and drew a following, white as well as black, and prevailed over slaveholders who aimed to stop his preaching; the new Baptist church he and his wife joined about five miles from his owners' place; and the nearby pond where Campbell was the first member to receive baptism, widely known as "Israel's pond."[140]

Slaves in the Black Belt in western Alabama struggled to keep up their ties with folks on adjoining plantations. During the late 1930s and early 1950s, exslaves in Sumter County told folklorists how people, forbidden by owners from visiting across plantation lines, kept in touch via calls that might carry as far as a mile off. Slaves sent out a holler, embellished with verbal phrases and musical tones appropriate to the feeling or intent of the message, to announce their presence, their whereabouts, or their mood; to inquire after friends; or to plan meetings.[141] In Greene County, Alabama, forty-nine slaves arrived from the Virginia Piedmont in 1840 to clear a new plantation for their owner, John H. Cocke. He offered them freedom provided they generated sufficient profits to repay their value and in the interim followed several rules without fail. Contrary to one of the standing directives, the slaves frequently stole off to go visiting on plantations adjoining Cocke family lands.[142]

In letters to Cocke, members of the Skipwith family described their new neighborhood as a site for both work and sociability. George Skipwith, foreman on Hopewell plantation, defended his management with the observation that Hopewell's cotton crop was in better shape than that on other plantations in the vicinity. Lice "have ingured the cotton cropes in our naberhood very much" but had done little damage at Hopewell. His daughter, house servant

Lucy Skipwith, was also inclined to view affairs at Hopewell in a neighborhood frame. During the Civil War, she assured Cocke that his relative who had fled to Hopewell from Mobile was settling in just fine. Mrs. Dorsey dispensed a good deal of "advice" to the slaves, though it was "serviceable to us all," and "nearly all the Ladies in the Neighborhood" had called on her.[143]

Slave neighborhoods in Alabama and elsewhere in the South undoubtedly had different contours from those in the Natchez District. First, neighborhoods in the district were probably larger than in some regions, smaller than in many others. A single plantation demarcated many neighborhoods in the Delta, and the same may prove true in other precincts newly settled with large slaveholdings during the late antebellum decades, such as Middle Florida, the Black Belt in East Texas, and other sites in the trans-Mississippi West.[144] Time is an important dimension of place making. Slave neighborhoods in the Atlantic Seaboard states, settled during the colonial period, were two centuries in the making by the Civil War and likely bigger than in the Old Southwest. Relations of power in the low country may have afforded bondpeople sufficient room to maneuver to push back neighborhood boundaries further still. Slaves engaged in task labor; many possessed mules, horses, and other means of transportation relatively unobstructed by planters who withdrew to town seats at Savannah and Charleston for much of the year; hence, many slaves navigated a favorable terrain for expanding neighborhood limits. From the standpoint of the South as a whole, slave neighborhoods in the Natchez District were on the small side.

Nor did slaves everywhere in the South put their neighborhoods together the same way as folks in the district. As the terms of work and struggle in the low country suggest, different configurations to particular neighborhood ties could transform the entire social terrain. Kinship may have distinguished neighborhoods in the Upper South and the Natchez District. Spouses belonging to different owners were more prevalent in states that exported slaves via the domestic trade than in importing states, like Mississippi.[145] If those men and women also went further afield than adjoining plantations to find husbands and wives, that would have gone a long way toward extending neighborhood boundaries past those lines, too. If the size of neighborhoods did not grow apace with ties between spouses, however, then those ties fell beyond neighborhood grounds. In that instance, other bonds may have had the pride of place among the neighborhood ties that intimate relations occupied in the Natchez District. Whether marriage abroad enlarged neighborhoods or fell outside them, the consequences for bonds of marriage, for bonds of neighborhood, and for the relationship between them were potentially vast. When slave neighborhoods are mapped across the South, the human geography of slave society is apt to look highly variegated, with a different topography and new landmarks.

However neighborhoods differed, the sense of place pervaded the ideology of slaves. It constituted the foundation of slave society. It defined their collective identity. It even shaped their sense of time. It took concrete form in neighborhoods, which could be found across the Old South from the Chesapeake to southern Louisiana, connected at the edges yet separate and distinct. Here slaves grounded family, work, property, struggles with owners, and varied sorts of companionability, from sacred worship to profane carousing. In the Natchez District, neighborhoods were the nexus of all those ties.

A neighborhood was slaves' handiwork, though they would not have thought so exactly. They did not, to their minds, make the place alone. They recognized slaveholders were fixtures in slave neighborhoods. As much as they struggled with planters to carve a path to adjoining plantations, they readily understood the paths widened with planters' cooperation. Slaves acknowledged owners' place in the neighborhood, with its boundaries hewed to plantation property lines. Neighborhoods, then, were the terrain of slave society as far as the slaves were concerned, a terrain they shared with owners. As a place shared with owners, moreover, neighborhood defined a terrain of struggle where the balance of power was tilted sharply against slaves. For slaves, one of the most profound impositions of bondage was never having a place they could call entirely their own.

Slaves' sense of place also complicated their sense of agency because they never set out to make neighborhoods. They did not, after all, attend sermons on adjoining plantations, go visiting, go courting, work, or lay out there for the purpose of creating neighborhoods. Rather, neighborhoods were the unintended result of such everyday activities. Nor do the vagaries of agency diminish the strength slaves took from their sense of place. On the contrary, this complex, indirect brand of agency gave slaves some distance, so to speak, from the neighborhood and enabled neighbors to imagine the place with a sense of permanence despite all the vicissitudes of slavery, the caprice of slaveholders, and the attendant vulnerability of bonds between slaves. Largely unbeknownst to themselves, without ever intending to do so, slaves made neighborhoods in the course of making and remaking families, crops, and the field of struggle. Intimate relations, work, and struggle — the sinews of neighborhood — have more to tell us about how slaves made this terrain and understood their society.

Intimate Relations

Mary Ann Helam was a reluctant bride, perhaps because she had endured a great many separations in her day. There were her parents and her daughter away off in Kentucky, and she had already lost two husbands. She buried one and was sold away from Robert Helam but kept his name anyhow. Now, in 1845, her owner, Latham Brown, was asking her to marry William Madison. She refused, but Brown would not take no for an answer. "I was told to marry this man by my master," Helam recalled. "I got 50 lashes on my back to make me marry him." And so a pledge exacted at the whipping post was taken as a vow at Belle Grove Church, "a colored peoples church."[1]

At the wedding, the bride, the groom, and their neighbors somehow made a start at consecrating the marriage, despite its unlovely beginnings. Among the slaves in attendance were two from the Brown place. The rest, she noted, were slaves "in the neighborhood." Over twenty years, Helam and Madison turned a forced concubinage into an enduring marriage, even if she maintained a certain distance and marked it by keeping the surname Helam. Her old friend, Rose Ballard, married at Belle Grove that day, too, and Helam and Madison named their first child a year later after Ballard's husband, Sidney. The boy died at just one month, but their two other children, Eli and his younger sister, Elizabeth, survived to adulthood. The baths Helam gave Madison were less a romantic interlude than a wifely service. "I done it to Keep him clean when he would come in from the field tired hot and dusty," she explained. Yet there was a touching intimacy to this chore as well, and she "washed him all over *many* times." When he enlisted in the Union army in 1863, he bought her some lumber, and she built a house in Natchez, where his regiment camped for a time. Madison returned to her from Vicksburg in May 1866, his face "hollow and sunken," with a feeling that told him he was "sick in his heart." He was only skin and bones: "He asked me to wash him. I washed him all over, and the next day he died."[2]

Intimate relations were fraught with tension for slaves because the weight of mastery bore heavily on even the most personal bonds. In the absence of legal recognition for spouses, forever subject to separation and vulnerable to the sexual predations of owners and their agents, men and women sought order for their attachments by contriving a structure of intimate relations. Comprising that structure was a set of understandings about different types of conjugal relationships—how they were created, what a couple could expect of each other, and how these unions related to one another.

In the Natchez District, slaves made fine distinctions between "sweethearting," "taking up," "living together," and marriage.[3] Sweethearting—neither permanent, nor monogamous, nor subject to the neighborhood's sanction—was an open-ended relationship for the young. Taking up was temporary, too, but was for mature couples prepared to submit to neighbors' informal recognition. Living together, by contrast, was a permanent bond, perhaps the most familiar to modern eyes, and entitled men and women to share a surname as well as a cabin. Marriage was permanent as well, yet distinguished from cohabitation by the formal recognition of weddings. The boundary between living together and marriage, slaves believed, was essential to the integrity of the bond between husband and wife.[4] Rights and duties did not set unions apart. Sweethearting and taking up overlapped from that standpoint. So did living together and marriage. What distinguished them was how slaves and owners sanctioned these unions. The endless task of creating and re-creating this structure, of articulating its rules and enforcing them as norms, was a neighborhood undertaking. As neighbors fastened bonds between men and women, they clinched the most binding ties in the neighborhood.

Romantic pursuits lent the neighborhood bond much of its ardor. They brought a steady traffic of men, who were expected to initiate courting, across plantation lines in every neighborhood.[5] Young men and women ventured into the neighborhood with new purpose when they went courting on adjoining plantations. Such visiting inflamed the daily struggle over passage between plantations because it had both costs and benefits to planters. The child of a slave belonged by law to the mother's owner. So planters might welcome their bondwomen receiving suitors from the neighborhood as a potential increase in property. A man who went visiting on an adjoining plantation, however, might beget children for another slaveholder. Slaves perfectly understood the slaveholders' calculations. Harry Alexander knew full well why his owner, William Foules of Adams County, tried to superintend the comings and goings between Mandamus and adjoining Beechland: "Squire Fowles wanted to keep the babies on his own place." Foules required his slaves to have a pass to go visiting and often turned down requests. Yet no force of man or nature could prevent neighborhood visiting by Alexander's account. "[I]t was just like stock, they could not keep them from mixing," he explained. "I would go over myself sometimes on a pass, and when they would not give me a pass *I'd go myself*."[6]

The pass system itself arose in part from owners' resolve to police the boundaries of intimate relations.[7] As Alexander suggested, refusals did not stop slaves from asking for passes. The bonds of neighborhood — in particular, the most intimate ones — required constant tending. They could not subsist on clandestine visiting alone, and slaves contended for owners' permission to clear the widest possible path between plantations.

Bonds between men and women survived even the worst calamities that befell a neighborhood. Foules could no more stop his men from taking a wife on Beechland than he could keep them from visiting there. For five solid years, Delila Clasby's husband, Thomas Parker, was a regular presence on the place to stay with her and after a time their two children.[8] Then, in June 1857, Parker and Alexander's brother killed the overseer on Mandamus. Both men hanged for the crime. Visiting in the neighborhood subsequently resumed with its customary pace and conventions. Elisha Clasby began to "step over" to visit Parker's widow on Beechland, sometimes with a pass, sometimes without. Clasby was already well known there to slaves who had kept abreast of the previous generation of intimate relations. Eliza Harris had known Clasby all his days. "He belonged to a neighbor here," she mused, "on the next plantation. I knew him when he was a baby." Delila Clasby went to great lengths in 1884 to obtain a pension as his widow, including paying witnesses to testify. Insisting that Parker was her husband undermined her claim to a pension as Elisha Clasby's widow. Yet she had no intention, even at that late date, of disavowing him. "I wish to say that Thomas Parker and I were man and wife before I picked up with the soldier," she said pointedly. "Parker killed a white man and was hung."[9] When neighborhoods reeled under heavy blows, the bonds of intimate relations persisted.

Slaves fashioned the structure of intimate relations as they came to terms with the conflicting desires of men and women as well as the capricious interventions of owners. Planters as well as their drivers and overseers forced themselves sexually on bondwomen. Slaves knew all too well that no couple was master of their own fate when owners had the power to sell, bequeath, or hire out either party as an exercise in discipline, as a bequest to children upon marriage, to settle a debt, or to divide an estate among heirs.[10] Some measure of the toll these transactions exacted can be reckoned from Union army registers of marriages performed in 1864 and 1865 at Natchez, Vicksburg, and Davis Bend. Among 3,846 men and women reporting previous spouses, nearly one of every six aged twenty or over reported a forced separation by an owner.

The likelihood of separation increased over time. More than a third of all couples with one partner at least forty years old had come through at least one broken union — one in five women thirty years old and over, one in four men.[11]

Yet the lessons of experience were as complex as the powers of owners were broad. Slaves were keenly aware owners could also keep intact what they rent asunder. Planters might permit, even force, couples to make a union — or forbid it.[12] Slaves defined intimate relations with the expectation that owners could respect or trespass on those relations and were likely do both at one time or another.

This was a lissom solution to an intractable problem. Bondmen and -women engaged owners, the greatest threat to all ties, in the enterprise of safeguarding them. Slaves also appropriated for themselves authority to sanction ties between spouses and to regulate intimate relations as a whole. As neighbors took notice of couples on adjoining plantations, mulled over, and gossiped about this one and that, they elaborated the rules and meanings of sweethearting, taking up, living together, and marriage. They took couples' measure, categorized them accordingly, and conferred or withheld recognition. Slaves forged a consensus about intimate relations that crossed plantation lines, prevailed in neighborhoods across the Natchez District, and added to the power of these bonds to hold couples together. Where slaves struggled to impart order to ties between men and women, they imposed it on folks in the neighborhood. Slaves devised a structure of intimate relations that enabled and obliged them to collaborate with and discipline both slaveholder and neighborhood.

The structure also accounted for some of the heavy lifting the slave family had to do. Families of every type rested in some measure on ties between parents.[13] Marriage produced a great many nuclear families everywhere in the South.[14] In the Natchez District, living together did so, too. By the same token, sweethearting and taking up engendered single-parent families, most headed by women, in every neighborhood. These transient unions offered up many of the children and mothers incorporated into extended families. The durability of the slave family, then, was not solely the product of the most enduring bonds between men and women. It resulted instead from hitching up the most open-ended ties in the structure to its most stable ones.[15] The permeability of intimate relations, which enabled couples to cross over from temporary to permanent unions — living together or marriage — transformed single-parent families into nuclear families. The variety of intimate relations enabled single parents and their children to form stepfamilies as well as mixed and extended families.[16] Slave families had to be works of ingenuity because they had to incorporate newcomers delivered by the slave trade, protect families from the impositions of owners, and ground folks unmoored by temporary intimate relations.

Like a painted portrait, the depiction of intimate relations in testimony before the U.S. Pension Bureau is burnished. Many witnesses polished blemishes to help claimants qualify for pensions. Congress provided in 1866 for widows of "colored" soldiers to receive pensions based on "satisfactory proof that the parties were joined in marriage by some ceremony deemed by them obligatory, or habitually recognized each other as man and wife, and were so recognized by their neighbors, and lived together as such up to the date of enlistment" by the soldier.[17] Thus it was partly at the bureau's cue that ex-slaves talked in terms of marriage and living together and distinguished those unions along lines of ceremony and the recognition of neighbors. Yet neither the categories nor the distinction were mere artifacts of federal law. The statute declared a widow equally entitled to a pension whether she and her husband had married or lived together. No one's claim depended on the difference between these two categories.

Former slaves were, if anything, more attentive to this distinction than the bureau was. According to an official reviewing the claim of Eliza Hutson, she "asserts that she was married to John Hutson by a slave ceremony." In fact, she had said just the opposite: "John and I were never married but were told to live together," she insisted. "I could not state that we had a ceremony of marriage because we did not."[18] Nor did Congress prescribe what ceremony constituted marriage. Rich, detailed accounts of the pains taken to orchestrate weddings and the myriad ways spouses sought and received neighbors' recognition all vouchsafe for the importance slaves placed on marriage, living together, and the distinction between them.

The incentives of the pension system, which underscored living together and marriage, prompted witnesses to lay a veil over sweethearting and taking up. The congressional provision that a widow had remained a soldier's wife until he enlisted raised the question of whether either spouse had other intimate relations either before or afterward. Bringing to light a couple's transition from sweethearting or taking up to living together or marriage raised nettlesome questions better left unasked. Even a bona fide widow did her cause little good by revealing a prior sweetheart, whether her husband's or her own. If either party had previously taken up with someone else, she likewise did well to keep that to herself. Women who contrived a widow's claim to obtain the pension of a former sweetheart or a man she had taken up with obviously had no incentive to talk frankly about the relationship. Still, voluble witnesses told some sweethearts' stories.

Sweethearting was a youthful bond. The very name evoked the first bloom of affection. It was a relationship of beginnings: the beginning of a couple, the beginning of new feelings and new passions, the beginning of sexuality itself. For a young woman in her late teens, sweethearting was a way of mediating desire in the interim between the onset of maturity and starting a family. Slave women typically reached menarche at age fifteen but had their first child at twenty. Many remained more or less in the dark about the facts of life as late as their first birth.[19] Others, feeling the pull of sexual attraction, took sweethearts. These couples were young, intimate relations were new to one party or both, and the relationship did not last forever. Sweethearts were thrust together as well by the sense their bond required no one's sanction but their own. Yet the feeling it was all their own affair was the most exclusive thing about this union, as sweethearts were not monogamous. Theirs was a compact of many pleasures and few obligations.

Thomas Green and Charity Dunbar were sweethearts during the 1850s.[20] Commitments were difficult to keep for slaves of Samuel Scott, who routinely transferred them among his three plantations and a fourth belonging to his son-in-law, all in Jefferson County. Martha Dudley, for example, was sent from Poplar Hill to Mount Vernon, David Creighton from Fair View to Cogen, the son-in-law's place. Charity Dunbar was still young enough to live in her father's house in 1855 or 1856 when Green began to spend nights with her on Poplar Hill.[21]

The immediacy of their relationship remained palpable some twenty years later as she explained they had not married, lived together, or sought their owners' permission. They "just took to sleeping together with out any bodies knowledge or consent." The sense of secrecy was their conceit. Other slaves learned all about them, beginning perhaps with her father, whose cabin was the quarters of their affair. That she could persist in the illusion she was secreting from him what was occurring under his own roof suggests he let the matter pass without comment. His silence, in turn, marked his sufferance of the relationship without conferring his recognition on it. Yet it also made him a collaborator in the secrecy and immediacy that bound together his daughter and Green. And it was from such shared illusions that sweethearting derived its fresh power.

Indeed, the secrecy around sweethearting was so widespread that many planters knew nothing at all of the bond, let alone the sweethearting couples in their midst. The practice came to light in two investigations of slave conspiracies in Adams County. In September 1861, sweethearting could scarcely compete for Lemuel P. Conner's attention with the astounding testimony he was hearing about an alleged conspiracy to launch a rebellion amid the crisis of the Civil War. Yet he managed to record, in his own shorthand way, a piece of gossip reported by a man named George: "Orange said he had Mitchell's Caroline Sweetheart." Orange, a prime mover in the conspiracy, was sweet-hearting with a woman on Palatine, one of the plantations in the neighbor-hood of George's plantation, Forest.[22] The disclosures in the other investiga-tion four years earlier were not as dire but were nonetheless disturbing. The novelty of sweethearting was only one reason the revelation about Dorcas, a slave woman on Cedar Grove, and John McCallin, a white carpenter, startled Alexander K. Farrar. The revelation lent credence to suspicions that McCallin had a hand in the murder of the overseer on Cedar Grove. "Dorcas was, and had been the '*Sweet heart*' of McCallin, for some 15 years," Farrar wrote dramatically to another concerned planter. Dorcas's relationship to McCallin was as open-ended as any between bondmen and -women. The carpenter also had designs to marry Dorcas's widowed mistress.[23]

The bond between sweethearts was as fragile as it was secret. It did not keep Green from running away as far and as long as he could. He made it clear to New Orleans before he was captured, and Dunbar gave birth to their daughter in his absence. Green was returned to Poplar Hill, then sent to Mount Vernon, where he took a wife. As for Dunbar, she was moved to Cogen. During her second year on the place, "Thomas went there a sweethearting after Charity," according to George Washington, who also lived, inevitably, on Mount Ver-non. Dunbar later claimed she had not known at the time about Green's wife, but that relationship did not infringe on hers because sweethearts were not exclusive anyway. The testimony is vague about just when Dunbar and Green parted for good, and it may not have been altogether clear at the time.[24]

Just as sweethearting gave a couple the fewest claims on each other, so it accorded parents the most tenuous hold on children. Green and Dunbar never did pull together much as parents. Around Christmas of the year he went sweethearting for her on Cogen, she was sent to Fair View, and their second child, a son, was born the following May. Green went to see her "once in a while" after that, Dunbar said. Occasional visits did not make him much of a presence to the children, Elsey and James.[25]

Owners broke Patsy Clayborne's precarious grasp on her children, too. She and George Smith belonged to the same owner in Adams County but lived on separate plantations, he at their "White folks great house," as Clayborne put it. They became sweethearts in the course of her Sunday visits there. The two babies taken away from her were "sweetheart children," Robert West recalled. Perhaps they were removed from her care to live with Smith and their owners at the home place, although the testimony does not spell out where they were taken or why. In any case, the arrangements estranged Smith from the children, too. Some fellow slaves had no inkling they were his. Grandisson Barton, for one, figured the father was a white man because Clayborne's color was dark and the children's was "bright."[26]

The bond between sweethearts and their children turned friable as two sets of power relations bore down on it — those between owners and slaves and between bondmen and -women. Even in nuclear families, women bore the brunt of the load when it came to the sheer work of parenting — the feeding, bathing, and comforting of little girls and little boys.[27] Where children lived with just one parent, it was usually their mother, so the care of sweethearts' children fell to her more or less in toto — as long as owners permitted her to live with the children, that is. Children taken away from parents, moreover, were especially vulnerable to sale.[28] These inequities were hardly privileges for men. Perhaps Thomas Green would have thought twice about absconding to New Orleans had he expected to take an equal part in caring for their daughter. But he presumably would not have run away in the first place had he already felt liberated by sweethearting.

Behind the distance between fathers like Green and their children, back of the inequities between slave men and women, were separations imposed by owners. Samuel Scott kept Thomas Green and Charity Dunbar on different plantations, and Patsy Clayborne and George Smith's owner separated that couple as well. The vast wealth of planters in the Natchez District only made it easier to come between sweethearts and their children. Multiple landholdings enabled slaveholders to separate these families on different plantations for any reason without the bother of selling them. Occupations that took men away from home on a regular basis — carriage driver or teamster, for instance — came between other sweethearts and their families.[29] Neighborhood sweethearts were divided by property lines. Sweethearting seemed a natural relation to young couples in no position to lay much claim to one another anyway.

Taking up was for sweethearts with endurance, figuratively and sometimes literally.[30] Men and women who took up were older than sweethearts, and their relationships tended to last longer. Sweethearting had its seasons but eventually ended or became another kind of union. Some sweethearts took up after their connection proved more durable than they or neighbors had expected. Many couples who took up eventually lived together or married and became husband and wife. Experience also gave taking up its own tone. This was a relationship for men and women who had outgrown the brash youthfulness of sweethearting. Of all the intimate relations, this one most squarely came to terms with owners' intrusions. Couples took up in the most acute awareness of the fragility of bonds between slaves, often from firsthand experience.

Bettie Wood and Daniel Robinson took up in Natchez. Their relationship during the Civil War was the point of contention before the Pension Bureau. She said they married, but he denied it. They still agreed on the nature of their antebellum affair, though he was dismissive about it in hindsight: "I just took up with her in old times — slavery."[31]

For Bettie Wood, taking up was a tough-minded accommodation to the grim reality that bonds like hers and Robinson's rested precariously on the whims of the slave trade, mortality, and two separate owners. She was sold south from Virginia so young she forgot her original owner's name, if she had ever known it. She was bought at the Natchez slave market by a local physician. In due time she took a husband, Winden Wood, who belonged to another owner, probably kin to hers. They had a son before Wood died. Two years later, "Daniel Robinson and I took up." Taking up was an open-ended solution to the perpetual vulnerability of intimate relations, driven home by her passage to Natchez, her husband's death, and the property relations that came between her and Robinson, a drayman who belonged to a different owner, a builder in town. They had two sons before emancipation.[32] For the generation of slaves born around 1830, the Civil War intervened to allow enduring couples to put their relations on a legal footing. But that possibility was nowhere on the horizon before the war, and couples took up for as long as circumstances permitted. Folks in previous generations spent lifetimes in this foreboding state.

Taking up was a product of several millstones grinding away at intimate relations on Sligo plantation in Adams County, from transfer between the owner's several properties to death and a licentious driver. Supervision over field laborers gave drivers a modicum of power over fellow slaves, and some used it to take sexual liberties with slave women. Emma Smith's claim as the widow of John Smith should be rejected, the commissioner of the Pension Bureau concluded after a special examiner decided she had been Barnett Baily's wife all along.[33] Perhaps her account of the millstones on Sligo was contrived as well, for they also served the interests of her claim. Transfer to separate plantations brought her prior relationship with Baily to an end with an air of finality. The driver's determined pursuit of her also suggested she was not his wife. Yet the bureau offered no opinion about those parts of her story, and drivers of that stamp were not unknown, while forced separations were commonplace.

During the 1830s, David P. Williams sent her across the Mississippi River to a Louisiana plantation he had an interest in. There she took up with Baily around 1839, and they had three daughters, lived together, became husband and wife. Williams removed his slaves from the plantation upon the division of an estate in 1845. He returned her to Sligo to nurse the Williams children and turned Baily over to another heir. That parted them for good, according to her, and Baily went back to his first wife. Whether or not her break with Baily was as clean as she made it out to be, their relationship afforded no protection back on Sligo, where "she was followed about by the driver and had a child by him."[34]

Other couples on Sligo also resorted to taking up. Nelson Grooms was in a position to know Emma's story and more about their owner's disregard for slaves' attachments. When Emma was a nurse on Sligo, Grooms was Williams's body servant—the man's "waiting boy," in Mrs. Williams's words. Grooms became a waiter in the dining room and tended his mistress's flowers. When he married Eliza Cotton, they had two sons and a daughter between 1847 and 1851, and then she died. When Grooms later contemplated his prospects with Zilla Johnson, he could tally up mortality along with the transgressions of owners and drivers among the reasons to keep their relationship on an open footing, at least initially. According to Anderson White, who also worked in the dining room, "Grooms took up with" Johnson. They eventually set up house together, and White considered them husband and wife, "as long as they lived together." But they went their separate ways after three years. Williams bought a new man, and Johnson "took up with him." White did not elaborate on the cause of the split between Johnson and Grooms.[35] Nor did he need to. Intimate relations on Sligo tended to be temporary, one way or another, which is why couples inclined toward taking up.

Taking up reflected a couple's determination to live with the temporary character of all intimate relations in slavery. Face to face with the vulnerability of all bonds to owners' impositions of every conceivable motive—greed, honor, vengeance, duty, lust—taking up charted a straightforward course subject to no one's approval and with few promises. Slaves took up in the knowledge that power relations in their society permitted owners to sell any man or woman at will, regardless of any bond he or she might fasten to another. Taking up was the most realistic intimate relation—more realistic than any intimate relation should have to be.

Sweethearting and taking up were the most similar of all these unions. Sweethearting was also temporary, if not in the same knowing way. Sweethearts might be off and on for the duration, which was not long. After a while, sweethearts broke up or took up, lived together, or married. Couples could take up, conversely, for years and years. Monogamy was the plainest difference between taking up and sweethearting, yet that distinction only underscores the overall resemblance between them, for slaves could not distinguish intimate relations solely in terms of obligations, fidelity included. Whereas sweethearts might well have two partners, slaves did not believe they could take up with two people at once. It was understood a couple had to split before one party took up with someone else, so taking up often ended up in serial monogamy. Sweethearting and taking up also shared the immediacy of a bond requiring only the sanction of the couple concerned. That mode of recognition, or lack thereof, contrasted sharply with living together and marriage, where couples went to some lengths to obtain the warrant of owners and other slaves.

The informalities of recognition made living together a bond all its own. To couples who had previously sweethearted or taken up, living together was a momentous change. It turned couples into spouses, obliged them to stick to one another for good and to remain monogamous for the duration. The exchange of recognition began with acquiring permission from parents and owners. The most powerful mode of sanction was the day-to-day acknowledgment of cohabiting men and women as spouses. This comprised a language of recognition in which neighbors called such couples by a common surname, talked about them as husband and wife, and bandied about whether they conducted themselves accordingly.[36] The couples performed their own roles in the drama, displaying their relationship on suitable occasions, soliciting neighbors' recognition, contending for it when withheld, employing it when proffered. Slaves across the South buttressed marriage by these means, too. Yet that did not make living together tantamount to marriage. In the Natchez District, slaves thought the language of recognition was one thing, the ceremony of marriage another, and they carefully maintained the distinction.

Slave spouses presented planters with pressing dilemmas of humanity and interest. Christian defenders of slavery who stringently formulated a master's duty deemed the inviolability of slave marriage essential to making southern slaveholding live up to biblical standards.[37] Henry Hughes, the secular proslavery theorist of Port Gibson, argued that marriage under church auspices would attain legal status as "warranteeism," his term for slavery in the South, advanced along the course of perfectibility.[38] The planters, though less exacting than either Hughes or the divines, judged proper spousal ties a mark of the "good master." Yet enduring ties between husband and wife ran at cross-purposes with slaveholders' right to dispose of people at will. Spouses also undermined the sexual prerogatives of mastery. The bond between spouses meant nothing if not that a wife shared her bed with her husband and him alone. For all these conflicts, humanity and interest also converged at particular points. Planters considered a growing slave population a touchstone of good management and dutifully recorded births and deaths in plantation journals. Some slave owners were well aware wives bore more children than single women.[39]

Slaveholders resolved these conflicting imperatives, to the extent they could, most readily on grounds of good order on the plantation. From this vantage point, planters found several virtues in the tie between spouses. It regularized sexual relations in the quarters, mediated competition for partners, and gave runaways pause.[40] Owners seized these advantages most forcefully when they directed recent acquisitions to take a spouse. William Madison, the husband Latham Brown chose for Mary Ann Helam, was a recent purchase.[41] George R. Dent personally conducted Archie Powell's wedding to a young woman "born & bred up on the Spring Hill," one of Dent's plantations in Jefferson County. "The master put them together & they stayed together," according to Lewis Griffin, who met Powell in the trader's yard where Dent purchased both men.[42] Planters also used marriage to manage problems engendered by neighborhood romances. Such couples, if kept apart, were prone to abscond and to labor poorly; if married, however, they were more likely to work steadily to maintain the husband's visiting privileges.[43] Accommodating spouses was a powerful tool in the ongoing struggle for control over space, more reliable than the pass system, less trouble than the whip. If it flattered master's self-image of benevolent paternalism, so much the better.

Yet such considerations did not entirely resolve the dilemmas posed by slave spouses. Planters added to those dilemmas with the broad claim to mastery combined with an inability to discipline themselves. The depredations of owners and their agents were rarely acknowledged, publicly or within plantation households. Nor did planters feel that upholding the bond in some cases and transgressing on it in others necessarily reflected poorly on them. They looked askance at peers who separated spouses for mere profit but were tolerant of those who did so under exigent circumstances, broadly defined. The planters were generally inclined to lay the dilemmas to the slave's purportedly bad character. Master's belief in the disciplinary benefits of the bond between husband and wife, for example, was based on the hoary notion that the potential for chaos lay not with slaveholders but within slaves. What spouses supposedly reined in was the slaves' lack of self-control, their reputedly passionate nature and inflated sexual desire.[44] In the end, owners tended to think what they did was best and the best they could do was the best that could be done. This gap between humanity and interest left slaveholders ample room to maneuver and thus left slaves with much work to do to put their intimate relations in order.[45]

Living together was a way of making the most of intimate relations at Ashburn, where the master reduced them to shambles. Austin Williams did not allow his people to marry. The prohibition suggests Williams, too, did not see marriage as synonymous with cohabitation and implicitly reserved a sexual claim on bondwomen, whom he wantonly violated, as did his overseer. In 1859 Williams's daughter, Eliza, and the overseer's son, John Hutson, decided to live together. William Henry Williams, a former dining room servant, declared the Hutsons "were never married excepting by slave customs," as if living together were tantamount to marriage for slaves. Then he made plain that living together was actually the closest slaves at Ashburn ever got to marriage: "No, there was no ceremony of marriage between them and there never was any ceremony on the Williams place — They would simply give their consent for them to live together and then they would celebrate with the supper." Slaves lived together because that was the only tie between spouses Williams recognized.[46]

As if to compensate for the prohibition against marriage at Auburn, slaves and owners contrived to put on more than the usual formalities for living together. Couples who lived together were rarely feted in the Natchez District, where suppers and similar festivities were reserved for marriages. Granting permission to share a cabin was a way for owners to recognize spouses everywhere in the South.[47] In the district, such permission was typically the only recognition owners extended at the outset to couples who lived together. Yet at Ashburn a supper of some kind was customary as well, William Henry Williams suggested. In the Hutsons' case, he added, it was "a big supper" given by their mistress, Caroline Williams: "[W]e had a big time," Eliza Hutson agreed. It must have been an ambivalent cause for celebration to Caroline Williams. She had lived in close quarters with her husband's slave daughter for Eliza's entire life. "I was raised right in the house with Mrs. Williams," Eliza Hutson recalled.[48] Many planter women bedeviled their husband's slave children.[49] Yet Caroline Williams, married to a man who degraded all intimate relations, master and mistress's included, took the unusual step of collaborating with slaves to put on suppers that dignified the bond between cohabiting men and women.

Neighbors recognized couples who lived together as spouses by exchanging stories about them and telling tales when circumstances warranted. Despite the thicket Thomas Green made of his affairs, slaves in his neighborhood kept sufficiently close track to know he lived with his wife, Mary Walker. After

Green stopped sweethearting with Charity Dunbar, his dalliance with Martha Dudley came to light. Susan Barefield, also a slave at Mount Vernon, agreed with George Washington that Dudley and her husband were married at the time, whereas Green and Walker lived together.[50] Neighbors on the adjoining Terry plantation were also alert to the particulars about Green and Walker. Emanuel and James Genifer, for example, knew Green and Walker "lived together." The Genifers were in a position to know, they explained, because of the constant visiting between the quarters, a mere quarter mile apart.[51] There was more to the exchange of gossip than mere nosiness, even if there was plenty of that to go around, too. Becoming known in the neighborhood as husband and wife was among the few tokens of recognition available to couples who lived together.

Surnames carried much of the freight in the recognition of husbands and wives who lived together. Mahala Knox contradicted her brother and a former fellow slave who testified she and William Knox were married.[52] They took up at first, she explained, and in time sought permission from their owner, Reverend Benjamin Chase, to share a cabin on the Mansion place in Adams County. They lived together some ten years and had four children — two girls and two boys — who also went by the name of Knox. A common surname, used throughout a neighborhood, neatly rendered intimate relations and family ties mutually reinforcing. It marked the Knoxes at once as parents and spouses.[53] The transitive property of a surname, assumed by a couple and affixed to them by others, conveyed weighty principles about intimate relations in general. Wherever couples who lived together assumed a shared last name and slaves on adjoining plantations spoke of the couple that way, it announced to the neighborhood that cohabitation sufficed to make men and women husbands and wives.

Of course, neighbors employed these informal modes of recognition with married couples as well. Neighbors often did so when drawing the distinction between marriage and living together. Married couples were typically known by the same name in their neighborhoods, too, and names were valued emblems of recognition for them as well.[54] The marriage bond took space in a neighborhood in everyday moments of recognition — the work of evaluating a couple and identifying them as married, making overtures for neighbors' sanction and conferring it, applying the label of marriage and making it stick. Yet marriage provided spouses with further recognition. Weddings exalted the tie between husband and wife by convening neighbors to bear witness to the bond in the making, to honor it by various ceremonies, to celebrate it with feasting, dancing, and sundry merriments. Between the everyday moments of recognition and the big times of weddings, slaves routinely heard tell of marriages in the neighborhood. That kept neighbors busy testifying before the Pension Bureau after the Civil War. Henry and George Randall could attest in 1867 to the marriage of Caroline and Benjamin Grim, "as they lived on adjoining plantations & in sight of each other for 4 years" in Jefferson County before Grim enlisted in the Union army.[55]

By these acts of recognition, slaves placed marriage at the pinnacle of intimate relations. Slaves regarded sweethearting, taking up, living together, and marriage as a hierarchy. Boundaries between these unions were permeable enough to allow couples such as Judy and Nelson Davis to run the gamut, but only in one direction. The Davises met in a trader's drove around 1842. Somewhere between Halifax, Virginia, and Natchez they "took up with each other," according to her half-sister, Lucinda Braziel. They began living together on Magnolia Grove in Adams County. Living together sufficed to make them husband and wife, but that was not to say they were married. The Davises could have merely gone through the motions of a ceremony two years later, considering the precious little homage to be paid them in the mass wedding their owner had arranged. Perhaps the Baptist minister performing the ceremony ennobled the occasion in their eyes. In any case, marriage meant something more than living together, and the Davises busied themselves with preparations for the wedding. Susan Swanson, who had also made the passage from Halifax to Magnolia Grove, "saw them getting ready."[56] A couple could go forward from sweethearting or taking up to living together and marriage, but there was no going back. If a husband and wife fell out, they did not retreat to living together or taking up; they parted for good.

Slaves distinguished marriage from living together by a formal sanction unique in their intimate relations. There was next to nothing in the attendant privileges and duties to tell the two relations apart. Both made a couple husband and wife, permitted them to share a cabin, and obliged them to be monogamous forevermore. Marriage also was no guarantee of those prerogatives. Husbands and wives who belonged to different owners, for example, were compelled to live apart. Had slaves defined marriage in terms of claims and duties, couples such as Rachel and Jackson Meguire would have had no business considering themselves married. Yet according to Rachel Meguire, "they had been married about 14 or 15 years when her husband died." In 1849, she recollected, "a squire," as slaves called a justice of the peace, performed a wedding for them on her owner's plantation just outside the Natchez District in Franklin County. Jackson Meguire traveled the four miles from his owner's place in Jefferson County to stay with Rachel Meguire in her cabin on

Wednesday and Saturday nights. That was not living together exactly, but the Meguires considered themselves married, and slaves who knew them agreed.[57] To slaves, what singled out marriage among all the intimate relations was the ceremony of weddings.

Susan Alexander and Louisa Woods were in perfect accord about the difference between marriage and living together, even though they disagreed on the particulars of the relationship between Alexander and her husband. Woods was emphatic the Alexanders lived together. Woods was no less insistent they were husband and wife for fifteen years or more, yet she wanted it understood living together was no marriage. The Alexanders "just took up with each other and lived together," Woods explained. According to Susan Alexander, however, marriage was one of several transformations their bond underwent. They were sent south from Virginia together as children before they were bought by the Whitmores in Adams County. The couple sweethearted at first during the 1840s and soon had two children — "sweet hearts children," she noted. Eventually, "they were married by Mr Whitmore." Though the ceremony had occurred "a great many years ago," she still remembered something of the vows he administered.[58] Woods and Alexander agreed about marriage in principle. Woods insisted the Alexanders were not married because no ceremony had occurred, and Susan Alexander said they were married because her owner had performed such a ceremony.

Alexander was hardly unusual in casting her owner in a prominent role at her wedding, for slaves in the Natchez District might engage owners at several junctures in making a marriage. Couples routinely sought owners' permission to marry,[59] even from a master of Prosper K. Montgomery's ilk. Montgomery presided over a Jefferson County plantation where he, his son, and his drivers tried the bonds between men and women. Montgomery's determined acquisition of land and slaves during the 1850s churned the quarters. He was often on the road to Natchez to buy slaves, and he moved some of his people across the Mississippi to a plantation near Providence, Louisiana, in January 1858.[60] Meanwhile, Montgomery's son, Frank, prowled the quarters on the Jefferson County place. Eliza Jones had her first child by Frank Montgomery. Nor were his advances the only ones she had to contend with. There was a time when driver Jerry Bingaman forced himself on women, too. By the eve of the Civil War, "he was a old man and had a wife and family of his own, but he was not above that in his young days," she recalled. "I remarked once in the quarters that if he was to bother me I'd kill him."[61]

Although some men and women circumnavigated this havoc by secreting their ties from Montgomery, enough couples asked his okay to make it seem conventional. He could not say for sure years later whether Eliza Jones and Elisha Grayson applied to him, though he figured they had "because it was the Custom of the slaves to ask my consent." William Fountain, who had also belonged to Montgomery, agreed: "The reason I am sure that they got permission to marry is because they had a regular wedding, while slaves that lived together without such permission had [to] do it on the sly." There was something chilling in how trespasses on women were embodied for the occasion by the notorious Jerry Bingaman, who also performed the weddings in his other capacity as a self-styled preacher. To Eliza Jones, Bingaman "was no preacher" at all, "but being the head man on the plantation and a member of the church he married me and Elisha."[62]

Owners' varied parts in weddings made capriciousness the norm.[63] More than a few masters officiated personally, some at the happy couple's request. Mistresses also performed weddings, some as "deputy husbands" in their absence, most as widows. Others took the trouble of hiring a minister. Religious ceremonies were the most promising to slaves during the 1830s. Clergymen expected couples to pledge themselves to one another for life. The Methodist ceremony, for example, convened the wedding party "in the sight of God," described marriage as a "holy estate," and joined bride and groom as husband and wife "until death parts you."[64] The Methodist vow also obliged owners to help slaves uphold it, and this encumbrance on master's property rights sufficed to make church weddings rare in the United States until the 1840s. After southern Protestants split off from their northern brethren — Methodists in 1844, Baptists in 1845 — ministers became more amenable to joining couples who might be separated and revised wedding vows accordingly. Many owners left the ceremony to slave preachers, drivers, or overseers.[65]

Slaves also prevailed on owners for clothes, food, and other means of celebrating a wedding in the high style they preferred for giving marriage its due.[66] Tishne Price recalled how "my mistress gathered up a lot of eggs and gave us a big dinner, and she dressed me in her dresses and jewelry," despite misgivings "we were only children."[67] Five couples on Basil Kiger's Buena Vista in Warren County had a yuletide wedding in the big house, followed by a supper of whiskey, pork, and cakes in the dining room and a dance in the hall. The fiddler nearly wore a hole in the floor keeping time past two in the morning.[68] Owners might accord a bride and groom some or all of these good offices, while others gave their consent and nothing more. The conventions of marriage, from the slaves' point of view, ranged widely across the neighborhood.

Consider the weddings on the Darden brothers' plantations in Jefferson County during the mid-1850s.[69] John Young and Margaret Dupee took vows administered personally by their owner, Buck Darden.[70] At Samuel Darden's place, a minister presided over some weddings, a slave preacher over others. James and Louisa Reed, for example, were married by a minister, their mistress's brother in-law.[71] Darden thought he extended this courtesy as well to Daniel Reed, James's brother, and Phillis Davis, the cook's fifteen-year-old daughter. A former fellow slave agreed, but the bride recalled her owners merely gave their consent, and a slave preacher on the place conducted the ceremony.[72] Old Jackson, another slave preacher, married Dicy and Oliver at Jesse Darden's, while their mistress took a hand in preparing a late supper spread — sausages, mutton, ham, coffee, and assorted desserts.[73] Slaves on the Darden plantations found their owners might perform a wedding, leave it to a relative or a slave preacher, give a party for one couple, or have just a few words of approval for another.

As the nuptials on the Darden places suggest, slaves assumed corollary parts to owners' roles in weddings. Couples routinely solicited their parents' consent, of course, and slave preachers often performed wedding services. Slaves did the lion's share of the work that went into the wedding feast, even when planter women pitched in, and the white family often retired when the dancing got started. After Old Jackson administered vows to Dicy and Oliver, a small party of a half dozen guests made the most of the occasion by tending to appointed roles. One couple waited on the bride and groom, while a fiddler called the figures for the dancers, who included three men from the neighborhood.[74] The most festive moments in the celebration of marriage were a neighborhood affair.

Although slaves and owners could play the same supporting roles in a marriage, they interpreted their parts differently. Consent, for example, had different connotations to the parties concerned. Chaney Johnson and Henry Sellers used Jacob Surget's consent to marry over her parents' objections. Surget was one of many planters who considered themselves qualified to judge the suitability of a prospective bride and groom, though he would not agree to the marriage without first consulting Johnson's parents. Her mother objected that Sellers, "a very stout man" who could lift as much as two men, by one account, was too big for her daughter. Surget agreed on that point but deemed Johnson's pregnancy the uppermost consideration, and the couple wedded with his approval around Christmas.[75] Slaves were determined to obtain consent from even the most irresponsible master because they understood that the permission of a mother and father was not on a par with the owner's. That is not to say slaves sought owners' consent with any notion master knew best.

For slaves, consent had nothing to do with the legitimacy of their bond as husband and wife. Rather, it was a matter of inveigling owners to place their imprimatur on a couple's own determination to stay together for good. Thus, many couples did not hesitate to marry over their owners' objections.[76] Permission was especially tricky to obtain for men and women belonging to different owners, for it required the approval of both, and either might demur. Yet a couple in Adams County received just the assurances they sought when they asked her owner, Reverend John G. Jones, a Methodist missionary, for his approval in the fall of 1834. Jones agreed to the marriage and agreed that when he left the vicinity, he would hire or sell her "in the neighborhood." Jones had only one condition, that the groom provide "a certificate of his good character" and of his owner's consent. When the owner refused, Jones considered the matter closed. The couple did not. Six months later, she "astonished" her owner with the revelation they "were married."[77] They, like others, sought permission to secure the prerogatives of marriage, nothing more and nothing less.

Even marriage itself had different meanings to slaves and owners. Jones and his slave's disagreement came to a head when he sold her in April 1835. At the moment of her departure with her new owner, she "burst into a great flood of grief" and declared she would rather die than leave her husband. Although Jones did not record her account of the circumstances of the marriage, she explained enough about them to persuade him they did not meet his criteria for marriage, but they plainly met hers. Her grievous objections derailed the sale, however, and her ensuing illness bought Jones time "to cry mightily to God" for guidance and then to persuade Bryan to purchase the woman "and let her and the man she loves get married."[78] This man and woman were obliged to take an unusually circuitous course to extract their owners' consent. Yet they were typical in collaborating with slaveholders, despite disagreements about the implications of owners' participation and the definition of marriage.

These disagreements were sharp, even if the parties avoided calling attention to them. For the planters as well as for northerners, Christian marriage was inseparable from legal marriage and its attendant rights and duties. Marriage conferred control over property and children, permanent obligations to support them and remain husband and wife. Slave marriage carried none of these implications as far as slaveholders were concerned. It accorded husband and wife no rights to property, to children, or to each other. Indeed, it bestowed no rights at all, only privileges, which were owners' to give or take away. Nor do the gendered inequalities of legal marriage mitigate the contrast with slave marriage. A slave wife did not owe her husband obedience, for that was a master's due from her and her husband alike. Whereas a husband had a legal right to physical chastisement, the slave husband who presumed to correct his wife was liable to get a whipping himself.[79] Slaves staked the claims of marriage not in law but in the wedding ceremony. They knew it held no guarantee against separation from spouses or children.[80] They believed a husband and wife ought to stay together by rights, but not as a right in law that belonged to them the way land, horses, or slaves belonged to white people. Weddings brought to the fore the underlying purpose of the entire structure of intimate relations, to put the bonds between men, women, and families on a stable foundation where it was not subject to constant negotiation and re-negotiation with owners.

Weddings in the Natchez District were anything but a ritual. Standardization is one of the definitive features of ritual, essential to its galvanizing work of directing thought and feeling toward particular ends and naturalizing them. Rites have a formidable power to give order symbolically to what is disorderly in society — the havoc, for example, that slavery wreaked on unions between men and women. Ritual can also reconcile antagonists to one another and to change by creating a sense of continuity among past, present, and future. It seems tailor-made to the problem slaves sought to solve — that is, to impose an order on owners in the future that had never existed in the past. One need not overlook the ambiguities of symbols or the often conservative nature of ritual to recognize that bonds between slaves could have been strengthened by ritual that declared the inviolability of slave marriage, dramatized, legitimized, and sacralized it.[81]

But planters got the better of the struggle over conventions of marriage. The slaves managed to carve out a space for weddings, like many rites, on the calendar. Most weddings took place during hiatuses in the annual routine of cotton agriculture — in July, after the crop was laid by, or around Christmas and New Year's, after the harvest.[82] Although some owners stuck with the Methodist matrimony through the 1850s, the inviolability of marriage did not fare well in the vows pronounced by most planters. Those Charles Whitmore administered to Susan Alexander and her husband were typical. "They stood up before him," she recalled, and Whitmore asked the bride "if she was willing to take Allen as her husband and do for him all that a woman should and he asked Allen" if he was willing to take Susan as his wife and do for her all that a man should.[83] Conspicuously absent was any pledge to unite bride and groom for life.[84] The vows most slaves took before owners, implicitly reserving the latter's prerogative to separate the couple, were all duties and no rights.

Despite the irregularities of weddings, slaves often put on elegant affairs.[85] Slaves in Tubb Robbins and Diana More's Wilkinson County neighborhood took care to give the couple a proper send-off in 1845. The event began just before dusk, according to a white observer, as slaves "from neighboring farms" began to arrive. Their first stop was the kitchen, where they paid their respects to More and Robbins. Guests chatted brightly—anxiously, too, when the slave preacher failed to appear at the appointed hour. Fiddlers were present, but the congregation remained still, as dancing before the ceremony was "a great indignity to the bride and groom." In the interim, the couple dressed. Robbins cut quite a figure in white pants, ruffled shirt, coat, gloves, and a stock high about his neck. Finally, two hours later, the parson arrived.[86]

The man gave his all to exalt this marriage between slaves. He took notice of the neighbors in attendance, submitted the couple's fitness to marry for their approval, and called on the father of the bride. He invoked Scripture, claimed to bestow the favor of God, and seized the authority of law. "By virtue ob dis writin' and dis holy book which I now hold in my hand," began the preacher, "and in dep presence ob all dese ladies and gemmen, I proceed accordin' to de constitution ob Wilkerson county, to marry, in a lawful manner, dese two niggers now before me." It was a bold stroke on the couple's behalf to appropriate the sway of law for the proceedings, even if Wilkinson County had no constitution. Denigrating the couple evidently struck the groom as superfluous, though, for his face and back tightened visibly at the mention of "niggers."[87]

"In de fus place," the preacher continued, "I ax who gibs dis girl away?" After a moment, the bride's father answered in a sharp voice: " 'Me! Peter,' Diana's daddy, *'guvs her up!'* " The preacher then invited the assembled neighbors to state once and for all any reason why the couple should not marry. Hearing none, he turned to the bride and groom. "You, Tubb Robbins, and Diana More, both ob you very plainly hear dat no one perjects to you marryin. Tubb Robbins, does you take dat omen you got by de right hand to be your loved wife, to nourish her, cherish her, and sakin all oders and cleavin to her alone, true and as well as good report assent." The groom bowed low in acknowledgment of his vow, and the bride smiled broadly in acceptance of hers. "Now, wid the grace ob God, Tubb Robbins, I pounce you man and woman, and yu de same Diana More. Salute your bride." The couple sealed their pledge with a kiss and retreated to their cabin accompanied by choruses of "Hurry on home my Diana gal" and the hearty congratulations of their neighbors, who remained for a supper and dance.[88]

Slaves were not simply standing on ceremony when they put on big weddings. They believed weddings honored marriage and added force to the bond between spouses. Diana More, Tubb Robbins, and their neighbors were by no means alone in the elegant dress and polite civility they displayed in celebration of "the matrimony," as former slaves often referred to wedding vows.[89] The "perfect propriety" of the slaves in attendance at Patrick and Mimi's nuptials on Melrose outside Natchez impressed even their mistress.[90] Slaves fashioned weddings into a singular recognition of the ties between husbands and wives.[91] Putting on a ceremony with all the trappings they could muster enabled a couple to make their owners, their kin, their neighborhood, and their God party to their vow and oblige them to respect it.

Slaves aimed the symbolism of weddings most pointedly at owners, the pre-eminent threat to spouses. Couples welcomed, even solicited, owners' partici-pation on the supposition slaveholders would hesitate to pry apart a union to which they had personally, formally acceded. If the slaves' notion was grounded as much in hope as fact, it found confirmation in some planters' re-luctance to separate married couples.[92] Betrothed slaves became all but price-less to Basil Kiger. Five recently purchased men got word to him in the fall of 1851 that they had made matches and wished to know whether he wanted them to wait until Christmas to marry. Their wedding came off in Kiger's house with high stepping into the early hours, as we have seen. In the mean-time, he dangled the prospect of marriage over their heads as reward and punishment. There would be no bride for Zeke unless he picked two hundred pounds of cotton daily, Kiger told the slave, "and he gets it regularly." Yet the prospect of weddings also made Kiger well disposed toward these slaves and boded well for their marriages. "You know it is against my principal to sell," Kiger reminded his wife, "but were I disposed to do so an offer of 10000 dollars would not buy them."[93]

A wedding, though not a ritual, seemed from the slaves' standpoint to symbolically mediate the conflict between slave owners' property rights and bonds between spouses. Marriage held out a promise of permanence, however implicit, and slaves did everything in their power to hold owners to that promise. The promise was explicit in the case of Sally and Ednoull, and he invoked it in 1849 when their owner, Dr. John Copes, made known his inten-tion to hire out Ednoull in Baton Rouge, Louisiana, and leave Sally behind in Mississippi. "Ednoull tells me," the owner's agent related, "that you and Mary Ann said when he and Sally married that they should never be parted and says that if I send him from her it will not do you or anybody else any good." Ednoull soon made his threat plain: "He openly said that he would kill himself if I sent him," the agent explained. Whether Ednoull's entreaties succeeded in the end is unclear. The threat certainly gave Copes second thoughts, however, and Ednoull did not accompany fellow slaves to Baton Rouge, although he too was sent within months. Copes's young stepson, heir apparent to Ednoull, urged Copes to reunite the couple and made the case on the same grounds Ednoull had pleaded to the agent.[94]

Though marriage did not in practice guarantee a couple's longevity, it staked a claim they could invoke again and again in the ongoing struggle to stay together. Warrick and Millie Hartwell were among the couples who made it stick. Armstead Hartwell, their owner in Rutherford County, Tennessee, went to some lengths to make their marriage possible, subsequently resolved to separate them forever, yet helped them remain together in the end. When Warrick Hartwell made known his intentions toward Millie Lanoing, who belonged to another owner, Armstead Hartwell agreed to buy her. The couple married around 1845 before a Methodist slave preacher who also belonged to Hartwell. Then, just three years later, their owner decided to sell Minnie Hartwell and wrest them apart. But Warrick Hartwell retained enough faith in his own powers of persuasion and his owner's susceptibility to them to ask that he and his wife be sold together, as we saw in chapter 1. Armstead Hartwell acquiesced and secured trader Sam Winston's pledge to sell them together, too.[95]

If the message of weddings was targeted primarily at owners, neighbors were critical to its intended effect. Weddings often convened slaves from around the neighborhood. A deputation from adjoining Monmouth was among the guests who impressed the mistress of Melrose with their decorum at Patrick and Mimi's nuptials. In fact, Mimi's bridesmaid, Viola, was a house servant at Monmouth.[96] Viola, in turn, married Marcellus, a slave on Melrose, the next spring. A flickering candlelight illuminated the service, as Viola, dressed in white, and Marcellus, in black, took their vows before a minister in Monmouth's opulent parlor, followed by a supper and dance.[97] Couples and neighbors needed each other at weddings. The presence of slaves from adjoining plantations put owners on notice the bride and groom were not the only parties concerned about the endurance of their bond over the long term and anyone who transgressed on the bond would have to contend with the neighborhood. Neighbors, for their part, readily seized their chance to exalt the bond between husband and wife, for this was part and parcel of the entire structure of intimate relations.

The feasting, dancing, and games that often ensued after the vows were, notwithstanding the marked change in tone, intimately connected to the solemn purpose of weddings. The air of gravity gave way to boisterous celebration, especially after the members of the white family took their leave. The prospect of a big time promised a large turnout to the general levy for Emily Wilson and Harris Stewart's wedding on Covington in Jefferson County. They could count on the attendance of Lewis and Alice Murray, who lived on the adjoining plantation and had known the bride for ten years or more. People with more attenuated ties to the bride and groom might attend with no higher aim than joining the party. Ben Lewis, a slave artisan from Adams County working near the Covington place, filled out the crowd at Wilson and Stewart's nuptials.[98] An elaborate wedding announced a marriage; a big time broadcast it across the neighborhood.

Marriage was a constitutive neighborhood bond. A large proportion of slave marriages across the South joined men and women belonging to different owners. Slave marriages across plantation lines comprised somewhere between one and three of every ten marriages, studies of the Works Progress Administration narratives suggest, and the proportion was higher in some states, such as South Carolina.[99] Scholars have yet to map the terrain of "abroad marriage" with any precision on the Atlantic Seaboard, but it evidently was not limited to adjoining plantations. The taboo against marriage between cousins compelled men and women to search far and wide for a suitable partner where slaveholdings were small and family trees could extend back a century. Slavery was founded during the seventeenth century in low country South Carolina and in Maryland, where about half of all slaveholding farms had fewer than three slaves by 1860. Many couples lived miles apart.[100] The proportion of spouses with different owners was comparatively low on large slaveholdings in states, like Mississippi, where planters bought more people than they sold in the domestic trade.[101] If testimony to the Pension Bureau is any indication, long-distance marriages were a rare thing in the Natchez District. With large slaveholdings and the constant influx of new slaves, women could take husbands and men wives at home or on adjoining plantations. Neighborhood, in short, encompassed the geography of marriage.[102]

Yet the variety of conjugal unions in the district placed the region in the mainstream of intimate relations in slave societies throughout the Americas. Even on tiny St. John, in the Danish West Indies, the spectrum was wide. Some men and women married; others formed enduring, monogamous unions without the recognition of law or the Moravian Church; while many were intimate with more than one partner during short-lived unions. One of the most important differences between intimate relations was spatial — whether couples got together on the same estate or, as occurred in large and growing numbers, lived on separate plantations. Provision grounds, typically located along the boundaries between estates, offered one arena where men and women met and talked and socialized. During the 1830s and 1840s, more than half the children baptized in the Moravian Church had parents living on different plantations.[103]

The sanction of marriage by church and state, in the absence of institutions to enforce it, contributed to the range of unions in the French Antilles and Brazil. Although recognition in canon and civil law had no counterpart in the United States, in practice it offered little alternative to informal bonds. Men and women still faced the forced separations, the sexual exploitation common in the Natchez District, and other obstacles besides. A large proportion of slaves had no intimate relations at all. Contrary to European laments about promiscuity, slavery was forced celibacy for many, including women who abstained from sex and men who never found partners in overwhelmingly male populations. High mortality also winnowed the field of eligible partners and cut short many unions. West Africans of different nationalities and American-born slaves married largely among themselves.[104]

Slaves entered into Christian marriages throughout Brazil, but only in small proportions.[105] Many had their own objections to marrying in the Catholic Church.[106] Most could not have done so if they had tried. Although the church supported slave marriage in principle, Brazilian priests were indifferent or hostile in practice. Slaveholders, whose permission was required for a priest to post a slave couple's banns, were reluctant to consent. Marriage protected husband and wife from separation in canon law, and violations could incur censure from the church. Slaveholders' control over plantation space raised another barrier in Bahia. Slaves did not extend marriage across plantation lines here because planters largely succeeded in confining field laborers to the grounds of their own estates. Christian marriage between slaves belonging to different owners was virtually unheard of.[107] The low incidence of marriage in Bahia was proverbial: "Negroes do not marry; they just live together."[108] Common-law marriage and concubinage were the norm for most free people as well in Brazil, where the vast majority of the population eschewed marriage.[109] Many slave couples maintained enduring bonds outside the church. Some women became owners' concubines in the hope of gaining freedom for themselves or their children.[110] Intimate relations for a great many slaves in Vassouras, a coffee-growing region, were mainly *amazia*, temporary unions.[111]

Slaves in Martinique and Guadeloupe, France's Caribbean empire after Haitian independence, engaged in marriage and polygyny, among other unions. Legal marriage was permissible yet rare. The Code Noir, Louis XIV's regulations on slaveholding, had placed marriage on a narrow foundation. It accorded slaves the privilege of marriage by a priest with the consent of their owners, who were prohibited from separating spouses. But neither the Catholic Church nor colonial authorities on the ground stopped planters from breaking up marriages at will. Most planters avoided running afoul of the code simply by withholding consent to marry. Thus, as in Brazil, the protection of marriage discouraged owners from permitting it and thereby prodded slaves to make other arrangements. Polygyny was practiced in every Caribbean slave society yet was also unusual, confined to a narrow stratum of skilled laborers, drivers, and others with means.[112] Little is known about what unions prevailed among the vast number of men and women untethered by marriage or polygyny. It is reasonable to suppose that the practice travelers consigned to *libertinage*, a term for concubinage and promiscuity in metropolitan France, actually constituted from slaves' point of view a more or less clearly defined relationship or perhaps many such relationships.[113]

Perhaps the closest counterpart to the Natchez District was the British Caribbean. Several varieties of marriage prevailed there. Polygynous marriage was not unknown. Christian marriage was widely practiced, though not universally popular, and many couples eschewed it. Such couples were engaged, in effect, in common-law marriages after the legal recognition of marriage in 1815.[114] The similarities were especially striking in Jamaica. Young couples inclined toward temporary unions with few obligations, something akin to sweethearting. Older couples with strong commitments cohabited. Slaves deemed legal marriage proper mainly for older couples of proven durability. Some of the prestige of age rubbed off on marriage itself. As in the district, men and women could pass through some or all these relationships as a couple or with different partners.[115]

In the Natchez District, neighborhood filled a place in slave marriage that African ethnicity had occupied in Spanish America during the era of the trans-Atlantic slave trade. There, the Catholic Church accorded marital rights directly to slaves, who need not gain owners' consent. In colonial Mexico, however, the church insisted on proof that the prospective bride and groom were single and unencumbered by ties of kinship to one another. To petition an ecclesiastical judge for a license, they produced witnesses intimately familiar with them to substantiate those claims. *Bozales* (African-born slaves) chose sponsors of the same ethnicity and with rare exceptions took marriage partners from members of their own ethnic groups. Thus, the typical wedding party comprised entirely Angolans, or Congolese, or Biafrans. In Mexico City, where slaveholdings were small, the bride and groom passed over acquaintances in their own vicinity in favor of sponsors of the same ethnicity from a different barrio at some distance.[116] In the district, by contrast, slaves carved out a geography of marriage in the proximity of adjoining plantations. Neighborhood defined the terrain where slaves found spouses, and spouses found recognition.

Indeed, no tie bound the neighborhoods of southwestern Mississippi more tightly than marriage. After the wedding, often a neighborhood event, the husband became a fixture over at his wife's quarters. The proximity of adjoining plantations facilitated more frequent visiting than was possible in an "abroad marriage," which typically permitted couples to spend weekends together. In the Natchez District, some married men had a standing pass to spend one night during the week, usually Wednesdays, as well as Saturdays and Sundays with their families.[117] Edward Hicks beat the path every day between his cabin on Oak Ridge and his wife's, only three-quarters of a mile off on the adjoining Grant place.[118] The relationship between spouses naturally created other bonds of kinship that crossed plantation lines. Henry Hunt, who was sold from Virginia to Warren County in his early teens during the mid-1830s, got around as a teamster but married a woman in his neighborhood in 1848. She already had a son, Jefferson, who was nine years old by then. Marriage thus made Hunt both a stepfather and a husband.[119] As husbands and wives became mothers and fathers, they begat new connections in the neighborhood—among generations, among families, among kin of all kinds.[120]

Men shouldered many burdens to bring together spouses and neighborhoods. The mandatory negotiations with owners, for example, were conducted by the groom. When it came time to request permission to live together or marry, he was obliged to do the asking.[121] If a couple belonged to different owners, he talked to her white people as well. This diplomacy was no easy task. Couples had a lot riding on his words, and testy slaveholders could get unpleasant even about the best intentions. Henry Lewis's owners cast aspersions on his request to marry Tishne Price, although they eventually agreed. When "my husband asked my old master for me," she recalled, Lewis was dismissed as a neophyte. "You have only been here four years, and you want to marry your mistress' body servant." Lewis, who had nerve but not the cheek his owner implied, stood his ground. "Well, she loves me and I love her," he responded. Price was not spared the abuse, but it seemed to take her by surprise, particularly when master asked whether Lewis was the best she could do. "I might do worser," she ventured.[122]

If a man's duty to beseech owners' cooperation subordinated his woman to him, it subordinated them both to owners and placed him in an unenviable position at best. Men in neighborhood marriages also had the often delicate task of obtaining passes because visiting was also the husbands' job.[123] Mobility had its advantages, no doubt. Leaving owners on a regular basis gave a man some distance from their discipline and enriched his congress with neighbors.[124] His wife, by the same token, had less access to adjoining plantations than her husband and less respite from owners' overweening presence. Yet women recognized the dangers visiting held for their men, who were compelled to run the slave patrol's gauntlet, and their safety in transit between quarters was a source of constant worry for wives.[125]

Slave women and their men could agree that a husband's responsibility to visit his wife accorded her womanhood a dignity it deserved. Furthermore, husbands routinely visited because they agreed the obligation was proper to manhood. This division of labor made sense to men and women alike, considering the prerogatives of gender denied to slaves. To be sure, owners would not have had it any other way. Because the ownership of slave children followed that of the mother, the right to slave property itself rested on denying the father the rights of paternity. For the planters, the bondman's obligation to visit his wife was implicit in her owner's right to their children. Yet it hardly stood to reason among slaves that sending wives out into the road to visit husbands would be liberating in a society where respectable free women rarely traveled unaccompanied by men either. On the contrary, the countless white men who could prey on a lone bondwoman constituted an abiding fear in every neighborhood.[126]

The structure of intimate relations, though sound on the whole, did not encompass all prevailing unions, and some fell by the wayside. Hager Johnson and George Washington were by no means unique as unmarried spouses belonging to different owners. After emancipation, some women later tried to shoehorn such relationships into the qualifications for a widow's pension by claiming to have "lived with" a soldier before the war, but their witnesses rarely spoke in those terms.[127] Cohabitation was quite a stretch in Johnson's case, as she and Washington lived apart for half the year. In fall and winter, when he took his owner's horses to train under her owner, they "passed these seasons together," she explained. In spring and summer, when he tended the horses at Pharsalia, the racetrack outside Natchez, Washington could visit only on Sundays.[128] Nevertheless, he talked about Johnson as his wife. Three old friends agreed, as one put it, the couple was "[k]nown in the neighborhood as man and wife." Yet the witnesses were at a loss what to call the relationship. Taking up did not quite do justice to the commitment between Johnson and Washington. They had three children, and he was on his way to visit her when a Confederate sniper shot him dead.[129] But they were not exactly married either. When colliding obligations to owners and spouses made for untidy relationships, neighborhoods set conventional definitions aside and recognized couples on whatever grounds were possible. Couples such as Johnson and Washington were husband and wife if only because they said so and neighbors went along.

Nor could slaves impose their version of orderly relations, especially duties of monogamy, on the drivers. Daniel, the driver on Walnut Hills in Warren County, took the liberty of keeping two wives. The women's abiding loyalty to their husband obliged their owner to put them under lock and key when Daniel ran away in 1832.[130] Others were notorious for forcing themselves on slave women.[131] That was more than enough for slaves to regard these men with scorn and dread. Yet some drivers also scandalized the neighborhood by their contempt for the tie between spouses. When a driver sexually coerced a woman, he violated her person, the bonds she had made, and their prerogatives, including those of her husband. If the driver had a wife, he dashed her expectations of fidelity, too. Intimate relations were most vulnerable to disruption by slaveholders, to be sure, yet many neighborhoods had to contend with transgressors inside the quarters as well.

No one confounded the order slaves tried to impose on conjugal unions more than planter men. The ravages of the planters were too numerous to catalog. They turned a blind eye on drivers and overseers who had their way with slave women. They raped their people, seduced them, and imposed on them with a combination of force and cajolery that defies latter-day distinctions between consensual sex and sexual coercion.[132] Some slaveholders were deterred by a husband's presence.[133] Mary Ann Holmes had a husband belonging to another owner at the time she bore her daughter, Eliza, by Austin Williams.[134] But neither the bond between spouses nor the proximity of husbands accorded much protection to women belonging to planters of Gabriel Shields's ilk. He gave his consent for two house servants, Eveline and James Perano, to live together but had her sleep in the big house. For Shields, the arrangement conveniently kept his nurse close by his children and preserved his own easy access to her for nearly a decade. Eveline Perano bore one child by Shields while she had two with her husband. Then in the late 1850s, Shields sent him to another plantation in Louisiana and broke up the Peranos' tenuous union for good.[135]

When the structure failed, when its strictures were most outrageously flouted, the slaves' last resort was force or silence. James Perano was not one to let such transgressions pass quietly. Shields may have exiled him in fear of retribution, though he claimed, ever the paternalist, it was for his black family's safety. "James Perano had a frightful temper," Shields's daughter related, "and my father did not consider the life of Eveline or the children safe with James Perano nearby."[136] However self-serving such fears were in the Shields family's case, some slave men blamed their women for master's advances. Courts in the Natchez District prosecuted several cases of husbands who turned violently on their wives or the men, bond or free, who wronged these women.[137] Such dramatic bursts of rage aimed to teach someone a lesson only in the narrowest sense of the term. Yet they were revealing about the ultimately delicate balance between the order slaves struggled for and the chaos slaveholders wrought in conjugal unions. The prerogatives of husbands and wives could be violated, but not with impunity.

The silences surrounding the sexual abuse of slave women kept everyone from putting too fine a point on that particular vulnerability of intimate relations.[138] The silence also protected perpetrators more than the victims, however. Eveline Perano never acknowledged to the Pension Bureau her owner was the father of her daughter, Aurilla. If she concealed the fact, in part, to maintain the Shields family's support for her claim, that support also reflected complex loyalties that had kept her working in their household throughout the Civil War and Reconstruction. During slavery times, she was part of the small circle of bondpeople in every neighborhood who, as they made cotton, made clothes, made meals, made beds, made children stop crying, and made visitors feel at home also made plantation households work and made paternalism a lived experience for the planter class. Perano slept in the nursery with her owners' children, traveled with the Shields family, and kept her distance from other slaves. "I had no acquaintance with the common negroes of the neighborhood," she intoned.[139] Perano concealed her feelings about her master from the Pension Bureau along with Aurilla's true paternity, but her intimate relations with Gabriel Shields, whatever she felt about them, were inseparable from the intimacies of paternalism. Although the hush about sexual relations between masters and bondwomen sometimes began in paternalist relations, it did not end there.

Secrecy enveloped the children bondwomen bore their owners. In the case of Eveline Perano and Gabriel Shields, even their child, Aurilla, betrayed some doubt about her father's identity. "I am reported to be a daughter of Gabriel Shields," she said, choosing her words carefully.[140] Many children grew into adulthood never knowing the truth with certainty. During the 1840s, the people on Linwood went along with the notion that the father of Polly Crawford's daughter, Diana, was an overseer, at least to the extent of calling the child by his surname. Eventually, some people allowed she was really the daughter of her owner, James Surget. A half century after emancipation, she still could not say for sure which man was her father. "I suppose I took the name Johnson after my own father and he was an over'seer on the old Surget place before the war. Some said my father was the old man James Surget a very wealthy white man, and I guess he was my father."[141]

The paternity of Eliza Grayson's firstborn was a closely held secret on the Montgomery plantation. Before the Pension Bureau, she laid the child to Elijah Hall, but he was not the father, though he was in a position to know who was. Hall was driver at one point and later had a daughter with Grayson after her husband enlisted. Yet there was some ambiguity about Grayson's first child in Hall's mind, for he guardedly related "it was a Mulatto, said to be by her Masters son." The news did not spread far in the neighborhood. Willis Latham, who spoke assuredly about intimate relations on the place, including the Graysons', also could not say who had fathered the child.[142]

Neighbors' careful monitoring of the structure of intimate relations flinched at owners' slave kin. Mothers taught children how to deflect queries about their paternity or told them nothing at all. Most people accepted the cover stories or knew when to stop asking questions. Slaveholders, too, were loathe to tell the secret, for the matter was almost unspeakable between master and mistress. The hush neither was a social construction nor had a design, much less an architect. It was patched together with dissembling, forgetting, and averted eyes.

The hush had a variety of important if unintended consequences for the slave neighborhood. It protected children from the assaults of planter women, who were prone to rage about their husbands' betrayals with slave women yet dared not speak openly of the subject. Silence also helped slave families incorporate children whose troubling paternity might otherwise have caused their ostracism.[143] Of course, the silence could be revealing to neighbors who paused to think about it, as some presumably did. Ambiguous parentage might set a child apart, given that mothers, fathers, and their ties were usually well known in the neighborhood.

Slaves made their structure of intimate relations prevail in many ways, all of which constituted victories, moral and practical, of a high order. This structure hissed and sputtered with contradictions, to be sure, and breaches opened up in the quarters. Drivers placed themselves outside it, and some unions were not incorporated into it. Nowhere in the Americas did slaves entirely protect conjugal life from the trespasses of owners and their agents, and the Natchez District was no exception. Slaves did not even have a tenable means of calling owners to account for the worst outrages. That slaves managed to give any structure at all to unions between men and women, considering the powers that bore down on them, was no mean feat. That they imposed this order, imperfect as it was, on their owners was an ingenious work of social engineering. That they obtained owners' cooperation was the most difficult maneuver of all, a tactic slaves used to good effect in other struggles as well. Slaves achieved all of these ends by making the most personal bonds profoundly social. A wedding only gave formal, full-blown expression to the regulating of intimate relations that took place in every neighborhood. Sweethearting, taking up, living together, and marriage dispersed affinities throughout the neighborhood and grounded them there.

Divisions of Labor

The fifty-four men and women who cultivated the fields of Nannechehaw in Warren County felt their owner's scrutiny at frequent but unpredictable intervals. James Allen, like most planters in the Natchez District, expected his people to increase production from one year to the next and hired overseers to free himself from much of the work of supervision. The trash gang spread guano, a fertilizer that reeked of bird excrement, across the fields in the spring of 1860, and the men cleared twenty acres of new ground for cultivation in 1861. Slaves encountered Allen at different points of production, depending on where in the work routine he chose to insinuate himself. Upon his return after a brief absence in 1860, he rode over the plantation, deemed the "place in horrid condition — gates open, fences broke — cotton in grass," and promptly fired one of the three overseers he went through that year. Gangs worked under Allen's direct superintendence only in exigent circumstances. "I have taken charge of corn plows," he announced in his journal when they replanted the crop. "Corn looks well but wants work, work, work."[1]

The slaves' progress was monitored constantly, reckoned by the acre, compared to past performance, and often found wanting. Twelve plow hands opened forty-five acres in two and a half days in April 1860, Allen recorded, and planted forty-five acres daily the following week. Fitting in all this work obliged slaves to work closely in tandem. The folks planting worked in two teams of six, plowing the same row in opposite directions, with one team digging a furrow for drainage and the other opening the ground, planting seeds, and covering them with a harrow. Eight slaves barred dirt off the rows in advance of another team scraping weeds off the cotton plants in late May. For all their labors, Allen deemed the hands a week behind their pace of the previous year by late May, ten days by early June. In the taut coordination of work, though, field laborers made Nannechehaw the focal point of their neighborhood.[2]

They put up with their owner's interventions in virtually every aspect of work on their own account as well. Men and women were paid for overwork on Sundays and produced beeswax, baskets, chickens, potatoes, corn, and cotton. Allen kept sufficiently close tabs on these endeavors to know how many people dug a pond on a nearby place and what they were paid (ten dollars for ten people); Nate and Lige's daily output of baskets (five); what cottonseed the men planted (Vick); the number of hands (twenty-two) "breaking out their potato patch" one day in 1860. Allen shaped the terms of trade as well as work. Men gained some proprietary claim over land their owner deemed the "boys' Potato Patches" and "the boys old field." Women were subordinated in exchange relations by Allen's willingness to trade primarily with the men. And all slave families were cut off from potentially lucrative trade routes by his various stratagems to monopolize their commerce. The advances of flour they received from Allen, for instance, obliged them to sell him some of their produce to settle the debt. Jerry and Dave might have squared their accounts themselves, but Allen made it a three-way deal by paying Dave the five dollars Allen owed to Jerry for making boards.[3]

Slaves on Nannechehaw recognized their owner would have a hand in defining the parameters of their enterprise. He had his say about when they worked on their own account, what crops they raised, and where they traded. Richard Eastman, a teamster and driver, did business in nearby Warrenton, a small town south of Vicksburg, procuring goods for the plantation and on one occasion "for his family."[4] Many years after emancipation, Eastman recalled, "[m]y master gave me the privilege of raising a little corn and cotton for myself every year and I would sell it and use the Money to buy pigs and would put them in a pen and fatten them, and he would allow me also to work away from home, on the neighboring plantations."[5] The terms of independent production kept other folks from raising all the cotton and swine they would have liked. The overseer caught slaves pinching cotton twice in the fall of 1860, once from wagons en route to the gin. Big Henry stole an untold number of pigs in May 1862 and distributed the meat to at least two other slaves before he was discovered.[6] Nannechehaw people knew they had to contend with Allen in all their relations of labor. Slaves understood that while many rewards distinguished work on their own account from staple production, the relations of power were much the same.

Work distilled all the relations of power in slave society because slavery was, first and foremost, a system of labor.[7] It was a critical tie between adjoining plantations because neighbors did all manner of chores together. Yet the demands of tending King Cotton kept field hands, the vast majority of slaves, at master's crop most of the time and made their own plantation the locus of neighborhood. In the fields, in their own gardens, in the big house, at the wagon, or at their trade, slaves also cultivated understandings of the power of slaveholders and the nature of power in their society. Planters fixed the division of labor, determined when slaves worked, what they produced, and how much they worked in staple as well as independent production. Here slaves reworked the lessons of intimate relations. The definitive exercise of a slaveholder's power was not to control slaves' every act, thought, and feeling but to step in where critical bonds between slaves were made. They located an owner's mastery at work in the capacity to put men and women in the house or the fields, at the plow or in the hoe gang, to shuffle the crop mix in the people's gardens, and to redirect their lines of trade. The terms of labor impressed on slaves, day in and day out, how owners exercised power by inserting themselves at will in slaves' every social relation.

Slaves worked the annual routine of plantation labor so deeply into their consciousness it marked their sense of time as well as place. Independence Day and Christmas were common time markers, partly because they also marked the year's two customary respites from work.[8] The tasks of raising cotton offered a passel of time markers familiar in every neighborhood — preparing the soil in winter, planting in spring, cultivation in summer, harvest in fall. Sam Davis could not say what year he parted from his first wife, but he knew their daughter was starting to crawl, and that was around cotton-picking time.[9] Jerry Rainey thought he left his owner in 1861, or maybe it was 1862 or 1863, but it was most surely "in cotton scraping time."[10]

Until the Civil War, slaves went to work at the conjuncture of four divisions of labor: between owners, overseers, and drivers in the task of supervision; between men's work and women's work; between staple and independent production; and between occupations in the fields and out. Planters in the Natchez District wielded much of their clout, as slaves saw it, in drawing these lines.

Of all the divisions of labor, slaves wielded most influence over that between house and field. Domestic service was a family trust. It belonged neither to the servant's family nor the owner's but to both. Slaves and owners agreed house service was rightly the province of families with long-standing ties to master, mistress, or their kin. Amos Wright of Claiborne County recalled how the lot of a "house boy" fell to him from the boughs of three family trees. He and both his parents, Joe and Rebecca Eddins, belonged to the Powers family until they were bequeathed to their owner's granddaughter, Delia Wright. When young Amos landed in the Wright household, her family's connections to his went back three generations, and he gave the tie its due by taking the Wrights' name.[11] Thus, Amos Wright became a house servant neither by an owner's fiat nor by a favor curried on his own but rather by a trust among the Eddins,

Powers, and Wright families. The children of maids, cooks, gardeners, and other servants often took up their parents' line of work.[12] As a credential, family ties reserved domestic service for one stratum in the quarters.

The family ties that put slaves to work in the house ran, more often than not, between women. Many slaves entered domestic occupations by way of women in the family, thanks in part to the gendered occupations of house service. Most domestics were women. Although men also held positions as cooks, waiters, and body servants, other jobs — maids, nurses, and midwives — were women's preserves. It is unclear whether Matilda Anderson's mother, a midwife, delivered their mistress's daughter. But it made sense to all parties concerned that the midwife's daughter should become the baby's nurse. Anderson eventually cleaned house and waited in the dining room, too. She and her husband marked the family tie to her owners by naming their child Nettie, after the young mistress Anderson had nursed.[13]

The entitlements of slaveholding women also lent a hand in making family ties a qualification for house service. Women received slaves as dowry and as inheritance. Planter families felt obliged to endow newly wedded children with substantial property — land for sons, cash and slaves for daughters.[14] A young plantation mistress typically took some of the slaves bequeathed by her family to work with her in the house. In the Natchez District, where more than a few men of common birth married their way into the planter class, many women setting up house had few but dower slaves to choose for domestic service.[15] Eliza Turner was an heiress to a sizable estate in land and slaves when she married an ambitious young lawyer in town, John A. Quitman, a recent migrant from the North. When she needed another domestic twenty years later, in the spring of 1845, she sent for her brother's house servant, Celia Brown. Family ties conferred no lifetime tenure in house service, and Brown had returned to the fields, condemned as a tippler, a thief, and a sharp-tongued liar.[16] Yet family ties had marked Brown as an obvious candidate for domestic work.

Planter women took it upon themselves to impress the importance of those ties on men in the next generation. Ann Barnes Archer of Claiborne County feared her nephew might neglect the family connection to his late mother's slaves after thirteen years of litigation over his title to them. When it appeared the court would award the slaves to a contending party, she urged her nephew to buy them if need be. "The negroes are nearly all family negroes of the Barnes family, & the few that are not have been owned by the family for more than twenty years," she explained. "It is very distressing to negroes to be sold at any time, but more so to be sold from their *old* family, or from their *own* families."[17] Keeping the credentials of house servants in order was the work of many hands — planter women who promoted the status of family slaves; sons, daughters, and other kin who upheld it; slave families who accepted the peculiar obligation to their white people; and fellow slaves who respected it.[18]

As children followed parents into the great house, the nexus between slave women and plantation mistresses encompassed a bond between families. In 1840, when Caroline and Peter Ramsay belonged to different owners, they surmised that the division of an estate in his white family could separate them for good. Caroline, nurse to Eliza Scott Purviance's family, made the predicament known to her owner and expressed a desire to marry. Purviance bought Ramsay forthwith, and Purviance's husband, a Presbyterian minister, married the couple in the parlor.[19] The ceremony fastened Peter Ramsay's ties to his wife's white family and cleared his way out of the fields. He became a gardener and hostler while his wife ironed and washed. The Ramsays' firstborn, Dennis, followed his father into the garden and then became a cook. "He was always raised in the house he never worked upon the plantation," his mother pointed out, "always Cooked for the family after he got big and old enough to do so." Dennis's brother and sister became domestics, too. "Father mother boys & girl," Eliza Purviance mused, "They were all house servants." Working in the house, a bequest of womenfolk at first, appeared to be a family legacy by the second generation.[20]

Yet this was less a perquisite seized by a few families than a duty they accepted. House service cannot be mistaken for light work. Cooks harvested, peeled, and washed vegetables and dressed and plucked game and poultry before the cooking even began, to say nothing of cleaning up afterward. Both cooking and laundering required hauling water and wood and tending fires. Badly soiled clothes, which had to be soaked overnight and then boiled the following day, required two days of heavy lifting. Laundresses needed fifty gallons of water — four hundred pounds — per week. They wrung out each article of clothing as they transferred it from kettle to kettle to soak, boil, wash, and rinse and finally hung it to dry.[21] No one worked more closely under owners' supervision, moreover, than house servants, mainly under mistress in the division of labor between planter men and women. Planter women kept some tasks of household reproduction at arm's length. Cooks, for example, worked in kitchens detached from the big house.[22] In the production of clothing, mistresses cut the cloth; bondwomen sewed it.[23] For domestic servants, slaveholding women were a constant presence, issuing instructions, scrutinizing completed work, and in the interim looking in on labor and laborers in the kitchen, the nursery, the ironing room, and wherever else bondwomen went about the varied, heavy, dirty, thankless tasks of cleaning house.

The tight quarters of house service put slaves in the way of the plantation mistress's notorious temper.[24] Eliza Quitman banished two slaves from the house in storms of pique, worsened by her confinement with a nursing infant, in early 1836. In January she returned Lydia, a recent purchase, to the slave traders in Natchez for being "lazy and impertinent" and generally "very troublesome to me." The following month, Fed and Alfred were the object of her bitter complaints to her absent husband for neglecting their work, for leaving home at will, for getting drunk — for becoming, in short, "perfectly lawless." Alfred, the vexing carriage driver, seemed to ignore her every command and left her waiting so long on one occasion she could not get to church. "I have borne with him until I can bear it no longer," she declared, and sent him to Springfield, one of the Quitmans' working plantations.[25] Corporal punishment was by no means the sole province of slaveholding men and their agents; women were responsible for their share of outrages and set upon slaves with switch, whip, fist, and knife.[26]

Working in the big house was more burden than privilege. No amount of leftovers from master's table, hand-me-down clothing, or occasionally expensive gifts compensated for the rigors of this life. The magnanimity of paternalism in the Mississippi style was such that few slaves had reason to expect manumission to be their reward. The 1860 federal census enumerated just 363 free people of color in the Natchez District, less than 50 per county, save Adams.[27] Elizabeth Green of Jefferson County deemed the status she bequeathed to family slaves a cut above slavery, but it was still a closer approximation to bondage than freedom. In 1833 she made special provisions in her will for "several old and faithful servants" whom she was "extremely anxious shall not serve as slaves after my death," including the families of two men bequeathed to her by her late husband twenty years earlier. Tom, his wife Lear, and their two children as well as Jerry, Rebecca, and their four children were to receive wages and a "guardian and protector" in the person of one of Green's sons. Yet each family was also to live with an heir, and when the youngest child turned ten years old, all the children were to be sold to the highest bidder in the Green family and the proceeds distributed among Elizabeth Green's grandchildren. As much as Tom, Lear, Jerry, and Rebecca presumably welcomed getting paid for their labor, they might not have agreed with their late mistress that they were no longer slaves, given that they were compelled to live with her family and their children were to be sold for the Greens' benefit. The favor bestowed on these two slave families and the strings attached were equally the product of the special place planters reserved for family servants. As much as Elizabeth Green wanted to reward what she called their "dutiful & obedient" service, she was determined to keep them in the family. Reproducing her family's ties to Jerry, Tom, and their people required nothing less.[28]

Owners' special considerations for house servants wreaked much havoc short of sale on the latter's families. Although planters avoided selling family slaves to strangers, house slaves were compelled to cede control over their families in singular ways. Their children suffered more punishment than those of field laborers, for example.[29] Many were obliged to give their personal attention to planter families at slave kin's expense. While Gabriel Shields had Eveline Perano sleep in his children's room and sometimes in his own bed, her husband occupied a cabin in the yard, and their children lived in the quarters with the plantation nurse.[30] Women in house service were the most vulnerable of all bondwomen to sexual abuse. Their children were twice as likely as field hands' children to have white fathers. Indeed, the sexual predations of slave-holding men played no small part in reproducing the family ties between owners and house servants. The enslaved daughters and sons of planter men formed a large cadre in the ranks of domestic laborers.[31]

The work of house service tied the Gordian knot of family ties between slaves and owners. Reproductive labor inevitably required house servants to work with owners on intimate terms and inevitably fostered hostile as well as kindly sentiments.[32] Family ties in the next generation were also fastened in domestic labor. In some households, wet nurses suckled owners' children, and house boys and house girls slept at the foot of owners' beds.[33] As mothers and fathers cooked, cleaned house, laundered clothes, and tended the garden, they kept their children in tow and apprenticed them in the skills of the parents' craft. The children, for their part, pitched in here and there and became familiar figures to the white family as playmates, nurses, and personal servants for young mistresses and masters.[34] In a matter of years, slaves and owners worked up family ties, with the attendant affections, antagonisms, and shared experiences, across two generations or more.

As a qualification for house service, family ties imposed constraints on all parties concerned. These connections relegated owners' proper choice of do-mestic servants to a small circle of people. A lack of ties undercut the claims of the vast majority of slaves on the largest category of employments outside the fields and undercut the claims of house servants themselves in the event they were sold to other owners. Four years of domestic labor on the Jakobi place in

Wilkinson County gave a sixteen-year-old woman no guarantee she would stay in that line of work. In 1845 her owner offered her for sale with a warrant she "will answer well for either a field hand or a house servant."[35] House servants themselves knew their occupations did not belong to them, like a skill or a piece of property, and they could not necessarily take their titles with them to other owners.[36] Field hands as well as house servants had a stake in the family qualification to the extent it gave slaves some say in the division of labor.

Reproductive labor outside the fields was critical to making and remaking neighborhoods. Certain occupations smoothed new arrivals' path into a neighborhood. Older slaves only magnified the difficulties of incorporating the people sold into every neighborhood: the longer their past, the deeper their ties to distant parts. Over the course of the antebellum period, big planters throughout the South increasingly assigned nurses to look after slave children, and many preferred older women for the task.[37] John Knight, a merchant in Natchez who owned a plantation across the river in Louisiana, asked his father-in-law to find him "a good, sound, intelligent, middle aged woman of experience, not only for midwife purposes, but as a constant *nurse* for my plantn children, that they may be properly taken care of and attended to regularly, especially in absence of their mothers at work in the field."[38]

Mary Ann Helam's employment as a nurse helped make her a fixture in her neighborhood in Jefferson County. Her third owner in Mississippi began calling her Aunt Mary as soon as he bought her in the late 1830s, her son recalled. Slaves on the Brown place followed suit in time. When Jefferson Hakes arrived there from North Carolina during the 1840s, "[s]he was called Aunt Helam." Nurses worked their way into neighborhoods by deeds as varied as the needs of their charges. Helam's namesake, a young girl named Mary, later told the U.S. Pension Bureau simply, "I was raised by" Helam.[39] A newly arrived nurse quickly became an important person to the mothers and fathers who relied on her to succor, protect, amuse, and discipline their children. And because intimate relations bound families across plantation lines, nurses cut a figure throughout the neighborhood. The ministrations of nurses compounded the resonance of titles such as "aunt" and "uncle" and the power of adoptive kinship to make strangers into neighbors.[40]

Nursing was one of many labors that forged neighborhood bonds. The concentration of property in the Natchez District multiplied opportunities for neighborhood work. Slave labor was a valuable largesse planters bestowed on lesser farmers. Henry Shaifer, a slave in Claiborne County, worked on the Foster place, a thirty-acre farm next to his owner's.[41] Work on adjoining plantations was most common where they belonged to the same family. Slaves beat the paths between James Metcalfe's three estates in Adams County during the 1840s to cord and haul wood, spread hay, harrow the rows, pick cotton, and pull cornstalks.[42] Slaves on William Mercer's four plantations worked together now and again as well. Grandisson Barton left Buckhunt, which also adjoined the Metcalfe places, to work on Mercer's Ellis Cliffs plantation, where Robert West was often sent from Laurel Hill. According to West, "when either set of hands would get behind those from the other places were brought to help work it."[43]

A good deal of neighborhood work took place during slack seasons, in winter before planting, and in summer before cotton picking. Slaves on the Harris plantation in Warren County often lent a hand on John Alverson's place, mainly with off-season chores, curing fodder, killing hogs, and salting and hanging meat in the smokehouse. "Mr Alverson never had poor things about him," John Turner told the Southern Claims Commission, "he had a large Range & pasture, bought the best Groceries, & made the best Meat & lard about." Turner, even if he was giving a fillip to the Alverson claim, came by his admiration honestly in his own toil.[44]

Road duty also engaged slaves periodically in just about every neighborhood. Counties singled out roads for construction or repair and planters to furnish slaves for the work each year. Folks on plantations near well-traveled routes worked them a few days annually over several years. Men performed most but not all of the labor. In Warren County, the board of police designated about sixty stretches annually in the mid-1840s and accepted only men for roadwork.[45] All slaves aged fifteen to fifty were subject to road duty in Adams County, however, and half of those offered up from the Metcalfe places were women.[46] Slaves often performed road labor with neighbors. Two dozen slaves from the adjoining Palmyra and Wood plantations cleared a road through a forest patch of Warren County for four days in July 1833. Fourteen people from the Wade place and nine from McCorkle's repaired the lower half of a major thoroughfare in Jefferson County in April 1852.[47] Planting was well under way by then, and road duty often carried over into busy periods of the crop year.

Slaves might be called to work out in the neighborhood in any season. In Adams County, a blacksmith on the Campbell place went to work on the adjoining Nevitt plantation in July 1830, and eight men went over in the fall at the height of cotton picking.[48] Circumstances inevitably arose that forced slaves on adjoining places to work together. Slaves were the only property around who understood the principle of property itself, and the livestock in their charge often wandered heedlessly across plantation lines. Retrieving wayward stock was one way John Wade became so well connected in his Jefferson County neighborhood. He spent enough time separating his owner's stock from Louisa Harper's to know her draft animals by sight when foraging Yankees brought them into Natchez during the war.[49]

While slaves fastened binding ties to adjoining places in work, they also moved the center of gravity of every neighborhood toward their owners' plantations. Owners took the lion's share of slaves' labor. That required field laborers to cooperate with a consistency and intensity unrivaled in any of their social relations with slaves on adjoining plantations. Cotton planting, for example, required close coordination between people opening the soil with plows, sowing the seeds, and covering them with the hoe.[50] In March and April 1832, field laborers marched through the Covington plantation in Adams County with trash gangs cleaning up and hoe gangs rolling cotton stalks before the plow gangs close behind.[51] Keeping gangs pulling in the same direction, at a pace that convened them at the right moment at the proper place, compelled slaves to discipline one another — if not by the driver's whip then by the rhythm of a song, a quiet admonition, or a knowing gaze — and produced conflict as well as cooperation. Tending cotton cultivated a thoroughgoing coordination, both within and between gangs, of hoes and plows, of minds and bodies, in action and purpose that made the fields the tightest quarters in the neighborhood and field laborers the closest of neighbors.[52]

Slaves understood that the authority to allocate them to productive or reproductive work belonged to masters based on their own division of labor with overseers and drivers. Assigning some slaves to the house consigned others to the fields. Owners also fixed the sexual division of labor in the fields; assigned slaves to plow, hoe, or trash gangs; and set the length of the workday. Slaveholders decided the days of work and rest, lay down the rules of the plantation, and determined the methods of cultivation. Slaves knew their ultimate obligation to work was to their owners, but the men to contend with at the point of production were drivers and overseers, who parceled out daily assignments to the gangs, scrutinized their work, and punished them when it was not up to snuff.

Several conditions converged in the Natchez District to make overseers prevalent there. The region had more than its share of absentee owners, virtually all of whom retained overseers. As many as half the plantations along the Mississippi River belonged to men who lived elsewhere. Planters with more than one property were common in the interior, too.[53] Natchez Nabobs presided over holdings in the district as well as across the river in Louisiana or to the north in the Yazoo-Mississippi Delta.[54] There were more elite slaveholders in the five counties of southwest Mississippi than in any state save Louisiana and South Carolina. More than 9,000 slaves—nearly 1 out of every 7 in the district—belonged to planters who owned more than 250 people in 1860.[55] William Mercer, master of 450 slaves in Adams County, confessed to his factor that "an extensive planter rarely attends to the details or even manipulations of his crops. Such operations are entrusted to the Overseers."[56]

Resident planters with thirty slaves or more typically hired overseers as well.[57] Slaveholdings were larger still in the district, where the median slaveholding was about twice that size by 1860.[58] Large slaveholdings and absenteeism also made overseers fixtures in the rice swamps of the low country, on the sugar estates of southern Louisiana, and along several stretches of the Black Belt, including northeastern Mississippi and the Delta. Thus, the Natchez District was one of several locales where slaves worked mainly under the direct supervision not of owners but of overseers and drivers.[59]

Field work put slaves face to face with overseers because superintending labor was their first order of business. Overseers were expected to see to the good order of plantation buildings, livestock, and crops, yet their primary duty was to keep a close scrutiny on slaves in the field and make sure their work was timely and correct. One old-timer, striking the pose of the ideal overseer in 1840, fashioned this obligation into a credo: "Wherever the negroes are working, I shall consider it my duty to be frequently with them, in order that I might see how they get along. I shall not content myself with doing this once a day, but I shall do so repeatedly observing every time what they are doing, and how they do it. I shall never permit them to do any work wrong, if it takes them the whole day to do it right." Monitoring was especially exacting at harvest, when overseers weighed and recorded the cotton picked by each hand daily. People on the Monette place in Adams County could expect the overseer to administer punishment at the scales if they failed to measure up. They were ordered by the overseer then and there to lie face down and bare their backs for between ten and fifty lashes, depending on how slim their pickings were. If the overseer's place in theory was with the hands, in practice he could not be everywhere at once—in the fields when he was looking over the cotton gin, with the hoe gang when he was looking in on the plow gang.[60]

So it also fell to drivers to keep slaves hard at their labors. Some drivers' obligations ran the gamut. Lewis Pinkney, the self-styled "Boss Colored man" on the Sessions plantation in Warren County, "overseed all the hands and had general charge of everything." A "head man," as slaves called drivers with some of an overseer's responsibilities, was in some cases accountable for the good order of the crop or buildings but usually the livestock. Balor Hill of

Claiborne County, for one, had charge of draft animals as well as field hands.[61] Most planters kept only as many drivers as they had hoe and plow gangs. The work of the gang was the typical driver's domain.

The driver's narrow jurisdiction circumscribed field hands' control over their labor, as a comparison to the low country suggests. There the relatively expansive powers of drivers cleared the ground for field hands to set the pace of work in the rice kingdom. The low country driver distributed rations and kept the keys to the smokehouse, provision rooms, toolhouses, and barns. He protected his owner's property, kept machinery in working condition, and looked after draft animals. He was expected to mediate quarrels between spouses and set a moral example in the quarters. He allotted jobs in the fields and determined whether labor was done properly and when it was complete.[62] Slaves worked not in gangs but by the task. Under the task system, every job had a customary stint recognized as a full day's work: an eighth of an acre for clearing new ground, a half acre for digging trenches, a quarter acre for hoeing.[63]

The driver's control over the parameters of task work was a dominion over space, not time. Indeed, the task itself was a unit of space — a quarter acre, or 105 square feet, to be exact.[64] Long after slavery, low country people talked about distances in interchangeable terms of tasks and acres. Every morning, drivers staked out plots as the task of the day for each slave. Drivers had the prerogative to reduce tasks depending on the condition of the soil, fields, or laborers — for ditchers working a riverbank mottled with roots, for slaves hoeing a field in the grass, or for everyone to an area the least able hand could manage. When laborers finished their task, the driver looked over their plots and ordered them to rework poorly tended patches or allowed them to leave the fields for the day. The strict division between the time field hands owed their owner and that belonging to themselves was the linchpin of the uncommon control slaves exercised over their labor in the low country. And that independence rested heavily on the drivers' control over slaves' place of work. The difference between drivers in the two regions was suggested by badges of power they wore: a ring of keys strapped to the waist in the low country, a whip tucked into the belt in the Natchez District.[65]

Direct supervision of field laborers by overseers and drivers required slaveholders to take some pains to get into a workaday relation with the vast majority of their slaves. Planters made their presence known to field hands by keeping an eye on their progress. Dr. Walter Wade's personal supervision of slaves in the field on his twelve-hundred-acre plantation in Jefferson County was rare enough to note in his journal, once with the telling phrase, "overseeing all day." Wade had his overseer report to him regularly, daily recorded the number of field hands engaged in different tasks and how much they accomplished, and frequently "rode over my crop" — on three straight Saturdays in June 1855. He was suitably impressed with the crop to show it off to an associate on another occasion.[66] As for absentee owners, riding over the crop was part of a repertoire on periodic visits to their working plantations, including strolling through the quarters, asking after a few of the people, inquiring into the overseer's conduct, and dispensing gifts, discipline, or both.[67] Slaves were sensitive to owners' direct scrutiny. In 1830 a Wilkinson County newspaper reported the results of a wager demonstrating slaves picked more than twice their usual amount of cotton in their owner's presence.[68]

For slaves, dictating the sexual division of labor was among the planters' most impressive interventions. The prerogative to determine so elemental a feature of work — of society itself — was a formidable display of an owner's power. Slaveholders distinguished men's work and women's work most sharply in slack seasons. In winter before planting and summer after the cotton was laid by, the several tasks of cloth production (spinning, carding, weaving, sewing) were women's work, while the heavy work of clearing new ground (felling trees and hacking through canebrake) was men's work.[69] Men were hard at it on most plantations every year, girdling trees, chopping them into cordwood, hauling it to the river for sale to passing steamboats, lumbermen in Natchez, or nearby planters.[70] The monopoly on chopping gained some men possession of axes. A dozen men complained loudly in 1842 when they were sent to Palmyra, the Quitmans' plantation in Warren County, before axes were handed out on Springfield, the Quitman place in Adams.[71] Planters made occupations in artisanal crafts and transportation — carriage driver, teamster — men's preserves as well. That, combined with women's slim majority in domestic service, meant a larger proportion of women than men worked in the fields.[72]

The sexual division of labor wrought by planters gave men and women different relationships to the entire terrain of neighborhood. The allocation of jobs outside the fields blocked paths abroad for women. Some regularly left the neighborhood in the capacity of midwife, nurse, or body servant. Yet transportation and crafts took the most slaves out of the neighborhood, and men's monopoly over those employments closed those avenues to women.[73] Although only a small minority of men plied the mobile trades, the sexual division of labor gave other men reason to think they might someday. All slaves knew that the boundaries of neighborhood, while affording men some room to maneuver, comprised especially close quarters for women.[74]

Owners' most imposing division of labor in the fields was at the plow.

Cotton demanded plowing throughout the year — to open the ground, to bar off ditches on either side of a row for drainage, to scrape away weeds that throttled young plants.[75] Plowing was men's work on many plantations.[76] Some men took some pride in their plowing.[77] The play of memory may have distorted Anthony Cooper's recollection that all the slaves plowing while Union soldiers foraged on the Bobo plantation in the Delta in 1864 "were man hands": at least one woman plowed that morning.[78] Perhaps Cooper, like other slave men, found it tempting to arrogate the skill of an able plow hand to himself. Pushing a plow down into the loam as a draft animal lunged forward was no easy task. Plowing a straight row demanded physical strength, a steady hand, and a rapport with headstrong animals. Planters increasingly replaced plow horses with fractious mules during the antebellum period.[79] Keeping a mule in harness was part cajolery, part browbeating — in sum, an irksome test of wills. Slave men were inclined to regard plowing as men's work because they liked to think of the qualities of a good plow hand — steadiness, common sense, bodily strength, force of will — as attributes of manhood itself.

Yet plowing was every bit as much women's work on some plantations as it was men's work on others. Women filled out enough plow gangs to evoke comment by northern travelers. A carpenter from Iowa found "the women as often driving a team before a plow as the man" on plantations outside Natchez.[80] According to Frederick Law Olmsted, "plowing, both with single and double mule teams, was generally performed by women" in Mississippi. Twenty women who adroitly turned their plows from one row to the next at the crack of a driver's whip on a large estate near the Mississippi River disabused Olmsted of any notion women were unfit for the work. "[T]hey twitched their plows around on the head-land, jerking their reins, and yelling to their mules, with apparent ease, energy, and rapidity."[81] Slaves on two of Dr. James Metcalfe's plantations in Adams County saw just how arbitrary the sexual division of labor could be. In 1848, plowing was men's work on Bourbon and women's work a few hundred yards away on York.[82] From the slaves' standpoint, the sexual division of labor at the plow — women's work on one plantation, men's work on the next, and the burden of both on another — typified the planters' arbitrary mastery.

The planters, aloof though they were, wielded enough power over the fields to extract more and more work from slaves after 1830. Planters adopted new methods of cultivation as soil erosion cracked the landscape throughout the period and the price of cotton hovered around its nadir during the 1840s. Slaves could not share their owners' enthusiasm for the new practices. What owners adopted in the name of "reform," "progress," "scientific agriculture," or simple "improvement" only increased the demands on slave labor. Not only did slaves work the soil more intensively over the antebellum period, evidence suggests they worked more acres per person as well.

The impositions of agricultural reform on the slaves of the Natchez District are obscured by its general failure everywhere in the South. At the level of political economy, reformers never resolved the contradictions of their enterprise. Some recognized the most immediate problem in the 1840s as a crisis of overproduction, for example, yet the methods of intensive cultivation they advocated were likely to increase the quantity of cotton raised as well as reduce costs of production. At the level of practical husbandry, few systematically adopted the reformers' agenda. Edmund Ruffin never gained a following outside piedmont Virginia and southern Maryland for his program of abating soil acidity with marl (fossilized calcium dug up in shell deposits).[83] Nor were southerners prepared to follow northern pioneers of convertible husbandry, which involved converting land to pasture, then restoring its fertility with nitrogen-rich manure, because doing so would have diverted too many slaves and fields from the staple.[84] Finally, planters were unwilling to provide the supervision of field work needed for the new regimens.[85] In the Natchez District, then, the planters' own division of labor with overseers was yet another obstacle to comprehensive reform.

Still, compared to most of the Deep South, the region was fertile ground for new methods of cultivation. Agricultural reform in the South was less a movement than an archipelago of like-minded men convened around short-lived periodicals and institutions. In Mississippi, reformers coalesced around Martin W. Phillips in Hinds County, just east of the district, and around Jefferson College, the *Southern Planter*, and Thomas Affleck in the vicinity of Natchez.[86] Reformers gained influence among planters in the Natchez District because it suffered from both of the crises that stimulated agricultural reform in the Upper South.

First, generations of staple production had depleted the soil of nitrogen and decreased fertility. Rich soil piled up into hills and bluffs by thousands of years of wind and flooding fell away in a matter of decades. The problem, apparent in the hinterland around Natchez early in the nineteenth century, was well advanced by 1835. "Every slough furrow becomes the bed of a rivulet after heavy rains," a northern visitor wrote. "[T]he impalpable soil dissolves like ice under a summer's sun."[87] Cultivation opened the ground. Rains pelted the exposed dirt and carried it off bit by bit. The foundation of clay under the soil dissolved into sand. Rills opened, stretched out, and plunged down, and gullies cut swaths across the fields.[88] Erosion in Jefferson County converted Everard

Green Baker to agricultural reform a year after he settled in at his new plantation, Richland. "I am daily more impressed with the necessity of planters in this
country paying more attention to the stopping of breaks upon their land," he
confided to his journal in April 1850. "To preserve the land," he vowed to raise
livestock and "vary my crops as to add vigor instead of inducing exhaustion."[89]

By the time of Baker's oath, planters in the Natchez District had also come
to terms with a second impetus to agricultural reform — economic depression.
Cotton production had grown dramatically across the South in tandem with
textile manufactures in New England and Great Britain until the late 1830s.
While cotton prices were high, slaveholders in the district devoted their land
to the staple and bought foodstuffs in the market. A bank in Natchez was
among the first in the nation not to honor drafts in the Panic of 1837.[90] Credit
tightened over the next two years, and the price of cotton collapsed and rarely
rose above ten cents per pound during the 1840s.[91] A few planters pulled up
stakes and migrated to fresh lands in Louisiana or the Delta.[92] Most stayed put
and tried to drive the cost of making cotton below its new low price by wrest-
ing more labor from slaves.

Agricultural reform transformed cotton culture for slaves. Mississippi planters widely adopted a minimum program of advanced farming in lieu of the
systematic regimes.[93] They outfitted plow gangs with new implements to cut
deeper into the ground and tap its remaining fertility.[94] They diversified production.[95] They devoted as much as one-third of their acreage to corn, planted
cowpeas between the stalks, and used the new rotation of crops to increase
production of swine.[96] Everard Baker reduced the program to a list of the
"First Elements of Planting" — "Deep Cultivation," careful selection of seeds,
and "rotation of crops." Most planters in the Deep South objected to fertilizer
as too costly and laborious. Baker went further than most when he listed
manuring among his first elements of planting, but others in the Natchez
District thought they had the means in capital and slaves to experiment with
fertilizers.[97] The addition of corn to the crop mix accounted for much of the
additional work. True, planters gave over some of their cotton grounds to corn,
which required less work than the staple. But planters also increased the total
acreage under cultivation. Corn competed with cotton for field laborers' attention in spring and added a harvest before cotton picking in summer.[98]

Agricultural reform tightened the slack seasons. Of course, other chores had
always remained after the cultivation of cotton ended in July while the staple
was left to mature — clearing new ground, hauling wood, mending fences,
repairing barns and other outbuildings. Yet the pace of work slowed in the four
to six weeks before picking began in mid-August. After the cotton fields were

picked out before Christmas and a few days of rest around the holiday, slaves, in addition to cloth production and clearing new lands, began to prepare the fields for planting in early April. Men and women knocked down old stalks or burned them, while "trash gangs" of children, nursing and pregnant women, elderly and infirm adults cleared away brush. Gangs made collars, harnesses, and traces and got their plows in working order.[99] Slaves had fashioned the respites before planting and picking, though never a lark, into seasons for weddings, balls, revivals, and other neighborhood pursuits. New chores added up over the years, and periods of rest, nudged aside in an increasingly crowded schedule of tasks, shrank. Slaves felt compelled to quicken their pace.

Slaveholders placed a host of new tasks in the interstices of the crop year.[100] During the 1850s, some planters extended the picking season beyond its natural endpoint of the first frost with a new cottonseed, Mastodon, that produced a boll that clung to the fiber through January. Slaves resumed picking after the Christmas holiday. Owners devised new jobs to prepare the ground for planting. As they came alive to the value of corn and cotton stalks as fertilizer, slaves who had once simply put a torch to the fields had to plow the stalks under.[101] Where owners saw the chance to make two corn crops each year, slaves had to plant the first one early. And winter sowing was liable to create more work down the road. If frost killed the crop, slaves planted it again. Richland people began planting corn on March 14 in 1850, but the crop came to naught after a snowfall two weeks later. Replanting kept the slaves busy into early June.[102] Slaves on the Darden place replanted for two years running.[103] Diversification obliged field laborers to plant corn in addition to cotton—sometimes two crops of each.

The mix of corn and cotton accelerated the pace of work in spring. On top of the work tending cotton, corn required slaves' attention to keep it out of the grass as well. Fitting in all that labor between April and July was a tall order. Each crop typically needed three cultivations—more when rains were heavy and weeds grew thick. By John Knight's estimate, the rains increased the work twofold one year, four the next. "We are all now in the very midst of the most pushing time of the crop," he reported in May 1846 to his father-in-law, who had procured most of Knight's slaves in Maryland and Virginia. They "are now put to the full test of their skill, strength and willingness and ability to bear fatigue & labor, which they have never before probably experienced."[104]

Plow gangs got saddled with much of the extra load of crop rotation. Planters shifted tasks from hoe to plow gangs after 1830. New practices made some jobs less work. Plowing hillsides in horizontal instead of vertical rows slowed erosion and spared gangs the trouble of working uphill. Yet horizontal plowing created chores, too. Wherever a row was uneven in depth, water collected, spilled over, and threatened new gullies, so slaves dug ditches to drain the water before it did any damage. Men on Bourbon put down their axes and picked up their shovels to ditch for a week in late winter 1848. At the peak of the work, fifteen men each dug some 450 cubic feet of earth daily. After "barring off" drainage ditches with a bull-tongued plow, gangs went back through the rows "molding" — throwing earth back up against the cotton beds so the plants could spread their roots through it. Plow gangs used scrapers to shear weeds away from the rows, side harrows to loosen the dirt between the rows.[105]

The new husbandry filled out summer with heavy work after the cotton was laid by. Tending corn and cowpeas followed the staple in quick succession. Field laborers planted peas in July. There was no slack season to speak of on Bourbon during the summer of 1847. Hoe gangs finished in the cotton on 30 August, and picking began just over a week later. Slaves planted a second crop of corn two weeks thereafter, then shucked, shelled, and ground the first crop the week after that.[106] Shifting work from the hoe to the plow gang required more draft animals, and much of the increased production of corn was fed to them. When the ears matured, slaves went into the fields to "pull fodder," the green blades on corn plants — between three and four hundred pounds per day. Slaves tied the leaves into bundles, stacked them to dry in the sun, then laid them up in sheds as winter feed for the mules and horses. Even planters recognized these jobs, performed at the height of summer when the air was thick, as sick-making work.[107] As boom times returned to the cotton market during the 1850s, planters commissioned mansions, especially in Natchez and Vicksburg, and slaves in the hinterlands went to work meeting a new demand for bricks. Men and women on the McCall place in Claiborne County made between four and six thousand bricks daily in summer and hauled them in winter.[108]

Slaves saw the increase of work in expanding and contracting spaces of land as well as time. Intensive farming required slaves to cover more and more ground from year to year.[109] Clearing new ground in the Natchez District, though one of the oldest regions in the Southwest, remained a fixture in the annual routine on the eve of the Civil War. Slaves in the region cleared more than 130,000 acres during the 1850s.[110] Census returns offer only a rough indication of how much land slaves worked because enumerators counted meadowlands as improved acreage. But improved acreage rose substantially between 1850 and 1860 in every county — from 15 percent in Wilkinson to more than 30 percent in Claiborne, Adams, and Jefferson and 40 percent in

Warren. Moreover, slaves cleared new ground faster than their own numbers increased. While improved acreage increased by 30 percent in the district as a whole, the slave population rose just over 6 percent. Slaves worked something on the order of 20 percent more land over the course of that decade alone, if census figures are any indication.[111] Slaves saw their growing labor obligations etched into the landscape, as fields and crops encroached on swamps and forests. Signs of more work on the horizon were plain at the edge of fields, where wild places in the neighborhood gave way under slaves' own hands to cleared forests, drained swamps, and a new stretch of rows to crop.

It is hard to fathom how just plain hard it was to slave away in the fields of Mississippi. The unusually precise calculations of Francis Terry Leak, a planter in Tippah County, north of the Natchez District, afford a glimpse, however, of the lengths to which slaves had to go in a day's work. Leak began to task plow hands in 1846, then the hoe gangs at their insistence. Not content to reckon their progress collectively by the acre, as most planters did, Leak measured it by the length and number of rows worked by each person. Over the next two years, he and the field hands came to terms on daily tasks that amounted to astounding amounts of labor. Working the plow on the Leak place was a long march—between fourteen and sixteen thousand yards for each slave planting, eighteen thousand yards for scraping—more than ten miles a day. Labor obligations differed by sex for the hoe gangs—3 miles for women and 3.75 for men keeping the rows out of the grass, anywhere from 4.5 to 6.5 miles chopping out the cotton.[112] Field work on cotton plantations was a footsore business.

Reform agriculture heightened the centripetal effects of work that made the home plantation the neighborhood epicenter. Fitting new tasks into finite periods of time obliged field laborers to increase coordination in the workplace. Slaves executed a growing number of operations, in sequence, over larger, more intensively cultivated grounds. As one season of work abutted another on Aventine plantation in Adams County, trash gangs, plow gangs, and hoe gangs synchronized picking, planting, and cultivating corn and two crops of cotton in 1859. Two elderly women and three in the "family way," as the overseer put it, were still burning cotton stalks in early March when slaves began sowing the corn. Two crops of cotton came to a head during the same week in April when the hands manured the cornfields. Four men pressed thirty bales of the preceding year's cotton while the rest of the field hands finished planting the next crop the week after that. Aventine people gave the cotton four cultivations by mid-July, working the corn all the while.[113] The rigors of increasingly close collaboration engendered new conflicts as well as solidarities and embedded the plantations where slaves worked in the heart of the neighborhood.

Slaves did not accept the stretch-out of their work without a struggle. Take the battle over Sunday labor on John Nevitt's plantation in Adams County, for example. In 1830, several men and women were at the cotton press on the Sabbath repeatedly in January and from October through early December. Three people absconded within a week after Sunday labor. Jerry worked the press the first Sunday of the new year, promptly ran away the following Wednesday, and returned home that Friday. Dan ran away in May, the Monday after he and Jerry had made 150 pickets. Dilly helped press seven bales on the first Sunday in November, left on Tuesday, and stayed out for nearly four weeks. Sunday labor was not the only point of contention.[114] Dilly, for example, had laid out twice earlier in the year. Nor did all the men and women concerned find money entirely adequate compensation for overwork. Nevitt occasionally paid them for working on the Sabbath in 1830, but some people ran away nevertheless. Dilly and Jerry were recipients of Nevitt's supposed largesse at different times that year, and Dan was paid for his trouble on the day before he absconded.[115]

The struggle over Sunday labor resulted in an elaborate compromise on the Nevitt place. Members of the press gang signaled their willingness to reach an accord when Jerry and Rubin brought Dilly home in early December 1830. There was little Sunday labor at all in 1831, and when Nevitt resorted to it again the following year, he no longer felt he could call the slaves out to work at will. When men and women gave up the Sabbath to plow, ditch, and make or haul pickets and posts, Nevitt had to "hire" them for "wages."[116] Nevitt undoubtedly got the better part of the bargain. He needed more work from his slaves, and he got it cheap — typically, three or four bits a day per person. The slaves prevented their owner from annexing Sunday to the regular workweek, but that was a rearguard action, for the Sabbath already belonged to the slaves across the South. Slaves on other plantations in the district bargained for paid Sunday labor, too.[117] Their victory was to appropriate Sunday labor to the relations of independent — or auxiliary — production.

Struggles over Sunday labor offer a clue to how owners brought slaves around to working harder over the antebellum period. As the burdens of work increased, the balance between staple production and reproductive labor shifted. Of course, slaves always worked for their own subsistence. Even when owners bought pork and corn in the market, slaves made the cotton that paid for their rations. As planters adopted mixed agriculture, field laborers worked harder, yet more of their labor time went to raising crops for their own consumption. Slaves understood that the corn and pork they made was not their property, and owners underscored the point by having the food handed out as rations. Still, the very experience of labor changed as long stretches opened up in the annual routine when slaves grew their own food.

Negotiations over Sunday labor were one overture in a struggle that played out across the Natchez District: Slaves converted a portion of their free time into compensated labor time. As the demands of field labor increased, slaves gained new opportunities to make, buy, and sell goods on their own account. The expansion of auxiliary production was a corollary to planters' calculations to make cheap cotton pay by extracting more labor from slaves.[118] Assigning slaves garden patches for raising corn, potatoes, beans, and other produce to supplement weekly rations was yet another way to reduce the costs of production.[119] When planters mixed corn, peas, and swine with their cotton crop, they also integrated staple and auxiliary production.

Auxiliary production was a substantial enterprise in almost every neighborhood. The work slaves performed on their own account was family labor.[120] The Southern Claims Commission rejected Samuel Chase's claim on the grounds he could not have accumulated all his property in a few weeks after the Union army's arrival in Warren County. Yet Chase made clear his entire family worked for what they had. While he hauled water for the Federals, "my wife washed for them and it was for the work that my wife, my self and my Son done for them from which we earned the money to buy" three mules.[121] Families earned money for overwork, small manufactures, and farm produce. Some traded well beyond plantation and neighborhood. A few were initiated into the market in the commodities they worked with or exchanged.[122]

Yet slaves in the Natchez District worked for themselves under constraints that were more pressing than those in the low country. The terms of auxiliary production were inextricably bound up with those of staple production throughout the Americas.[123] The time slaves labored for owners determined how much they could work on their own account. In the low country the task system established a clear division of labor time. It enabled slaves to set the pace of their work in the rice and cotton fields, to raise these labor-intensive crops for themselves, at night by torchlight if need be, and to exchange these valuable staples for ready money.[124] In Liberty County, Georgia, more than two-thirds of former slaves compensated by the Southern Claims Commission grew rice.[125] Slaves' control over their labor was a bulwark in trade. Planters' attempts to keep slaves' commerce at home by buying up their produce and setting up plantation stores failed on the whole.[126] Men and women crowded the Charleston marketplace until the Civil War.[127] Livestock, draft animals, and wagons became a conventional progression in the accumulation of property for low country families.[128] Nearly all Liberty County claimants owned hogs, more than half had horses and cows, and more than a quarter had buggies or wagons.[129]

Slaves in the Natchez District, by contrast, ran up against the boundaries owners imposed on auxiliary production at every turn. Planters had their say about when slaves worked on their own account, what they produced, how much they planted, whether they traded in kind or in cash, and with whom. Although families cultivated a variety of crops, making cotton was a rare privilege. Constraints on what slaves sowed limited what they reaped. Most families exchanged most of their produce with their owners, who eschewed market relations.[130] Unable to produce valuable crops like the staple, few slaves accumulated the means to acquire productive property such as draft animals before the Civil War. The independence that slaves achieved for their commodity production in the low country eluded men and women in the district, where they never managed to wrest control of the terms of work and trade from owners.

The difference between the Natchez District and the low country began with the division of labor time. The line between the time slaves owed their owner and that belonging to themselves was by no means fixed in either region. Task labor might go until midafternoon or into the evening, but men and women determined the pace of their labor, and families gained control over their time.[131] In the district, however, owners blurred this division of labor time. The boundary often broke down on Saturdays around noon. The people usually but not always had the rest of the day as their own. Keeping slaves at master's crop on Saturday afternoons was one way to get through the bottlenecks of work created by agricultural reform. Some worked full Saturdays even during slack seasons.[132] Slaves on Bourbon were clearing new ground until nightfall on Saturday during the week their owner's son began managing the place in January 1843. The men cut and hauled eleven cords, while the women and children burned the brush and cleaned up.[133] All hands on the McCall plantation in Claiborne County were at the brickyard one Saturday in June. The six thousand bricks they made were, their owner judged, "a Good days work."[134]

Planters also imposed limits on what slaves could produce. Slaves made baskets and grew vegetables, beans, hay, and other fodder in quantity. The mainstays of auxiliary production were corn, potatoes, chickens, and eggs,[135] items that readily did double duty as supplements to weekly rations or goods in trade. Corn was the staple of the slaves' husbandry because it was also feed for livestock, equally convertible to chickens, hogs, and cash, though at different rates.[136] Families had to make large crops of corn to raise pigs. Swine marked a step up in auxiliary production because they reproduced themselves and yielded more meat and fetched higher prices than did fowl. Indeed, hogs were the most valuable goods produced extensively in the quarters.[137]

Slaves in the Natchez District never made the staple a fixture in their gardens. Few grew cotton on their own account. Slaves on the Templeton plantation in Warren County stored their cotton in a shed by the gin, where Union soldiers seized it for bedding in April 1864. "There were 10 or 12 bales there belonging to different colored people," recalled William Foster, who owned two of these bales. Other witnesses put the slaves' crop at sixteen or seventeen bales. Making cotton for themselves, observed D. H. Alverson, a young master in the neighborhood before the war, "was the custom with most of the hands on that plantation." Alverson, by singling out the Templeton place, alluded to the rarity of auxiliary cotton production in general. J. W. Fowler of Adams County instructed his overseer that the slaves had leave to raise potatoes, tobacco, and chickens, but the staple was forbidden. Fowler had the law on his side. The Mississippi code prohibited slaves from growing their own cotton. The law reflected a fear, widespread among planters, that cotton in the gardens encouraged theft from master's bales.[138] Such prohibitions also aimed at cutting off lines of trade between slaves. The few slaves permitted to raise cotton were expected to let their owners market it.[139]

Some planters went beyond fixing limits on labor time and crop mix to stake subtle claims to supervising auxiliary production. To be sure, slaves exercised far more control over their work in their gardens than on the staple. Applying their skill to the soil without the overweening superintendence of drivers, overseers, or owners was a valuable reward of auxiliary production. Yet slaves often had to put up with some scrutiny. Walter Wade, who seldom noted the work of individual hands, recorded the names of twelve people who planted their own corn on one Saturday afternoon in April 1851. The following Saturday, he tersely recorded having "[r]ode all over corn," presumably taking a look at the slaves' corn along with all the rest.[140]

Slaves in the low country did not have to brook such monitoring. A comparison with the British Caribbean suggests why. In Jamaica and the Windward Islands, slaves typically worked provision grounds on backlands, often several miles from their owners' plantations. Planters and their agents knew precious little about how the slaves' crop was coming along.[141] Owners and drivers in the low country also were in no position to monitor the gardens. Planters repaired to Charleston for much of the year, and drivers were kept so long supervising staple production they had a customary right to other people's labor to tend their patches.

Slaves in the Natchez District gained no comparable mastery over auxiliary labor. Owners' power to determine when slaves worked for themselves and what they made hemmed in production down the line. Planters' control over the division of labor time fixed the terms of production to a great extent. Slaves who often gave up Saturday afternoons at the behest of owners or overseers were bound to raise smaller crops than low country folk who worked on their own account for half of most Saturdays, Sundays, and every weekday afternoon they could get for themselves. In the district, prohibitions against the staple reduced the volume of trade and truncated the circulation of goods.

There is little evidence, for example, of trade between slaves on adjoining plantations. Perhaps this is an artifact of the historical record. Exchanges between slaves are not documented in plantation journals, but owners and overseers were unlikely to record trade they were not a party to, even if they knew about it. More surprising is the dearth of neighborhood trade in Southern Claims Commission files. When claimants were asked how they obtained their property, they usually talked about work rather than trade, about how they accumulated the resources to buy property rather than who sold it to them. Perhaps neighbors conducted more trade than meets the eye in these records. Freedpeople may well have expected the commission to doubt any claim based on extensive trade between slaves and decided the less they said about it, the better. Yet the evidence at hand suggests most trade was between slaves and owners.[142] When slaves could do business off the plantation, they often bypassed the neighborhood and headed into town, where prosperous buyers and a wide selection of goods made for better terms of trade.

Owners saw to it that trade routes led back to them. Henry Hughes, the Port Gibson lawyer and proslavery theorist, argued that exchange fell to owners in their own "division of labor" with slaves. Acting as slaves' agents in the market, Hughes explained, was part and parcel of owners' responsibility over work, health, and public order.[143] Planters' admonitions about contraband trade focused on liquor and staple crops because valuable, uninhibiting commodities embodied the dangers free trade posed to discipline and productivity.[144] Control over trade sustained slaveholders' sense of mastery in other roundabout ways. Plying slaves with clothing and a few addictive goods — tobacco, sugar, coffee — stocked them up with guilty pleasures that suggested they lacked self-restraint and needed a master's guidance.[145] Imposing boundaries on trade, moreover, was another front in the struggle over space intrinsic to the master-slave relation. Permitting exchange relations off the plantation put slaves at risk of incurring obligations to other slaves, owners, or strangers. The state supreme court threw its weight behind owners' determination to insert themselves in exchange relations with the axiom that a slave "has no more right to purchase, hold or transfer property, than the mule in his plough."[146] Trade was a critical part of owners' struggle to keep slaves body and soul — their goods, their associations, their desires — within plantation boundaries.

The circulation of goods and cash among slaves was limited because planters bought most of their people's produce and sold them a large portion of the sundries they could afford.[147] Slaves collected substantial revenues annually from owners intent on their trade — $200 for hay on Elgin, $145 for corn on Highland, and several lump sums of between $60 and $90 for wood on Buena Vista.[148] Planters circumscribed trade merely by purchasing the bulk of slaves' produce. Owners recouped their outlays by selling goods to slaves in return. Joseph Davis famously permitted Ben Montgomery to keep a store, although few went to such lengths. Twenty men on Buena Vista bought tobacco by the plug from their owner in 1849–50, and forty-nine men bought tobacco by the pound in 1857.[149]

The terms of trade between slaves and owners engaged the parties in an array of different exchange relations from barter to debt to gift. Slaves traded with owners in kind as well as cash.[150] Barter had the advantage of inviting negotiation over the value of goods at both ends of the bargain. Paton haggled with Susan Sillers Darden to exchange thirteen yards of Lowell cloth for his chickens, though the two parties left undecided exactly how many. Paton thought his four chickens were worth $2.50, an amount his mistress thought exorbitant. They eventually compromised on $2.37, nearly 60 cents each, a welcome premium over the 50 cents apiece Darden paid another slave around that time. Barter had its disadvantages, too. Slaves entered auxiliary production under the burden of debt, for example, when they received goods in advance. More commonly, slaves advanced their produce, but that did not necessarily put their owners in debt to the slaves.[151] Owners could always recast payment in more congenial terms.

Slaveholders often transmuted their debts into gifts. The transformation was accomplished in a sleight of hand, as owners simultaneously doled out payments and presents. Amid the struggle over Sunday labor on the Nevitt place, slaves may not have appreciated their owner acting like he gave them "a treat" when he closed their accounts on Christmas Day 1830 and handed out gifts of old cloth. The following year, he distributed presents without making any payments for auxiliary production and chalked it up again in his diary as "a treat." Handing out presents with payments or without was all the same to

Nevitt. A great many slaves could expect owners to wait until the Christmas season to pay up in toto for overwork, garden produce, and other goods advanced over the year.[152] Slaves received pay for goods in trade as well as gifts at the Darden place on Christmas Day 1855 and at Fonsylvania on New Year's Eve 1858 and pay alone on Forest in Adams County on Christmas 1859.[153]

Slaves were hardly taken in by the subterfuge. Gabriel Shields took the occasion of a visit to Aventine in May 1859 to pass out hats and handkerchiefs while the slaves handed over ducks and eggs. Simon was not content to let the exchange go at that, however. Whether he demanded to be paid for his two ducks on the spot or merely announced a preference for payment in cash over kind, he made clear "he likes to have the money," according to the overseer's record.[154] As slaves collected on their goods, they found the meaning of trade converted, too. Planters stripped the act of payment of any sense of obligation to slaves and recast it as a favor bestowed upon them.

The terms of exchange with owners, then, had nothing to do with market relations as far as slaves could see. Slaves also did not necessarily receive market prices in the South Carolina up-country or in southern Louisiana.[155] In the district, the terms of trade slaves hammered out with owners for a particular good often tended toward a plantation-wide price. Although Paton's hard bargaining earned him ten cents more than what his mistress usually paid for chickens, he later settled for the same fifteen cents she gave all the hands for chicks.[156] The prices slaves received for corn were fixed across the district during the 1850s. Slaves on the Wade plantation got the same fifty cents a barrel for their corn between 1852 and 1857, even though their owner kept abreast of fluctuations in corn prices at Rodney. Fifty cents was the going rate on Aventine, too.[157] As slaves compared trade on plantations in their neighborhood, they could not help but notice that corn, the staple of auxiliary production, had settled at a customary price.

Experience with trade off the plantation was broad but not deep. A great many slaves enjoyed an annual outing, usually around Christmas, to trade in Vicksburg, Natchez, and other towns. Sunday commerce made a picturesque scene around Natchez during the 1830s in Joseph Holt Ingraham's telling. Slaves "leave their plantations and come into town to dispose of their produce and lay in their own little luxuries and private stores." Roads in the suburbs were "filled with crowds of chatting, laughing negroes, arrayed in their Sunday's best, and adroitly balancing heavily loaded baskets on their heads," with men and "their dames or sweethearts riding 'double-jaded' behind them" on "mules or miserable-looking plough-horses" loaded up with goods. Authorities tried to clamp down on but never stamped out slave vendors.[158] In 1836

Woodville prohibited slaves from marketing there on Sundays, but slaves were at it again by the fall of 1839, when the ordinance was republished.[159] Reuben Cunningham's memories of a store in Grand Gulf where he traded as a slave afford a glimpse of these heady excursions. The sight of Hutchinson's store, packed to the rafters with boots and shoes and tobacco and whiskey, still impressed Cunningham years later, when he recalled the place "was very long and the shelves were very high — It appeared to me that the store was full of goods — I saw no empty shelves — no vacant room and it was filled with all kinds of goods calico, groceries and everything."[160]

Only a small corps of slaves regularly traded outside the neighborhood. Teamsters sold more varied goods to a wider range of buyers over a larger territory than anyone else. Lewis Jackson conjured up something akin to a grocery on wheels in his recollection of Samuel Chase's wagon. Chase was their mistress's "Market man," Jackson explained, "and was allowed to raise corn, potatoes, garden truck, hogs, poultry, and market it for himself."[161] A teamster could often sell to planters whose paths he crossed. Dan sold three chickens to Susan Sillers Darden, his owner's in-law, who also bought four pullets off a passing wagoner from the Montgomery place on another occasion. Fellow slaves also gained access to buyers outside the neighborhood through a teamster willing to hawk their wares. Henry Hunt made a tidy profit buying goods in Vicksburg and selling them to slaves in his neighborhood. "I made a good deal of money that way," he boasted, enough to buy "a fine sow pig" in the mid-1850s.[162] Providing access to markets abroad was a valuable service with high returns for teamsters.

Slaves on the banks of the Mississippi River also turned a profit on a comparative advantage of the Natchez District. Traffic on the river offered slaves a potentially large market. Many traded extensively, mainly with small peddlers who bought and sold from flatboats, some with steamboats passing between New Orleans, Memphis, and points north. Slaves on Davis Bend shut planters out of the poultry trade and cornered the market at times. Henry Turner, who managed Palmyra there, complained in 1845 that "chickens are scarce at this time — the negroes sell all they have to the boats."[163]

Yet planters adroitly stepped in to dominate riverine commerce as well. Slaves on many places along the Mississippi were forbidden from trading with steamboats.[164] Other planters did not bother to stanch the trade and merely inserted themselves between buyer and seller at the point of exchange. Thomas Bradshaw, a teamster in the Delta, recalled buying wood from fellow servants to sell to the steamboats on Saturday afternoons and "moonshining nights." Yet Bradshaw's owner had the overseer transact the sale.[165] On the river, as in auxiliary production as a whole, planters' control over labor time reduced slaves' leverage in trade. Selling wood to steamboats was a lucrative enterprise for slaveholders. Slave men extracted payments for overwork cutting or hauling wood, but owners retained a firm grip on the trade itself by having the wood cut on their time.[166]

Knowledge of markets never extended much beyond a cadre of men familiar with the trade in a few of the goods they worked with. The Southern Claims Commission determined the amount of compensation for goods seized by the Union army based on their "fair market value" at the place and time they were obtained.[167] Some witnesses — generally men — who differentiated antebellum prices by the particular characteristics and quality of goods had evidently gained some experience before the war with the judgments, negotiation, and rough equality of the cash nexus. James Smith saw enough of the steamboat trade in Claiborne County to know the going rate was between $2.00 and $2.50 per cord "owing to the kind of wood." A cord "cut from the heart of the tree," Smith added, "would sell as high as $2.50 or $3." Smith was not just driving up the commission's award to his old master, who claimed a flat $3.50 for all his lumber. Despite Smith's keen eye for cordwood prices, however, he knew nothing of, for example, the market price for corn before 1863.[168] William Johnson, a groom in his owner's stable at Port Gibson, likewise recalled prices for seemingly every grade of horse but knew nothing about market prices for other goods that were everywhere around him. Prices for eight horses taken by the Yankees varied in his judgment according to their age, use, and provenance: $85 apiece for two unbroken bay colts; $175 for a sorrel wagon horse; $275 for a six-year-old bay saddle mare from "the upper country"; and $300 for the gray with a "nicked" tail. Yet Johnson had "no idea" what buggies were worth.[169]

For most slaves, trade escaped the market scot-free. Given that planters bought most of what slaves had to sell, trade with owners amounted in no small measure to the terms of exchange itself. Cyrus Lee of Warren County, like most ex-slaves who testified to the commission, could not estimate the market prices of any goods he routinely produced or consumed before the Civil War: "I was a slave then & will not say what articles of any kind were sold for in those times."[170]

While trade with owners isolated slaves from the market, it accorded men some control over exchange relations. Slave men did most of the selling to owners, among others. Two-thirds of the slaves who sold corn to Walter Wade in 1852 and to Basil Kiger in 1857 were men.[171] The Ramsay family transacted business in cakes and pies on a strict division of labor. Caroline Ramsay baked the goods, while her husband, Peter, sold them to the students at Oakland College, where their owner was president during the 1850s.[172] Some women conducted a brisk trade with owners, too. Nine of the twenty-five slaves on Aventine who sold corn in 1859 were women, including three with accounts separate from those of their husbands. Nancy Berry sold her owner a barrel and a half of corn, and the eggs she turned over during his visit to Aventine in May made three shipments that month.[173] In the egg and poultry trade on the Darden place, women took part in nearly equal numbers, but the men had the more valuable part of the business. Nine of the ten sellers of eggs were women, but ten of eleven chicken peddlers were men. One need not believe in tales about geese laying golden eggs to appreciate how the men's trade in chickens afforded them control over the supply of eggs.[174]

As the trade on Aventine and the Darden plantation suggests, owners shaped a sexual division of exchange relations among slaves. Men represented families at the point of sale partly because owners were willing to do business with men. Some slaveholders extended men's control over selling on the plantation to buying goods off the place as well. The men got permission to go to Fayette the day after slaves on the Darden place settled up with their owners on Christmas 1855.[175] Planters in Warren County also reserved for men the permission to shop in town.[176] The prerogative of trading came to some men hand in hand with a proprietary claim to garden patches. Such a claim appears implicit in the overseer's notation about the division of labor on Aventine one afternoon in July 1859: the women washing, "the men working *their* patches."[177] Planters indirectly strengthened men's control over trade where the sexual division of labor in auxiliary production duplicated that in staple production. Men's part in the wood trade with steamboats, for example, followed the convention that clearing land was men's work. Men may have sold most of the corn on the Wade place because they did the plowing to plant it, at least when their owner was watching.[178] According men trade preferences was an adroit maneuver, for it gave half the slaves a stake in the owners' goal of keeping the traffic in goods at home.

Women's accommodation to their men conducting family trade is under-standable in light of what little they gave up. Trading with owners was no privilege. Women recognized the indignities men suffered when an owner doled out hard-earned cash at the discount of a condescending gift. Nor did women surrender title to family property. Jane and her husband, John, chose the day Benjamin L. C. Wailes paid off Fonsylvania slaves for their corn in July 1858 to ask permission to divorce, probably because they thought the crop belonged to both of them. They no longer agreed on much else, and it must have been a trial waiting for the appointed day, for the hard feelings brimmed over into "a scene outright" when they paid court to Wailes. What exactly was said, we do not know, but one gets a feel for the tension of the moment from Wailes's observation that Jane was intelligent, "high tempered and has a most abusive and vulgar tongue which is impossible to silence." It was plain to all parties concerned that if the couple parted for good that day, Jane would take her share of the corn with her.[179] It was a matter of principle among slaves that women retained ownership of property they brought into a marriage. Slaves' recognized women's title to property by the convention of neighborhood couples keeping their property on the wife's place.[180] Teamster Henry Hunt, for example, took the sow he bought to the adjoining Chappel plantation where his wife lived. Fannie Hunt and her son bred the pig for more than five years before Union troops took the offspring in 1863.[181]

For all slaves — women, men, and families alike — staking claims to property and making them stick was neighborhood business. Slaves followed a similar procedure to marriage in the absence of legal standing for rights of ownership and sought recognition of their title to property from neighbors. They displayed their ownership of goods and solicited acknowledgment when goods, crops, poultry, and livestock were counted, compared, praised, or admired.[182] The exchange was almost effortless for slaves in town or on the same plantation, where living quarters and yards lined up tight. Louisa Lattimer of Vicksburg was well versed regarding Andrew Black's property. "I knew that Andrew owned some stock two mules and a horse because he used to brag of it."[183] Emory Anderson and Elvira Holly's owners were brothers, and their quarters were half a mile apart. Anderson had his eye on Holly's cow and calves even before her father gave them to her during the Civil War. "I knew the Stock well," Anderson recalled, "knew them before [her] Father purchased them . . . from a Drover who staid in the neighborhood Some time selling to black, & white."[184] Charles Burnam admired the horses Benjamin Stinyard inherited, for the men lived on adjoining plantations and saw each other weekly, sometimes daily. Both horses were "large and full grown," one roan or sorrel, the other a bay mare, "good work and riding Stock" and "in good order for the Season" in the summer of 1863 when the Yankees seized them.[185] The gaze and language of recognition did their work in chores and talk in every neighborhood.

Draft animals were beyond the means of typical field laborers in the Natchez District. Enough planters objected to slaves keeping cows, horses, and mules for state law to prohibit it.[186] Much of the slaves' earnings went to stocking up on necessities — tobacco, sugar, molasses, flour, cloth, and clothing.[187] Some people accomplished impressive feats of accumulation, though. George had saved a bag of money by October 1843 when he left Palmyra for another Quitman place. Several slaves on the Acuff plantation in Warren County saved enough cash—up to five hundred dollars in a few cases—to loan money to their owner, or so he told the Southern Claims Commission. Russell Giles owned hogs as well as a cow and mule.[188] Belfield Hicks told the commission such contradictory stories about himself and his property that neither his claim to have inherited draft animals from his father nor Elijah Sharkey's corroborating testimony should be accepted at face value. Still, Sharkey had a reasonable explanation for why a slave who owned draft animals stood out. "It was such a rare thing for colored men to own property that when one did own any he became Known all around the neighborhood."[189]

Most owners of that species of property held occupations above the common rank. William Scott was a slave foreman. Anthony Lewis, an elderly gardener in Claiborne County, needed his horse to get around. Nelson Finley, a blacksmith in Wilkinson County, belonged to the West Feliciana Railroad and earned as much as five dollars a day for overwork.[190] The overwhelming majority of former slaves who claimed mules, oxen, or horses before the Southern Claims Commission had hired their own time during slavery or obtained the animals during the Civil War, when the antebellum terms of work and trade were transformed.[191]

By contrast, draft animals were a ubiquitous property among slaves in the low country. Ownership of horses, by no means restricted to slaves of any particular occupation, was common in the ranks of field laborers.[192] Productive property—horses, mules, and wagons—was essential to the slaves' agronomy. The singular advantage of task labor was the ability to carry on independent production regardless of whether other slaves were engaged in staple production. Owning productive property or borrowing it from other slaves guaranteed families access to draft animals even when the master's teams were in use. In the Natchez District, however, the progression in the accumulation of property stopped short at cash and livestock—mainly poultry and hogs.[193] Some planters prohibited slaves from owning productive property such as cows and horses. But slaves hardly needed to be told they could not own property they lacked the means to obtain, given the time available to them. Planters' control over labor time and productive property gave them a tight hold on the scope of auxiliary production.

Owners' role in auxiliary production was all too familiar to slaves from routines of staple production. The difference between the power owners appropriated in these overlapping spheres was one of degree rather than kind.

Owners did not entirely dictate the sexual division of labor or the crop mix in the gardens as they did in the cotton fields. Yet the boundaries of space and time — namely, the plantation and the crop year — made reconciling the competing demands of fields and garden a zero-sum game. The time owners appropriated for their crops inevitably reduced that available to slaves for work on their own account. Planters tightened the margin when they adopted reforms that increased the obligations of field labor. Owners did not stand vigil over the slaves' work in the gardens, but then planters did not do so in the fields either. Slaveholders, in their attempt to monopolize trade, subordinated women to men in exchange relations. In auxiliary as in staple production, owners exercised their authority mainly over when slaves worked, what they grew, and what was proper for men and women to do.

In no line of work could slaves transcend the property relations of bondage, including the small corps of slaves who hired out their time. They went to their labors under two very different arrangements. Most were hired out by their owners to another employer for terms ranging from a day to a year. A few paid their owner a fixed monthly sum for the prerogative of finding their own employers and keeping the rest of their earnings for themselves.[194] From the slaves' standpoint, the monthly dues they paid were a rent for the use of their own time.[195] Working outside the neighborhood was part privilege and part burden. Amos Cooper wore a gold ring with his sister's likeness when he hired himself out in 1845 to an officer in the Mexican War.[196] Although most found employers closer to home than Mexico, all spent long periods away from kin and neighbors.

Slaveholders across the South resorted to hiring out where the demand for labor was uneven. Hiring out was most extensive in the Upper South, where disparities between farms and between town and country were especially sharp.[197] Hiring out was perhaps most pervasive in Virginia, where the transition from tobacco to grain and livestock created a surplus of slaves who were sent to textile and iron factories in Richmond and other towns voracious for labor.[198] In the district, by contrast, the increase of work on cotton plantations stanched the growth of hiring out. There the supply of rented labor was reduced mainly to owners who had lost their land and estates in probate, while the market consisted mostly of the construction of railroads and the limited needs of plantations and mercantile county seats unmet by white artisans.[199]

Slaves had different conceptions of self-hire, neatly captured in two formulations of the practice. Slaves who hired themselves out said they hired their time from their owners, while other slaves said such folks simply hired their own time.[200] Robert Johnson and William A. Bailey were typical. Johnson recalled his friend "was allowed to hire his own time" in Woodville. As for Bailey, he described himself as "a Jack of all trades," a carpenter and hack driver, "hiring my time from my owner."[201] Practitioners used Bailey's formulation consistently before the Southern Claims Commission after emancipation, and antebellum court records provide contemporary evidence of the usage. When John Allen asked a slave who crossed his path in the spring of 1843 what he was doing on the road to Vicksburg, the man declared he was going to town "to work having hired his time from his master."[202] The precision and consistency of these formulations hold clues to how slaves understood hiring out. Practitioners such as Bailey cast the practice as a relationship to owners, whom outsiders such as Johnson elided.

Slaves who hired their own time had good reason to talk about the prerogative in terms that invoked their owners. They harbored no illusions they were free. The arrangement was illegal in every state in the South. The law in Mississippi, though rarely enforced, fined the permissive owners. If they failed to pay, however, the slaves could be sold. More important perhaps than the state law were local ordinances, like Woodville's, prohibiting slaves from hiring their own time.[203] The mobility that went along with hiring out only exacerbated slaves' need for their owner's authority. Untethered to law, distant from owners, slaves who hired themselves out were open to seizure of their chattels or their person. John Allen seized the man he met on the road to Vicksburg then and there and held onto him for a day or two until Allen was arrested for horse stealing. Allen was questioned at his arraignment about stealing the man as well but insisted he had merely taken up the slave as a runaway. Be that as it may, a slave who announced he hired his time from his owner also reminded people up to no good, without putting too fine a point on it, that they were courting more trouble than they bargained for. Ironically, the very independence of hiring one's time required slaves to resort to their owners' authority.

Keeping hold of property likewise occasioned resort to that authority. Benjamin Edwards began hiring his time from his owner in 1845. That permitted him to "have what I could make, but I had to hold it in my master's name." Albert Johnson, a free black man who got to know Edwards during the 1850s, understood his friend's predicament from his own experience. Johnson also could not legally own property and said of Edwards that "in case any one inquired whose property it was he would have been obliged to say his master's."[204] Edwards, like other slaves who hired their own time, could find his title to property challenged by unscrupulous trading partners, by suspicious constables, or by any other white person who had the nerve to make an issue of it. Staking claims to property in an owner's name was an expedient way to defend them on the road.

Slaves such as Edwards knew the prerogative of hiring their time did not belong to them as much as it pertained to the relationship between them and their owners. Thus, it was not transferable from one owner to the next. After Amos Cooper returned from the Mexican War, his owner in Vicksburg sold him to a lumberman in the Delta. Hiring his time with his old owner gave Cooper leverage with his new one, but not enough to hire his time again. Instead, William Whiteman agreed to free Cooper after he worked off his purchase price of $850 at a rate of two dollars for every day of work, minus the cost of his board. It took Cooper fully nine years to free himself. Unless he was served some very fine fare at Whiteman's table or rarely worked at all, that was several years more than his owner was owed.[205] Although the rental slaves paid their owner for their time varied from ten to twenty-five dollars, the monthly pay period was a fixture in the arrangement. Embedded in the relations of hiring their time was a regular reminder they still worked for owners.

Slaves who did not hire their own time had their own notions about the practice. Matilda Anderson, though intimately acquainted with hiring out, formulated it in the same terms as the vast majority of slaves. Her mother, a midwife, "hired her own time," Anderson said. Her husband "always hired his own time," too. Although her account combined the affections of daughter and wife, Anderson's admiration for her mother's and her husband's frugality and generosity, their skill and enterprise were common in recollections about slaves who hired their own time. Mother "was thrifty and made and saved money." Some went to helping Anderson's sister buy a horse and cow. Anderson's husband, who belonged to another owner but kept house with her, was a carpenter and "a good workman." He took his pay for building gin houses and other work in cash or kind, mainly livestock. He left the animals with Anderson, breeding some, selling others, and "speculating in other ways."[206]

Other slaves saw men and women who hired their time as unusually independent. Anderson knew her mother was no free woman. By Anderson's reckoning, her mother hired out her time, not her person. Of course, time was no small thing for a slave to call her own. Anderson's mother also stood out among slave women for the mobility that went along with her prerogative. Midwives typically attended birthing mothers for several days and might visit periodically for weeks. Most people who hired their own time were artisans or teamsters and therefore men.[207] Demand for skilled labor drew slaves who hired their own time into Natchez and Vicksburg to ply their trade in lumber mills, hammer away at anvils in small shops, and lay bricks into mansions.[208] Men such as Anderson's husband were likely to work in their plantation neighborhood, in town, and anyplace in between. Her mother, "[k]nown and sent for all over the country — by the white Ladies," according to Anderson's brother,[209] traveled as widely as any man, a rare perquisite given women's relatively few chances to leave the neighborhood.

To field laborers, whose work confined them to neighborhood grounds, the ability to operate routinely over a far larger terrain shifted the balance of power between owners and slaves who hired their own time in the latter's favor. Jack Hyland, who found plenty of work as a teamster hauling goods in Vicksburg, divided his time between town and his owner's plantation eight miles into the hinterland. Slaves who hired their own time routinely accumulated property beyond what field laborers eked out of their gardens, including draft animals. In Warren County, Daniel Murfee related, "I used to hire my time from my mistress" for $12 a month. He had nearly $300 in 1858 and bought two mules, Jack for $150 in the spring and Jenny for about three bales of cotton, $120 worth, in the fall.[210]

Some people who hired their time parlayed their earnings into freedom. That required the resources of an entire family in the Natchez District, as elsewhere.[211] Murfee recalled that when the Union army carried off the last of his mules, "I just sat down & cried." His tears were not just for himself but for his wife as well, for they had both "worked night & Sundays for what we had. . . . I thought we had a hard time of it," he lamented, and "she worked as hard as I did."[212] In the 1840s, Richard Dorsey paid his owner $18 a month for his time and $15 for his wife's. They earned enough in Natchez to clear between $20 and $30 monthly, and within a year the full scope of the possibilities before them came into view. "I intended to have laid up enough to have bought myself & wife," Dorsey explained. In two or three years they saved enough to buy "a Span of Mules," a dray, and harness. Dorsey used the team to peddle as well as haul — "I traded in any thing that there was money in" — but he and his wife never carried off the plan to buy their freedom. Isham Lewis of Vicksburg cleared enough after his $20 monthly dues to buy himself for $1,400 when he was still in his thirties. Freedom never came cheap, but the elderly could get a discount. Jackson French, a drayman in Port Gibson, was over sixty when he bought himself for $500.[213]

Small wonder most slaves left owners out of the equation in their reckonings of hiring out. To live apart from owners, to work routinely outside the neighborhood, to accumulate cash and property beyond the means of other bondpeople, perhaps to buy freedom itself — all this added up to getting as free and clear of masters as a slave could get. Yet hiring out, like all social relations, looked different from the inside. Practitioners needed their owners' authority to engage employers, to keep their property, to navigate the terrain outside the neighborhood, where they were liable to find themselves on shaky ground. What they received for their monthly dues was their time. The slaves themselves belonged to their owners, and they knew it.

Slaves distilled the social relations of their society in work. Men and women in every occupation molded the contours of neighborhood. Teamsters, carriage drivers, artisans, and other mobile slaves operated over a wider terrain than the rest of their neighbors. The sexual division of labor that excluded women from those pursuits also confined them within the neighborhood to a greater extent than men. Field laborers, men and women alike, and the vast majority of slaves made their owners' plantations the hub of the neighborhood in the routines of cotton culture. Thus, slaves on adjoining plantations fashioned not one but several centers of every neighborhood.

At the same time, slaves conceived of staple and auxiliary production as a single field of power relations. The relations of labor impressed on slaves owners' ability to exercise power at a distance. Planters in the Natchez District held aloof from the daily routine of the fields. Yet they exacted increasing amounts of work by inserting themselves where men and women came together at their particular point of production. Slaves felt their owners' heavy hand when they put bondpeople to work in the house, at the wagon or in the fields, at the plow, or in the hoe gang and defined the sexual division of labor on their own capricious terms. Slaves likewise felt the weight owners threw around in work on their own account, setting the parameters for auxiliary labor time, the terms of trade, and the accumulation of property. Slaves learned all too well how owners exercised power by stepping in where the divisions of labor were drawn, the mix of crops was fixed, the fruits of production were handed out or exchanged.

Terms of labor defined the terms of struggle in critical ways as well. The division of labor between planters and their agents confronted slaves with drivers and overseers in the fields. That, in turn, confronted slaves with the problem of engaging owners in struggle.

Terrains of Struggle

The people on Fonsylvania broadcast their grievances across their Warren County neighborhood to get the overseer fired. Their owner, Benjamin L. C. Wailes, spent most of his time in the hamlet of Washington at the other end of the Natchez District, so getting him to take the matter in hand took some doing. Sophy told white people on the Gee place, next to Fonsylvania, things had gotten so bad she wanted to remove to Dr. Beall's at Rocky Springs, eight miles distant. Mrs. Gee warned Sophy to mind how she pursued that scheme, lest she find herself sent further away than she intended. Sophy somehow made her wishes known to Dr. Beall, who was advised by A. Pettit, owner of another plantation adjoining Fonsylvania, to write to Wailes.[1] Finally, John and Clem spread the alarm next door on Kensington, which belonged to Wailes's niece. When the overseer brandished firearms at John and Clem, the two brothers fled there, whereupon both overseers on Kensington and Fonsylvania also wrote to Wailes, who promptly made his way out to the place. Sophy, John, and Clem made the people's quarrel with the overseer known on three plantations in the neighborhood.

Their campaign ensured Wailes had gotten quite an earful by the time he arrived. Pettit, with whom Wailes crossed paths en route, told him of "great abuses at the plantation" and related "the current opinion of the neighborhood that my overseer had not been acting correctly." The overseer at Kensington confirmed the "unfitness" of Wailes's manager and said the crop was in the grass besides. John and Clem took the opportunity of Wailes's return to come in under his wing. Jane, John's wife, was working their corn patch when Wailes rode onto Fonsylvania and told Wailes Clem had just passed by her. Clem walked out from the bushes after Wailes rode on, calling after him. John joined the procession moments later. Along the way, John and Clem told their side of the story, and it rang true to Wailes, if only because "sources not altogether friendly to them" said much the same. After hearing out the overseer, Wailes was inclined to think the conflict a misunderstanding, at least as far as Clem was concerned, but resolved to "make further investigations."[2]

Other slaves did not wait for Wailes to solicit their opinions and stepped forward to put in their two cents. "A number of the negroes called in to-day to give their account of the causes of the disturbances on the place during the past week or two," he noted in his diary.[3] Even those who had bones to pick with fellow slaves spoke up for John and Clem, and all roundly denounced the overseer. The slaves had circulated their complaints so broadly Wailes could scarcely distinguish the slaves' story from that of slaveholders in the neighborhood, who had heard it from the slaves in the first place. Having outflanked the overseer, they exposed him to Wailes as "indolent . . . deficient in judgment and temper, and brutal . . . neglectful and inattentive to the sick . . . passionate and profane, and in short brutish in his disposition towards the negroes." Wailes slept on what they told him, then fired the overseer in the morning.[4]

When slaves' contentions are mapped on neighborhood grounds, several landmarks stand out on the terrain of struggle: determined campaigns to draw owners onto the field and to draw together adjoining plantations; the rebels' uphill battle; conflicts with runaways; points of contest in all the relations of power where neighborhoods were made. Neighborhoods were the arena for battles of every sort with slaves' every antagonist. This is where men and women confronted drivers, overseers, owners, slave patrols. Here slaves found allies, runaways lay out, plotters crafted and set in motion plans to kill white people. The terrain of struggle also illuminates how blurry, how porous, how downright messy neighborhood boundaries could become in times of strife. Neighborhoods were places of conflict as well as solidarity among slaves. Indeed, conflict was intrinsic to forging solidarity. Men and women established this principle most pointedly in capturing runaway strangers from outside the neighborhood. Nor did slaves confine their struggles to adjoining plantations. Some of their most powerful gambits involved hammering away at alliances between plantations and forging links between neighborhoods.

Boundaries between neighborhoods were by no means impermeable, and protracted struggles were liable to extend beyond adjoining plantations. Three killings, five years and just a mile or two apart in southern Adams County, hint at bonds of struggle that broke over neighborhood bounds. By January 1852, Bill had taken more abuse than he could stand from his owner, Matthew Lassley, who had rained down fire and blows on the slave. A doctor's examination of Bill's injuries laid bare the magnitude of Lassley's savagery — fractured bones and burned, bruised, and wounded flesh. During another attack, Bill, fearing for his life, as he later claimed in court, drove an axe below Lassley's ear, three inches deep into his skull. Lassley instantly fell dead. The circuit court, in contrast, was neither swift nor certain in punishing Bill. The testimony of several of his fellow slaves adduced some evidence that others on the Lassley place wanted their owner dead and perhaps even conspired to kill him. In the spring and fall, the judge set aside guilty verdicts against Bill for murder and manslaughter on technical, though provocative, grounds.[5]

Five years later, in 1857, three men in that neighborhood killed an overseer for outrages against slaves. Perhaps Henderson, Reuben, and Anderson on Cedar Grove, which adjoined the Lassley place to the east (see map 2), had forgotten Bill's deed by the time they acted.[6] Henderson later told planters investigating the overseer's death that he got the idea from a conversation with a white carpenter, John McCallin. There was nothing unusual about the sound of whipping carrying from the quarters that evening, Henderson told McCallin, when the carpenter asked what all the fuss was about. McCallin suggested the boys on Cedar Grove should "get rid" of the overseer, "put him out of the way," or words to that effect. The next morning, McCallin asked how long the whipping had gone on the previous night, but Henderson could not say. It happened all the time, he replied, and he tried not to pay much attention. McCallin taunted him and the other Cedar Grove men for tolerating such abuse and even went so far, Henderson later claimed, as to say they would all be better off if they did away with the overseer. Then McCallin could marry their mistress, widow Clarissa Sharpe, and there would be no overseer at all. The investigating planters later made much of these conversations and accused McCallin of masterminding the killing. McCallin had designs on marrying Sharpe for her fortune, even while he was sweethearting with her house servant, Dorcas. Yet the slaves had their own controversy with the overseer — the constant whipping — and killed him for it.[7]

The overseer was still in his nightclothes when Henderson, Reuben, and Anderson jumped him in his bed in the dark of the morning on May 14 and beat him unconscious with a club. They carried him a half mile to the woods at the edge of the plantation. Intermittent signs of life indicated their work was not done, and Reuben, a carpenter, wrenched Skinner's neck from time to time until all the moaning and twitching stopped. Anderson went back to Skinner's cabin and returned with some of his effects — horse, clothes, gun, and game bag — to make his death look like a hunting accident. The three men together dressed the body before Henderson, the carriage driver, went to begin his daily rounds. Anderson hoisted Skinner onto the horse, rode further into the woods to a tree, scuffed up the roots, put the body over them, and sent the horse on its way. Reuben fired one shot and dropped the gun and other effects nearby, as if Skinner had died from a fall after his horse had reared and thrown

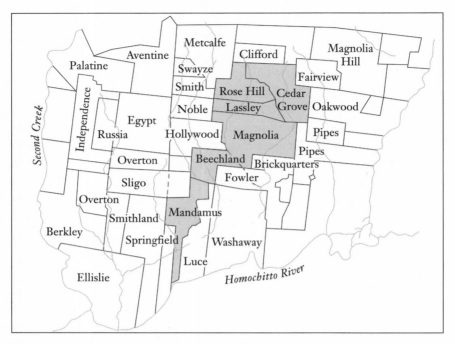

Map 2. Slave Neighborhoods East of Second Creek

him. Anderson and Reuben made one more trip between Skinner's cabin, where they collected his money, and his corpse, where they placed the key to his trunk in his pocket.

The men enlisted other slaves in the neighborhood to help cover their tracks. They took the bloody nightclothes and club to the cook, Jane, who burned them and scrubbed down the bloody floor in Skinner's cabin. Dorcas hid twenty dollars for Reuben, and Anderson hid himself on another adjoining plantation, Magnolia, where his neighbors provided shelter and a sounding board for his remorse.

The slaves' campaign against their tormentors in this section of Adams County spilled over neighborhood boundaries before summer was out. Mandamus was not, strictly speaking, in the neighborhood of the Lassley place, Cedar Grove, and Magnolia; it was closer but not contiguous to the latter. Beechland, where people from Mandamus went visiting, went courting, and fashioned abiding ties of kinship, did adjoin Magnolia. Thus, if people on Mandamus were not part of the neighborhood where slaves did away with their antagonists, their neighbors on Beechland were. Ties did not exactly stop at the perimeter of adjoining plantations but rather became attenuated. That sufficed for slaves on Mandamus to receive word slaves on Cedar Grove had killed their overseer and, moreover, had gotten away with it. Or so it seemed nearly four weeks later when white folks still considered the overseer's death an accident. Thomas Parker and John Baker of Mandamus thought they could get away with settling the score with their overseer, their trial later revealed, just as folks on Cedar Grove had.[8] On June 7, Parker and Baker wrestled the overseer to the ground, punched him, kicked him, threw him in a pool of water, and tried and failed to drown him. They finally landed a wooden club square on the side of his head, a mortal blow at last.[9]

Planters in Adams County resolved to make an example of the five men on Cedar Grove and Mandamus, despite some disagreement about how to do so. The usual procedure for executing slaves was to hang them, publicly but discreetly, inside the courtyard of the jail in Natchez.[10] Yet that would not suffice for Henderson, Reuben, and Anderson, duly convicted of murder by the circuit court; their apparent ability to kill with impunity had emboldened Parker and Baker to try, too. Alexander K. Farrar, who led the investigation on Cedar Grove, warned that making a spectacle of hanging the culprits could incite still more killings. "If the Negroes are brought out in public to be hung," he warned, "and they get up and talk out that they have got religion and are ready to go home to heaven, etc. etc. — it will have a bad effect upon the other Negroes."[11] Authorities hanged Henderson, Reuben, and Anderson on Rose Hill plantation anyway, adjoining the Lassley place and Cedar Grove, across the road from the woods where Skinner expired. The site was chosen, a newspaper reported, so "the slaves on all the neighboring plantations can witness the certain vengeance of the law."[12]

When Parker and Baker were hanged on Mandamus a week later,[13] other slaves from the place were in attendance. The memory was still insistent twenty years later for Baker's brother, Harry Alexander. Parker "was hung," Alexander told the Pension Bureau. "My brother was hung at the same time. His name — my brother's — was John Baker, was hung on the same gallows for the same offense. . . . I saw them hung."[14]

The three killings were episodes in a protracted struggle extending across two neighborhoods east of Second Creek. All parties concerned recognized the connection between the two 1857 murders. Baker and Parker themselves had traced their inspiration to the Cedar Grove men's example. Planters, convened for a public meeting in support of the investigation on Cedar Grove, also took note of the killing on Mandamus "and the general restless state of the slaves in that vicinity."[15] Although no extant testimony connects those killings to Bill's on the Lassley place, they are linked by, in addition to their proximity in time and space, some striking patterns. Bill never denied killing his owner, yet the court failed to convict him during a year of legal proceedings. The Cedar Grove men's ability to pass off a murder as an accident persuaded Baker and Parker they too could get away with it. Most important, all six men exacted the same penalty (death) for the same offense (brutality to slaves).

Neighborhoods, no matter how much their boundaries could be stretched and crossed, posed intractable problems for slave rebellion. To muster a force of any consequence, rebels had to unite across neighborhood lines. Yet slaves typically cultivated solidarity within those lines, and slave society was everywhere divided along them. Moreover, any insurrection had to get around dangerous obstacles inherent to the neighborhood terrain, which slaves necessarily shared with slaveholders. Slave neighborhoods not only overlapped with the slaveholders' neighborhoods but were contained within them. Slave rebels, surrounded by their enemies, were in constant danger of discovery. In early 1861, as the Civil War was just getting under way, slaves west of Second Creek, on the opposite bank from the executioners of the 1850s, began to plot against their owners on a grander scale. Their plot did not get far before it was discovered. Although it was investigated by a self-appointed "Executive Committee" of district planters, it was undone by the hazards of neighborhood — the limitations of solidarity among slaves as well as detection by owners and their epigones.[16] The terrain of neighborhood, with its inextricable constraints and obstructions, all but doomed slave revolts.

Slave men put the plot together from one plantation to the next. They worked the neighborhood ties, especially kinship, in the evenings, on Sundays, and during other off hours along the creeks, at parties, in the woods, and in other liminal places. Slaves on Brighton plantation were the prime movers in the business. All five men there were involved.[17] Orange and Harvey, father and son, carried their planning from adjoining plantations, Waverly and Grove, to another neighborhood around Forest. (See map 3.) Orange talked over the plot with men on Waverly; he and Harvey discussed it at Grove and next door on Forest. Orange also envisioned the rebels making a circuit, counterclockwise, through his neighborhood from one adjoining place to the next, beginning at Brighton and ending at Grove. According to Frederick Scott of Waverly, Orange planned to strike Brighton, Waverly, Fair Oaks, Beau Prés, Forest, and then Grove. Men on Forest — Dennis, Simon, and George — also plotted their course by a neighborhood compass. They talked with men on Palatine, right across the creek, and planned to kill owners on adjoining Fair Oaks and Beau Prés.[18]

Men around Second Creek made some headway at cobbling neighborhoods

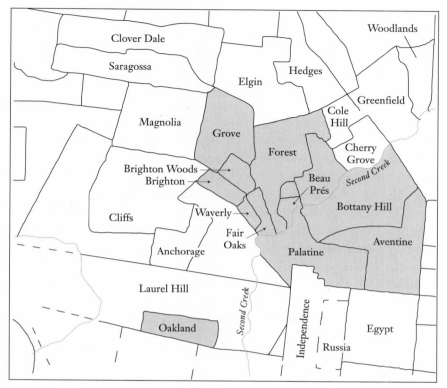

Map 3. Slave Neighborhoods along Second Creek

together along with the plot. Forest was the hinge for opening up the field of struggle onto this new plane. Even by Orange's circuitous route, rebels would have briefly left his neighborhood around Forest. Other Brighton folks carried their talks to Forest as well.[19] The collaboration between men on these two plantations amounted to an alliance between neighborhoods. Forest was the nexus for other recruits from other neighborhoods.[20] During the summer, slaves from Brighton attended a dance at Forest. There they talked with several men from the place — Simon, George, Dennis, Peter, Dick, Paul, Albert, Harry — about killing the mistress of Forest, Mary Dunbar, among other slaveholders, and about weapons to do the job. Simon and George declared they had firearms. So did David Bradley, a French-speaking runaway who came to the party with Harry Scott from Waverly.[21] Men on Forest also looked abroad for collaborators and targets. George astutely targeted Levin Marshall, one of the wealthiest planters in the district, on Poplar Grove, two miles north on the opposite bank of Second Creek.[22] Simon talked over the war on Oakland, a mile or so to the south, with the driver, Edmond, who confidently predicted, "If the black folks were turned loose with hoes and axes they would whip the country."[23]

Neighborhoods, however, did not readily coalesce. For plotters navigating this social geography, good contacts among the outsiders were necessarily few and far between. Nelson, a Brighton man, alluded to these limitations when he claimed to have discussed the plot solely with other men there with just one exception. It took time for slaves to cultivate enough trust for any common endeavor, let alone to risk all, as all rebels must. Edward, the carriage driver on Bottany Hill, across the creek, was the only "Strange" slave to whom Nelson spoke directly.[24] When the plot was uncovered, some men were not even on a first-name basis with slaves they had approached outside the neighborhood. Some witnesses who said so were perhaps trying to protect comrades, but that could be more convincingly accomplished by giving interrogators incorrect names, as runaways often did.[25] Doctor, a man on Palatine, seemed willing to tell what he knew about two runaways, one named Davy Williams and another from Fatherland plantation outside Natchez. He added that the latter was "a yaller" man but did not give his name, evidently because Doctor had never known it.[26]

As men combined in neighborhood circles, they arrived at different notions about how the plot would unfold. Men on Brighton, Forest, and Waverly, for example, deliberated the fraught question of what to do with the planter women. Bondpeople understood the power of slaveholding men entailed control over slaveholding women. These plotters imagined their own control over those women as a hallmark of their future mastery over their late owners' dominions. There was disagreement, though, about whether the women would make willing partners or whether the rebels would have to impose themselves by force. On Brighton, Alfred put his plan simply: "[K]ill all the white men and take the young ladies and women for wives." He did not say exactly how he expected to appropriate the women, but he imagined it would involve their consent to some degree, for he repeatedly insisted they would become "wives" to rebels.[27] On Forest, Simon at one point expected the planter women to seek the rebels' protection. Dennis, Simon's neighbor on Palatine, recalled him saying "the white women would . . . run to the black men to uphold them." Orange, conversely, expected rebels on their tear through his neighborhood to rape planter women. According to the abbreviated notes of another Waverly man's testimony, Orange himself intended to kill both his owners on Brighton but not their daughters, for he meant to "have young ladies to self." When the rebels struck at Waverly, Orange testified, Harry

Scott "would ravish" his mistress.[28] Scott — who often greeted people with an enigmatic "Hell kicking up!" — had his own brutal euphemism for rape: "I kill master and ride Mrs." The rebels, he said, would "ride the ladies" at Forest, too. In addition to Brighton, Forest, and Waverly, the one place the plotters talked about rape was Grove, where Henderson declared against it.[29]

The necessity of organizing across a broad field inevitably required men around Second Creek to venture into unfamiliar neighborhoods, and the terrain was not promising. Charlie Davenport's testimony affords our only available glimpse of such encounters. Like other Works Progress Administration narratives, Davenport's recollections in the late 1930s related experiences from childhood, long after the fact, from the perspective of old age.[30] To these familiar vagaries, Davenport added the novel claim he had received a wartime visit on Aventine plantation from Abraham Lincoln himself.[31] So it is entirely possible Davenport's account of a visit from a Second Creek plotter was just another tall tale. But then the contemporary testimony before the Executive Committee suggests conspirators, unlike Lincoln, were actually in the vicinity. The backdrop to the encounter on Aventine is also well documented in the plantation journal and by witnesses before the Pension Bureau. As we have seen, the exactions of reform agriculture had the slaves working harder and harder. They were whipped to their labors, thrown into the stocks, and as Eveline Perano and her husband could attest, the master of Aventine sexually exploited at least one of his bondwomen and broke up her marriage to do it.[32]

Aventine people, though they had no shortage of grievances, would have no truck with rebels, if Davenport's testimony is any indication. "One night a strange nigger come en he harangued de ole folks but dey wouldn't budge," Davenport recalled. "While he wuz talkin up rid de sheriff en a passel ob men. He wuz a powerful, big black feller named Jupiter, en when he seed who wuz comin he turned en fled in a corn field."[33] Jupiter was caught the next day, hiding in a bayou, and hanged without trial. Davenport heard about Jupiter's capture secondhand from his "granny," who was the source for the entire episode in another draft of Davenport's narrative. Yet Jupiter's swift execution would account for the absence of any witness by that name in the Executive Committee's extant records and the absence of any mention of Aventine plantation. Nor is it surprising slaves there would have rejected Jupiter's overture. From the standpoint of Aventine, like any unfamiliar neighborhood a rebel tried to enlist, the call to insurrection demanded slaves jeopardize their lives, their families, their neighbors, all on the word of a stranger. If some might be willing to take the risk, others were bound to decide, this they could not do.

The men around Second Creek were betrayed not by a slave, however, but by a white boy. The risks of discovery by slaveholders and their agents, like the rejection of rebels as strangers, went with neighborhood territory. Slave neighborhoods were shot through with white people, who were bound to pick up on all the talk of insurrection as it carried on through spring, then summer. And it is indicative of just how unfavorable the balance of power was for slaves, especially for rebels, that the plot was uncovered not by an owner, not by an overseer, but by an overseer's son, little Benny Austin, just eight or nine years old. Men on Brighton seem to have paid him no mind at all while they talked with Louis, a driver belonging to the Metcalfes, who employed the boy's father as overseer on Montrose, two miles away. The master of Brighton kept a school on the place, and if Benny was a student there, the men were likely used to seeing him around. On this occasion, when Orange expectantly declared "whipping colored people would stop," Benny asked why. Alfred probably thought his cryptic reference to a "resting place . . . in hell" would go right over the boy's head. Perhaps it did for a time, but Benny had heard enough to somehow put planters on notice about talk of insurrection in the quarters along the creek.[34]

When all was said and done, men around Second Creek had not gotten all that far with the tactical questions of revolt. A number of men had volunteered for the business. Several had pledged their arms. Some were thinking about where to strike and how. Yet they had arrived at no consensus about even so elementary a question as when to launch their rebellion. Most had yet to consider the matter of timing at all. Those who had given thought to the matter looked to the Union's arrival in New Orleans — September 10, they reckoned. But others planned to wait until the Yankee army arrived in Natchez, whenever that might be. All in all, the conspirators were not very good at insurrection because the politics of neighborhood afforded them little experience and less chance of success. It took the outbreak of civil war and the prospect of armies from the North to make these men think the balance of power could shift in their favor. They were not unusual in these calculations. The combination of political crisis and powerful allies, real or imagined, is so consistent a leitmotif in the planning of slave rebels throughout the Americas as to constitute a veritable precondition for rebellion.[35] For slaves in the Natchez District, divided as well as united along neighborhood lines and enveloped by slaveholders' neighborhoods, a successful rebellion was hard to conceive except in the most extraordinary circumstances.

The divisions rebels had to contend with prevailed within as well as between neighborhoods. Conflicts within a neighborhood could be as common as they were prosaic. Even collaborations as wide ranging as those between neighbors on the Nevitt and Campbell places broke down on occasion. Three men from Nevitt were caught stealing with Sandy. Before he and Rubin were ferreted out from a swamp, Peter helped them steal a hog. Afterward, Sandy and Bill purloined some bacon and liquor from a warehouse. When Bill confessed their crime to his owner, Sandy testified against him in court. When Logan, a newcomer to Nevitt, was taken up in the Campbell quarters, Sandy and another man turned him in.[36] Such episodes were hardly unique to their neighborhood. Slaves were prone to complaining to owners about fellow slaves as well as about overseers.[37] Such conflicts were not so much lapses in neighborhood solidarity as part and parcel of it. The very density of relationships that held neighborhoods together also provoked struggles among slaves. The binding ties pulled taut, overlapping loyalties clashed, disputes broke out.

Runaways afford a plain, sometimes stark, view of neighborhoods as twin fields of solidarity and struggle. Slaves lay out inside neighborhood bounds, and newcomers ran back to old neighborhoods. Yet the solidarities of neighborhood, like any solidarity, defined potential foes as well as allies. A measure of antagonism went hand in hand with carving out neighborhoods as the grounds of solidarity because this carving required slaves to discipline one another. Slaves drew neighborhood boundaries most sharply against fugitive strangers.

Fewer slaves lit out for freedom than absconded to old neighborhoods.[38] To be sure, fugitives from the Natchez District were not unknown in the North. Benjamin Savage, a free black man in Natchez, reputedly forwarded several slaves to Chicago before he was arrested and sentenced to ten years in the penitentiary.[39] Yet assistance from a purported Ohio abolitionist proved little help to three slaves in Vicksburg, including a man and woman belonging to former governor Charles Lynch. Their escape was foiled before their boat got under way to Cincinnati. A twenty-five-year-old fugitive from Warren County who went by the name of Jack made it clear to Illinois, only to land in jail there in 1848.[40] Runaways who made it to the North were still liable to capture, even before the Fugitive Slave Law of 1850.[41] So it should come as no surprise that escape to the North seemed beyond the realm of possibility to most would-be fugitives surveying their prospects from the Deep South.[42]

Slaves who ran away to old neighborhoods were hardly taking the path of least resistance. Slaves often ran away soon after they were purchased in a campaign to return whence they came.[43] Sam would have to use his wits going by steamboat. But it helped that he had worked the boats for years as a cook before his owner in Arkansas sold him down the river to Woodville. Sam "will no doubt aim to get to the river," his owner predicted in 1840, and board a boat "passing up, as he was heard some time since [to] express a wish to get back to Arkansas."[44] Lige, like many fugitives, probably headed east when he set out on horseback from Jefferson County, although he supposedly had the hair and complexion "to pass for a freeman." His old home was "in the southern part of Alabama," his owner pointed out in an advertisement for his recapture, and Lige "may endeavor to make his way back again." Henry had a long trip ahead when he left Adams County in 1847 if, as his owner surmised, he was "making his way to near Lexington, Ky., where he originally came from."[45] Fugitives aiming to return to the border South set themselves a daunting task that might take years to accomplish. The trip took months even at the double-time pace of a trader's drove. But runaways were not free to march the highways at any hour of the day and made their way uncertainly along less traveled routes, often under cover of darkness. They were vulnerable to seizure anywhere along the way, of course, and might not give up even then.

Determined runaways put off jailers with aliases for their owners as well as themselves. In fact, all parties concerned expected runaways to give aliases, which is why owners and jailers routinely provided physical descriptions in notices for fugitives.[46] When Caroline disappeared just a month after she was sold in Natchez, her new owner suspected foul play. But he allowed she might be trying to return to her former owner in Kentucky: "She will perhaps claim him for her master."[47] State laws required unclaimed fugitives to be sold at public auction after a certain time — six months in Mississippi.[48] Runaways might fabricate owners' names from whole cloth in the hope of getting sold to local owners and then escaping again at the next opportunity.

Others gave the name of their previous rather than current owners on the chance authorities would speed them on to their destination. Isaac's new owner in Wilkinson County thought he might have absconded with such designs in 1836. His accomplice turned up chopping wood for a lumberman nearby. The owner offered one hundred dollars for the conviction of anyone who might be harboring Isaac and provided the name of his previous owner, "Seth Jones of Amelia County, Virginia," whom Isaac would "in all probability claim . . . as his owner." In 1837 the fugitive James also claimed to belong to a Virginian. The jailer in Amite County, knowing James's current owner was more likely a local slaveholder, placed a notice in the newspaper in adjoining Wilkinson County.[49]

Fugitives tried to return to neighborhoods in the Natchez District, too. Three men sold out of Wilkinson and Jefferson Counties absconded together in 1830 from new owners in the Louisiana sugar country. Tarver "may be lurking about Laurel Hill, as his wife lives in that neighborhood."[50] William tried desperately to get back to Warren County. Born in southern Virginia, he evidently had been caught up in the backlash against Nat Turner's Rebellion. He arrived in Mississippi badly scarred from a whipping, "at the time of the South-Hampton Insurrection," his present owner noted ominously. William had run away repeatedly in the two years since he was sold out of Mississippi to southern Louisiana. Each time William ran away, the name he gave for his owner was invariably "some gentleman in Vicksburg." When he ran away yet again in the fall of 1840, it seemed "probable that he is now making an effort to get to Vicksburg."[51] Archibald had become a skilled as well as determined runaway in repeated attempts to return to his old neighborhood in another section of Adams County. He had evidently received more than a few whippings for his trouble, for he was "seared on the back very much." Seven months after absconding once again in October 1846, he was still at large, probably near the Branch plantation, where he had formerly lived, "as he has run off before this . . . and has always been caught there."[52] Bondpeople went to remarkable lengths to return to old neighborhoods.

Runaways often lay out in their own neighborhoods.[53] The clandestine encounters where slaves extended aid to fugitive strangers are precisely the sort most likely to elude the historical record. Yet experience persuaded owners and their agents runaways often stayed close to home.[54] An overseer in the Natchez District told Frederick Law Olmsted he could assume runaways in his charge remained nearby. If he could not catch them immediately, they eventually put in an appearance at the quarters to see kin and get food. When they showed up, true to form, he soon found their tracks, put the dogs onto their scent, and captured them.[55] What fugitives needed most was sustenance and safe harbor, and slaves readily gave such aid to neighbors who absconded. Although many people on Palmyra took their grievances with overseers to their owner, John Quitman, in Adams County, his brother-in-law, Henry Turner, had a pretty good idea where they were if they did not turn up there. Dennis, Turner reported, "picked a basket of very dirty cotton and as soon as it was discovered he made off before a word was spoken, to him — he is still out, tho I think he is in the neighborhood."[56]

Runaways made ample use of adjoining plantations in the Adams County neighborhood of the Nevitt, Campbell, and Barland plantations in the early 1830s, notwithstanding the occasional disputes. The best places to lay out in every neighborhood were in the woods, swamps, and otherwise unimproved acreage at the edge of crop fields and between the fields on adjoining plantations. These areas changed from year to year, shifting and receding as slaves cleared new ground in winter. The Natchez District offered plenty of cover through the end of the antebellum period, but as men drained swamps and cut and girdled stands of trees, old hiding places were hacked down, obliging runaways to find new haunts. A swamp on the Nevitt plantation was a favored hideout in that neighborhood, even if it was an unlovely spot. It took half a day to extricate a horse from the mire in the nearby "swamp field."[57] After slaves had chipped away at the swamp for cordwood, timber, and pickets for a year or more, the hideaway was uncovered in the spring of 1830. Sandy and George from the Campbell place, along with Rubin and Little Sal from Nevitt, were found one day in late May when John Nevitt and several others ventured into "the swamp to hunt runaways."[58] The ground was forever shifting under runaways' feet.

The transformation of the swamp into a workplace did little to stop the flight of runaways, who retreated to other parts unknown in the neighborhood. Cinthia absconded from the Nevitt plantation in November 1830 and was taken up four days later by the owner of the Barland place, near his house. Roads cleared paths between neighbors, from the edge of Nevitt's to Barland's and from the Nevitt quarters toward a fence opposite the great house on Campbell's. The latter route, passing by the Campbell manse, was ideal for approved visiting that could bear Campbell's scrutiny. Runaways, however, may have preferred other byways. Dilly and Albert from the Nevitt plantation were found in an outbuilding on the Campbell place.[59] Logan, though new to the neighborhood, must have cultivated some strong ties at Campbell's in his first several months on Nevitt. Purchased in May 1832, Logan had already absconded several times before he decamped in November and turned up in the Campbell quarters three weeks later.[60]

Neighborhood solidarities made runaways wary of other slaves as well as white people beyond those grounds. There runaways became suspicious characters, in both senses of the term: they were suspicious of slave strangers, who were equally suspicious of them. After Henry and Bob reconnoitered near Port Gibson in Claiborne County for a few days in 1847, they headed northwest toward Grand Gulf on the Mississippi River. Early one morning, they spied a slave crossing by boat from the opposite bank. If they ever considered enlisting his help, they had judged it too risky by the time he came ashore. They waited for him to land his boat and made off with it as soon as he was out of sight. It could have been worse. If the fugitives did not assume the other slave to be their ally, they also did not take him for an enemy. Upriver they saw a white man, James Young, who looked like he meant to take them up. They landed their boat. Bob advanced toward Young, as Young advanced toward

him. Young said, "Good Morning"; Bob raised a shotgun in reply and then
fired before Young could say anything but "Don't."[61] Bob thought he was
doing what was required to stay at large, just as he and Henry had done when
they stole the slave's boat. Canny runaways avoided strangers because they
could not take other slaves' protection for granted outside the neighborhood.

Furtive runaways understood the burdens they placed on a neighborhood.
Providing the food, shelter, and protection fugitives needed to avoid capture
was no small thing. Victuals were relatively easy to secure, if only because they
were portable, and runaways could abscond with enough food to tide themselves over for a while. Yet they had to impose on other slaves for provisions
eventually. Good Samaritans, for their part, could feed a runaway out of their
own rations, their garden produce, or purloined food. Stealing from fellow
slaves was frowned upon. "Taking" from owners, even if it raised no moral
qualms for slaves, brooked stiff penalties, which could befall anyone in the
vicinity of a discovered fugitive and could range capriciously from an upbraid-
ing to whipping or sale.[62] It was one thing to take these risks and impose them
on others for someone in the neighborhood, quite another to do so for a
stranger. When Jim Hanes ran away in 1845, he was not counting on slaves at
the Dunbar place in Wilkinson County for provisions; instead, he broke into a
cabin. Runaways were often discovered outside their neighborhood helping
themselves to food they dared not ask other slaves to give them.[63]

The encounter between slaves and runaway strangers tended to play out in
predictable ways, and fugitives who did not keep out of strangers' sight were
liable to be captured by them. That was Hanes's fate after he was spotted by
the overseer on the Dunbar place. The overseer ordered two slaves to the door
of a cabin where Hanes had secreted himself. Inside, Hanes rushed the overseer, who pulled a gun and got off an errant shot. Hanes pulled a knife and
stabbed the overseer, who stumbled out of the house, ordered the slaves to
seize his assailant, and died. The slaves captured Hanes in short order and
talked of burning him right there on the spot. A newspaper editor took their
fury as a measure of their high opinion of the overseer. A more straightforward
explanation is that it reflected a low opinion of Hanes.[64] Yes, slaves aided
runaway strangers on many occasions. The overseer on Bourbon did not
recognize the two runaways foiled twice in attempts to steal hogs in the fall of
1847, but they probably gained the cooperation of Charlotte, a slave on the
place who ran away on the day of their second attempt.[65] Slaves on the Ma-
gruder plantation in Adams County, conversely, may have felt plundered by
two runaways from Claiborne in 1857. After the fugitives took their supper in
the kitchen, they went to the quarter, stole into a cabin, and made up biscuits

to take with them. While the biscuits baked, the runaways slept, only to be discovered by several slaves on the place, who clapped at least one fugitive into the stocks forthwith.[66]

A number of slaves in Jefferson County went to some trouble to take up intruders in their neighborhoods. As many as ten men from the Beavin place gave their all in 1849 to chase down two fugitives who had stolen food from their owner's pantry the previous night and made off with a horse. The men got close enough at points to hear canebrake crackle under the runaways' footfalls. It was evening by the time the pursuers picked up the trail on Everard Green Baker's place and continued on after telling him "they had been all day in hot pursuit."[67] Susan Sillers Darden recorded several captures by slaves. Dick, a man on the McGee plantation, caught Betsy the day after she ran away from the Stampley place in 1857.[68] In June 1859, Tom, a slave on the Darden plantation, captured Henry, a virtual stranger to the place when he made his fourth runaway attempt in the five weeks since the Dardens had purchased him. He absconded the first time in dread of field labor after just four days and was retrieved in Fayette, where he had previously worked in a livery stable. Tom had reason to think he was taking his life into his hands the day he followed the newcomer into town, considering Henry had tried to slit the jailer's throat the last time he was taken up. Tom went to the livery stable, where he fetched Henry's former owner, and they retrieved Henry from a cornfield. Ten days later, the day the news about John Brown's raid on Harper's Ferry reached the Darden household, Henry was returned to his old owner — evidently his goal all along.[69]

One runaway, "Sol, the Natchez bandit," as a newspaper editor dubbed him, solved the dilemma of the persistent runaway with flair, at least for a time. A gunsmith testing a rifle behind his shop one day recognized the notorious Sol and a companion. The smith gave chase and shot Sol, who continued on the run until he reached a crop field a mile and a half south of town. He was no stranger to Margaret, a bondwoman on the plantation who sold vegetables in Natchez, but he was no friend to her either. She called for help, set loose the dogs, then captured Sol herself. A bag containing the tools and proceeds of his trade also held clues to his troubles with people like Margaret. Along with many brooches and what a newspaper called "the plunder of negroes generally," Sol collected vivid emblems of his prowess — alligator's teeth, a lock of hair, and a dead man's fingers.[70] To compel cooperation he could not obtain voluntarily, Sol conjured up the misfortunes of those who underestimated his netherworldly powers.

Men and women captured the likes of the Natchez Bandit, Jim Hanes,

Henry, and the two fugitives from Claiborne County because solidarities of neighborhood could cast persistent runaways in a bad light. Their enterprise had a certain logic all slaves understood. The neighborhood was simply too small for a fugitive to remain at large there forever. Most fugitives, of course, never made it through the gauntlet of slave patrols and white people, all of whom had legal authority to seize runaways, or returned home on their own. Runaways determined to avoid capture eventually had to leave. At that point, resorting to theft, intimidation, and force simply went with the territory.[71] When slaves crossed paths with a fugitive stranger in their neighborhood, they knew they had someone in their midst who was willing to resort to such mayhem. The encounter might end with the stranger, one who perhaps had goods to trade or a sympathetic story to tell and told it well, gaining protection. Sometimes it gave way to a struggle with a slave who deemed runaway strangers a menace and dealt with them accordingly.

The capture of runaways testifies to the rough discipline slaves exercised over each other to turn adjoining plantations into neighborhoods. If the stranger who ventured into the neighborhood was a menace, neighbors who ran away from the field were problematic in their own right. During the 1830s, a northern visitor to the plantation hinterlands around Natchez recorded how one slave took up his own son, found "skulkin 'bout in Natchy." The father professed the hope, if John ran away again, their owner would sell the young man. John's mother, the father explained, had cried when she heard their son had run away, and John would "disgrace" his family if he did it again. We need not take the father's hard line at face value to recognize his exercise in discipline. (The father gave their owner a telling demonstration of the cruelty of selling his son for running away by pronouncing the sentence himself.)[72] A father's willingness to take up his son is punishment enough to suggest how slaves disciplined one another for letting bonds of neighborhood fall.

Furthermore, the encounter with fugitives underscores how slaves fashioned their neighborhood in struggles over other ties. Slaves often sought, provided, and denied protection with other bonds in mind, especially kinship. Runaways laying out in the neighborhood might rely primarily on kinfolk for provisions, even as other neighbors provided welcome help of various sorts — food, shelter, intelligence about where to hide or who was hunting them. Neighbors might aid a runaway family member for a time, then pressure her to return home if they feared a draconian punishment, like sale, was in the wind. Slaves who captured runaway strangers might do so with dangers to their own family uppermost in mind. Slaves' defenses of their neighborhoods were no less determined when they acted on the basis of the constituent ties binding the place together. Indeed, this defense was founded at the key-stone where the terrain of neighborhood and the entire terrain of struggle were joined.

For slaves made battlefronts of all the relations of power in which they constituted the neighborhood itself. Relations of property all but guaranteed slaves would clash with owners over the geography of neighborhood, the bonds of kinship, the terms of work and struggle. By right of ownership, slaveholders appropriated fulsome powers to their own persons: to keep families together or break them apart; to configure the parameters of staple and auxiliary production; to define transgressive behavior and punish it. Slaves encountered owners' power on property lines between plantations, at the altar, in the big house, in the fields, at the whipping post, by fiats of indulgence, in acts of cruelty and violence. If owners exercised their power with maximum force directly and individually on slaves, planters also wielded it to great effect by buying and selling people, performing wedding ceremonies, parceling men and women out in the divisions of labor, and policing neighborhood boundaries. From the slaves' standpoint, owners displayed their power most formidably by stepping in where slaves made ties between themselves.

Moreover, bonds of neighborhood shaped the terrain of struggle, which, in turn, reshaped neighborhood bonds. Owners used the bond between spouses to keep slaves at home; slaves extended the bond to adjoining plantations and shored it up with the recognition of neighbors. Slaves hewed methods of work and contention together in a similarly dialectical relationship. Men and women honed skills and tools of work into tools of struggle. Just as relations of labor made the home place the focal point of neighborhood, so work was the focal point of many conflicts. The division of labor between planters and their agents obliged field laborers to confront drivers and overseers face to face in the cotton fields and to work hard to draw owners onto the field of struggle. The terms of work, in short, overlaid the whole terrain of struggle.

Of all the neighborhood bonds, work was the most active site of contention. Because the purpose of slavery was production, slave labor cut across all power relations and produced struggles of every sort. Slaves' methods of struggle were shaped, in turn, by divisions of labor among owners, overseers, and drivers. For all the planters' professed concern for the well-being of their human property, slaves brooked owners' indifference as often as their wrath. Yet slaves persisted, implicating owners in conflicts with overseers and drivers, and skillfully played these parties off against each other.

Slaves were likely to put up a fight whenever the terms of labor changed for the worse. The increase in work was especially dramatic for recent arrivals from the Upper South. For slaves from the Chesapeake, whence Natchez merchant John Knight imported laborers for his Louisiana plantation, King Cotton proved a harsher taskmaster than the cereals they had formerly cultivated.[73] When they were pushed to redouble their efforts to get the cotton out of the grass, Knight could predict their response: "[T]he consequences will be, I expect, (as it is usual even with old hands,) that several will fly the track & run off again." Bill Sillman from Maryland was one of two recent arrivals who had already decamped.[74]

As owners heaped up the demands of field labor during the 1840s and 1850s, the terms of struggle became increasingly pitched, and slaves taught owners by bitter experience to expect contentions when the rules of work changed. Any increase was bound to cause a run-in to hear Solon Robinson, a northern agricultural journalist who traveled widely in Mississippi before settling there, tell it. Slaves "know what their duty is upon a plantation, and that they are generally willing to do, and nothing more." If pressed beyond customary limits, "they will not submit to it, but become turbulent and impatient of control." That the planters extracted more and more labor from slaves over the years suggests Robinson exaggerated the difficulties when he insisted "all the whips in Christendom cannot drive them to perform more than they think they ought to do, or have been in the habit of doing."[75] Yet whips alone, the planters agreed, rarely did the trick. By 1851, Stephen Duncan had learned from years of contentions with his people, including some two hundred slaves in Adams County, that they would not tolerate being "dealt harshly with—otherwise they will run off—and if once the habit of absconding is fixed, it is difficult to conquer it."[76]

As these planters attest, slaves contended mightily against worsening terms of labor. They did not discipline slaveholders to the extent of fixing direct correlations between particular impositions and specific acts of defiance. Instead, the intensity of labor, resistance, and punishment increased roughly in tandem. Provocations in this cycle followed in such quick succession the roots of any particular conflict were open to interpretation by all parties concerned. On Aventine, where the stretch-out was in full force throughout 1859, Simon ran away in January, before slaves had finished baling the previous year's crop, after the overseer put him in the stocks.[77] When Fanny complained about stomach pains in August, shortly after her arrival from another Shields plantation, the overseer endeavored to renew her appreciation for field work. Convinced she was feigning illness, he put her over the course of four days "in the jail house," "in the stock by the legs," "in the stock by the neck," back "in the jail house," and back "in the stock by the legs," where he gave her ten lashes and then turned her out.[78] Laying up and laying out afforded slaves immediate if temporary relief from punishment and labor just as respites were becoming sparse.

Woodchoppers honed a deadly power at the nexus between the sexual division of labor and the terms of struggle. Slaves found any number of ways to kill drivers, overseers, and owners — with hoes, knives, fence rails — but if there was one weapon of choice, it was surely the axe.[79] On the Tarleton place in Adams County, David killed the overseer instantly with one stroke in May 1846.[80] The following year, a slave named Tarleton was indicted for murdering his owner with an axe in Warren County.[81] Killing with an axe, as these examples suggest, was men's work, a difficult, if indelicate, operation. Axes were tricky to handle, and more than a few men had the scars to prove it.[82] Henderson, who had worked for four years clearing a swamp for his owner, died of lockjaw after cutting himself in the foot while clearing new ground.[83] In the annual routine of bringing forests into cultivation, men learned how to wield an axe with speed, accuracy, and a sure hand. When men, in the heat of some altercation, reached for an axe and brought it crashing down on an overseer's head, they brought to bear in a single moment years of training movements, nerve, and skill to work in concert.

For the vast majority of slaves in the Natchez District, planters' withdrawal from the fields made owners a remote set. Bondpeople realized Nabobs like the Archers could not even name all the several hundred people they owned, including 188 on Anchuca, the home place in Claiborne County. Richard T. Archer rarely discussed particular slaves in his correspondence, and his wife, Ann Barnes Archer, could not name all of those she wrote about. She knew it was Fed and Alfred who stepped up to the dining room window to send their respects to her son and nephew away at school in Virginia, but she neglected to name two other well-wishers from Pine Woods, another Archer place. Mary Ann understood her owners would not care exactly whose good wishes she was sending when she kindly said, "Mistress, the boys at Pine Woods miss Mas. Abe & Ned most as much as you do."[84] Men and women belonging to the Archers were not alone in their anonymity to owners. The names of Benjamin Wailes's people sometimes eluded him, too. Those mentioned but unnamed in his journal included "the cripple girl," "a little servant girl" with fever, and "[s]everal of our negro girls" who got into a row.[85] Wailes, about as dutiful as owners came, was on intimate terms with only a select group of his slaves.

Planters reserved their consistent personal ministrations for field drivers, carriage drivers, house slaves, and other family servants. Wailes took a keen interest in the family of Nat, his teamster. Nat, for his part, worked out the family trust with his owners in labor. Taxidermy was Wailes's avocation first, and he occasionally put Nat to the task. Nat eventually took to killing polecats on his own — four in one week — and put the skins in alcohol.[86] Ties of work and intellect and faith compounded one another to fasten deep bonds between the Wailes family and Nat's. He and his wife, Amanda, were Methodists, like the Waileses, and even named their son after a Methodist preacher. Their son's appointment as carriage driver was thus an auspicious occasion, at least for Wailes, who was gratified to place his refurbished old sulky — with a fresh coat of varnish and paint, neat trim, and new cushions — under fourteen-year-old Dubose, "a smart intelligent boy." Wailes took the occasion to record Dubose's namesake (the Methodist minister), his family tree ("the second son of my man Nat, by his second and present wife Amanda"), and his family resemblances (closest to his mother).[87]

Wailes also bestirred himself from time to time to do right by his people on Fonsylvania, of course, and not only when the overseer harry-ragged them. Wailes often looked in on folks in the quarters when he visited the place. He and his wife cut short a trip to New Orleans to visit "old man" Poole, who suddenly took sick.[88] He arranged for a Methodist preacher to minister regularly to the people. And he tried to keep in a hand where slaves fastened bonds among themselves. Wailes expected slaves to ask his permission to marry and tried to make it worth their while. When two couples applied to him, he promised them a wedding supper and clothing as well as suitable cabins to move into. At one woman's request, he bid $1,000 for her former husband, Jack. If she was aware of Jack's feelings — he vetoed the sale on the grounds he did not want to go back to her — she was using her owner's leverage to effect a reconciliation. Wailes was trying to live up to the paternalist duty of protection when he considered going to law over an outrage against Clem. After a passer-by stabbed Clem with a sword cane, Wailes consulted an associate for some way around the prohibition against slaves testifying in court against a white person. But all Wailes could do, they concluded, was hope the culprit incriminated himself.[89]

Given planters' distant brand of paternalism, the first order of business for slaves intent on getting grievances redressed was often to retrieve owners to the neighborhood. Wailes's vocations as scientist, educator, and improving planter kept him busy at his town seat in Washington, outside Natchez, where he was a college trustee, president of an agricultural society, and a working geologist. Other planters were preoccupied with their own welter of intellectual, political, and financial interests.[90] The vast wealth of the district's planters, grounded in multiple plantation holdings, required a great many bondpeople to contend with absentee owners. When slaveholders were off tending to other properties, politicking, or just visiting, the first beachhead slaves needed to secure was their owners' attention. As Fonsylvania people knew all too well, this could prove a tall order in its own right.

Just as relations of labor made the owner's plantation the center of the neighborhood, so they converged to pit slaves first and foremost against drivers and overseers. The planters' division of labor with their agents meant owners dictated the rules of slave labor, while overseers and drivers had the unenviable task of enforcing those rules. Yet slaveholders had contradictory ideas about proper management. Planters judged their plantation well run if it yielded maximum crops; improvements in buildings, equipment, and land; and a natural increase in slaves.[91] It dinted the planters' expectations not at all that the rigors of tending King Cotton exacted a toll on all productive property, especially land and slaves.

From such wide-ranging imperatives, planters issued contradictory instructions. They expected slaves to work vigorously from daybreak to first dark yet warned overseers and drivers not to overwork the hands; they expected certain, swift, commensurate punishment for any breach of discipline yet warned against cruelty to slaves.[92] Some owners synthesized these contradictions into a few pithy formulations in standing written instructions.[93] Nowhere were the contradictory rules on punishment put more succinctly than in the list of overseers' duties appended to the widely used account book and plantation journal published by Thomas Affleck of Adams County: "Be *firm* and at the same time *gentle* in your control."[94] Planters established the parameters of management for drivers and overseers, who predictably overstepped prescribed boundaries applying contradictory rules.

This division of labor thus defined particular terms of struggle among drivers, overseers, and owners. From the owners' perspective, overseers and drivers were mere intermediaries between master and slave. Slaveholders in the Natchez District, like their peers throughout western history, thought of slaves as mere extensions of their owners' will. "I picked yesterday more Cotton than I ever picked on the place before," Basil Kiger boasted to his wife — about four bales, he reckoned, or sixteen hundred pounds ginned. Of course it was a rare slave who could pick even three hundred pounds of seed cotton in a day, and Kiger was accounting for the work of many hands without having picked a boll himself that day.[95] The syntax would not have confused his wife; planter women likewise talked about slave labor as if it were the work of their own hands. "I finished Laura's under body, cut out Sleeves of Prene's calico Dress," Susan Sillers Darden wrote in her journal. "Maryanne made them,"

Darden added, specifying in addition what five other slaves had done that day.[96] Yet Darden often wrote as if mistress and master did all the work themselves.[97] In the slaveholder's ideal, the chattel's task was to execute an owner's will, nothing more and nothing less.

From that perspective, drivers and overseers, too, were mere extensions of the slaveholder's will. Owners charged these employees with responsibility for managing plantations on a daily basis yet insisted they submit to every directive, including ones that ran at cross-purposes. For the slave to do an owner's bidding properly, the owner's agents also had to follow orders to the letter, without revision and without fail. Planters deemed obedience the overseers' first duty, as it was the slaves'.[98] Slaveholders' understanding of the terms of struggle with slaves reduced drivers and overseers to mere animated tools as well.

The terms of struggle were not in practice what the planter class mandated in theory, however, because drivers and overseers reckoned these terms differently. Whereas planters tended to view overseers as extensions of the planters' own will, every overseer knew he had a will of his own and aimed to use it as he saw fit. The overseer expected slaves to obey him without question, as they should any white man, and felt entitled to considerable leeway to apply, overlook, revise, and extend his employer's rules. The planter's slavish notion of the overseer's duties was so objectionable neither party openly drew comparisons to the master-slave relation. Yet the inevitability of negating the manager's will to bring slaves in proper subjection to owners was at the core of the notoriously brittle relationship between master and overseer. Overseers came and went every year or two because they had little alternative but to quit and planters little alternative but to fire them. Either the overseer was dismissed because he failed to follow orders in the style to which slaveholders were accustomed, or the overseer quit when he could no longer tolerate the slaveholder lording it over him like, well, a slaveholder.

The driver's problem was how to exercise power over field laborers when he had no more than a slave's authority. For obvious reasons, he had to find more subtle solutions than did the overseer to the contradictions in the hierarchy of management. Drivers were no more accommodating than overseers about the planter's notion they were merely animated tools. The driver knew all too well, whatever owners decreed in theory, he was bound to make his own rules and enforce them by his own lights from time to time to make slaves work in practice. So was the overseer, as the driver saw it, even if there was no love lost between them.

The driver's paradox had at least two solutions, and each consigned him to a different place in the neighborhood. The one most widely adopted was to distinguish himself from other slaves. Placing himself outside the slaves' system of intimate relations, by practicing polygyny or imposing himself on slave women, was sure to put the driver at odds with his neighbors. Some of these men took care to look the driver's part, too, dressing in black boots and a greatcoat with a bullwhip — a tool of the trade and an imposing piece of apparel — tucked conspicuously into the belt. Planters encouraged drivers to strike the outsider's pose by providing the requisite clothing, appointing newcomers to the post, or according privileges that enabled drivers to exalt themselves in the quarters.[99] As we have seen, Richard Eastman, the driver on Nannechehaw, was permitted to go jobbing "on the neighboring plantations," to grow cotton in his patch, and keep livestock as well as draft animals — pigs, goats, a mule, and mare.[100] To keep the hands at their labors, to push them on day in and day out, to whip them when they fell behind, it helped if drivers looked and felt like outsiders.

Outsiders often had to make up for their lack of authority with sheer force. The largest flock and the sharpest clothes, much less the aloof owner, could not help a driver keep his gang moving when push came to shove, as oftentimes it did. Eastman was on his own when, as his owner put it, his plow gang "pitched into" him. After a man named Boss refused to take a whipping, Eastman dared the entire gang to have a go at Eastman himself: "[H]e told them he would whip all if they did not take him down." And take him down they did, though he gave as good as he got. Eastman, bruised and with cuts to the head, stabbed Elias in the chest with a pocket knife.[101] By a compounded power of will, personality, and physical strength, a driver could compel slaves to do things they would do for no one else. On Walnut Hills, Daniel commanded not only the loyalty of two wives but Sam's enduring awe. Daniel had lost his title when he killed their owner in 1832. Sam was terrified by the crime, but he was more terrified still by Daniel and dutifully helped dispose of the owner's body. Slaveholders came to Sam's defense on grounds he was merely Daniel's tool. Duly convicted as an accessory to the murder, Sam received the governor's pardon.[102] The most feared drivers exercised a power that slaveholders could regard with the shock of recognition.

Men who resorted to the other solution to the driver's paradox — cultivating the persona of a leader among fellow slaves — struggled to carve out a place for themselves in the neighborhood fold. Their first step was to work with their gangs. Instead of standing behind them, urging them on by the lash or command, this type of driver labored at the head of the gang and, leading by example, set the pace himself. Thus Edward Howard, a driver on the Crane place in Claiborne County, styled himself "the leader of the plows." Additional responsibilities added credibility to a driver's claim to leadership. Howard, for example, was also responsible for horses, mules, and livestock.[103] On the Hamilton place, Balor Hill also worked with his plow gang, had charge of the draft animals, and counted the mules morning and evening. "I carried the lead on," he explained. "I was a driver, and a leader for the hands." When Union soldiers confiscated all the corn on the plantation, Hill took it upon himself to procure enough for the people to get by for a few days. He borrowed twelve bushels, ground it into meal, baked it up into bread, then sold some to Yankee soldiers for greenbacks, which he then used to pay for the corn, one dollar per bushel.[104]

Fellow slaves did not ease the path into the neighborhood's good graces for any driver, insider or outsider. Field laborers had their own understanding of drivers, whom they detested for both their cruelty and their stance toward slave society. Many slaves did not recognize any distinction between the browbeating driver and the leader of the hands. In truth, the distinction often had less to do with a driver's personality than with his age. Hill and Howard, for example, were both in their fifties by the end of the antebellum period. In some cases, the self-styled leader was an outsider working toward a rapprochement with his neighbors. From the latter's perspective, then, the question was not whether the leader was a man different in character from the outsider but whether the outsider cum leader had really turned over a new leaf. Slaves on the Montgomery plantation certainly had their doubts about Jerry Bingaman, the driver who had preyed on women there in his younger days. When Bingaman took to performing weddings on the place, too, he staked some claim to be "a kind of a preacher," as William Fountain remembered.[105] Other witnesses before the U.S. Pension Bureau did not dignify Bingaman with the name of preacher in any fashion. The dubious character of his credentials hints at drivers' difficulties in acquiring authority in their guise as leaders.

Nor did slaves agree with either owners' or overseers' estimates of their respective powers. Indeed, had slaves followed their owner's logic, axe blows leveled at the overseer would have landed in master's head. House servants, as we have seen, believed their relations with owners were mediated by family ties. As for field hands, they could not even conceive of themselves as an extension of master's will. They saw on a daily basis how overseers revised his rules, appropriated new powers to themselves, modified slaves' duties and prerogatives. It was plain as noonday from their vantage point that between themselves and their owners stood many figures—overseers, drivers, family servants—all with wills of their own.

Slaves did not reckon the power of these parties on a par with that of owners. Bondpeople were dubious, for example, about the overseer's claim to their unquestioned obedience. Everyone in the neighborhood saw the proof of overseers' expendability in owners' habit of replacing them on a more or less regular basis. Women among the family servants could be positively flamboyant in their contempt for overseers. Mammy, a nurse, understood she was immune from the overseer's discipline. He finally learned this for a fact when he tested the proposition by seeking his employer's permission to punish her. "Why I would as soon think of punishing my own mother!" replied her mortified owner. "Why man you'd have four of the biggest men in Mississippi down on you if you even dare suggest such a thing, and she knows it! All you can do is to knuckle down to Mammy."[106]

For slaves, mapping the terrain of struggle was largely a question of probing the boundaries within which they could take on their antagonists. Their rules of engagement with the driver were arguably harshest of all. Slaves contested his claims to authority and leadership, regarded him, until he proved himself otherwise, as an outsider and tyrant who imposed his will by brute force. Most of the time, the imposition gave field laborers reason enough to follow his commands or, if he preferred, his lead. Sometimes, usually in response to some unusual, undue act of severity, they responded in kind.[107] Slaves felt free to do what they could to provoke an overseer's dismissal when they decided his time had come.

The pervasive threat of getting sold away from the neighborhood compelled men and women to approach the boundaries of permissible struggle with utmost care. If the overseer was disposable, slaves knew they were fungible, and consequently they had to use subtlety when engaging owners. Many of the slaves' favored and most ingenious and successful methods of contention seemed to involve no struggle at all but could be as dangerous as an axe. Poison was useful because cooks could disguise it in everyday routines of service. Arsonists could make torching an outbuilding or the great house look like an accident. Less dramatically, almost imperceptibly, field gangs could regulate their pace by their rhythm and cadence in song.[108] Slaves complained to each other about the powers that be, sometimes in stage whispers in the latter's earshot.[109] When slaves waged their struggles within carefully drawn bounds, owners were less likely to exercise the ultimate power of sale and instead mediated in slaves' relations with drivers and overseers. Keeping neighborhood ties intact often lay at the crux of slaves' well-documented knack for pitting drivers, overseers, and owners against one another.[110]

Slaves were likely to bring the neighborhood more directly to bear if they got no satisfaction from implicating owners in contests with overseers. Four plow hands tried to engage Walter Wade in their disputes with the overseer in early 1854, to little avail. What instigated the struggle is unclear, though it may have started in February with overseer Torry's attempt to discipline Harvey, who promptly ran away, came in, and presented himself to Wade around nightfall. Harvey's attempt to interpose his owner between himself and the overseer did not move Wade, who sent Harvey back to Torry with instructions to "beg off" and stay the night in the overseer's cabin. Harvey, evidently expecting more from his owner, waited for Torry to fall asleep, then absconded again. Four other plowmen also tried to enlist Wade's aid in March. Monroe reported to him after running away and promptly absconded four days later with Harvey, Charlie, and Extra. Monroe returned on Tuesday night. The dogs caught Harvey on Wednesday, and Charlie and Extra gave themselves up to Wade the day after that. Wade seems not to have intervened on behalf of any of them with Torry, who put Harvey in the stocks.[111]

Faced with the difficulty of getting satisfaction from owners, slaves widened their battles to neighborhood grounds. Confronting the same problem Fonsylvania people would face two years later, a neighbor on adjoining Kensington made a similar appeal in 1857. The man (whom Wailes did not bother to name in his account of the incident) drew an axe when the overseer on Kensington tried to discipline him. Having achieved a standoff, the slave ran away. His owner, Wailes's niece, spent much of her time elsewhere.[112] The slave consequently tried to outflank the overseer by making an ally of another planter in the neighborhood, Wailes. The man could not have timed his stratagem better, for Wailes was just then entertaining doubts about the overseer as "unduly severe and tyrannical." Wailes heard the man out and sent for the overseer, who took the slave back to Kensington. Yet the man got precious little protection from Wailes.[113] In the end, it was the slave's word against the overseer's. Sending for the overseer put him on notice Wailes would be watching his next move. More forceful action, however, would been more trouble than it was worth to Wailes, whose confidence in the overseer grew apace with his increasing dissatisfaction with overseers on Fonsylvania.[114]

Although this man had no luck bringing his complaint to Wailes, slaves on Fonsylvania, as we have seen, got their owner to turn out his overseer by those means. Indeed, Fonsylvania people may have learned from their neighbor's experience. When they resolved on a showdown with Wailes's overseer two years hence, they sought as much leverage as possible by broadcasting their grievances to everyone in the neighborhood they could.

Ties of kinship overlapped with those of labor on the terrain of struggle, although they were not entirely coextensive. The tool slaves used to get overseers dismissed and reduce the burdens of work and whippings was much the same they used to defend the bond between husband and wife. A wedding, after all, was merely the most formal way bondpeople courted owners' intervention to attain their own ends. Yet from the standpoints of work and family, slaves tended to face in different directions on the field of struggle. Relations of labor necessarily inclined slaves to focus their activities and ties on the home plantation, to conceive the place as the locus of the neighborhood, and to converge on battles with drivers and overseer. Owners hoped family connections would reinforce these inward-looking tendencies and upheld the bond between spouses partly to keep runaways at home.[115] Relations of property between slaves and slaveholders all but guaranteed family ties were thickest on the home place. Yet if people declined to leave conflicts with overseers on Fonsylvania, Cedar Grove, and Mandamus, among other places, kinfolk routinely took bonds of struggle across plantation lines.

Family ties, the strongest ties binding the neighborhood together, encouraged slaves in strife to look outward to the neighborhood. Intimate relations were a flash point on this field of struggle, and desire generated much of the heat. The pass system originated in some measure at the crossroads where ardent men and women courting across plantation lines ran up against owners' resolve to draw the boundaries of family life. Regulating intimate relations was among the kindest, most profound interventions neighbors made into any couple's life — and the most powerful, too. Bonds between spouses confounded a maxim at the foundation of slaveholding, that the only bond that counted for bondpeople was to master. Every neighborhood placed steely fetters on owners' property rights when it exalted the bond between husband and wife and upheld norms for intimate relations between men and women. Slaves also secured formidable bonds of struggle as they cultivated family ties on neighborhood grounds. Runaways seeking safe haven on adjoining plantations were quick to invoke family ties. Kinfolk felt a special obligation to respond to overtures from fugitive neighbors. When slaves intrigued to press struggles beyond adjoining plantations, kinship was among the first links they tried to fasten between neighborhoods.

Neighborhood occupied subtly different places in the social terrain of men and women, and this inscribed different contours on the terrain of struggle for them as well. The same gendered dynamics of space that made neighborhoods cramped for women and capacious for men help explain why women figured less prominently than men in certain modes of struggle. Constraints on a bondwoman's mobility, especially her exclusion from most mobile occupations, made her conspicuous on her own abroad, uncertain on that terrain, and less well known outside her neighborhood. All of these factors hemmed her in as a runaway.[116] They also left her with precious few contacts to contribute to any plot, let alone an insurrection, requiring links between neighborhoods. By the same token, the bondman's near monopoly on mobile occupations enabled him to hide many transgressions under the guise of doing master's business, to familiarize himself with the lay of the land outside the neighborhood, and to make contacts there. Men made the most of these advantages, modest though they were, to do most of the running away and plotting.

Relations of gender among slaveholders also marked the terrain of struggle as slaves conceived it. Men's duty to solicit owners' consent for couples to live together or marry, do the traveling required in a neighborhood marriage, and to conduct most of the trading for their families had parallel conventions in slaveholding families. Planter men were also expected to do the talking when it came to soliciting permission to marry. Planter women's participation in trade also was narrowly circumscribed — specifically, to their capacity as "deputy husbands."[117] Wives routinely bought supplies and even made contracts while husbands were away tending to business — legal, professional, political — at the county seat, the state capital in Jackson, or elsewhere for days, weeks, or even months at a time. For planter men to exercise the privileges of manhood to the fullest, they needed competent deputy husbands at home. Many women thereby gained sufficient experience to manage estates deftly as widows. Yet planter women rarely ventured into the market when fathers or husbands were available to do so on their account.[118] From the standpoint of slaves of either sex, those inequalities made it hard to see what business a woman had asking for her man's hand in marriage, conducting her own trade if her husband was available to negotiate for her, or traveling alone if a man could accompany her.

To be sure, gendered inequalities did not serve slave men and women well in many respects. They excluded women from mobile occupations and cost them a measure of control over goods their families made on their own account and over the terms of marriage and living together. We will never know exactly how much slaves lost in the way of marriages unmade, goods undersold, or potential unrealized in skilled crafts and other pursuits. It is reasonable to assume that the terms of intimate relations, trade, and work would all have improved had slave society been free to call on all the talents in its ranks. And such practical matters, of course, do not even begin to reckon with how inequities of gender undermined slaves' ability to stake other claims to equality. Inequalities between planter men and women narrowed the field of struggle not only between bondwomen and men but between slaves and owners.

But slaves, women as well as men, also gained a certain power by appropriating owners' conventions of gender. One way to contend against the inequities in slavery was to claim prerogatives of free men and women, inequities and all. Enslaved men and women knew full well their children belonged not to them but to the mother's owners. They understood, moreover, that slaves' very status and owners' corresponding rights to human property were based on denying bondmen rights that free men claimed as their birthright, starting with paternity. From this standpoint, slaves—women included—saw good reason to confer whatever prerogatives they could on men.[119] It would not have put slaves' claims to travel, marry, or trade on a surer footing to stake them in terms that also challenged owners' gendered sense of propriety. Owners were unlikely to grant bondwomen prerogatives denied to planter women. Observing owners' conventions of gender bordered on the subversive to the extent it bolstered slaves' intimate relations and ability to buy and sell.[120] Law did not recognize a slave's rights to marry or trade precisely because they contradicted her status as property. When slaves accorded men privileges (which doubled as burdens) to arrange marriages or traffic in property, they also encroached on slaveholders' rights of ownership.

Slaves' appropriation of owners' notions of gender was not tactical but ideological. It was neither the product of utilitarian calculations of costs and benefits nor a mask slaves donned to fool master and mistress. If the appropriation had its advantages, they only added to slaves' conviction that their understandings of manhood and womanhood were right and proper. Slave women undoubtedly said their piece about how men transacted negotiations over marriage or trade. Yet bondwomen felt compelled in their own way to cede to their men these prerogatives. Owners' conventions of gender gained some of their power in their capacity to mediate conflicts between slave men and women. For those conventions encouraged slaves to think, when men negotiated on women's behalf, they were merely giving manhood and womanhood their due.

As the appropriation of inequalities between slaveholding men and women suggests, slaves resorted effectively to powers outside the neighborhood, including at least one whose power knew no bounds at all. Christian slaves could recalibrate the balance of power when the Spirit moved them. They could take even minor accommodations of plantation discipline to religious scruples, observing Sunday as a day of rest, for example, as a planter's concession to God's sovereignty. The overseer's authority or lack of it was revealed in a new light to slaves on Palmyra after he began preaching to them in summer 1843. He stirred up "a religious excitement," their owner's brother-in-law reported, and now they were "determined if possible to have the upper hand." The embers cooled only after several months had passed, the overseer had been replaced, and at least five men — Abram, Dennis, George Evans, Lewis Hawkins, and William Smith — had run away and returned.[121]

Contentions were bound to spill over the perimeter of adjoining plantations because powers outside the neighborhood — the law and the slave patrol — did so much to constitute the place as the terrain of struggle. As slaves pushed out from their owners' property lines for access to adjoining plantations, the state and its emissaries pushed back. The law and the patrol were, if anything, more uncompromising antagonists than owners were in the struggle over space. The slaveholders, after all, had work for slaves to do off the plantation, wanted peace to go along with good order on the place, and therefore had their own interests in coming to terms with their people's claims to neighborhood grounds. Neither the patrollers, who did not have to live with the slaves on their beat, nor the law, invariably articulated in the language of universality, was similarly intent on compromise. And the law was quite specific in placing the border of its domain in what was, from the slaves' standpoint, the very heart of the neighborhood. By statute, law was set in motion where slaves departed their owners' property.[122] When men and women contended for neighborhood space, they took on not only owners, overseers, and drivers but patrollers and the law as well.

Space was a critical dimension of slave law.[123] The Mississippi code defined many slave crimes in spatial terms. Arson, for example, was burning a place: a "dwelling house, store, cotton-house, gin or out-house, barn or stable." To commit theft was to "carry away" someone else's goods. The prohibition against arms similarly forbade moving them from place to place, to "carry any gun, powder, shot, club, or other weapon whatsoever." The prerogative to trade was curtailed in part by imposing geographical limits on it in a statute forbidding a slave "to go at large, and trade as a freeman." The law against hiring out enjoined slaves not "to go at large" hawking their labor. The provision on unlawful assemblies also prohibited "trespasses."[124] An 1842 statute forbade owners from keeping more than six slaves over a mile from the master's residence without the presence of an overseer or some other white man eligible for patrol.[125]

The Mississippi code devoted five sections to runaways, including one provision that authorized "any person" to capture fugitives for a $6 reward, return them to their owner, or commit them to jail. Draconian measures applied in the case of runaways who passed through or reached certain places. Ferry operators and toll-bridge keepers were liable to a $25 fine for letting a slave use their means of conveyance without a pass. The leader of a slave patrol was authorized "to take such power with him" as he deemed sufficient to take up two or more runaways "lurking in swamps, woods, and other obscure places."[126]

The slave patrol thus was a force slaves had to contend with in their ongoing struggle over neighborhood space. When they eluded the pass system to run away, to attend neighborhood gatherings, or for any other clandestine purpose, they kept on the lookout for patrols. Jake Dawkins, formerly a slave in eastern Mississippi, cast patrols as a direct extension of plantation discipline when he identified their ranks with the meanest overseers around.[127] For slaves, the patrol distilled the capricious power exercised in their society by drivers and owners as well as overseers. By law, patrols had the power to search any quarter for slaves who were disorderly, unlawfully assembled, at large without a pass, or runaways; to kill all dogs kept by slaves; to collect information about owners who permitted slaves to own livestock; and, if they saw fit, to lay on a whipping right then and there.[128] Patrollers wielded broad, menacing powers.

Slaves gained some room to maneuver, however, from the difference in size between the slaveholders' neighborhood and theirs. The patrols hardly had the manpower to be everywhere at once. Each county board of police appointed at least five captains to organize patrols of five men or more, and the captains typically appointed patrols by neighborhood.[129] But these were slaveholders' neighborhoods, so each patrol was actually responsible for many slave neighborhoods.

The patrollers' own deficiencies widened the interstices between slaves' and owners' neighborhoods. Patrollers might visit only half a dozen places on any given night. It was not unusual for the men to do some drinking, retire to a warm place for the wee hours, or otherwise neglect their duties. Some planters, well aware of such mischief and jealous of their own sovereignty, banned patrols from their property. Slaves understandably felt much obliged for this aid to their struggle for mobility and fondly remembered such owners for decades after emancipation.[130] Yet even these slaves had to deal with the patrol on other places in the neighborhood. Slaves routinely posted sentries at the outskirts of religious meetings, dances, and gatherings of every sort. From the slaves' perspective, the patrollers constituted a power not because of some crack efficiency but because of a mercurial ability to turn up in the neighborhood at unpredictable intervals. The patrols, notwithstanding their lax approach and thin ranks, eventually made their presence felt in every neighborhood. And when they did, slaves knew all hell could break loose.

Slaves made neighborhoods a formidable redoubt and gained some high ground on the terrain of struggle along the way. If neighborhoods placed revolt largely beyond the realm of possibility, men and women compelled their most powerful antagonists, the slaveholders themselves, to come to terms with neighborhoods as the terrain of slave society, with the variety of intimate relations and the project of keeping them together, with the slaves' strenuous objections to the overseer and the principle his tenure would be brief. Runaways spared themselves whippings and days of hard labor and carved out the neighborhood as a relatively safe haven. Slaves were so persistent in contentions over the terms of work and kinship and sociability they crafted struggle itself into an everyday neighborhood tie.

Slaves' most enduring accomplishment in their pervasive battles was the creation of neighborhoods. For slaves in the Natchez District, neighborhood constituted the field of struggle. The sites of contention — labor, kinship, worship, and other modes of companionship — were the everyday relations of neighborhood. Slaves cultivated alliances to the folk with whom they worked, formed families, worshipped, and fraternized — in short, with their neighbors. The contentions themselves were yet another neighborhood bond, and a powerful one at that. Slaves made neighborhoods in struggle with owners, overseers, and other slaves. And their struggles gained impetus from neighborhood ties. If these were largely unintended consequences, they were not automatic and demanded a hard line with owners and overseers as well as runaways and other slaves. By these means, slaves cleared some ground to stand on. That was no mean feat, considering planters' claims to own most everything in sight.

The boundaries of neighborhood were permeable, and it is further testament to slaves' tenacity in struggle that they sometimes pressed on beyond adjoining plantations. Runaways kept going, even into unfriendly territory. Men and women circulated grievances and broached alliances with slaves as well as owners outside the neighborhood. There slaves approached the source of the unfavorable balance of power in their society. Slave patrols cut a figure in the neighborhood and were the most local arm of law and state power, bulwarks of slavery. Some bondmen, regularly navigating the broad terrain outside the neighborhood, had to map its political geography and develop their own understanding of the powers that be there.

Beyond Neighborhood

Anthony Stafford was a cosmopolitan, well traveled, well connected up and down the Mississippi River, well informed about politics. He lived in New Orleans, attended his owner in his travels, thrice to Natchez. Stafford had some firm attachments in town, especially to Peter Ramsay, whom Stafford knew "mighty well." Both men had belonged to Abner Ogden before Ramsay fell to Ogden's sister. Stafford served his owner in several capacities, including dining room servant, and evidently cocked up an ear when the white people were talking politics around Judge Ogden's table. So it was second nature for Stafford to fix the time of his trips to Natchez by a political calendar — namely, William Harrison's brief presidency in 1840, the administration of James K. Polk and Vice President George M. Dallas in 1845–48, and John C. Frémont's canvass for the new Republican Party in 1856. "The first time was in President Harrisons time, the next was in Polk & Dallas time and the next was when Fremont ran for President," Stafford recalled.[1] Neighborhoods were the focal point of slave society, but they were not the horizon of slaves' experience. There were folks in every neighborhood who were also men and women of the world.

To map the place of neighborhood in slave society, we need to chart slaves' travels beyond its bounds. Most bondpeople left their neighborhoods occasionally. A sizable cadre did so routinely. They decamped for much the same purposes they went to adjoining plantations — to preach and worship; to visit spouses, children, and other kinfolk; mostly to work. Outside the neighborhood, one tie could lead to another. Stafford's work in Natchez led to an enduring friendship with Ramsay. What defined the neighborhood as a social terrain was the nexus of social relations it encompassed — labor, kinship, struggle, worship, and socializing of every variety. Bonds were rarely as thick outside the neighborhood as they were inside. Even the most mobile slaves, like Stafford, were fortunate if they could maintain a couple of strong ties abroad. Yet the world outside the neighborhood occupied no small part of the collective experience and collective consciousness of slaves in the Natchez District. As they navigated that world, they encountered new powers and familiar ones in new guises — law, the state, and God. To explore slaves' notions of these powers, we must follow their paths out of the neighborhood, repeatedly trace and retrace their courses on the circuit between town and country, as they did, at work and leisure, on journeys mundane and profound.

A Christian's walk of life had interior moments when slaves transcended the neighborhood without setting foot outside it. Neighbors did much to constitute and sacralize the place when they worshipped. In its spiritual dimension, too, slave religion was fervently spatial. When Christians tapped into their faith at its deepest wellsprings — at the moment of conversion, when they felt moved to shout or heard preaching about God's kingdom, whenever they contemplated the promise of salvation — they trained their sights well beyond neighborhood horizons. If these moments were, chronologically speaking, few and far between, they could last a lifetime. Salvation was many things, and one of them was a place.

Slaves experienced this feeling most deeply at the moment of conversion. In the late 1920s, ex-slaves, most from Tennessee, told scholars from Fiske University stories of antebellum conversion with a profound sense of place. Morte was at the plow when he heard the call to preach. A voice called his name — surely his owner to chastise him for plowing up the corn — and Morte ran off. "I come to bring you a message of truth," the voice summoned. Suddenly darkness fell, and "a great roaring" sounded. "I looked up," Morte recalled, "and saw that I was in a new world." Here the plants, the animals, even the water spoke, and they spoke as one: "I am blessed but you are damned!" He prayed for mercy and felt an angel's touch, whereupon he saw his hands and feet were new, his old body "suspended over a burning pit by a small web like a spider web." Morte prayed again, and the voice, softly now, invited him on a journey: "I will guide you unto all truth," the voice promised. "Go, and I am with you."[2]

The course of Morte's life somehow changed for good when, as if shaken from a trance, he returned to the field he was plowing. His owner was there, too, but Morte had lost his fear of whipping, and his owner "seemed to tremble" in fear of the slave. Down the corn rows Morte found Gabriel, standing at the base of a great mountain, clearing their path ahead. "Gabriel lifted his hand," Morte recalled, "and my sins, that had stood as a mountain began to roll away." Morte came to after an hour or so, and when he told his owner what he had seen, the terrain of the master-slave relation was altered, too. "Morte, I believe you are a preacher," his owner said. "From now on you can preach to the people here on my place in the old shed by the creek. But tomorrow morning, Sunday, I want you to preach to my family and neighbors." Morte thanked his owner, then thanked God — "for I felt that he was with me" — and went through the quarters cabin by cabin, "rejoicing and spreading the news."[3]

Slaves were continually beckoned to the Lord's places, where the neighborhood and all its relations of power were nowhere in sight. As good evangelicals, slaves grounded this Christian geography in Scripture. As much as they were moved by the spirit of the Lord, they yearned for the Word as well.[4] Slave preachers who could read were exalted above all others. Even those who could not sometimes preached with the Good Book in hand to avail themselves of its authority. The intense desire to learn Scripture facilitated a sectarian compromise between Baptist slaves and Methodist planters in the Black Belt. Slaves appreciated Methodist missionaries for preaching by the book, notwithstanding doctrinal disagreements such as the relative merits of immersion and effusion.[5] Astute Methodists like Charles Colcock Jones of Georgia recognized Scripture held slaves' attention and as a result concentrated instruction on the Bible — verses as well as parables, events, and biography.[6]

Learning Scripture from slave preachers, planter women, and missionaries, slaves took to heart the lesson that heaven was a place. Reverend John A. B. Jones took pains not only to preach from the Gospel but also to record the passages during his plantation mission in the Natchez District and vicinity.[7] Jones, like other white ministers, tried slaves' patience with exhortations to obedience thinly veiled as biblical exegesis. Yet he also preached from verses where Jesus spoke to slaves' condition with empathy and hope: "Come unto me all ye that labor & are heavy laden and I will give you rest."[8] Jones again and again mustered slaves to a world apart from the planters' thralldom, the "kingdom of God." There "all these things shall be added unto you" — not merely food, drink, and shelter but also "righteousness & peace & joy." This was no earthly place at all, for as Jesus told Pilate, "My Kingdom is not of this world." No one could enter "the Kingdom of heaven" unless they had been "born again."[9] Methodist slaves around Vicksburg looked forward to renewing their fellowship in the kingdom. "During their protracted meetings," according to one slaveholding woman, "after becoming pious, they would work themselves into a frenzy, and begin their shouting by walking up to each other, taking and shaking the hand with words, 'I hope to meet you in heaven.' "[10]

Some Christians left the neighborhood in body as well as spirit. Men with a call to preach were forever going hither and yon. Harrison Winfield, a blacksmith by trade, worked for other planters in Warren County when he finished his owner's business. He went to Sophia Fox's plantation at first to sharpen plows, among other chores: "I was also engaged by her to preach to her servants on the Sabbath, which I did regularly."[11] Although the plantation mission made neighborhoods the locus of religious practice, some went to country churches or those in town. Migrants from the Atlantic Seaboard, where African American churches had been well established since the early republic, presented letters of demission from their old congregations to new houses of worship in Mississippi.[12] Slaves from the McCall place in Claiborne County attended a Methodist service with the white family one Sunday in July 1852, but George, Charlie, and Squire were sent home for some transgression, real or imagined.[13] Nancy Roberts regularly traveled five miles to a Presbyterian church near Port Gibson. These were social occasions, too, of course, and she became close with at least two of the minister's people, Caroline and Peter Ramsay.[14]

Slaves could pursue various relationships beyond adjoining plantations along many routes. The way through the neighborhood also led out. Footpaths between plantations opened onto public roads, stretching out through other neighborhoods, into town and out again. In many neighborhoods, one boundary between plantations was a public road. Henry Leach, a stock tender at the east end of Warren County, noted his owner's place was on a road going clear across to Vicksburg in the west.[15] In the suburbs of Natchez, the Old Courthouse Road bounded several plantations, including the Whitmore place, Windy Hill, before crossing a puncheon bridge, passing hard by the slave market, and leading onto St. Catherine's Road straight into town.[16] Other major roads connected county seats through the intervening countryside — Natchez and Fayette to the north and Woodville to the south, for example. The Woodville road started at Natchez, doglegged at Fort Adams on the Mississippi River, turned south toward Bayou Sara, and continued on to Baton Rouge and eventually New Orleans.[17] The broadest thoroughfare of all, the Mississippi River, connected the district to points of interest from the Crescent City to the Delta, Memphis, and the upper reaches of the Mississippi Valley to the north.[18]

Some left the neighborhood to cultivate family bonds. Where slaves' and owners' kin overlapped, broad avenues could open up not only within but also out of the neighborhood. At least a dozen slaves went visiting in 1859 on plantations connected by ties of marriage between the Surget and Shields clans in Adams County. Seven men, women, and children from the Surgets' Highland brought New Year's greetings to Montebello, the home place of Catherine Surget Shields. An elderly slave couple, Polly and Abram, went to visit one of his relatives on Aventine, the Shields plantation across Second Creek, in September.[19]

The road between families rent by sale was harder and less traveled, but more than a few people took it out of the neighborhood. When Eliza Warren's sister was sold south from Tennessee, they had reason to wonder whether they had seen each other for the last time. But some years later, Warren herself was "sold & carried" to the Patterson place in Claiborne County, not far from the Humphreys plantation, where her sister had landed. "From that time on," Warren recalled, "I used to see her occasionally all along until freedom came."[20] Jerry and Rubin crossed the Mississippi to visit family in Louisiana in 1831, though less often than they would have liked. Two days after their owner (John Nevitt) settled a debt by sending their wives to the Minor place near Concorde, Louisiana, Jerry and Rubin ran away. Although they got passes to go together a few times as well, they also absconded again.[21] Rubin was gone for five or six weeks before he returned in May. That put him in leg irons for a month and ended his travels for the year. Jerry also had a rough time navigating Minor's turf. In the fall, the overseer opened fire on Jerry with a rifle but missed.[22]

Slaves traveled outside the neighborhood most often and most extensively to work. Artisans, though relatively few in the Natchez District, plied their trade over a wide area, on hire from owners or at overwork on their own accounts.[23] The many grandees with several landholdings obliged slaves to work abroad more often than their peers in much of the Black Belt. Planters shifted men and women between their own places and shared laborers with kinfolk — across the county, across the district, or across the river in Louisiana. In 1842, more than a dozen slaves were on the move between John A. Quitman's Springfield plantation in Adams County and Palmyra up in Warren on Davis Bend. Both Grace and Sophy suffered the deaths of infant children during their stays.[24] In 1849, men and women went back and forth between the fields on Richland and Villa Gayoso, the Baker brothers' places in Jefferson County, to pick cotton and dig potatoes, among other tasks. Yet most of the work field laborers did off the plantation was on adjoining plantations, and they left the neighborhood less than domestics did.[25] Judy and Hannah, house servants in Claiborne County, waited on their owners during a visit to the latter's plantation up in the Delta.[26] Body servants, carriage drivers, and teamsters went to the north, to town, and everywhere in between.

No one ventured to more distant parts than body servants. Some went as far as Mexico. Harry Nichols did two tours of duty in the wars there. Planters in the Natchez District avidly supported the annexation of Texas, a field of vast ambitions — to speculate in land, to expand slavery, to win military glory. After Anglo-Texans launched a rebellion for independence from Mexico, Nichols boarded a steamboat at Natchez with Quitman, who commanded the volunteers aboard, and proceeded up the Red River in April 1836. The shooting was over by the time they reached San Jacinto two days after the Texans routed Santa Anna's army.[27]

Nichols and other bondmen saw a good deal of action ten years later in the Mexican War at the Battle of Monterey. Slaves had embarked in numbers with planters from the Natchez District in a regiment of Mississippi volunteers.[28] Three months later, on September 21, Nichols came under heavy fire at the rear of the column while Quitman urged his brigade into Monterey through a gauntlet of imposing defenses. Nichols had his own war story to tell when he rendezvoused with Quitman after the first long day of fighting. "[T]he Mexicans kept shooting cannon balls," Nichols declared. "Sometimes," Quitman related, "he avoided them by dodging, sometimes by jumping & some times by laying flat on the ground."[29] Similar stories made the rounds among slaves attending other officers. Jim Green, who served Jefferson Davis of Warren County, colonel of the Mississippi volunteers, talked likewise of "balls & bombs that were flying about as thick as hail." Green said he was "obliged to *dodge so much* that when night arrived he was so sore & stiff that he could scarcely walk."[30]

Nichols spent the next fourteen months with the army on a long march to Mexico City, punctuated with intervals killing time in camp. He had his share of military duties, though. "Harry's days are entirely taken up with orders, drills, reviews and alarms," Quitman reported in February 1847. His wartime adventures were sometimes bandied about in the Quitmans' correspondence with a wink of condescension. Yet Nichols understood his exploits had placed both him and Quitman on a historic plane where he had seen and done things his family and neighbors, white and black, could scarcely imagine. Nichols assured fellow servants and the Quitmans back home "that master & [I] will come back covered with honor." On his return, Nichols could fairly marvel at how far he had come. When Quitman mused one summer day in 1855, "No one knows all we have been through Harry do they," Nichols could only agree: "That's a fact sir."[31]

Foreign wars aside, peregrine slave women got as far from the neighborhood as men. Women and men alike tended planter households on excursions north as well as south. Eveline Perano, the Shields family's nurse, attended them regularly on their annual tour of the North.[32] A maid and another servant started out with the Roach family on a trip from Adams County to the Virginia springs in 1853. Both made it as far as St. Louis, and one continued on at least to Baltimore by way of Chicago and Pittsburgh.[33] That summer a servant of Sarah Dunbar's was traveling widely, too. The slave's humanity was discounted along with her room at hotels in New York, New Haven, and Boston, where her mistress was billed for "3½ persons."[34] Free soil was not necessarily liberating to slave visitors, but it could be. The Quitmans' servant, John, used to say, according to his young master, "if it were in the power of these abolitionists to give him a *thousand freedoms he would not desert us & his wife at home*." Yet John, accompanying some of the Quitmans on vacation to Newport in 1846, left his Boston boardinghouse one day and was gone for good.[35]

New Orleans was a common destination for women as well as men who worked in transit. This was the Natchez District planters' commercial nexus with the Atlantic world, where they exchanged bales of cotton for the staples of the Americas, the manufactures and finery of Europe and the North.[36] Two generations of men in the Gray family had rare prerogatives there. During the depression years of the early 1840s, while some elite planters obtained fresh land in the Delta and Louisiana, Andrew Brown opened a retail outlet in New Orleans for his lumber mill in Natchez. Simon Gray retailed lumber from flatboats along the Mississippi between the two cities, "coasting" with Brown's son. In 1845 Gray began to captain crews of between ten and twenty men, with charge over the slave and free laborers alike, on two- or three-week trips coasting or delivering lumber directly to Brown's yard in New Orleans. Gray got boatman's wages of twenty dollars monthly after 1853 and sold sand by the barrel on his own hook. His son, Washington Gray, spent enough time in New Orleans after 1856 to find a sweetheart there and marry her a year or two before the Civil War.[37] More conventional than the Grays were house servants — maids, nurses, cooks, waiters, body servants — who tended owners on a spree or during a temporary residence in the city. Dora, Susan, and Harriet, for example, worked on the Francis plantation and in New Orleans in 1839.[38]

Women, though they went as far afield as men, worked away from the neighborhood less frequently — and less independently from owners, at that. Consider the Francis slaves. The two men who also went from the Francis plantation to their owners' town seat in the Crescent City presumably worked under much the same close scrutiny as Dora, Susan, and Harriet. Ryall, the plantation teamster, spent long stretches without supervision on the road to Vicksburg. He was gone for four days once in February and for eight days on one of his three November trips. In December he got home after four days away and within a few days turned around and went back to town again. Ryall often paired up with one of several other slave men on the Francis plantation, and their travels were unusual only in length.[39] He and his fellow slaves were otherwise typical of the sexual division of labor outside the neighborhood.

With rare exceptions, women worked there as house servants, whereas men left home most often as teamsters.

And teamsters often left the neighborhood for a day or two unaccompanied by white people. Men belonging to planters with more than one place carted goods between plantations constantly. While field laborers occasionally moved between Quitman's Palmyra and Springfield, teamsters regularly brought butter, meat, and garden truck from the latter to the home place at Monmouth.[40] For all the visiting between slaves of the Surget and Shield families in 1859, the traffic was heavier from one Shields plantation to another. Ellick left Aventine for Montebello, the home place outside Natchez, weekly in the spring. Little Washington delivered medicine, molasses, writing paper, and cash in small sums to Montebello from Aventine and Natchez. Horace hauled meat, oats, corn, nails, and other supplies monthly from town to Aventine.[41] Nor was unsupervised travel the sole province of the grandees' teamsters.

Between two and four men on any given plantation carted produce and goods back and forth to town. Fall and winter were the busy seasons, when field laborers picked, ginned, and packed the cotton, and then teamsters took it to market a half dozen bales at a time and returned with provisions. Both Andy and Ben wagoned from the Darden place in central Jefferson County. Andy made three overnight trips south to Natchez in January 1855, two with Ben. They mainly went north to Rodney in the fall, usually for two nights each trip, four times in November alone. Twice they set out for the next trip the day after returning from the last. Men on similar errands crowded the roads. The same morning Andy and Ben returned from one trip, four other wagons passed by their owner's house.[42]

Teamsters and other rural slaves entered an altogether different social space in town. The landscape of the hinterlands, chockablock with slave neighborhoods overlaying planter neighborhoods, gave way to the ordered symmetry of a street grid. This was an urban geography dominated, defined, and divided by white people along lines of core and periphery and increasingly function and respectability. Nowhere in town could slaves, scattered wherever owners lived, outnumbered throughout, call their own. Here the most freewheeling places were those where slaves rubbed shoulders with white people. On the outskirts of town — at crossroads into the countryside, in a corner of Vicksburg called the Kangaroo, tucked between riverbank and bluffs at Natchez Under-the-Hill — slaves found the less respectable establishments where they too could drink and gamble and carouse. Further on, slaves proceeded along residential streets with churches and private homes. Social distinctions were not especially sharp in these precincts. Houses varied in size and splendor, from modest clapboard houses and neat cottages to ornate villas and hulking brick mansions. Towns expanded or contracted with the trading district near the center, and the largest combined the functions of county seat and commercial entrepôt. Public houses (restaurants, taverns, boardinghouses, hotels), workshops, and stores lined commercial streets. The courthouse, the tallest building around, rising from a hill in Vicksburg and Natchez, loomed over the heart of town.[43]

Here the opportunities for transgressive behavior were greater and more varied than those back in the rural neighborhoods. Slaves who visited regularly and knew their way around found arenas for clandestine trade, drinking, and conviviality on the outskirts of towns. Towns of any size had white people who were willing to trade contraband with slaves, small shopkeepers who bought stolen goods without asking too many questions, proprietors of taverns, grog shops, gambling dens, and bawdy houses who dispensed liquor to anyone, bond or free, with ready money.[44] "Hundreds of negroes," a newspaper editor fretted, "are nightly drunk in consequence of the attention paid to them by the grog shops on the roads leading out of Natchez."[45] Some of the many teamsters chastised by slaveholders for coming home drunk had presumably discovered these haunts. At least three teamsters on the Nevitt place knew where to get a drink in Natchez, including Dan, who got caught in 1829, ran away for four days, and came back to leg irons.[46] In the sleepy hamlet of Washington, outside Natchez, slaves drank at Brewer's Tavern, where Henry Walker and Jane talked freely over their drams in December 1836. There was nothing unusual about their imbibing until Walker threatened to kill a local grocer.[47] As Walker's threat suggests, slaves' dealings with whites, surreptitious by nature, stealthy in practice, were not all in good fun.

If the possibilities for carousing were greater in town than in hinterland neighborhoods, so were the risks. The tension between slaves and lowdown white people was only heightened by periodic campaigns against the clandestine trade. In Vicksburg, slaves bought alcohol by the glass or the jug from the aptly named Charles Dollar or Henry Swaps. Slaves got whiskey, gin, wine, brandy, and other spirits from Dollar or did their drinking with the boisterous company at the "ill governed & disorderly house" where Swaps presided, at least until the spring of 1837, when both men got indicted.[48] The mayor of Woodville had issued an ordinance the previous year to clear out slaves who passed Sundays around disreputable taverns and stores in town. The patrol and constable were directed to give as many as twenty lashes to any slave, residing in town "or in the country," found "loitering about the streets, or about any shop or public house" on the Sabbath. Anyone selling "spiritous liquors" or anything else to slaves that day was liable to a fine between $20 and $40. The crackdown had evidently waned by the fall of 1839, when the ordinance was published again.[49] Authorities had little success in Vicksburg or Natchez, where groups of white people were prosecuted periodically for selling alcohol to slaves during the 1840s and 1850s.[50]

Although urban precincts had their pleasures, neighborhood divisions made navigating the terrain between town and country tricky. Andy, one of the teamsters from the Darden place, learned this lesson the hard way, if he did not know it already, when he stopped to feed his mule team at the corn stand near the Hoggatt plantation. While the mules ate, Andy dozed, and several Hoggatt slaves helped themselves to sundry goods from his wagon — four pairs of shoes, three hams, two gallons of vinegar, some sugar, and a tin bucket. If Andy remonstrated with the slaves when he awoke, he got no satisfaction and enlisted their owner's help. They held ranks under Hoggatt's persistent questioning and handed the goods over from nearby thickets, denying any part in the theft all the while. Perhaps they regarded this show of unity as a transgression against their owner, if anyone. Yet they could have predicted the whipping meted out to Andy back home.[51] Neither their rough handling of Andy nor his telling tales on them breached any solidarity these slaves recognized. On the contrary, this clash between neighborhoods was par for the course.

It followed from the solidarity of neighborhood that past its boundaries lay a potentially hostile territory. Indeed, neighborhood scarcely made sense apart from this exterior arena and gained significance set against it. The two spaces implied one another, just as "inside" implies "outside" and "here" implies "there." Slaves also felt the sense of place, moreover, in the difference between their relations with people on adjoining plantations and beyond. Contentions with strangers on the road were yet another site where slaves created, reproduced, and exalted the neighborhood. Differences between slaves, in turn, came along with the difference between places inside and outside the neighborhood. We will never know exactly what calculations Andy and the Hoggatt people made at different junctures in their confrontation. Yet they shared a sense of neighborhood in which the Hoggatt slaves needed only to regard dozing Andy long enough to determine he was a stranger to know he was fair game. By the same token, once Andy awoke to the fact he was in the midst of strangers, his wagon pilfered, he had reason enough to suspect they had done him a bad turn.

Slaves could feel the difference inside and outside the neighborhood, along with the antagonism between strangers, because the two places were built differently. To be sure, slaves made them in similar ways, even at the same time. Both were unintended consequences of making families, crops, friends, congregations, and other sorts of fellowships. To the extent one place implied the other, as slaves followed those pursuits on adjoining plantations, they were, unbeknownst to themselves, defining the terrain beyond neighborhood, too. People who worked outside the neighborhood made friends or had family on the road. David Gant, hauling freight between Natchez and Fayette, sometimes paid a call on his aunt and four cousins on Seltzertown plantation, six miles from his owner's place.[52] Anderson Watson and William Madison, teamsters who lived five miles apart in Jefferson County, worked, socialized, and prayed together. They crossed paths from time to time between Fayette and Rodney. Watson sometimes "stopped over" on the way home at Madison's house, where he got to know Madison's wife, and on Sundays Watson attended Belle Grove Church, where the Madisons married.[53] Folks such as these often ventured outside the neighborhood and even forged various bonds there that overlapped somewhere along the way. Yet no matter how much slaves traveled, comrades, family, and Christian sisters and brothers were scattered over a wide territory at best. Slaves invariably had fewer ties there than in the neighborhood, where bonds of sociability, labor, and kinship all converged.

Slave society was less dense outside the neighborhood than inside because the places were constructed from different bonds. Work was the most critical tie between slaves outside the neighborhood, intimate relations inside. Living together was an oxymoron for men and women in different neighborhoods, and marriage abroad was rare in the district. Watson knew his relationship to the Madisons was forged in work: "You know me and her husband wagoned together," he explained. Yet work did not yield as many compounding ties abroad as intimate relations engendered between families and generations on adjoining plantations. Teamsters, carriage drivers, and body servants, the most mobile slaves, went abroad to work and established whatever connections to friends, kin, or church their duties permitted. Solidarities there were bound to be attenuated, given that most slaves worked inside the neighborhood.

As slaves ventured out from their neighborhoods, they also crossed paths with new powers more treacherous than any slave stranger. These powers spanned the landscape and were liable to crop up anywhere. Law was a power to contend with for slaves because it took up where owners left off. Southern legislators defined the jurisdiction of slave codes as the arena off the plantation, as we have seen.[54] Even within the neighborhood, slaves placed themselves under the state's jurisdiction as soon as they pushed their social terrain onto adjoining plantations. Law, moreover, animated an extensive disciplinary apparatus. Slave patrols were its most forward deployment, from the slaves' standpoint, and its most remote outpost was the county courthouse, where the hand of the state was most plainly in evidence. Slaves had prosaic encounters with government, too, at work on public roads or even traversing county lines, although the hand of the state was not easily discerned here. As a rule, law and government stood out in increasingly bold relief from the personal power of owners as slaves left their neighborhoods further behind.

Slaves' familiarity with the state was limited by its contradictory role in the peculiar institution. It decisively shaped the relations of power by handing off to slaveholders the right to dictate slaves' duties and privileges.[55] Slaves forged neighborhoods in struggles aimed at constraining the vast powers the state granted to owners. But the state never showed slaves its hand in this accord. They saw the rights conceded to slaveholders instead as powers owners appropriated for themselves. To make master's powers stick, law restricted slaves' access to the bar. Thanks to the statutes prohibiting black people from testifying against white folks, slaves never testified in civil litigation, even when it turned on their motivations — whether they were habitual runaways, for example, and therefore had been sold under false pretenses about their "good character."[56] Crimes against slaves seldom went to court.[57] Slaves could not initiate suits at law, but criminal proceedings could be brought against them.[58] So slaves were understandably most impressed by the force of the state. Their experience, after all, was weighted heavily toward police powers.

Slaves in the Natchez District left few accounts of their impressions and did not elaborate much after emancipation, yet occasional references in postbellum testimony to antebellum politics marked junctures where slaves encountered the state. Dropping a plumb line at those junctures, we can tease out something of what these encounters were like and some of the conclusions slaves might have reached. Understanding slaves' notions of the state is thus a speculative exercise that, in one sense, brings us closer to their cast of mind, for they had to draw their own inferences from limited evidence, gleaned from an episodic experience with government. Their conclusions too were limited and provisional. Some already realized, however, that government, by no means simply benevolent, presided over an arena where slavery could be hotly contested.

The compass of local government was inscribed on the landscape in county lines. Slaves were clearly alert to them, if not necessarily to the jurisdiction they signified. In postbellum testimony, slaves' awareness of the boundaries is apparent in recollections of crossing county lines before the war. For slaves who came to Mississippi from the Upper South, their old county of residence was worth keeping in mind as long as they harbored any wish of seeing those left behind. Burl Lewis had to resort to time markers to get a fix on his date of birth, but he knew the place exactly. "I was born in Williamsburg Co. Va. at a place called Hickory Fork," he recalled.[59] In the Natchez District, some slaves routinely forded county lines. The Compton place, slaves well knew, was near three such boundaries. Caroline Christian, a slave there during the 1840s, noted that the boundary between Jefferson and Franklin Counties ran right through the plantation. Rachel Meguire, whose husband regularly trekked four miles from the Compton place to visit her, pointed out it was near the Adams County line, too.[60]

The county officers whom slaves encountered most often were hard to recognize as representatives of government at all. Under most circumstances, it was not readily apparent whether planters such as Jesse Darden acted at the behest of the county board of police, which appointed them to supervise work on designated roads. But perhaps Dick figured out roadwork was a government enterprise when he dropped off Darden's report to the Jefferson County board.[61] When slaves put in their day or two each year building or repairing stretches of public road, they typically worked under the supervision of planters and overseers from the neighborhood. Of the fifty-five slaves from six different plantations working the road near the Wade place in April 1852, more than half (twenty-nine) worked under their own owners or overseers.[62] The title of the planter in charge, the "overseer of roads," neatly evoked the continuity with ordinary routines of labor. From the slaves' point of view, work under such government auspices differed little from an exchange of labor among planters.

Slave patrols, also organized by the boards of police, cloaked their government authority as well. By statute they were empowered to turn wayward slaves over to justices of the peace to "be dealt with according to law" or to appropriate judicial power to themselves and whip slaves on the spot.[63] Patrollers, of course, were notorious for their arbitrary resort to the whip. Tom Granville and another Darden slave secured a pass to go to a party during the 1856 Christmas holidays, but their fellow slaves, Ellen and Dicy, who neglected to get permission in writing, got a whipping when the patrol showed up at the festivities.[64] At these moments, patrols seemed to embody modes of power that pervaded the neighborhoods.

The jurisdiction of law was murky from slaves' standpoint. Contrary to the statutes, men and women hired their time from owners. The pass law stayed the hand of law itself by providing for slaves, in effect, to carry an owner's authority with them as long as they had master's permission in writing.[65]

Slaves often eluded the patrols, which could turn up only occasionally, if unpredictably, given the difference in size between slaves' and planters' neighborhoods.[66] Not only did slaves evade the law, but slaveholders were quick to step in where they found legal justice wanting. Planters disciplined slaves for transgressions away from home and formed vigilante committees rather than allow the law to run its plodding course with rebels. Thus, slaves recognized only some agents of the law as such.

Judges and justices of the peace, although they embodied a seamless connection between law and planter, tended to stand out to slaves in the neighborhood. Slaves knew justices of the peace by their official title or by the slaves' version of it, "squire." Long after emancipation, Harry Alexander still referred to his former owner as "Squire Foules."[67] William B. Foules was engaged as a justice of the peace in several noteworthy cases involving slaves, but he took no official part in the prosecution of Alexander's half-brother for killing the overseer in 1857.[68] Ties of kinship gave Rachel Meguire an appreciation for a magistrate's good offices. She and her husband were married by "a squire" named Guise.[69] Slaves recognized a judge by his official title whether or not he was their owner. Benjamin Stinyard, who belonged to William Sharkey, chief justice of the state supreme court, recalled selling horses to "Judge Sharkey" during the war. When Union troops confiscated Henry Banks's hack in Vicksburg, he noted, it was near the courthouse, "in front of Judge Springer's house."[70]

Slaves had reason to take note of a squire in their midst, for he dispensed the rule of law, such as it was, directly to them more often than did anyone else. His jurisdiction was closer to the neighborhoods than any other standing officer of the law. Between twenty-five and fifty justices of the peace stood back of the patrols, arrayed across the district to adjudicate lesser offenses and collect evidence about capital crimes for prosecution in the circuit court.[71] Offenses subject to penalties of thirty-nine stripes or less, from carrying a weapon and theft to trespass and unlawful assembly, fell under the squires' authority.[72] A squire's court found Bill, the teamster on the Nevitt place, guilty of larceny while his accomplice got off without punishment after testifying against him. The proceedings, which concluded with Bill's sentence of thirty-nine lashes, could not have impressed him much for fairness.[73] Few records are extant from trials like Bill's, presided over by a justice of the peace and two slave owners. Slaves' depositions in felonies submitted to the grand jury of the circuit court hint at what it was like for slaves to go before justices of the peace. They were men of average wealth, a cross-section of owners of land and slaves in Warren County. The sites where slaves were questioned by a squire — out of doors, in his house, in a store — betrayed no hint he was an emissary of government or any other political institution. Slaves would have found much in the encounter to suggest the squires' power fit hand and glove with that of owners.[74]

Squires announced the presence of law menacingly. Southern jurists decreed that slaves, lacking the independence and honor to uphold an oath, must have their duty to tell the truth impressed upon them by other means.[75] Mississippi law required justices of the peace to preface slaves' testimony with instructions crafted to show them the draconian face of law. A twenty-five-cent fee added a modest pecuniary incentive to administer the charge. On a bill for services rendered in the case against Henry Walker for assaulting a grocer, the justice appended a note: "The fees are very meagre & it would be hard not to get them." Thus, Jane was duly "charged as the Law requires" before she recounted Walker's threat to kill the grocer.[76] "[B]y the direction of the law," the squire began, "I am to tell you that you must tell the truth, the whole truth and nothing but the truth." If she was subsequently found to have lied, "you must . . . have both your ears nailed to the pillory, and cut off, and receive thirty-nine lashes, on your bare back, well laid on, at the common whipping post."[77]

The magistrate's charge revealed the law as a cruel taskmaster, another reflection of the discipline exacted on slaves in every neighborhood, only worse. Authorities merely exacerbated this impression when questioning continued in the same intimidating tone. David confessed not once but twice in 1846 to killing an overseer. Although the precise circumstances of the interrogation are unclear, he was compelled to confess by some mix of cajolery and threats from a squire and parties unknown. The circuit court directed the jurors to ignore David's confessions if they believed his statements had been extracted "by any threat or inducement." The court implied both were in evidence when it also instructed jurors to consider his second confession only if they believed he no longer expected favorable treatment at the time he made it.[78] Whether the justice of the peace held out the inducement of fear or favor, David might well have recognized the squire's collaboration in the effort to coax and browbeat him to confess.

Criminal trials initiated a small but growing circle of slaves into the rule of law at its most exacting. Prosecutions of slaves in circuit court increased over the antebellum period.[79] Slaves were also called to testify by defendant and prosecutor alike and kept in attendance at court for as long as either side required.[80] They saw no evidence the law protected them from the impositions of slavery. Even when courts followed the rule of law, slaves were on trial for their lives.[81] Only capital crimes — arson, rape, murder, insurrection — were tried in circuit court after 1833.[82] Three slaves were separately sentenced to hang on 30 November 1849 in Warren County — Granville for arson, Frank for murder, Washington Brown for rape.[83] Yet southern jurists often extended slaves the right to procedural due process.[84] Protecting owners' right to human property demanded nothing less, especially when master's people were accused of crimes carrying the death penalty. Slave defendants often received new trials on account of technical errors in indictments or verdicts deemed contrary to evidence or law by the circuit court or on appeal to the state supreme court.[85] A court that granted slaves due process in practice was bound to display the rule of law to them as the process played out. Court was no place for slaves to seek relief from the abuse of slaveholders, but some found protection from the abuse of law.

Criminal proceedings were intimidating from the outset. Slave defendants were entitled by statute to notice of the charges against them and were routinely served with a copy of the indictment while they were in jail. Slaves who could read or had the document read to them likely found bewildering the abstruse terminology and inane detail, such as the price of the murder weapon.[86]

The courtroom's singular economy of space set the place apart from the familiar, neighborhood sites of discipline. Here white men were consigned to their proper place — the dais, the jury box, the gallery — in orderly fashion according to their part in the proceedings. Seated on high at a dais, iron in Vicksburg, wooden in most courthouses, was the judge. Flanking him on one side was the jury, selected from a pool of twenty-four men, at least half of them slaveholders. The defendant sat before the judge at a long table with attorneys for both sides. Behind them was the spectators' gallery, lower than the floor of the proceedings in some courthouses, noisier at times as well. Authorities in Wilkinson County spread sawdust on the floor to muffle footsteps. Witnesses testified from a raised platform near the judge.[87] Slaves regarding the crowd from that vantage point might have thought it a passel of low white people before the judge drew the defendants' attention.[88] In circuit court, too, law was invoked most explicitly in the same brutal threat administered by the squires — slaves were admonished not to lie lest they have their backs lashed and their ears nailed and cropped.[89] Defendants and witnesses took in an imposing courtroom spectacle.

Slaves could not see the law at work where lawyers and judges neglected to follow it. Even the prosecutor thought better of the death sentence Stephen received in 1832 after confessing to shooting at his owner "to 'scare him to make him treat him better.'" Defense counsel made little of how Stephen's alleged intent to kill was mitigated by his professed intent merely to frighten. "I prosecuted him," R. M. Gaines wrote to the governor, "and the defence was altogether inadequate to the importance of the case, as the defence of negroes always is."[90] The circuit court tried Eliza three times before fixing up a conviction for "assaulting a free white person with attempt to murder." When the third jury seemed on the brink of failing to reach a decision as well, a juror was "withdrawn," the requisite guilty verdict returned, and Eliza was sentenced to hang.[91] The court discreetly submitted to the disposition of the mob in the case of Peter, who had allegedly assaulted a white woman and threatened to knock her "to hell." Released to his owner pending trial, he had failed to appear in December 1837, probably because he was already dead. In June 1838, unnamed parties produced unspecified evidence proving "to the satisfaction of the court" that Peter "hath departed this life."[92] Courts ignored legal rules, gave their imprimatur to lynch law, and otherwise dispensed justice unworthy of the name.[93]

When courts heeded rules of procedure and evidence, however, slaves took part in motions to invoke their rights and heard attorneys and judges debate, interpret, and explain the law. Slaves' right to counsel, to compel testimony in their defense, to challenge the seating of jurors, and to appeal verdicts were all guaranteed by statute in trials of capital offenses — in effect, all cases in circuit court.[94] The legislature and state supreme court extended protections against coerced confessions during the 1840s and 1850s.[95]

In due form, criminal proceedings were scripted to give slaves a walk-on part in motions before the court. Bill was unusual among slave defendants only for the number and complexity of his motions during three trials in 1852 and 1853 in circuit court at Natchez. At the first trial, he was acquitted of murder in the death of his owner, the savage Matthew Lassley, but found guilty of manslaughter. The judge ordered a retrial when Bill's counsel pointed out the indictment had neglected to mention the charge. Manslaughter raised the vexed question of whether slaves could ever justifiably kill owners. In a motion for a continuance, Bill took a hand in presenting the argument he had rightly defended himself against Lassley's abuse. The motion was "Sworn to & subscribed in open Court" by Bill and from the outset invoked him as its prime mover before the court: "The Said defendant comes into open court and makes oath that Dr Luke P Blackburn," the physician, examined "the [defendant's] wounds . . . Burns fractures & C."[96]

Slaves might well have taken seriously their momentary standing before the court. The formalities of a motion, if anything, exaggerated the defendant's role in the proceedings. Slave defendants such as Bill did not argue, of course, on behalf of motions, which were instead filed as affidavits and read out in court by counsel. Yet motions were carefully fashioned to speak in the defendant's name at key points. Bill's motion thus cast him as the one who would "attempt to Show" he was "greatly maltreated wounded and endangered." The motion "is not made for delay but that he may have justice according to the Laws of the Land." Although slaves could not bring criminal charges to court, they could initiate motions in proceedings brought against them. In formal legal proceedings, slaves briefly attained a legal standing denied them in substance. Yet some may have recognized, especially when their motions and arguments prevailed, that a court took some pains to hear slaves' side of the story. Perhaps Bill recognized, when the judge granted a continuance for the physician's testimony, the jurors would finally hear what Lassley had done to his slave. If so, Bill presumably thought the court's decision right and proper.[97]

Slaves could also get a grasp on the proceedings from lawyers' rough-hewn eloquence, fashioned vividly to reveal the law even to unlettered jurors. Joseph G. Baldwin, who practiced widely in Mississippi during the 1830s and 1840s, thought S. S. Prentiss had a gift for "knowing and being able to show to others what was the law."[98] Prentiss's summation for the state in the case of Mercer Byrd, a free black man accused of collaborating with slaves to kill their owner in Warren County, was reputedly his best performance ever in a courtroom. If lawyers in the case of Bill and other slaves were not of Prentiss's caliber, the exegesis of the law nevertheless could be first rate. Many attorneys had their own keen knack, as Baldwin put it, "To start *in medias res* — to drive at the centre — to make the home-thrust — to grasp the hinging point — to give out and prove the law."[99] If any white person in the courtroom could follow the arguments, so could many slaves.

In November 1852, Bill's trial addressed another intriguing question — whether law could countenance his owner's murder. If the jury deemed Bill guilty of murder or party to a conspiracy to murder, he would go free because the first jury had already acquitted him of that charge and manslaughter was another matter entirely. Legally, the difference between murder and manslaughter was malice, which was of two kinds, express or implied. Express malice was a calm, deliberate design revealed in the circumstances of the killing — in Bill's case, if he joined a plot to kill Lassley or in his use of an axe if the jury deemed it well suited to kill and concluded that Bill had acted alone. There was no malice in killing immediately upon provocation, and this was manslaughter. Between the testimony of the physician and eight fellow slaves, Bill evidently had good reason to fear for his life at the moment he killed

Lassley. Yet many of Lassley's slaves and even some of the witnesses had apparently wanted him dead and perhaps combined to murder him.[100] To slaves alert to the implications of the testimony, including their own, the law exhibited some provocative tendencies — to justify killing an owner, to exonerate a bondman innocent of murder or, most delicious of all, because he was guilty.

Elaborate proceedings to instruct the jury distilled these tendencies. Slave witnesses had likely departed the courtroom by the time the jury's instructions were given, and only the defendant remained. Instructions were limited by statute to "points or principles of law." The defendant heard the instructions twice, first when attorneys for each side read out their proposed instructions and again when the judge repeated those he accepted — thirteen in Bill's case — to the jury.[101] The judge reminded jurors to look to Bill's axe for evidence of implied malice; that the "provocation where a murderous weapon is used must be great indeed to reduce the Killing to Manslaughter"; that even an intent formulated instantaneously in advance sufficed as "premeditation in law." We can only imagine what Bill thought when he heard the judge's instructions to let him get away with murder. Jurors were directed to acquit Bill if they believed he committed any offense other than manslaughter, even if "the offence Committed was murder."[102] The jury, returning the only verdict carrying a punishment, found him guilty of manslaughter. The decision also implicitly censured his owner, whose savagery provoked Bill's crime, yet the judge set aside this verdict, too, and granted Bill a new trial. The court record is silent on the outcome.[103]

Other slaves prevailed more conclusively than Bill did against fraught charges. Grand juries often indicted slaves for the most heinous crimes the jurors could construe from the facts alleged. As a practical matter, procedural due process often amounted at trial to acquitting a slave of charges overdrawn or carelessly stated in the grand jury's indictment. In Henry Walker's case, the jury found him not guilty of assaulting grocer Daniel Dexter "with intent to murder." Phil was acquitted of an "Attempt to Poison," while Harriet was found innocent of the same charge just one day later. In 1840, jurors in Adams County declared Harriet (presumably not the same woman) not guilty of arson "in the manner and form as she stands charged in the indictment."[104] These slaves were by no means unique in gaining acquittals at trial for capital crimes. In other cases, judges set aside jury verdicts in the name of due process, or the state supreme court overturned convictions improperly charged in indictments.[105]

One can only speculate about how slaves interpreted the power of law from such proceedings. Many witnesses could be excused for regarding the law as nothing more than a savage threat. After all, the only time they were sure to hear the law invoked was when they were charged to tell the truth under the penalty of having their ears cropped. A woman compelled to testify against her husband in Hinds County, across the Big Black River from the district, wept with each incriminating question posed to her by the prosecutor.[106] Some slaves who knew owners, like Matthew Lassley, for the sadists they were must have thought it a hard thing to try one of the owners' victims on pain of hanging. That does not mean all slaves party to criminal proceedings necessarily regretted conviction or welcomed acquittal in every case. The turn of events landing slaves in court — the murder of one slave by another, for instance — was liable to arouse conflicting loyalties.

Yet anyone who perceived that the rule of law compelled white men to stay the hand of punishment would have found the courtroom a striking contrast to the exercise of discipline back in the neighborhood. Planters congratulated themselves on the supposed consistency and restraint of their paternalist mastery. Slaves saw little in their owners' capricious exercise of power to bear out such claims. And for some slaves who landed in court, the experience revealed the quality of justice there to be no better. To others who had their days in court, however, it became apparent that the rule of law in court did indeed involve rules. These rules were based on principle, not the whim of slaveholders; the principle had something to do with fairness; and the principle of fairness was encompassing enough to take in slaves — even slaves who killed owners. In some slaves' experience, the law occasionally did what no power in the neighborhood could ever do — bring white men to heel, no matter what a slave did, no matter what white people thought about it.

Nor was law the only power of the state that slaves encountered, for better or worse, at the courthouse. There slaves were put up for sale as well as on trial, and politicians held forth about the sectional controversy over slavery. The courthouse was also a hub of government, politics, and commerce where people in many pursuits and many classes, even slaves, convened. A considerable proportion of local sales of slaves took place at courthouses — 50 percent in South Carolina, by one estimate.[107] Mississippi sheriffs had statutory authority to auction property for debt; to ensure a good crowd of bidders, the law required that such sales take place at the courthouse door on the first Tuesday of each month. Many estates in probate, slave property included, ended up sold here.[108] Political events of every type — stump speeches, debates, party rallies, mass meetings, processions — took place or began at the courthouse, too, and slaves joined the crowds.[109]

The exercises of popular democracy initiated a slave cadre, women as well as men, to electoral politics. Elections were annual affairs in Mississippi, which had one of the longest slates of elective offices in the Old South, including county boards of police and all judicial officers from justices of the peace to the state supreme court.[110] But county elections turned on picayune questions, agitated at gatherings indistinguishable from the round of hunting parties, fishing trips, and other events in the social life of planter neighborhoods.[111] Contests for state and lesser offices made little impression on slaves, if time markers are any indication. Rose Ballard used a political time marker of the highest rank to approximate her son's birthday. For years to come, she used it to keep track of other milestones—his age as well as that of the son of her friend, Mary Ann Helam. "My son Robert is 43 years old, he was born in April 1844," Ballard recalled, "the same year Mr. Polk was elected President. There was only a week or two's difference in the ages of my son Robert Ballard and Eli Madison."[112] When former slaves looked back on slavery times, the politics that stuck out in their minds were strictly presidential.

Work drew slaves, especially house servants, into politics, if only at the periphery. Slaves in town or on plantations in the suburbs were best situated as political observers. Rose Ballard was enslaved in Rodney, a town on the Mississippi River, before she landed on the Brown plantation out in the country. Natchez was a busy electoral center where political events often took place and processions assembled before making their way to barbecues on plantations in the hinterland.[113] Slaves, conveying planter families by carriage, tending to their care and feeding, were conspicuous amid the throngs at barbecues during the 1844 presidential campaign. "In every neighborhood there were always certain old negro cooks who had special secrets in the management of barbecued meats," recalled Mississippi Democrat Reuben Davis, "and these were always installed chiefs of that department. Besides these were coachmen with their horses, maids in attendance upon 'old mistis' and the young ladies, 'boys' waiting on master, nurses with the children."[114]

If democratic pageantry introduced slaves to electoral politics, contention over slavery gave them reason to take note of the proceedings. When President John Tyler presented the Senate with a treaty for the immediate annexation of Texas in April 1844, electoral politics turned, as if on a dime, from economic controversies over tariffs and banks to the expansion of slavery.[115] Jefferson Davis and Henry S. Foote campaigned for Polk and Texas across the Natchez District. Foote castigated Clay and the Whigs as abolitionist allies and even as abolitionists in their own right. Robert J. Walker, a Natchez lawyer and U.S. senator from Mississippi, established the tone of the Democratic campaign across the South when he similarly condemned Clay as an abolitionist and opposition to immediate annexation as tantamount to abolitionism.[116] Burl Lewis was but a child at the time, yet something about the election marked that moment in his life for the rest of his days. "I do not know anything about dates," he said, reckoning, "I was about 10 years old when Henry Clay ran for president. I was then nursing the children."[117] Lewis had yet to leave Virginia for Natchez, though the election was striking to other slaves around town. William H. Williams, the dining room servant at Ashburn plantation in the suburbs, was then sixteen years old by his estimate. "Do you Remember when Clay & Polk Run for Presdent?" Williams inquired in a letter to the commissioner of pensions years later. Commenting on the intensity of his interest in politics as well as a paucity of recollections to determine his age, he wrote, "if you Do i was a good Big Felowe then the Democrats and whegs was all that i Could Remember."[118]

The politics of slavery was hardly beyond the comprehension of slaves in earshot. Clay, who had family downriver in New Orleans, was a frequent visitor to Natchez, and his reputation as an antislavery man may have intrigued some slaves, like Lewis and Williams, who followed the election. There was much talk of slavery and liberty in the contest between Clay and Polk. And in politics, as at the bar, orators excelled at distilling first principles from arcane disputes.[119] Prentiss's skills as a litigator made him a celebrated political speaker, too. Any experienced politician could explain government and "its workings so simply and clearly that a practical workingman can understand it," according to Reuben Davis; "every question was made clear even to men otherwise uneducated." Debates over the Wilmot Proviso and the Compromise of 1850 reverberated in a new sectionalist politics in Mississippi, where candidates mobilized against northern insults in a vituperative defense of slavery along with southern honor.[120] It is not hard to guess what was provocative about the new antislavery Republican Party to slaves who heard tell of it, such as Anthony Stafford. George Bright took note of the Republican standard-bearer in 1860. Bright landed outside Natchez on Montebello "4 years before Lincoln's election."[121]

If many folks traveled outside the neighborhood, came alive to institutions whose power exceeded its bounds, some people developed collective identities that transcended place itself. Slaves in the Natchez District conceived of themselves most broadly as "a people." This notion, too, was grounded in social relations and identities that had their nexus in the neighborhood. The owner of Lewis, a bondman in Warren County, thought his last words were, strictly speaking, a plea for his kinfolk. Lewis was surely in dire straits on the night of July 8, 1846, bleeding from several stab wounds to the face, shoulders, and back as well as a mortal slash through his side clear to the spine. "O my people," he cried. His oath, of course, was grandly ambiguous. The state supreme court concluded it was no oath at all, and his ensuing accusation against a fellow slave as his assailant could not be admitted as testimony in court. Lewis's words, the court ruled, did not conclusively demonstrate the recognition he was on the brink of death, which was necessary for a dying declaration to stand in for an oath for legal purposes. According to his owner, Lewis's oath was a simple request to see his family.[122] It may not have been entirely clear even to Lewis, mortally wounded, betrayed by a fellow slave, precisely who his people were at that moment.

Yet some freedpeople in Jefferson County were talking of peoplehood in stentorian tones shortly after emancipation, as Merrymon Howard's correspondence with the Freedmen's Bureau suggests. He invoked peoples of many sorts in a letter to the commissioner, including "our poor People," "the people in back & midel Countrys," "the freedmen and free people" (people emancipated during and before the war, respectively). Despite all these distinctions of wealth, region, and prior legal status, he implicitly conceived of freedpeople as a body in references to "the Cullerd People freed & free," the "Cullerd people of Mississippi," and "a people of our Culler." And with force and eloquence, Howard asserted their collective identity as a body politic in his succinct formulation of their predicament: "Despised by the world, hated by the Country that Gives us birth denied of all our writs as a people."[123]

Beyond neighborhood lay a terrain of critical importance in slaves' experience and political thought. Most folks ventured there once in a while, many had business to attend to more or less regularly, and some forged strong personal bonds along the way. Slaves did not invest this territory with the sense of place that they cultivated on adjoining plantations, where they fastened social ties of depth and density that made neighborhoods a singular place. Men and women did some of their most important work exalting the neighborhood in travels outside the place, in struggles with strangers and other travails there. Yet for some folks who routinely navigated the terrain abroad, it acquired resonances quite apart from neighborhoods. They conjured up collective identities that coexisted, cross-cut, and rose above that of neighborhood. The slaves of the Natchez District conceived of themselves not only as neighbors but also as kinfolk, Christians, men, women, and a people. The territory beyond neighborhood was also the seat of formidable powers. They were neither benign nor solicitous to slaves but were impressive still. In the Civil War, slaves crossed neighborhood boundaries with new frequency and purpose. As men and women became more familiar with the new terrain, they came alive in growing numbers to the law, the state, and other powers and regarded the possibilities with new eyes.

War and Emancipation

Slaves in Natchez learned a good deal about the Civil War by watching and listening to the lumberman, Andrew Brown. Richard Sullivan joined the crowd lining the streets for a torchlight parade on Washington's Birthday in 1861. He was struck by the sight of the float Brown contributed, for the contraption — "a large Pall . . . rigged up as a Ship and called the Ship of State" — tellingly captured the rebel enterprise. Randall Pollard kept abreast of Confederate victories and Union defeats by eavesdropping on Brown, even though doing so brooked an outburst of his owner's volatile temper. "I would sometimes get around at such times to hear what was said, though at such times we were not allowed to stand around." Brown rejoiced over the Yankees' every setback, Pollard recalled, and said they would never succeed. Anderson Thomas, whose wife belonged to Brown, noticed her owner was in a fighting mood when Federal gunboats came within sight of Natchez after the capture of New Orleans in 1862. As Thomas made his way through the crowd on the bluffs overlooking the Mississippi River, he heard Brown upbraid an associate for a leery prediction: the Confederates, Thomas heard the man say, "would never catch Old Farragut asleep."[1]

Telltale signs of Brown's faltering resolve began to show. As Federal boats came and went during the spring and summer, Brown ran a Confederate flag up and down the pole atop his mill. As Jacob Robinson, Brown's head sawyer, observed, "whenever a Gun Boat made its appearance the flag would be hauled down and as Soon as the Gun Boat would be Out of sight the flag would be hoisted this was by Mr. Brown's Orders." During the siege of Vicksburg in the summer of 1863, Brown took the Confederate flag down for good.[2] Slaves saw Brown complete his passage from fervent Confederate to fair-weather patriot and then beaten rebel when the Union army occupied Natchez in July.

They scrutinized his demeanor closely the day the Yankees commandeered his mill. Robinson recalled that Brown, usually a man of few words around slaves, lashed out savagely at John, even talked of burning the man alive, and for the trifle of grinding too little meal, or so Brown said. Brown hit John so hard upside the head he bled from the nose. It was a good thing John was an

old man, Robinson heard Brown say, or "he would measure him on the spit."
Burl Lewis stuck around to see just what Brown would do when a Union
officer called at the mill for lumber. "Mr. Brown hemmed and hawed and said
he would not let him have it," Lewis noted, but was powerless when the officer
returned with a detachment of soldiers. "I staid there until the guard came and
commenced taking the lumber."[3] Not long thereafter, Lewis took leave of
Brown once and for all and enlisted in the 58th U.S. Colored Infantry, Company A. "I was one of the first volunteers go up here in town," he recalled
proudly. In due time, several of Lewis's comrades from the mill also joined up
with the regiment.[4]

Slaves looked at their society with new eyes during the Civil War, and what
they saw told them new powers were afoot. As neighbors caucused about the
war, they arrived at the conclusion, like slaves across the South, that this was a
struggle about slavery and freedom. Yet in the Natchez District, the consensus
was not monolithic but plural. The war counsels of 1861 and 1862 resulted in a
cascade of ideological change — in the boundaries of neighborhood as well as
in ideas about the nature of power, what freedom was, and how it might come
about. Power, slaves recognized, was no longer located in persons in the same
way it had been. They heard tell of new forces, largely peripheral to their
experience until now, massing in distant parts to converge on their corner of
Mississippi. As slaves came alive to these powers — law, state, and nation —
they worked up certain expectations about what freedom would look like and
when it would be theirs. By these lights, freedom came not in a single stroke
but in several moments of emancipation.

Freedpeople vividly recounted the war to the Southern Claims Commission
during Reconstruction. Their testimony portrayed in concrete detail what
slaves did, what they said, and what they heard, saw, and thought. The commission awarded compensation only to Unionists for property confiscated by the
Federal army. In addition to queries about how claimants had obtained their
property and what it was worth, therefore, the commission asked a battery of
questions about slaves' political sympathies. Witnesses traced out lines of
communication in reply to questions about when, where, and with whom they
had conversed about the war. They sketched the evolution of their views while
considering interrogatories about the "causes," "progress," and results of the
fighting. Their answers to the question, "When did you become free?" served
as time markers and more;[5] witnesses marked the advent of freedom by a conjunction with well-known episodes and recounted just how the siege of Vicksburg and other turning points impressed them as moments of emancipation.

The struggle over Unionism and secession in the district briefly split planters' ranks in late 1860. In the presidential election, Wilkinson, Jefferson, and Claiborne Counties went with the standard-bearer of southern rights, John C. Breckinridge. Adams and Warren, conversely, voted Unionist and chose "co-operationist" delegates to the secession convention at Jackson. Secessionists rightly understood the cooperationist platform — a united southern front to demand guarantees from the North — as a gambit to forestall disunion. But even cooperationists urged secession should the North prove unforthcoming. The convention, citing the defense of slavery as the bedrock purpose of independence, voted on January 9, 1861, to leave the Union. Within little more than a month, representatives from Mississippi withdrew from the U.S. Congress, Jefferson Davis of Warren County ascended to the Confederate presidency, and planters convened a mass meeting at the Natchez courthouse to display their unity and resolve.[6] As slaveholders closed ranks, a wide-ranging, far-reaching debate among the slaves was just beginning.

In 1861 and 1862, they watched and listened and pooled their intelligence on the aims and prospects of civil war. They fashioned lines of communication, connecting circles of men and women, drawn together in relations of kinship and work, sociability and worship in every neighborhood. Attentive slaves made unwitting owners serve as especially revealing informants. The ability to read enabled some folks to collect information abroad. Dick Green, for one, took cues from literate slaves. "I heard people say who could read & write that the Yankees were going to free the niggers & I wanted to be free." Teamsters, artisans, preachers — mobile men — were the most important investigators and messengers in the slaves' ranks. They made themselves into homespun military experts by their ability to reconnoiter over a broad terrain, canvassing informants, sifting opinion and fancy, separating rumor from fact. Slaves in transit, gathering and dispensing information from neighborhood to neighborhood, connected them along the way.[7]

"Times were ticklish and a black man's life wasn't worth more than a chickens," according to James Hyman, a drayman in Natchez who was especially pithy about the risks of investigating the war. But no slave could ignore those risks.[8] Slaves confronted a police apparatus of unprecedented scope by the spring of 1861. Antebellum slave patrols gave way to an extensive mobilization of local provost marshals, vigilante committees, and paramilitary groups, self-styled the Minute Men in central Jefferson County, the Adams Troop around Kingston, and the Washington Troop outside Natchez.[9] Slaves hewed close to neighborhood ties, at least at first, as they navigated this new terrain. Military assessments gained credibility from connections across plantation lines, which made sources familiar and therefore trustworthy. Benjamin

Stinyard and Charles Burnam lived on adjoining plantations, had known each other since childhood, and saw each other weekly, sometimes daily during the war. Slaves in the neighborhood of the Sharkey plantation in Warren County waited for the cover of darkness to exchange what they knew. "Conversations of this Kind generally occurred during the night," Burnam recalled, when "we often met and talked at the Corner of the fence."[10]

Bonds of kinship, trade, and religious fellowship brought Clem Harde-man, Lloyd Wigenton, and Anthony Lewis together in their neighborhood in Claiborne County. They took heart at Yankee victories, and "we had rather long faces on" when battles went the Confederates' way. Lewis was nearly thirty years Hardeman's senior and uncle to Wigenton's wife. He ground corn for the two men and was "a sort of a preacher among us and we looked up to him and advised with him," Wigenton explained. Trips to Rodney, where Lewis marketed vegetables, likely made him well informed, too. So he did much of the talking—about "how they come to fight," as Hardeman put it, and about their own stake in the outcome. Lewis came to the attention of soldiers and members of a nearby church "for expressions . . . amongst his colored neighbors about the Union cause," Wigenton related, "something about his telling them, that the Yankees were fighting to free them, but if the Confederates were successful they would still be in slavery." Lewis disavowed such talk when his tormentors took him to the woods, debating whether to shoot him or hang him. Lewis's disclaimer saved his life, but they had pegged his discourse right. Lewis told Hardeman, "if the Yankees whipped the Con-federates we all would be free."[11]

Much of the information circulating in slave neighborhoods originated with owners. Planters read newspapers, corresponded with sons, husbands, kin, and friends who were soldiers, officers, and officials. Even men and women of discretion talked over what they knew in the garden or the yard, on the porch, and at table, where house servants picked it up and passed it along. A tirade on Yankees rampaging over some distant corner of the Confederacy, hell-bent on destroying slavery, might speak volumes about what was at stake to slaves within earshot: cooks, waiters, gardeners, carriage drivers. Some slaveholders, at ease in their family ties to house servants, imprudently told slaves what they wanted to know. In the neighborhood of the Fox plantation in Warren County, Samuel Chase spread the good tidings he picked up from confiding white family members. Chase talked about the war with "the other Slaves on the place and the Slaves on the adjoining plantations," Lewis Jackson recalled. "Sam being a favorate of Old Mistress and her family, Soon learned from them, after the beginning of the War, that if the Union army succeded in whiping the South, that all the Slaves would most likely be set free." Chase, working his contacts in the big house, became an informant for the entire neighborhood.[12]

Nor was Chase the only person spreading the good word in this neighborhood. Harrison Winfield, the blacksmith and preacher from the Messenger plantation, canvassed opinion among most of the men on the Fox place, where he had visited regularly since the 1850s, sharpening plows and spreading the Gospel. "It was generally believed by all the Slaves of my acquaintance," he found, "that if the federal army conquered the South, that the Slaves of the U.S. would be set free."[13] Although Winfield did not reveal what views he contributed to this consensus, a preacher's calling lent his reckonings of the war a unique authority. His exegesis of the causes of the war, its turns on the battlefield, and its likely outcome could take on the import of revelation, allegory, prophecy.

Preachers also possessed skills and prerogatives that added to their sway. Many were inspired to literacy, for example, which gave preachers the ability to glean information about the war from newspapers and other texts.[14] Most important, having leave to preach gave them mobility throughout their neighborhoods and beyond. Winfield, for example, lived on the Messenger place, three miles distant from the Fox plantation. Preachers, who were mediators in a neighborhood's relationship to God as well as literate and mobile, brought unique attainments to the task of forging ties between neighborhoods and had a special importance among the conduits.

Other slaves on the move — carriage drivers, artisans, teamsters, body servants — also contributed to this nexus.[15] Thomas Turner, a messenger servant for the Surget family in Adams County, was typical in harnessing neighborhood ties to an extensive network of contacts. He was a regular visitor on the plantations of his owners' in-laws, like the Shields place four miles away. On one visit, Turner conveyed what his mistress had said about the possibilities of freedom. According to George Braxton, Turner "told me once during the war that the Union Soldiers were going to gain the day that he heard his mistress say as much, and that if they did we would be free."[16] Louisa Lattimer put store by the advice of Andrew Black, a teamster in Warren County. He often paid her a call when he came to Vicksburg to sell vegetables. "I was determined to take the first opportunity for my freedom and used to ask advice from Black," she recalled. He often warned her to mind what she said about the war, "or his life and mine would not be worth a Copper. and then he used to say just pray to God for help. that the Yankees were fighting for us and that we would soon all be free."[17]

Mobile slaves, especially those with access to means of transportation, became new focal points in the ongoing battle over space. That struggle opened
up on new fronts against fresh adversaries during the war. Confederate authorities were alert to the wide influence of carriage drivers, teamsters, and
hackmen. In Claiborne County, a carriage driver on the Crane place got a
vicious beating, according to Edward Howard, a former slave there. Bailer
"had been talking about the war and a lot of Confederates came here and took
him and a whipped him nearly to death and was going to hang him."[18] Planters
in Jefferson County hanged at least four carriage drivers implicated in a purported insurrectionary plot in May 1861.[19]

Bailer was spared, but the struggle against bondmen like him often threatened to turn violent during the war. The Confederate police apparatus was
most effective in towns, which confined hackmen like Henry Banks as well as
everyone else to narrow streets and reduced the tactical advantages of mobility. Authorities in Vicksburg took note that Banks's horses were not stabled the
night a slave couple escaped to Union lines in 1862. Banks spent the next three
days in jail. Only the intervention of his wife, his owner, and another slaveholder, he thought, prevented his captors from whipping a confession out of
him. Banks emerged from the episode with renewed appreciation for the
dangers of speaking out of turn. "If I had opened my head but once about the
war," he recalled, "there is no telling what would have happened to me. I'se
sensible of these things and kept these things to myself."[20]

His ordeal is revealing as well about how the war raised the stakes in the
struggle over space. Mobile slaves had always cut a figure in every neighborhood, not only marketing goods but also at moments of crisis when conflicts
with owners became pitched. From a slaveholder's point of view, such slaves
had long pushed at boundaries in the relations of slavery. They moved contraband, facilitating theft and other transgressions against plantation order. Yet
that was petty mischief compared to the power they held now that owners
were fighting for their political lives. As hackmen, carriage drivers, and teamsters went about their business, they also trafficked in the prospects for emancipation. Banks even carried slaves bodily to freedom. Confederate authorities
could not put an end to the movement of people, plantation produce, and
other goods conveyed by mobile slaves. Indeed, war only increased the volume
and quickened the pace. Unable to detach the productive role of mobile slaves
from their subversive capacities, the quick resort to violence was a blunt in-
strument to stanch the flow of information.

In the deliberations of 1861 and 1862, slaves reoriented their neighborhoods in subtle yet elemental ways. A congeries of struggles — to clear paths

across plantation lines, monitor intimate relations, protect and discipline run-aways — had directed inward the collective energies of every neighborhood. As neighborhoods turned to the task of interpreting the war, they looked outward as never before. Extending communications beyond adjoining plantations was critical to evaluating a conflict playing out well afield of the district. This process required slaves to cross plantation lines as well as overstep long-standing boundaries between neighborhoods. The more slaves learned about the war, the sharper, more urgent the new perspective became. The growing conviction they would gain their freedom if the Union whipped the South joined them by their highest aspirations to events in faraway places.

The new orientation of neighborhoods, furthermore, prompted realignments within them, too. Slaves who proved themselves valuable in the exchange of intelligence gained stature among neighborhood folk. House servants gained credence among field hands, and both looked to folks who got around. As slaves gathered around a returning wagoner or carriage driver to get the news, he became first among equals in a circle of confidants and gained new prominence as they circulated his views through the neighborhood and beyond.[21] The mobility that had given some slaves one foot in the neighborhood and one foot out placed them at its center during the war.

The neighborhood debates resolved that the war was, first and foremost, a struggle over slavery. Minerva Boyd of Vicksburg neatly summarized this consensus along with her own part in its making: "I thought & said the Union Armies would make us free."[22] Ironically, this prescient conclusion benefited from limitations on the slaves' communication lines as well as their reach. Slaves across the South knew the North was fighting for emancipation, even as responsible parties in the Federal government denied that goal.[23] In the Natchez District, where men and women exchanged information from person to person, neighborhood to neighborhood, intelligence-gathering facilities fell well short of Washington, D.C. Expectations grew and spread undeterred by the authoritative statements of Northern war aims. Slaves evidently received no word of President Lincoln's First Inaugural Address or Message to Congress on Independence Day 1861, wherein he declared preserving the Union to be his government's sole and entire purpose.[24] The conviction that the Yankees were fighting to free the slaves fed not only on what they had learned but also on what they did not know and could not know thanks to the constraints of their terrain. The personal exchange of information, moreover, introduced variations in the interpretation at many points.

The conspiracy around Second Creek in Adams County was one trajectory in these debates. The conspiracy began when the debates were just getting under way in May 1861 and perhaps as early as April.[25] The plotters, like slaves everywhere in the Natchez District, convened across plantation lines to share what they knew, cultivated ties between plantations and between neighborhoods, and picked up intelligence from owners.[26] Slaves on Brighton first heard about the war from their "young missus," who provocatively suggested they fight to protect her.[27] Two men on Palatine, unaware of the firing on Fort Sumter, speculated that "the fighting would begin in New Orleans." The men along Second Creek wanted the South "whipped" as much as anyone. The North would win the war, Simon and George assured their neighbors across the creek on Palatine. The debates, in turn, must have partaken of the earthy euphemisms bandied about among the plotters, even if witnesses declined to repeat them before the Southern Claims Commission. The North would "make the South shit behind their asses," Simon and George declared.[28] The plotters were thinking along much the same lines as everyone else debating the war in the spring and summer of 1861.

Only when the rebels came to the practical matter of how the war would lead to freedom did they veer off from the debate at large. Those who had considered the matter thought that the time to strike was approaching, even if they had not decided exactly when. A circle of teamsters was inclined to wait until the Union captured Natchez. Yet the date most widely mentioned, September 10, 1861, was appointed for General Winfield Scott's expected arrival in New Orleans.[29] The conspirators' sense of urgency was compounded by their singular conviction the balance of power had already swung irrevocably against the South. Louis, a driver, introduced a rare note of pessimism when he told Harry Scott the South was "whipping the North." Scott, who perhaps appreciated having a namesake in command of the Union army, boasted in reply that "Genl Scott would eat his breakfast in New Orleans." They "were all bound to be free," he told others confidently. Edmond, the driver on Oakland, predicted that the slaves, given their superior numbers, would prevail with their axes and hoes.[30] On the basis of such improbable estimates of the order of battle, the plotters began to address the tactical questions of revolt.

The conspiracy also reveals just how far the debates it sprang from had gone. From talk about what owners said of freedom to plans to kill them for it was no small step, to be sure. The differences between the debates and the conspiracy, however, involved means rather than ends. They diverged around points of strategy. Most slaves had a much higher estimate of the planters' strength than the rebels did. Where the rebels peeled off to plan their rebellion, the debates went on to consider exactly what powers the war was bringing into play. The debates ultimately concluded to wait and see what came of the war. Yet slaves across the Natchez District had trained their sights on freedom, espied a rival power to their owners, and made up their mind to throw in their lot with that rival at the proper time. The conspiracy might well have tacked back to the mainstream of the debates had the planters not brought the plot up short.

The conspiracy impinged sharply on the debates in the end. In September 1861, the rebels of Second Creek were not in revolt but under interrogation. At least twenty-seven slaves hanged by the time the "Executive Committee" finished crushing the plot in October. Some people caught up in the investigation and probably some of those executed were likely engaged in the debates rather than the conspiracy. Few ex-slaves directly brought up the plot before the Southern Claims Commission.[31] George Braxton may have alluded to the plotters when he attributed his reluctance to talk about the war to Colonel A. K. Farrar, who "was always looking for a chance to get hold of some of us." Farrar, whom Braxton identified as provost marshal, was also a leading figure on the Executive Committee.[32] George W. Carter, a freeborn drayman in Natchez, had no doubt that the hangings at the racetrack were "a warning to the other Colored people what they had to expect if they did not keep quiet." James Hyman referred to those ghastly proceedings as a cautionary note to his friend, Richard Dorsey: "I told him to be mighty careful about his talk," Hyman recalled, and warned that if anything he said "would get out that the gallows at the race track would get him."[33] The fate of the conspiracy put those debating the war on notice that loose talk would get them hanged.[34]

The debates also ventured into advanced discussions about freedom and what it meant. Slavery was a hard school for freedom. Men and women enmeshed in the myriad relations of slavery and embedded in the binding ties of neighborhood were poorly situated to think freedom all the way through in theory and practice. Yet their thinking on the matter was nothing if not concrete. Freedom meant no more lashes; an end to buying and selling the people and to breaking up their families; and sweeping away the pinched boundaries of the neighborhood terrain. Here again the rebels of Second Creek spoke for many. When they succeeded, Orange told other conspirators on Brighton, "whipping colored people would stop."[35] The mobility Henry Banks enjoyed as a hack driver made him more sensitive than most to the confines of slaves' neighborhoods, but he spoke eloquently to common hopes when he "told other colored people that should the Yankees succeed, we could go where, when & how we pleased and our children would no longer be sold, and that negro-trading would be played out."[36] The slaves' notion of freedom was, at its core, a litany of negations of slavery.

By the same token, freedom was also an elaboration on prerogatives of slavery. On the Fox plantation, Samuel Chase's fellow slaves thought he was already taking liberties — to raise more or less what he pleased, to market it off the place, to travel back and forth to town — akin to freedom if not the genuine article. "We were all astonished at Sam, who seemed to be more anxious to be free than any the rest of us," Lewis Jackson recalled, "and frequently asked him about his great anxiety to be free, when he was already almost as free [as] any White man." Slaves did not speak in the language of rights, but Chase evoked its spirit when he insisted, "Still I am a Slave, as the rest of you are." What he wanted from freedom was not simply prerogatives but their inviolability. "Old Mistress cant live always," he pointed out, "and if she was to die I might fall into hands that would treat me very diferent to what she does."[37] It is unclear whether Chase's discourse was instructive to his fellow slaves or merely put into words what they already knew. Be that as it may, the struggle to build on the foundations of slavery had already begun in earnest on the Fox place, as it had all over the district, and some folks would find it heavy lifting enough.

The men around Nelson Finley, a blacksmith in Woodville, were among those who reckoned that the war had bound up the issue of slavery and freedom with a clash between states and nations. They expected God to take a hand in so prodigious a conflict. And they did not take his name in vain but in anguish, in gratitude, in awe, and in hope. "Whenever we heard that the Rebels had whipped the Union men," Mack Washington remembered, "we were down hearted & would almost cry & we prayed together that the Union troops would whip the Rebels & when we heard the Union troops would whip the Rebels we thanked God & prayed for them."[38] Many were the prayers sent up from the Natchez District for God's intervention.[39]

Finley sketched out for his comrades the full dimensions of southern nation-building. He told Washington "the Southern people wanted to do as they pleased & to keep the Colored people in Slavery & to keep the poor white Man down — & to have a Country of their own." Many slaves became acutely aware that their owners' defense of slavery entailed the parallel project of building a new Confederate nation and a government to rule it. Finley understood some apparatus would be required to accomplish the subordination of a stratum of white people along with the slaves, and he told William Harris that creating a new government went hand in hand with creating a new country. The "rebels wanted to keep the colored people in slavery forever & didnt want to allow any poor man a chance & wanted to have a government separate from the North — so that they could keep the yankees out of it."[40]

Some slaves first encountered the new powers that be in the public rituals where slaveholders celebrated their new Confederacy and stoked nationalist sentiment. In a society where literacy was low, Confederates made their appeal by means that could be seen and heard and hence were as well suited to slaves as anyone else. The South was quick to seek legitimacy in appropriating the icon of George Washington for its new purposes. Natchez glowed with torches on Washington's Birthday, as we have seen, and it thundered as the town seized the founder's mantle with a reading of his Farewell Address and a one-hundred-gun salute.[41] After the procession, Andrew Brown mounted his "Ship of State" over his mill, allowing slaves more than a year to mull over this evocative symbol of state power.[42]

And the symbols of the nation-state were neither the only nor the easiest way for slaves to learn about it. The transformation of towns into centers of Confederate government and fulcrums of nationalism gave people in Vicksburg, Natchez, and county seats such as Woodville a better purchase on the politics of the war than was available to slaves in the hinterlands. Yet the latter were well aware of the new relations of power, too. On the Green plantation in Warren County, Cato Rux gathered the South was creating a new nation with its own body of law because his mistress said as much: "She told me that she was for the union and had been all her life. but now she had to obey the laws of the country in which she was then living."[43]

The war also changed long-standing relations of labor in short order in 1861 and 1862. Slaves confronted new figures at the point of production, as enlistment and conscription removed owners and overseers from many plantations. The management of field labor fell suddenly to plantation mistresses, elderly men, or boys on the cusp of manhood.[44] Authorities took some pains to keep able-bodied white men at home. When the Confederacy enacted conscription in April 1862, Mississippi exempted anyone who could claim to be the last white man on a plantation with twenty slaves or more.[45] Wartime mobilization collapsed the managerial hierarchy to a planter or overseer and elided the antebellum division of labor. Across the Natchez District, field laborers thus confronted greenhorn overseers, mistresses, young masters, and old masters in unaccustomed roles of direct supervision. Slaves were quick to try the authority of these newcomers in the fields.

Slaves on James Allen's Nannechehaw plantation persistently contested his discipline when he took an uncharacteristically direct hand in managing their labor in April 1862. As usual, they failed to work as hard or as assiduously as he demanded. Tom registered his objections to shelling thirty bushels of corn one Sunday in May with complaints to a fellow slave, loud enough for Allen to hear. He cracked the whip often and hard that summer and into fall, though he had not recorded using it during the previous two years. Tom got a whipping for his "impertinence"; Ambrose and Morris for going tardily into their gang and leaving a gate open; Aaron for failing to bring the carriage promptly on one occasion and again for tarrying to start the gin. The people refused to sit still for such abuse. Ambrose and Morris ran away after they got whipped. So did Big Joe after Allen chewed him out for not pitching in to fix the gin.[46] Although he did not relent with the whip, the slaves brought him to terms on rations. Big Henry's May whipping for stealing pigs did not deter other folks from killing a shoat. They butchered part and buried the rest, as Allen discovered in August. He initially intended to reduce everyone's meat allowance for the next five days but soon had second thoughts and instead gave them an extra ten pounds.[47]

Slaves increased auxiliary production under wartime conditions. Labor obligations diminished on plantations where the crop mix changed to provide provisions for the army. Authorities encouraged but did not require a shift from cotton to food crops. The state legislature urged planters to reduce their cotton crop by three-quarters, while papers in Natchez and Vicksburg carried paeans to "King Corn."[48] Many planters were not eager for King Cotton to abdicate. In June 1862, James Allen and even Joseph E. Davis, the president's brother, resisted a Confederate commander's order to torch bales liable to fall into the hands of the Federals plying the Mississippi.[49] The shift from staple to food crops continued apace from 1862 to 1863. Where land was converted from cotton to corn and grain, slaves worked more on their own account. Some used the proceeds to buy mules, horses, and other draft animals. Thomas Turner acquired a mule early in the war. When he arrived in Natchez in the latter part of 1863, Richard Dorsey recalled, "I heard from him and others that he had owned her two or three years."[50]

When slaves acquired productive property, they changed and expanded the antebellum terms of auxiliary production. A draft animal, long beyond the typical field laborer's grasp, was still prized for plowing, hauling, and undercutting owners' control over the time slaves worked for themselves. As neighborhood boundaries became more permeable, slaves created new trade routes that bypassed owners. Mules thus became more valuable tools than ever, not only to plow the rows but also to increase mobility, improve the terms of trade, and eventually to turn the fruits of agricultural labor to other kinds of enterprise.

In towns, some men and women were already seizing opportunities to enter new lines of work. A few even hired labor as they continued to hawk their own. Henry Banks, who hired his time from his owner and drove a hack in Vicksburg, also turned a few dollars on the increased auxiliary production in the hinterland. "Whenever I took people into the Country," he recalled, "I bought butter Eggs — chickens fruit & whatever I could sell at a profit and in this way I made considerable money." There was a good deal of work in Vicksburg, where new commissary storehouses and other Confederate facilities required carpenters to build them, draymen to haul the raw materials, and hackmen to get the new personnel around. Banks did so much business in town he took on his friend, Albert Webster, to drive, too. Banks, Webster noted, "always had enough to pay me my wages" — and more besides. He owed four hundred dollars on his hack in 1859 but had amassed a tidy four hundred dollars in gold in 1862.[51] Hauling, generally men's work, was presumably new to Minerva Boyd. She had hired her time from her owner since the 1840s, though, and in late 1861 she hired Moses White from his owner to drive her dray.[52] Enterprising types such as Boyd and Banks were increasing their trade, embarking on new endeavors, and entering into wage relations with other slaves.

By the slaves' calibrations, the balance of power shifted against owners in confrontations with Confederate authorities in 1862. The army appropriated slave labor for all manner of tasks, from one-day chores hauling supplies to long stints putting up breastworks.[53] Impressment suggested slaveholders' power paled against that of the Confederate state, especially its military arm. When the army put bondmen to work, it removed them from neighborhood, kin, and the control of slaveholders, often against the owners' will. Impressed slaves took notice of Confederate indifference to owners' objections and the powerlessness it implied. Several men belonging to O. M. Blanton saw his authority go into eclipse when the army brought them down from the Delta to build fortifications at Vicksburg. When Blanton came to look in on them, he "said he would do all he could to get us home," Jeff Claiborne noted, "but it was not in his power to release us."[54]

Slaves were alert to other implicit acknowledgments of Confederate supremacy. Standing orders from owners to take to the woods when officials showed up, for example, spoke volumes about the slaveholders' diminished sway. Those orders were good advice on the Acuff plantation, where at least two slaves were supposedly in league with their owner, collaborating with the

Union army. Nelson Ashby, a slave in the vicinity, heard the report of gunfire when Confederates went through the quarters, whipping the people and killing the driver. "They did this because they thought Mr. Acuff was in connection with the Union troops and that his driver and this other Colored Man Was Connected with him in that way," Ashby explained.[55] Slaves were tough-minded in their estimates of owners who put up a fight against Confederate authority. Some bondpeople took open conflict as a damning sign of weakness. Slaves on Sycamore plantation in Warren County were not impressed when their owner resisted other planters' suggestions to send his people away. "Some of them when they heard these things, would believe they were to be free," observed Benjamin Jones, "and would not work, and would talk Saucey to white people."[56]

The balance of power tilted further still against owners when the Union army made incursions toward the Natchez District in the fall of 1862. The North had gained the upper hand in the lower Mississippi Valley in April. The capture of New Orleans gave Federal gunboats the run of the Mississippi River below Vicksburg, and the victory at Shiloh poised Grant's army on the state's northern border. The Federals crossed into Mississippi and took Corinth in May, but there they remained. Confederate troops regrouped to the south at Holly Springs and Tupelo, fought the Yankees to a draw at Iuka in September, and pushed the invaders back to Corinth in October.[57]

Some slaves were impressed by what they saw of Federal power in May. Alex, a teamster on Nannechehaw, thought the shelling from Union boats did more damage to towns downriver in Claiborne and Jefferson Counties than other observers had led his owner to believe. By Alex's account, women and children were compelled to leave Grand Gulf, and at Rodney the Yankees caused "worse destruction than first reported — visiting all the house[s] & destroying even Negro clothes & furniture."[58] Two thousand soldiers alighted at Grand Gulf, appropriating food, livestock, and men to dig a tunnel south of Vicksburg. Some slaves on C. D. Hamilton's plantation in Claiborne noticed his loyalties shift northward when Union legions were around. Balor Hill, the driver, found his owner's allegiances hard to pin down. When Hamilton confided he was a Union man, Hill "asked him what that meant; but he never gave me any satisfaction." Reuben Cunningham found Hamilton's opportunism illuminating, however. Hamilton, Cunningham shrewdly observed, was a Union man "when the Federals were too tight on him and a Confederate when the Rebels were tight on him."[59]

By the end of 1862, the collective investigation of the war had laid the groundwork for a range of views about when freedom might break out. To be sure, there would be no direct correlation between which new forms of power slaves discerned and the particular moment they later claimed their freedom. The consensus that the destruction of slavery depended on the outcome of the fighting pointed to the end of the war as the moment of emancipation. That selfsame notion only gained vitality among slaves who also recognized the war as a struggle over law, government, and nationality, for they understood that making emancipation stick would require uprooting these new forms of power, too. Yet the process of interpreting epoch-making change from its subtle outward signs — an owner's solicitous demeanor, stray terms from the lexicon of the nation-state like "country" or "government," and suggestive images in the iconography of nationalism such as the ship of state — inevitably led to varied understandings of these powers and their potentialities. More-over, the North made its presence felt in different ways in 1863 — as invader, conqueror, occupying power. Slaves saw emancipation at the conjuncture be-tween those interventions and the slaves' own particular circumstances.

Some took the Emancipation Proclamation as their moment. Lewis Jackson had shared in the consensus around the Fox plantation that the Union would have to whip the South for slaves to gain their freedom. But the edict changed Jackson's mind, and he considered himself "freed by Abraham Lincoln's Proc-lamation."[60] The proclamation did not simply speak for itself but gained or lost authority depending on owners' mastery or lack of it. The proclamation was especially promising, for example, to folks abandoned by their owners. For these slaves, who reaped the fruits of their own labor, worked without super-vision, and even in some cases had possession of plantations, the announce-ment of emancipation gave new liberties an august imprimatur. Thomas C. Drummond's owner withdrew from Jefferson County across the Mississippi to Louisiana in March 1862 and sent his slaves east of the Natchez District. Drummond collected wages as a railroad brakeman, traded widely, and rapidly accumulated livestock and other goods. Under these circumstances, news of Union victories made Drummond feel "like a free man." By 1863, he had many reasons to think he was "let free by President Lincoln's Proclamation." But few slaves were in such enviable circumstances by that time.[61]

To the great mass of slaves in the region, the Emancipation Proclamation was, to their way of thinking, remote. First, word of it did not circulate widely among slaves in some areas far from Union lines, including the Natchez District. Word of Lincoln's Unionist war aims in 1861 did not arrive in the neighborhoods of the district, and his edict of emancipation was known only to some.

Second, the proclamation moved few slaves from the belief they would gain their freedom if the Union won the war. From that vantage point, two men in Vicksburg who scrutinized the preliminary proclamation in the fall of 1862 found it wanting. What struck George W. Walton, a carpenter, and drayman Ambrose Holmes was not the declaration that slaves in rebel states would be "thenceforward, and forever free" come New Year's Day but the offer to rejoin the Union before then and thereby evade emancipation. "We were afraid they would accept the terms offered & slavery would not be abolished. We wanted the rebels to be conquered," Walton recalled. Like most slaves, he and Holmes had come to believe emancipation hung in the balance with the outcome of the war, and they saw nothing in the proclamation to alter that conviction.[62]

Third and most important, Lincoln's proclamation failed to measure up to slaves' conceptions of power, old or new. His declaration changed little for those who had begun to apprehend the significance of states and nations. At first glance, the notion that Lincoln had destroyed slavery at will seems well suited to slaves who located power in persons. But it dovetailed not at all with the spatial dimension of that understanding. Slaveholders' myriad powers acquired much of their potency in the ability to decide the fate of families, dictate the terms of labor, and impose discipline and punishment on the ground. As far as slaves in the district could see, Lincoln was in no position to exercise such authority. The president, far off in a place called Washington, exercised none of the prerogatives that they identified with real power. His edict, in sum, was peripheral to most slaves, peripheral to their neighborhoods, to their understandings of the war and of power itself.

Civilians in the Natchez District encountered the Union army at close quarters during the siege of Vicksburg in the spring and summer of 1863. Grant's attempts to drive on the Natchez District over the winter had briefly touched down north of Vicksburg at Chickasaw Bluffs, where General William T. Sherman's troops disembarked from boats on the Yazoo River and menaced Confederate defenses for a day. All Grant's effort and ingenuity finally bore fruit on April 30, when his troops crossed the Mississippi River south of town, marched northeast to the state capital in Jackson, and doubled back due west toward Vicksburg. They drove twenty thousand Confederates off Champion's Hill on May 16 and crossed the Big Black River the next day. Then they dug entrenchments in a broad arc around Vicksburg and battered the city. Grant's swift march began with his willingness to slough off supply lines, and his troops subsisted off the neighborhoods of Warren County throughout May and June. The soldiers swept over nearby plantations in small detachments, seizing cattle, sheep, chickens, wagons, fodder, fence rails, and whatever livestock, food crops, or movable property could feed, shelter, or otherwise provision the army. The confiscation of property made for an awe-some display of power.[63]

Many slaves who saw the Union army in the throes of impressment in their neighborhood deemed this the moment of emancipation. Edward Hicks watched squads of Union troops go relentlessly about their business on the adjoining plantation where his wife lived, Absalom Grant's place. They emp-tied Grant's smokehouse, led away his horses and mules, carried off his corn, and killed his hogs. "They killed his hogs for weeks, must have killed in all 70, or 80 head or more," Hicks recalled. "I saw them at it every day until they got all he had."[64] Slaves in the neighborhood of the Sycamore and Brooks planta-tions took note of similar exhibitions of Yankee wherewithal and efficiency. On Sycamore, Esther Cameron watched soldiers take a dozen wagons of corn on the first day and molasses, salt, fodder, fencing, sheep, hogs, and cattle over the next two or three weeks. It was a striking sight to Cyrus Lee on the Brooks place. "I saw them constantly driving" cattle from Sycamore to army "Butcher Pens," Lee recalled, "& killing, & distributing the Beef to the Officers & Men, & Same way with his Hogs & Sheep."[65] After Squire Myers watched two such expeditions drive off virtually all the stock on his owner's place, "I Knew that Mr Johnson was jist broke up."[66]

In addition to the planters' hold on their property, what broke in the act of impressment was planters' control over neighborhood space. The Union army's ability to carry off livestock, break open smokehouses with impunity, and literally disassemble property lines was vivid proof slaveholders no longer commanded the place.[67] When a Union detachment confiscated fence rails, it took down the most visible boundary between plantations in the neighbor-hood. Charles Anderson noticed soldiers uttered not a word as they led a wagon, several horses, ten mules, and as many cattle off Fanny Green's plan-tation. For a full week, he watched soldiers take down the boundaries of his owner's property, removing two miles of fence rails by the wagonload: "I have seen as many as four and five army wagons carrying rails off the place at a time."[68]

Union incursions into neighborhoods transformed the entire terrain of struggle. Many slaves left owners in short order.[69] In effect, they ran away, an act as old as slavery, of course, yet in the aftermath of confiscation as different as it could be.[70] Neighborhood suddenly ceased to define a perimeter for runaways or the terrain of struggle in general. Instead of laying out on an adjoining plantation, they made their way to town or to army camps, perhaps first one in the neighborhood, then another further off. Anderson left the Green place when the fences came down.[71] Cyrus Lee departed the Brooks plantation in late June after foraging parties cut a swath through from Syca-more. Like others, he enlisted in the Union army forthwith.[72] When Union squads made a show of force in the neighborhood, it fell away with the fences as a boundary of struggle and a place of confinement.

For some slaves, a Union squad was a sufficiently powerful presence that they could partake of its emancipatory effect without leaving the neighbor-hood. Samuel Chase still had no intention of abandoning his mistress, but he changed his mind about the Federals having to win the war to gain his free-dom. Soldiers camped in the woods on the Fox place and foraged widely there and in the vicinity. And at some point he decided emancipation was at hand: "I became free about the time the Federals were besieging Vicksburg."[73]

The fall of Vicksburg on Independence Day resounded across the Natchez District as a clarion of freedom. To slaves residing in the city, the Federal victory looked conclusive. Albert Webster claimed to speak for himself, the hack driver he worked for, and everyone else they knew in town: "[A]fter the surrender of Vicksburg he as well as all of us were positive that we were free."[74] The import of the event issued forth into the countryside — dramatically, on many plantations. In Jefferson County, the end of the siege was a moment of truth on the McCoy place, where slaves circulated the news while the overseer prepared to refugee them to Texas. At least eleven slaves decamped for Union lines before others were carried off, despite the wrenching separations this step entailed. Judy and Nelson Davis left without her sister, Lucinda; Emily and Harris Stewart never saw their nineteen-year-old son again.[75]

Aftershocks from the fall of Vicksburg, like the Emancipation Proclama-tion, were compounded by slaves' whirlwind changes to their own circum-stances. Reunion with kin, payment of wages, a new freedom of speech all substantiated the liberating tendencies of the moment. Olive Lee, who had lived separately from her husband, considered herself free when he left their owners' plantation in the hinterland and joined her in town. Peter Jackson, enslaved on the Acuff place, decided he was free as soon as the siege ended and he went to work for himself. Confederate police powers collapsed with the surrender of the city, and the danger that had hung over the war counsels of 1861 and 1862 suddenly lifted. William Green, who had left his owner's place to wait on a Union colonel during the siege, finally took the liberty of speaking his mind. "We could not have expressed our opinions in public, before the yankees Came, after that we talked very openly."[76] Slaves were only begin-ning to break the silences around the worst outrages of white people, mend breaches in intimate relations, and make the transition to free labor. The work would continue for a decade or more, yet those who got started in the aftermath of Vicksburg had all the more reason to judge this the moment of emancipation.

Reverberations from Vicksburg carried south into the district when a Union brigade captured Natchez without a shot on July 13. The events came so hard on each other's heels it is unclear whether some folks in Adams County acted in consequence of Vicksburg's fall or in anticipation or the aftermath of the Yankees' arrival in Natchez. One hundred slaves finished working their potatoes on York plantation and left on the Saturday after Vicksburg surrendered, two days before the fall of Natchez. The rest of the slaves departed two days afterward. Roley Washington's recollections suggest he, Mahalia Dorris, and her son were among the second group. "When the federals came to Natchez Miss. in 1863 — about July — we all left the plantation & came to Natchez. I Mahalia & Foster all come to gether."[77] Thomas Turner had a decision to make when the Yankees came to town. His mistress, having predicted emancipation would arrive when the Yankees won, now made clear that the day had come and offered to pay wages or rent land to anyone who stayed on the place. But Turner went to Natchez for a while instead, as did his son, Wallace: "I Knew that after the union soldiers Came here. that the war gave us our freedom."[78] Slaves from plantations across Adams and Jefferson Counties made for Natchez. By the third day of the occupation, reported the Union commander in town, they were arriving by the thousands. Another 20,000 had converged on Vicksburg by the end of August.[79]

The siege of Vicksburg was the most critical moment of emancipation before the end of the war. In point of fact, it was not one such moment but several. Slaves deemed freedom at hand when they took in the act of confiscation or got wind of the surrender of Vicksburg or the capture of Natchez. The emancipating effect of the Union army spread with the occupation.[80] The Union commander in Natchez betrayed some doubt about the status of the thousands of men, women, and children entering his lines when he asked his superiors for "some instructions as to what policy I shall pursue with regard to the negroes." "With regard to the contrabands," replied General James B. McPherson, "you can say to them they are free." But many who grasped confiscation, enlistment, and other encounters with the army as the end of slavery days did not need to be told.[81]

Yet most slaves in the Natchez District did not consider emancipation an accomplished fact in the summer of 1863. For one thing, the majority remained on their owners' plantations. Among the thousands who lit out for Natchez or Vicksburg, many did not equate leaving their owners with the destruction of slavery. Some did not consider themselves free because they had left behind family and friends who were not. Some drew a further distinction between their own freedom and the fate of slavery itself. Despite impressive Union victories in the region, slaves had long recognized the war was playing out in a larger theater. After the siege of Vicksburg, they rightly understood the war was far from over and held fast to the view that slavery would not be destroyed until the Union had won the war.

Thousands of men enlisted in the army on the conviction that the war between the Confederacy and the Union — between slavery and freedom — could still go either way. Anthony Lewis harbored no illusions the war was over that summer and urged his two sons to enlist.[82] As early as May, the sons of the Natchez District began to muster into three infantry regiments, starting with the battered remnants of the Ninth Louisiana, reorganized at Vicksburg. In June 1863, the regiment helped repulse the Confederate attack at Milliken's Bend, Louisiana, one of the war's first trials of black soldiers on the battlefield.[83] Louis Dixon, enslaved on the Lum plantation in Claiborne County, died of wounds he received in the battle before his name was even entered onto the regimental rolls.[84] "We were might near destroyed at Milli-kens Bend," recalled Tobias Orey, a duty sergeant from the Delta in Company B, "only 13 men left in my Co." The remnants of the Ninth Louisiana made their way to Vicksburg the day after the city fell "& went to work reenlisting the Regmt."[85] Three men left the Montgomery plantation in Jefferson County and together joined the regiment in October.[86]

In Natchez, soldiers enlisted at the slave trader's yard, including many men lately bought and sold there. In late summer, men joined up with the first two regiments organized in town, the 6th Mississippi (later redesignated the 58th U.S. Colored Infantry) and the 6th U.S. Colored Heavy Artillery.[87] "I enlisted in the army out here at the forks of the road," Burl Lewis recalled. Women were also alive to the resonance of joining army ranks at the old soul driver's depot and mentioned it to the Pension Bureau years later as a telling detail about their husbands' military service. Phillis Reed did not know the date of his enlistment, but she knew the place for sure: "the fork of the Washington and Liberty road."[88]

All told, the region contributed more than a dozen units of U.S. Colored Troops: eight regiments of infantry, one cavalry, two heavy artillery, and two batteries of light artillery. By Christmas, five more units had mustered in Vicksburg and vicinity, including the 3rd U.S. Colored Cavalry, which did the most fighting of all the regiments from the district.[89]

For the duration of the war in the Natchez District, slavery and freedom seemed to hang in delicate balance. Men and women throughout the region made considerable headway in the reconstruction of intimate relations, work, and the terms of trade. Many embraced legal marriage, wage labor, and market relations with enthusiasm. Others recognized familiar outcroppings from the terrain of slavery as they navigated the transition to free labor. Even the Union army was hardly liberating in many ways. It both compromised with slavery and transformed it in the act of enlistment. Enrolling officers foisted owners' names on soldiers, who mustered into the ranks with an oath of loyalty to the nation-state. The Union's military hold on the district was breached by Confederate raids through 1864. Most slaves did not see the moment of their emancipation until the end of the war.

At enlistment, the Union army hearkened back to slavery when enrolling officers imposed owners' names on soldiers. Across the South, men enrolled in the army under their fathers' surnames as a mark of emancipation. Yet recruits sometimes confronted an officer impatient with their scruples about names. William H. Williams joined up in Kentucky, where he decided not to go by that name, which he reckoned could connect him to his former owners, the Williams family of Adams County, if the Confederates won the war. He gave his name as "Wesley." "Is that all?" he was asked. "I said Lord, God ain't that enough?" "Wesley Lord" it is, the officer decreed.[90] Harrison Willis had no luck joining the 66th U.S. Colored Infantry under his family's name. Willis had long used his owner's last name but presented himself to the enrolling officer as Harrison Barnes, after his father, Mike Barnes, who belonged to another planter in Claiborne County. The officer promptly asked his master's name and then enlisted him as Harrison Willis.[91] A name was hard to shake off after the army affixed it. Officers called the soldier by that name and read it out daily at roll call, so comrades heard it, repeated it, and used it routinely.[92]

Yet enlistment also commenced a newly powerful engagement with the nation-state. When soldiers mustered into the Union army and married under its auspices, they marked the occasion with ceremonies that explicitly invoked law, government, and nationality. Military service immersed troops in these new forms of power, placing them under a military law binding on officers and enlisted men alike.[93]

Enlistment initiated recruits to national loyalty and the rule of law. Within six days, every soldier took an oath pledging his "true allegiance to the United States of America," to "serve them honestly and faithfully," to obey orders "according to the Rules and Articles for the government of the armies." Swearing in at the courthouse in Vicksburg dramatized the rule of law for troops in the 52nd U.S. Colored Infantry in the spring of 1864. Enlistment routinely underscored the rule of law with a reading of the Articles of War, and each regiment was required to read them out again every six months. That mandate was observed only in the breach in some regiments, and the rule of law was imperfect at best. Still, soldiers understood military law as a critical break with the personal exercise of power under slavery. Punishment according to military law, for example, contrasted sharply with slaveholders dictating the terms of discipline.[94]

The Union army engaged civilians as well as soldiers in legal marriage in 4,627 weddings performed around Natchez, Vicksburg, and Davis Bend in 1864 and 1865. Matrimony was something of a command performance where Union authorities in the Mississippi Valley, refusing to recognize marriages consecrated in slavery, urged couples to wed. Weddings became urgent at Natchez in April 1864, when officials exempted soldiers' wives from an order requiring anyone without gainful employment to leave town. Yet liberated slaves across the South believed that weddings under military auspices gave a new authority to the bond between husband and wife.[95] Ceremonies performed by military officers permitted couples who had fallen outside the system of intimate relations to place them on a proper footing. Hager Johnson and George Washington, having lived apart as unmarried spouses, married at long last before the regimental chaplain of the 58th U.S. Colored Infantry.[96] Isaac and Fanny Sloan, who had duly married before a slave preacher in 1847, renewed their vows before an army chaplain on July 3, 1864, the eve of both Independence Day and the anniversary of Vicksburg's fall.[97]

Men and women also believed a military wedding conferred the sanction of law and nation. Indeed, they were sufficiently impressed with the import of the ceremony to give the new institution a name, marriage "under the flag."[98] At its most literal, the phrase referred to the location: flags often hung nearby at weddings performed by regimental officers.[99] Yet marriage under the flag also had more resonant meanings that spread beyond the ranks of couples so joined. It is unlikely the American flag was anywhere in evidence at the home of Bettie Wood's employer in Natchez when she married Daniel Robinson, but her friend in attendance, Jennie Williams, deemed it marriage under the flag nevertheless. "When Dan was a soldier he and Bettie got married 'under the flag,'" Williams recalled.[100] Military weddings marked a new bond between husband and wife, wrought of stronger mettle than the antebellum sanction of neighbors and slaveholders.

Patsy Clayborne clearly described the political meanings of marriage under the flag, though she must have had mixed feelings about undergoing the ceremony herself. She and Dudley Payton had already married "in a colored church" after they arrived in Natchez. The Union dragnet of the unemployed gave her little choice but to marry again. Yet she had her own reasons to be alert to just what constituted this particular bond of matrimony, having had two sweetheart children taken away from her before the war. She knew what a military wedding was all about when she heard the soldiers drumming women out of Natchez say "those who had wifes must get married by the United States Laws."[101] Clayborne's understanding of the ceremony as legal marriage under national auspices elaborated on the resonances implicit in the very phrase marriage "under the flag."

Within army ranks, Union soldiers reconstituted old neighborhood ties. Many served with comrades from adjoining plantations. Fellow slaves departed their owners together and joined up in the same company or regiment.[102] Others left in groups across plantation lines or followed a few days after neighbors left and ended up in the same unit. There they built on antebellum affinities in the comradeship of army life, from mundane chores such as picket and guard duty to events of a lifetime, skirmishing and battling with rebels. Five slaves from the neighborhood of the Terry and Scott plantations in Jefferson County served in the 58th U.S. Colored Infantry. There were hard feelings between Silas Dudley and Thomas Green after Green was caught in a compromising position with Dudley's wife back on the Scott place. Perhaps Dudley, having remarried before he enlisted, had put those feelings aside by the time he died in the pest house. Their neighbor from the Terry place, Emanuel Genifer, helped bury Green when his time came.[103] Some neighbors made pacts: should one man fall, the other promised to get the awful news to the dead man's family. Many had to carry out their end of this grim bargain, as men died in the fighting or were carried off by disease.[104]

The work of forging bonds between neighborhoods continued on a wider scale in Union ranks. Soldiers recombined the old neighborhood ties with new bonds to comrades from distant parts. The 63rd U.S. Colored Infantry brought new recruits from the Natchez District into the ranks with battle-scarred veterans from Louisiana and subsequently with fresh recruits from Memphis in the fall of 1863. The soldiers' far-flung origins were reflected in the regiment's succession of designations: the 9th Louisiana, the 1st Mississippi Heavy Artillery, the 63rd U.S. Colored Infantry. Mississippians in the 3rd U.S. Colored Cavalry served with comrades from Virginia and half a dozen other southern states. The units raised in the Natchez District were slated for garrison duty along the Mississippi. The 58th U.S. Colored Infantry was one of four regiments from the district that spent the war in Natchez and Vicksburg, save for occasional expeditions. All the other units did stints in one town or the other and were posted for months at other points on the river in Louisiana, Arkansas, or Tennessee. Men in the 51st U.S. Colored Infantry ventured as far off as Florida, Alabama, and Texas.[105]

Whichever the regiment, wherever the post, these men did a soldier's duty, broadly construed. Like all Civil War soldiers, they were often on fatigue — doing manual labor, that is — and like all black soldiers, they did more than their fair share of it.[106] Up and down the Mississippi, U.S. Colored Troops built and defended fortifications. The army ran the 52nd U.S. Colored Infantry ragged in Vicksburg during the fall of 1864. Day after day with the spade and shovel left little time for training with the rifle and bayonet, "no chance for improvement in Discipline, Instruction and the duties of a soldier," a captain lamented. Their officers felt compelled to excuse their "unsoldierly appearance," he added, given their "heavy guard and fatigue duty."[107] Garrison duty entailed fighting, too, since fortifications inevitably came under attack. Regiments from the district gave battle in skirmishes at Natchez, across the river around Vidalia, and along the Big Black, among other locales, as well as in the heavy fighting at Milliken's Bend, the siege of Fort Blakely in Alabama, and Yazoo City in the Delta.[108]

None of these regiments was more battle tested than the 3rd U.S. Colored Cavalry. Black cavalry, employed as scouts, on reconnaissance, and raids, generally saw more fighting than the infantry. By the time the 3rd U.S. Colored Cavalry joined the occupation of Yazoo City in the late winter of 1864, the unit had already made expeditions to battles at Tallulah Courthouse and Satartia.[109] On the morning of March 4, some 2,500 rebels surrounded the city, defended by a mere 1,200 Federals. Pickets from the 3rd U.S. Colored Cavalry took the initial brunt of the rebel advance, one of their officers wrote, and the "report of their carbines, volley after volley, as they met the attack, was the first sound to break the stillness of the early morning." Rebel artillery on the hills laid siege to the Union fort while Confederate troops advanced and tightened their cordon. Two companies of the 3rd U.S. Colored Cavalry took up a position outside the fort to the west, where they confronted a Texas regiment notorious for taking no black prisoners. As Union troops, outnumbered and outgunned, struggled to hold their ground, another detachment of men from the 3rd Cavalry, caught outside the fort, fought its way back in and rallied with other troops to turn a rebel flank. As these Confederates retreated, the Texans west of the fort broke, pursued at a dash by the two companies from the 3rd U.S. Colored Cavalry, "firing and yelling" until the rout was complete. Even the Confederate commander conceded "the Negroes . . . pressed our forces so hard that we were compelled to withdraw."

Officers as high as the adjutant general's office claimed bragging rights for the exploits of the 3rd Cavalry, a "superb body of men," their regimental commander boasted. "I almost believe they could whip the whole Southern Confederacy."[110]

The Federal occupation of the Natchez District also cleared the ground for a dramatic reconstruction of work. When the Yankees took Natchez, members of the Reed clan left their neighborhood in Jefferson County and served the Union army as soldiers and military laborers. Brothers James and Daniel Reed enlisted with two cousins in the 58th U.S. Colored Infantry, where they earned $10 per month (seven in cash and three in clothing). Their uncle drove a wagon at the regimental hospital, where both the Reed brothers died of smallpox in early 1864. Phillis Reed, having tended her husband, Daniel, during his illness, became a nurse after his death. The ten dollars she got each month was the official rate for military laborers, nurses, teamsters, laundresses, cooks, and men who built fortifications. As far as the terms of work were concerned, military labor was far less exacting than soldiering. For military laborers, too, the wage relation sheared away the powers — to whip, to break up families — that owners had employed to put slaves to work. Yet troops remained subject to corporal punishment and owed the army far more than their time — from martial loyalty to risking life and limb — in return for a soldier's pay.[111]

To women and men on the plantations, wage labor under Union supervision seemed to look both forward and backward. Union commanders in Louisiana and Mississippi used new rules for plantation work to cultivate loyalty among local planters. Adjutant General Lorenzo Thomas assured those he consorted with in the district that the new regime would be modeled on terms of slave labor. Thomas's Order No. 9, issued in March 1864, codified obligations slaves and owners had contested before the war in several particulars. Thus, free labor also obliged field hands to work sunup to sundown and entitled them to a day of rest on Sunday, adequate rations, separate dwellings, and plots for each family to cultivate on its own account. Even Yankee planters worked free laborers in gangs supervised by overseers. The regulations also threw the army behind the planters in the struggle over mobility. A provision to withhold half of monthly wages until the end of the year aimed at keeping the labor force in place. The people's consternation at the likeness between slavery and free labor was apparent to John Eaton, general superintendent of freedmen, at his Vicksburg headquarters. Laborers hesitated to contract with either "their old masters" or lessees, he wrote, due to "their terror of finding themselves tricked into some form of bondage."[112]

Yet Order No. 9 had transformative effects as well. It prohibited flogging, set wages at $7 per month for women and $10 for men, and termed free labor a "revolution." Federal authorities extricated slaveholders from the management of plantations along the Mississippi by requiring planters of "doubted loyalty" to take on Union-minded partners, typically northerners. A Treasury Department official counted 244 plantations in the countryside around Natchez and Vicksburg operated by lessees when the order went into effect. The attempt to build on conventions of slavery might have dovetailed with liberated slaves' own notions of freedom had it used their prerogatives rather than owners' as the point of departure. Yet women — the majority of laborers in the fields at this point — as well as men secured better terms in practice than Thomas offered on paper. On the Hawkins place in Warren County, for example, Julia Ann McCaskill rented a tract in exchange for a share of the cotton and corn she raised. Philip Hart and Gabriel Boger paid rent of $170 for thirty-four acres they worked together and cleared land in return for use of a pasture.[113]

Even the Union army's most radical enterprise displayed continuities with slavery. During the siege of Vicksburg, Grant aimed to make Davis Bend, where Joseph Davis had presided over his own version of a paternalist utopia, the site of "a Negro paradise." The people on the bend, as before the war, were subjects of a society in microcosm and an experiment in social engineering, the reconstruction of Davis's model slave society into a model of free labor. In 1864, 110 freedpeople worked for a northern lessee under Order No. 9. Under separate regulations pertaining exclusively to the bend, another 600 people formed "companies" to lease land. Each member covered part of the company's expenses, received a share of its profits, and had a say in choosing a representative to other companies, which combined to form "colonies." A Union officer presided over each colony as superintendent with authority to subject every member to his orders, his notion of proper field work, and the punishment of work without pay. On the Home Farm, more than 1,000 worked merely for rations.[114]

Though a majority of people on the bend received no wages, they had no doubt they were slaves no more. At an Independence Day celebration, they sang,

De Lord he makes us free indeed
   In his own time an' way.
We plant de rice and cotton seed,
   And see de sprout some day:

We know it come, but not de why, —
    De Lord know more dan we.
We 'spected freedom by an' by;
    An' now we all are free.[115]

The army expanded the experiment in 1865. The ranks of communal tenantry grew from 76 to 181 companies, and laborers on the Home Farm collected some wages. Authorities got the antebellum court back up and running with an elected panel of three freedmen. Regulations enjoined the judges to decide cases "according to their Ideas of justice." One implied he did not exclusively weigh his own views, however, when he castigated two defendants as "the cause that respectable colored people are slandered, and called thieving and lazy." The new court, like the Union venture at Davis Bend on the whole, was built on antebellum foundations, yet to thousands of men and women who passed through there in 1865, the court and the rest of the proceedings were unprecedented.[116]

Across the Natchez District, liberated slaves pushed at the antebellum boundaries of auxiliary production. A market in free labor on the plantations remained in the future in 1863 and 1864.[117] The terms of work under slavery reproduced in Order No. 9, the enlistment of military laborers and soldiers in the overriding cause of winning the war, and the compulsory air military occupation cast over the entire terrain of labor — all this gave liberated slaves little reason to mistake free labor for a market relation. Still, men and women who worked for wages were obliged to buy what they needed to keep body and soul together. People who combined plantation labor with occasional work for the army or soldiers also gained the means to buy goods. Many used wages earned in the army's employ to set themselves up as independent producers.[118] Owners of means of production, in turn, often bought means of subsistence as well. As substantial numbers of men and women ventured into the cash nexus to hawk their wares and to buy draft animals and food, they honed varied understandings of markets.

Some families embarked on determined strategies for accumulating productive property. Draft animals such as mules and horses, restricted largely to slaves who hired their time before the war, became signposts on a relatively well traveled path of accumulation. The Southern Claims Commission awarded George Washington just $30, insisting he could not have accumulated $1,090 worth of property in just one year despite detailed testimony both he and his wife, Millie, were hard at work for fifteen months. The Washingtons used the proceeds of his work for the army to farm and trade on their own hook. After the fall of Vicksburg, he served as a guide and officer's cook. The Washingtons may have squatted on the three or four acres just past the city limits where they grew vegetables, for he put his army pay toward getting a stall at the market, according to his wife. She often worked the stall, too, and peddled their vegetables elsewhere. Between the stall in the center of town and the farm on the outskirts, the Washingtons were well situated to trade on favorable terms with white people leaving Vicksburg and used their advantage to accumulate a small stable of livestock by the fall of 1864: a cow and calf, two horses, and four mules.[119] Horses and mules were essential to the Washingtons' household economy, not only as draft animals to work their small farm but also for the mobility the Washingtons needed to transport goods between their distant points of trade.

Many families shifted long-standing boundaries in the sexual division of labor as well. Men had done most of the selling before the war, yet Millie Washington was one of many women who were trading extensively by the end of it. Thomas Drummond's mother launched a new endeavor after their owner sent them down the tracks to Scott County. She used a cow her son bought with the proceeds of his work for the railroad to make ice cream and sold it to passengers around Morton.[120] Sarah Burton conducted a brisk trade in Vicksburg on her own account. She was single when she went to work cooking for the 47th Illinois at the bridge over the Big Black outside town. She saved enough money to buy a mule, then a cart, which she used to sell fruits and vegetables.[121]

She extended her prerogative to trade by harnessing it to one better established before the war. Slave women had long retained control over property they brought into a marriage, and Sarah Burton swapped her cart "and gave $75 to boot for a Wagon" after she married John Burton. She continued buying and selling on her own, too, although she allowed he "helped me to make some of the Property." Her husband used the wagon to haul wood from nearby swamps for sale in Vicksburg, she recalled. At the same time, "I had a little Store, and bought Sugar to Sell again." She was sufficiently engaged in the hauling business as well to know it fetched $10 per load. After a while, the Burtons bought a sow, which bore six pigs. Purchase of two more draft animals fit out their four-horse wagon with an incongruous team of a horse and three mules.[122]

Many liberated slaves cottoned to market principles and conducted trade along those lines. Some folks kept close tabs on fluctuations in prices for corn, wood, or mules of a particular grade. Gold, silver, and greenbacks were all common currency during the Union occupation. Some people kept track of prices in more than one medium of exchange. Edward Hicks, for example, noted the price of horses in "U.S. money" ($125) and corn in gold ($1 per bushel).[123] In the sudden onrush of trade, hack driver Henry Banks took to an objectified notion of market relations that imbued money with all their ostensible power. Money's uncanny ability to gather men in commerce and move goods between people verged on alchemy in Banks's mind. After the fall of Vicksburg, money seemed to take different physical forms, even take flight, at least metaphorically: "The Cotton Buyers were thick and spent money like water and the soldiers had just got paid, and their money just flew around, especially the big officers who didn't appear to care anything about it." Banks and other carriage drivers in town were quick to charge whatever the traffic would bear. "They would pay anything you asked," he mused, "and we asked all we thought we could get."[124]

Engaging slaveholders — as opposed to soldiers, cotton brokers, and other strangers — in market relations was a potentially sticky business. Liberated slaves had long taken customary prices for their produce from owners, who had grown accustomed to paying such prices. Henry Hunt began to change the terms of trade with planters in his Warren County neighborhood. He sold the fine sow he had bought before the war to his wife's owner for $12 in silver, a tidy profit.[125]

Yet some came to wonder whether occupied territory was really free soil. Henry Watson, like his fellow slave, Samuel Chase, thought himself a free man early in the siege of Vicksburg. Yet Watson seemed to find his freedom precarious during the summer and fall, when he often told his friend, James Puckett, that he was trying "to Keep free." And between the vagaries of wage labor and the heavy hand of the Union army, keeping free was a struggle. Within days of the capture of Natchez and Vicksburg, the Union army began to confiscate horses, mules, and conveyances and took up many of the draft animals slaves had painstakingly acquired early in the war. Foraging troops confiscated Watson's livestock in October. After a month spent cooking for the company that took his property, he tried to enlist, was deemed physically unfit, and joined the Pioneer Corps for a year. He was promised a soldier's pay, which was the going rate for military laborers in late 1863, but "I never got a cent of pay for what I done." We will never know whether Watson believed he was keeping free during that year of unpaid labor. When Puckett saw him then, Watson said, appropriately enough, "that he was a pioneer."[126]

The Yankees' uncertain control over the district made freedom tenuous for other former slaves. In Adams County in December 1863, Confederate guerrillas raided the plantation where Dudley Payton and his wife were making a crop and carried him off with several other laborers. She retreated to a place outside Natchez until Payton got away to join her in town and enlist.[127] Rebels engaged union troops just a mile and a half outside Woodville, the Wilkinson County seat, in the spring of 1864.[128] Confederate scouts were still making forays into Warren County, the very heart of occupied territory, later that year. In August, they captured Gabriel Boger on the Hawkins place just eleven miles outside the city and put two shots through his hat as he made his escape.[129] Richard Eastman, refugeed to a saltworks in Alabama in May 1863, returned to Warren County only in May 1865, after the surrender at Appomattox. "I was a Slave all the time during the war and became free at the close of the war," he recalled.[130]

The perils of 1863 and 1864 gave people in the Natchez District good cause to take the end of the war for the moment of emancipation. Some hesitated to put too fine a point on it in testimony before the Southern Claims Commission years later. "I was made free by the war," Boger said. Many witnesses spoke in much the same terms when asked when they had gained their freedom. Others, however, made clear they had the end of the war in mind. In Claiborne County, Anthony Lewis considered himself "freed by the war," which was to say, "I became free when the war ended."[131] Elvira Anderson said something similar: "[T]he war freed me." She lived on a plantation in Warren County, washed and ironed at a nearby army hospital during the summer of 1863, and left for Vicksburg in September, after she married a soldier. "I was threatened because my husband belonged to the Union Army & was compelled to leave the Noland place." She finally "[b]ecame free at the close of the war."[132]

How did slaves know they were free? During the Civil War, they formulated the question in a different, more urgent form: "When will we be free?" In 1861 and 1862, they forged a consensus they would gain their freedom when the Union won the war. A good number broke with that accord in 1863 when it appeared at different junctures that freedom was at hand, even while the war remained a going concern. The Emancipation Proclamation was the first moment of emancipation, but it was neither the last nor the most important. A great many more people resolved they were free at some point around the siege of Vicksburg — at the commencement of the bombardment, a foraging party's show of force, the surrender of the city, the fall of Natchez. While slaves were inclined to take hold of a single moment of emancipation, several such moments took place in the Natchez District. Those moments, considered together, make plain that emancipation was not a single instant at all but a process. The slaves had recognized that fact at the outset, and most stuck to those guns to the end. That is what they meant when they said, from start to finish, that the Yankees would have to whip the South and that the war freed them in the end.

Slaves, moreover, embarked on a journey of ideological change amid wartime social transformations. Many quickly recognized this was not a simple clash between men but rather a conflict between nations, governments, and laws. Soldiers in the Union army committed themselves most powerfully to the nation-state and the rule of law. Men and women embraced the nation-state and rule of law most intimately by reconstructing bonds on the foundation of legal marriage. They also began to lay out new ways of production and trade to extricate themselves from the thicket of ties to slaveholders that had so long encumbered all relations of labor.

Indeed, slaves redrew the entire map of their social terrain. They crossed the prevailing boundary between neighborhoods as they collected intelligence about the war. Men and women who decamped for Union lines, enlisted, labored for the army, or went to work on more or less distant plantations severed some of the ties — of intimate relations, work, struggle — to adjoining plantations that together had formed the sinews of neighborhood. When they reconstituted those ties on new ground, they broke the bonds of neighborhood itself. That rupture was temporary. After the war, freedpeople in the Natchez District made the reconstruction of neighborhoods groundwork for the transition to freedom.

Epilogue

Merrymon Howard, a former slave in Jefferson County who had gained his freedom during the mid-1850s, was disappointed in what he called "the new order of things" as it took shape in early 1866. Already in January it was enough to make him question the meaning of freedom itself. "[W]ell what sort of freedom is this," he asked the Freedmen's Bureau commissioner in Washington, D.C., "and what kind of free Country is this?" Recently enacted black codes, the letter continued, had pitted the law against the freedpeople, "and now we are for bid & denide the right of renting" land, doing business in town without a license, buying whiskey ("even for sickness"), and educating children.[1] Howard was flabbergasted at the Yankees' tardiness in coming to the defense of their allies by April, yet what he wanted from the government just then was a school. He volunteered propertied black people to pay a small tax to support the teachers, field laborers to throw in a share of their wages, and planters to administer the deductions. The planters, he suggested, "might establish Scholes in every neaborhood."[2] Howard envisioned a school system organized along neighborhood lines.

Neighborhoods persisted during Reconstruction, and they resembled their antebellum counterparts in important ways. As in slavery times, neighborhoods served as the locus of many different social relations after the Civil War, including some of the same relations, especially work and intimate relations. The reconstitution of neighborhoods was an unintended consequence of freedpeople's other everyday activities, just like the creation of slave neighborhoods. The very work of remaking neighborhoods was familiar to freedpeople, for that was a constant of slave neighborhoods, too.

Yet freedpeople did not simply re-create slave neighborhoods, not to a tee, anyway. Intimate relations were the most binding tie in the neighborhood before the war, but afterward relations of labor were most important to neighborhoods in the making. Freedpeople's neighborhoods, moreover, were bigger than slave neighborhoods. Bigger neighborhoods meant fewer neighborhoods. And because the social terrain was less divided by neighborhoods, folks coalesced more readily than ever across those lines. Freedpeople also laid the groundwork for new institutions in the neighborhood: schools, churches, the Republican Party, and its offshoots. As former slaves politicized neighborhoods in new ways, they transformed the terms of struggle with former slaveholders. Freedpeople's mobilizations around election time made neighborhoods a fulcrum in the struggle for state power. And this democratic reconstruction of the neighborhood terrain helps to account for the violent character of the opposition to Radical Reconstruction.

Freedpeople were quick to return to their old neighborhoods after the war. From the outset of the fighting, slaves across the Natchez District had breached the boundaries between neighborhoods and cobbled them together into extensive lines of communication to gather military and political intelligence. After the Union army rolled into the neighborhoods, men left to enlist or join the ranks of military laborers, women followed to work in the camps, and many went back and forth with impunity. Their social terrain seemed to know no neighborhood bounds at all for a time. John Wilkes and Robert Banks of Jefferson County were among thousands of other freedmen and -women who made their way back to old neighborhoods shortly after surrender. "I have known Robert Banks all his life," Wilkes recalled, "we lived on adjoining plantations before the war." They did not see much of each other during the war, as Wilkes served in the 6th U.S. Colored Heavy Artillery in Vicksburg, while Banks was in Natchez with the 58th U.S. Colored Infantry. Banks looked well when Wilkes saw him again. "After his discharge," Wilkes said of Banks, "he returned to this neighborhood, and I saw him in 1866."[3]

The neighborhoods freedpeople returned to were already different, starting with the personnel. Many people never made it back to the neighborhood: soldiers who stayed where their regiment mustered out, especially Vicksburg or Natchez; women who joined soldiers there or went to town for their own reasons; people who took to the road to return to family in the Upper South. Men and women who did not return to their old neighborhoods but settled down somewhere else in the district became newcomers in other people's neighborhoods.

Freedpeople from the Adams County neighborhood of Mount Pleasant and Windy Hill made all these moves. Across the South, dramatic numbers of former slaves repaired to towns and cities after the war. In Vicksburg the African American population multiplied from 1,400 in 1860 to 6,800 by 1870; in Natchez, from 2,300 to 5,300.[4] The Mount Pleasant and Windy Hill neighborhood, only a few miles outside Natchez, probably lost more people than most to the town. Philander Perry returned to Mount Pleasant for three years after his discharge and then moved in town. Nellie Jefferson also left for Natchez, where she joined her husband, who had visited her from town for years before the war. Isaac Sloan, on the other hand, returned from the army to his wife on Windy Hill and stayed for the next ten years. More common were freedpeople, women and men both, who did not remain for long in any one place. After Susan Alexander's husband died in the service in 1864, she left Natchez and returned to Mount Pleasant. She went back and forth between there and Windy Hill every year or two. Thus, even as she changed places five times in seven years, she remained on the familiar ground of her antebellum neighborhood except for two years on the Flemming plantation. These relocations, frequent yet in close proximity, enabled Alexander to keep up old neighborhood ties. She and the Sloans, for example, saw each other frequently — often twice a month. She finally left that neighborhood in the early 1870s for Aventine plantation on Second Creek.[5]

By this roundabout course, freedpeople enlarged and re-created antebellum neighborhoods. New arrivals such as Susan Alexander were numerous in postbellum neighborhoods. Yet the reconstituted terrain was defined by a persistent core of men and women, like Charlotte Grant, whose roots in the place went back to the slave neighborhood. She and Peyton Grant had two children on the Mayberry plantation in Jefferson County before the war. After the fall of Vicksburg, the family left for Natchez, where he enlisted in the Union army. Within a year, their daughter had died, and he was killed in a skirmish outside town. Charlotte Grant began living with Richard Lewis about a year later, although she later told the Pension Bureau they never married.[6] In the nearly ten years she lived with Lewis, they moved every year or two to a different plantation near the Mayberry place.

The dimensions of the old neighborhood grew slowly as she and other freedpeople made roughly parallel moves near the plantations where they had lately been enslaved. While she moved with Lewis and her son from the Stewart to the Stampley and then Jones places, she found many longtime acquaintances nearby. Henry Brooks had lived near her when he belonged to Thomas Darden. George Chaney, who had belonged to her owner's kin, may have lived for a time on Mayberry. Grant and Lewis quarreled a heap over the years. When they finally went their separate ways in 1873, she recalled, Lewis "left the Neighborhood."[7] The five miles or so separating Grant on the Jones plantation and Lewis on the Miles place were not far beyond neighborhood bounds in the 1870s. But she had her reasons for keeping her distance from Lewis and measuring it precisely. If she was cutting the contemporary boundaries close, they were far beyond the antebellum limits of adjoining plantations.

People moved from one plantation to the next to reconcile varied, often conflicting aspirations. Especially compelling were impulses to preserve the old ties yet settle at some remove from former owners. Charlotte Grant, like a great many others, lived on several places around her former owner's plantation but conspicuously avoided taking up residence on the old place itself. Nevertheless, freedpeople generally reconstructed neighborhood boundaries as they hammered out the terms of free labor.

The struggles over free labor and social space were joined from the outset of Reconstruction. The black codes, pioneered in Mississippi and South Carolina in the fall of 1865, resembled antebellum slave codes in the determination to control freedpeople's mobility. The law against vagrancy, punishable at the maximum by a $100 fine and ten days in prison, placed certain venues off limits, especially the urban establishments where slaves had formerly drunk and fraternized with disreputable free people: "houses of ill-fame, gaming-houses, or tippling shops." The laws empowered municipal authorities to keep freedpeople out of the cities by prohibiting them from taking up residence without a license from the mayor, who could revoke it at will. The statute's broad definition of a vagrant included several categories for people with untoward mobility: "vagabonds," "common night-walkers," and "runaways." Any citizen or official could "arrest and carry back" freedmen and -women who left their employers before their contracts expired. A provision reminiscent of fugitive slave laws offered arresting parties $5 plus ten cents per mile "from the place of arrest to the place of delivery." Now, however, freedpeople would have the costs of their retrieval deducted from their wages.[8] To secure planters a reliable labor force, the black codes aimed to circumscribe freedpeople's movement from place to place.[9]

After federal authorities suspended the codes with the advent of Congressional Reconstruction, the struggle over free labor continued to shape the rebuilding of neighborhoods, especially its pace and tempo. Freedpeople made winter the season for relocation because the system of annual labor contracts more or less dictated it. To leave their place of employment before the cotton was gathered, accounts settled, and the contract fulfilled was to jeopardize any claim to their accumulated wages or share of the crop. Freedpeople did not set out to change employers with the intention of creating a market in labor power, but that was the result.[10] Reconstituting slave neighborhoods on new grounds was still another unintended consequence of freedpeople's determination to better the terms of employment. In the seemingly small step of hiring onto different plantations, freedpeople created new neighborhoods and fundamentally altered their social terrain.

The place of intimate relations changed as much as that of work in the making of neighborhoods. One might even say the two switched places. To the degree freedpeople rebuilt their neighborhoods in the course of forging the terms of free labor, work supplanted intimate relations as the foremost constitutive bond in the place. Intimate relations even had the centripetal force that work had generated before the war. Then, field laborers had worked on adjoining places from time to time but labored mainly on their owners' plantations, which became neighborhood focal points. After emancipation, intimate relations no longer engendered other bonds of kinship across planta-tion lines because husbands and wives were no longer separated by slave-holders' property lines. Freedmen and -women enjoyed new liberty to go courting in the neighborhood at large, while husbands and wives, parents and children were free to live together.

Postbellum neighborhoods also quartered a structure of intimate relations at once remade and transformed. A structure hewed in no small part against the impositions of owners could not hold together long after slavery ceased to come between freedmen and -women. Still, many couples who had lived to-gether in good standing during slavery days saw no reason to pronounce themselves husband and wife in law after emancipation. The state constitu-tional convention accommodated this preference in 1869 with a clause pro-nouncing "[a]ll persons who have not been married but are living together, cohabiting as husband and wife" to be "married" for all legal purposes.[11] Romantic unions persisted in some variety through the 1870s. More than a few men and women who got together in those years preferred taking up or living together to marriage. The federal pension system unwittingly encour-aged the profusion of intimate relations. The rule prohibiting a widow from receiving a soldier's pension after remarrying provided ample incentive for women to settle into informal arrangements with men. Couples then had the awkward task of fashioning for the Pension Bureau elaborate accounts of their chastity, another qualification for a widow's pension. Widows who lost their stipends paid dearly for these new intimacies.[12]

Antebellum intimate relations at the boundaries of commitment — sweet-hearting and marriage — changed most radically after emancipation. Freed-people ceased to associate sweethearting with the first stirrings of youthful desire and instead attached its clandestine quality to infidelity. An unfaithful man was often said to have a wife and a "sweetheart." Faithless men thus received some of the indulgence neighbors had formerly bestowed on young lovers in slavery.[13] Young freedwomen who had children out of wedlock received an implicit rebuke in the discourse surrounding their progeny. Emma Hunt had four children with a man after the war but never married him because her father objected. "We just stole them," she recalled.[14] If witnesses before the bureau did not spell out just what these women had appropriated or from whom, they had clearly run afoul of their neighbors' sense of propriety. That sense of propriety, vividly displayed at antebellum weddings and other suitable occasions, was hardly new, but it gained added impetus and authority from the many new churches freedpeople founded after the war.[15]

Legal marriage, buttressed by the pillars of church and state, held considerable sway with freedmen and -women. Weddings performed by black preachers now also conveyed the authority of law. Couples were expected to put their relations on proper footing when they joined churches, which kept after folks who hesitated to marry. Wilson Turner was the preacher at a small church in Adams County and lived with a woman for a year until the members of his congregation objected. "The church got down on him and told him he had to marry," his wife recalled.[16] Freedpeople's reservations about legal marriage had nothing to do with any hankering for slave marriage. Couples did not deem themselves married solely on employers' and neighbors' say-so. The convention of brides and grooms prevailing on planters or their agents to perform weddings went by the boards. The days of slave marriage were gone for good.

The freedpeople's political mobilization in Radical Reconstruction was built on neighborhood foundations in some precincts. One Jefferson County neighborhood was the arena of political debates, a Republican club, and processions, too. Young Republicans convened at the schoolhouse for a debate in 1873. The men got up a parade along the way, and a good deal of drumming was heard. Local planters thought there was no telling what mischief such proceedings could lead to, and one complained to Merrymon Howard, by then in the capacity of a sheriff, that the laborers on his place included as many as 150 armed men. Howard went out to have a look but found nothing out of the ordinary in the debating, parading, and drumming. "I knew all about the neighborhood," Howard told an investigating committee of congressmen, "and there was no trouble."[17]

At election time, turning out the neighborhoods was an important part of getting out crowds and votes. Representative John R. Lynch's congressional district extended clear across southern Mississippi to the Alabama line, but his base lay in the counties of the old Natchez District below Warren County.

When Lynch's supporters in Jefferson County resolved to put on a grand demonstration for the congressman's visit to Fayette in 1876, they went to the grassroots by way of the neighborhoods. "I was careful to go to every neighborhood and send word out by every leading republican in the county that I could get hold of," Howard explained.[18]

The neighborhoods made a fine showing for the event. Between 1,500 and 2,000 freedpeople from the countryside paraded into town, first a procession of men, most on horseback and mules, and then women and children in wagons or on foot. They were not deterred when the meeting was shortly broken up by a phalanx of white Democrats with a wagonload of guns and an artillery piece. "I rode on my horse," Howard recalled, "and told the colored men who were still around the street to get their neighbors together and fall back to the creek." There, eight miles outside of town, near a railroad station, they rallied 400 strong—men, women, and children—hallooing and yelling and shouting for Lynch. After Lynch, standing in a wagon at the depot, delivered a mere five- or ten-minute speech, the train whisked him away, but the crowd marched off in high spirits. The parade traveled a good two miles, drums beating, flags flying for Rutherford B. Hayes and William A. Wheeler—the Republican presidential ticket—and John Roy Lynch. "We thought we had won a big victory," Howard testified. "We had had our meeting."[19]

Neighborhoods performed much of the disciplinary work of forging political unity. And in Mississippi that unity was formidable indeed. By Howard's estimate, just forty or fifty freedmen in all of Jefferson County threw their lot in with the Democrats. Charley Chester "had a good deal of trouble" when he joined a Democratic club, according to Howard. "The people in his neighborhood and himself were getting along very badly." Their skirmishing played out on several fronts, including the courthouse, where Chester was forever embroiled in lawsuits. During the 1876 election, on the Saturday before the vote, someone unloaded some birdshot into Chester, although he survived the shooting.[20]

Although these divisions on occasion played out dramatically, they were slight when it counted in the early 1870s. Two of the four African Americans in the first legislature of Radical Reconstruction represented the Natchez District. Adams and Jefferson Counties repeatedly elected former slaves to the post of sheriff. Republicans fairly swept local offices in Warren and Claiborne Counties, where freedmen formed a majority on the board of supervisors, occupied the sheriff's office, and policed many beats as constables and justices of the peace. Men in the latter offices, however modest they may sound, were the law's gatekeepers, empowered to originate criminal and civil cases as well as arrest and examine witnesses.[21]

Yet a certain distance prevailed between the officeholders and the neighborhoods, which rarely elected one of their own. From their standpoint, the leading black Republicans in the district were, to a man, outsiders. Many were newcomers to the region. Peter Crosby was enslaved in central Mississippi before he served with the 5th U.S. Colored Heavy Artillery in Vicksburg, where he rose in a circle of African American politicians, the so-called Vicksburg Ring, that dominated politics in the city until 1874.[22] Hiram Revels, born free in North Carolina, attended a Quaker school in Ohio and studied ancient Greek in Baltimore before the war, landed in jail for preaching to slaves in Missouri, and recruited black troops there and in Maryland. He arrived in Mississippi in 1865 but left for two years to recover his health before settling in Natchez in 1868. He parlayed his election as a town alderman that year into a seat representing Adams County in the state senate in 1869, a well-spoken prayer opening the legislative session into the nomination for Jefferson Davis's old seat in the U.S. Senate. H. P. Jacobs, enslaved in Alabama, escaped to the North, whence he arrived in Natchez during the war as a Baptist missionary. He cut a figure across the state as a peripatetic organizer of churches and Union Leagues before he became a state legislator from Adams County, a contender for the Senate nomination in 1869, and Lynch's main rival.[23]

The former slaves from the district who rose highest among officeholders were townsmen. Before the war, the slaves most attuned to electoral politics had lived in and around the county seats, especially Vicksburg and Natchez, where most government business took place. Former slaves from town were nicely situated to prosper in the political milieu fashioned by Republicans, who also set up headquarters in town. Lynch came of age in Natchez, where he was a house servant. Even as Merrymon Howard rose from justice of the peace to the state legislature and the county sheriff's office, he always traced his roots to the county seat of Fayette. "I have always claimed that as my home," he declared in 1877.[24] Falling in behind outsiders such as Howard, Lynch, and Crosby helped freedpeople sidestep old neighborhood divisions and coalesce anew along those lines.

Lynch encountered this distance from his constituents in his first office, justice of the peace, in 1869. Empowered to perform weddings, he routinely concluded the Episcopal rites with "a brief lecture" to the couple, elaborating on "the importance and sacredness of the relation upon which they were about to enter." He had laid it on thick for a couple from ten miles out in the country whom he found uncommonly bright and attractive, so he was surprised to find the bride back in his office ten days later recounting her husband's infidelities. Lynch told the woman to return the next morning and arrived at his office to find the couple sitting on the steps. Under Lynch's questioning, the wife repeated her bill of particulars. The husband readily confessed his errors and promised to make amends if he could have a second chance. The husband's apparent notion that Lynch could punish him for neglecting his vows was reasonable in light of his experience. After all, before the war, planters had taken that prerogative along with the power to perform weddings. Lynch did nothing to dispel the husband's notion and warned him he would "suffer the full penalty of the law" if he failed to do right by his wife in the future. She had no complaints when Lynch ran into her some time later, and he eventually became accustomed to freedpeople's exalted view of a squire's power. Many constituents, he found, had an "exaggerated idea about the office" and "magnified it far beyond its importance."[25] The distance between urban officeholders and rural neighborhoods covered vastly different understandings about the location and boundaries of power.[26]

A critical vulnerability of Reconstruction lay in neighborhood divisions of a different kind. Radical Reconstruction set off an unprecedented struggle for political sovereignty over neighborhoods. Democratic Party politics were, if anything, even more broadly grounded in neighborhoods than were Republican politics. With rare exceptions, antebellum political elections were determined by neighborhood loyalties.[27] Historians rightly argue for the political character of slaves' struggles with owners. But the planters, who thought such contentions were no more political than those with their wives, children, or any other household dependent, could not have agreed. As freedpeople consolidated neighborhoods and mobilized a Republican Party there, they ventured onto a political terrain where planters had long assumed they would never have to contend for power with black people. For planters alert to the change, Democratic electoral campaigns comprised critical battles in a campaign for unchallenged control over neighborhoods as a political field. The struggle for state power derived some of its force and blood thirst from this underlying conflict over political space.[28]

Neighborhoods were a formidable redoubt in the siege on Republican government. The Vicksburg troubles surrounding Crosby's reelection as sheriff in 1874 spilled over the Warren County line into the southern portion of Yazoo County, where white Democrats galvanized. During the week leading up to the August vote, Yazoo's Republican sheriff sent deputies to track down reports about armed white people drilling in the night, harassing the freedpeople. The deputies found two paramilitary groups, the sheriff related to a

Senate committee, one in the "Benton neighborhood" and another in the
"Dover neighborhood." The captain of the Dover company forwarded a letter
to the sheriff, declaring "that our object is simply to maintain the peace and
quiet of our neighborhood." Freedpeople there, the captain explained, had
begun "a movement" with good, limited intentions: "mutual assistance in
times of sickness." But then "bad men" managed to "convert it to their purpose of controlling the whites." These new leaders held meetings and tried to
collect arms, and "there has been turbulent colored persons going through the
neighborhood endeavoring to stir up strife by exciting the blacks." The sheriff
found no evidence of freedpeople arming themselves anywhere.[29] Yet the
challenge of the freedmen's political agitation — "going through the neighborhood," as the captain put it — was real enough. Such politicking threatened
white Democrats' sovereignty over the neighborhood, and that was a struggle
they did not intend to lose.

Freedpeople's neighborhoods were no more unique to southwest Mississippi than were slave neighborhoods, if congressional testimony is any indication. Although the sheriff of Yazoo County found no evidence of armed freedmen there, the paramilitary aspect of African American politics across much of
the South is well documented.[30] A freedmen's militia in the York District of
the South Carolina up-country was evidently a neighborhood organization.
The militia drilled once or twice a week, according to one freedman, who
noted that the captain declared he would sooner "kill from the cradle up" than
surrender his arms. The captain's declaration soon became common knowledge, the witness pointed out: "I heard it from other folks that it was a general
thing in this neighborhood." He had told two men himself on Sunday, while
on the way to church, another landmark political institution in the neighborhood. When word circulated the Ku Klux Klan "had been in the neighborhood," other freedmen "went about the church and lay out."[31]

The Ku Klux Klan had neighborhood roots in some locales. A Klansman in
up-country South Carolina insisted the organization was so pervasive he had
little choice but to join it. "Pretty nigh everyone in our neighborhood belonged to the organization," he confessed in federal court. According to another member inclined to minimize his own role, the Klans seemed like just
another vigilance committee: "[T]hey were getting them up in all the different
neighborhoods, and I said it would be very well for us to have one to protect
our neighborhood."[32] In Georgia, the Klan was under neighborhood discipline, organized and operated on those grounds, according to some witnesses
who testified to Congress. A freedman in the piedmont observed that Klans-
men tried to mask themselves behind "false-faces" with long beards, big eyes,

and long noses, yet he had seen them a dozen times and was not put off by the disguises: "I knew they were neighborhood men."[33]

Union Leagues in North Carolina flourished, at least for a time, in neighborhood soil. Some fiery talk was heard in the leagues around Chatham County in 1869. One freedman recalled hearing a speaker argue in favor of burning houses down if that was what it took to compel freedpeople's enemies to live and let live. The witness went to only three or so meetings, although others attended far more regularly than he. By July 1871, however, the leagues "had all died out a while ago in my neighborhood."[34]

The struggle over the terms of free labor in up-country Georgia played out on a neighborhood field, at least from one freedman's standpoint. Reuben Sheets confronted employers determined to fix the labor market at low wages. "All around me there men want me to live with them," but he rented land instead, worked his children, and accumulated "right smart of property." Daily pay for field work ranged from thirty-five cents to fifty cents and provisions. "Men in the neighborhood," he reported, declared that everyone would have to labor for the same price and "work cheap."[35]

As a political arena, neighborhoods in the Mississippi Delta survived the overthrow of Republican state government in 1875. Three years later, Louis Stubblefield was in his fourth term on the county board of supervisors when a man from Arkansas gained a following for an emigration to Liberia. "They came on down into my immediate neighborhood," Stubblefield recalled, "where I had been for ten years, and in all our political matters there was never a meeting called but that I must be there." He opposed the movement with the mixed motives of a substantial landholder anxious about his labor supply, about a potential backlash from the white planters, and about the fate of "some very near and dear friends" caught up in the whirlwind. At a meeting, he looked at the organizer and condemned him as a swindler. "Boys, you had better let that man alone," Stubblefield admonished. "[I]t is best to take a man from amongst ourselves to transact our own business, and not depend so much on strangers and foreigners." The speech put nary a dent in the agitator's influence, so Stubblefield and other opponents joined the emigrationist clubs sprouting up around the county and eventually did their part to stanch the movement.[36]

The neighborhoods freedpeople rebuilt after the Civil War did not occupy quite the same place in African American life that slave neighborhoods had. Emancipation had taken down a bulwark of the old neighborhoods. That bulwark, of course, was slavery itself. And many new ties that defined emancipation—legal marriage, electoral politics, trade, church—linked men and women to distant classes, institutions, towns, and other far-flung places. Yet many of those ties — party politics, family life, and family labor — also sank deep roots in the neighborhoods. Freedpeople still hitched together many different bonds there. Neighborhoods, no longer the locus of society, nonetheless endured as a cornerstone of Reconstruction.

Appendix: Population, Land, and Labor

Table A.1: Increases in Slave Population and Cleared Land, Persistence of Uncleared Land, 1850–1860

County	Slave Population		Improved Acres		Unimproved Acres (%)	
	1850	1860	1850	1860	1850	1860
Adams	14,395	14,292	77,675	103,394	93,766 (54.7)	125,619 (54.9)
Claiborne	11,450	12,296	96,896	127,260	152,398 (61.1)	153,265 (54.6)
Jefferson	10,493	12,396	93,817	123,368	135,868 (59.2)	159,159 (56.3)
Warren	12,096	13,763	78,472	110,480	134,825 (63.2)	186,089 (62.8)
Wilkinson	13,260	13,132	96,630	112,693	149,611 (60.8)	170,822 (60.3)
Total	61,694	65,879	443,490	577,195	666,468 (60.0)	794,954 (57.9)

Sources: U.S. Census Office, *The Seventh Census of the United States, 1850* (Washington, D.C.: Armstrong, 1853), 447; U.S. Census Office, *Statistical View of the United States: Compendium of the Seventh Census* (1854; New York: Ross, 1990), 262; U.S. Census Office, *Agriculture of the United States in 1860: Compiled from the Original Returns of the Eighth Census* (Washington, D.C.: Government Printing Office, 1864), 84–85; Joseph C. G. Kennedy, *Population of the United States in 1860: Compiled from the Original Returns of the Eighth Census* (Washington, D.C.: Government Printing Office, 1864), 267.

Table A.2: Increased Acreage under Cultivation per Slave, 1850–1860

County	Increased Improved Acres, 1850–60 (%)	Increased Slaves, 1850–60 (%)	Improved Acres per Slave		% Change, 1850–60
			1850	1860	
Adams	25,719 (33.1)	−103 (−.7)	5.4	7.2	33.3
Claiborne	30,364 (31.3)	846 (7.4)	8.5	10.3	21.2
Jefferson	29,551 (31.5)	1,903 (18.1)	8.9	10.0	12.4
Warren	32,008 (40.8)	1,667 (13.8)	6.5	8.0	23.1
Wilkinson	16,063 (16.6)	−128 (−.9)	7.3	8.6	17.8
Total	133,705 (30.1)	4,185 (6.8)	7.2	8.8	22.2

Note: All figures calculated from figures in table A.1.

Notes

Abbreviations

ACCCR   Adams County Circuit Court Records, Historic Natchez Foundation, Natchez, Mississippi

ACPRER   Adams County Probate Real Estate Record, Film 0886340, Family History Center, State College, Pennsylvania

AHR   *American Historical Review*

CWPF   Civil War and Later Pension Files, 1861–1942, Records of the Veterans Administration, RG 15, National Archives, Washington, D.C.

EE   Electronic Edition, Documenting the American South, University Library, University of North Carolina at Chapel Hill, <http://docsouth.unc.edu>

FSSP   Freedmen and Southern Society Project, University of Maryland at College Park

JAH   *Journal of American History*

JMH   *Journal of Mississippi History*

JSH   *Journal of Southern History*

MDAH   Mississippi Department of Archives and History, Jackson

NTC   Natchez Trace Collection, Center for American History, University of Texas at Austin

RASP   Records of Ante-Bellum Southern Plantations, ed. Kenneth M. Stampp, University Publications of America, Frederick, Maryland

RG   Record Group

SCC   Southern Claims Commission, Settled Case Files for Approved Claims, General Accounting Office, 3rd Auditor, RG 217, National Archives, Washington, D.C.

SHC   Southern Historical Collection, University of North Carolina, Chapel Hill

USCC   U.S. Court of Claims, Congressional Jurisdiction Case Files, RG 123, National Archives, Washington, D.C.

WCCCP   Warren County Circuit Court Papers, Old Courthouse Museum, Vicksburg, Mississippi

WMQ   *William and Mary Quarterly*

Introduction

1. Claimant's Request for Findings of Fact and Brief on the Merits, n.d., Naomi Fowler Claim, Case 13189, USCC.

2. John Weed, Deposition, 11 March 1896, Harriet Pierce, Deposition, 9 March 1896, James Pierce File, Widow's Certificate 321488, CWPF. Although some pension file documents identify Wade as "John Weed," he had not gone by that name since his service in the Union army. See Claimant's Request for Findings, Naomi Fowler Claim, USCC.

3. James C. Cobb, *The Most Southern Place on Earth: The Mississippi Delta and the Roots of Regional Identity* (New York: Oxford University Press, 1992), 3; Herbert Weaver, *Mississippi Farmers, 1850–1860* (Nashville: Vanderbilt University Press, 1945), 10, 18, 22; Christopher Morris, *Becoming Southern: The Evolution of a Way of Life, Warren County and Vicksburg, Mississippi, 1770–1860* (New York: Oxford University Press, 1995), 3; John Hebron Moore, *The Emergence of the Cotton Kingdom in the Old Southwest: Mississippi, 1770–1860* (Baton Rouge: Louisiana State University Press, 1988), 7.

4. Adam Rothman, *Slave Country: American Expansion and the Origins of the Deep South* (Cambridge: Harvard University Press, 2005), 193–96. For an account of Abd al-Rahman Ibrahima, a slave in Adams County kidnapped from West Africa and returned there in 1829, see Terry Alford, *Prince Among Slaves: The True Story of an African Prince Sold into Slavery in the American South* (New York: Oxford University Press, 1977).

5. Adam Rothman, *Slave Country*, 9–18, 24–26, 34–35, 49, 174.

6. D. Clayton James, *Antebellum Natchez* (Baton Rouge: Louisiana State University Press, 1968), 77, 102–3; John Hebron Moore, *Agriculture in Ante-Bellum Mississippi* (New York: Bookman, 1958), 13–27; Lewis C. Gray, *History of Agriculture in the Southern United States to 1860* (New York: Smith, 1941), 2:897–98, 903, table 34.

7. Herbert G. Gutman, *The Black Family in Slavery and Freedom, 1750–1925* (New York: Vintage, 1976), 19–20, 154.

8. Randolph B. Campbell, "Slavery in the Natchez Trace Collection," in *Inside the Natchez Trace Collection*, ed. Katherine J. Adams and Lewis L. Gould (Baton Rouge: Louisiana State University Press, 1999), 34.

9. William K. Scarborough, "Heartland of the Cotton Kingdom," in *A History of Mississippi*, ed. Richard A. McLemore (Hattiesburg: University and College Press of Mississippi, 1973), 1:321–22, tables 1, 2. Adams, Warren, and Wilkinson Counties yielded the most cotton in the seed. Measured by the bale, Jefferson County ranked fifth (Moore, *Emergence of the Cotton Kingdom*, appendix B). On the cotton boom during the era of the early republic, see Adam Rothman, *Slave Country*, 45–54.

10. Weaver, *Mississippi Farmers*, 18; Moore, *Agriculture in Ante-Bellum Mississippi*, 57–58; Moore, *Emergence of the Cotton Kingdom*, 30–36; Christopher Morris, *Becoming Southern*, 156–57.

11. Scarborough, "Heartland of the Cotton Kingdom," 321–22, tables 1, 2.

12. The average wealth (real and personal estate) of free men in Wilkinson County was $26,100; in Jefferson County, $22,740; in Claiborne County, $21,600; for free men in the South, $4,380; for all men nationwide, $2,700 (Lee Soltow, *Men and Wealth in the United States, 1850–1870* [New Haven: Yale University Press, 1975], 157, 166–73, tables 6.3, 6.6). On wealth in the Natchez District, see also William K. Scarborough, "Lords or Capitalists? The Natchez Nabobs in Comparative Perspective," *JMH* 54 (August 1992): 229–67; William K. Scarborough, *Masters of the Big House: Elite Slaveholders of the Mid-Nineteenth-Century South* (Baton Rouge: Louisiana State University Press, 2003), 444–47, 467–73, appendixes C, D; Morton Rothstein, "The Changing Social Networks and Investment Behavior of a Slaveholding Elite in the Antebellum South: Some Natchez 'Nabobs,' 1800–1860," in *Entrepreneurs in Cultural Context*, ed. Sidney M. Greenfield, Arnold Strickon, and Robert T. Aubey (Albuquerque: University of New Mexico Press, 1979).

13. In 1860, the combined median slaveholding was 70 in Wilkinson, Adams, Jefferson, and Claiborne Counties in the Natchez District as well as the South Carolina Sea Islands (Lewis C. Gray, *History of Agriculture*, 1:530–31, tables 10, 12).

14. Allan Pred, "Place as Historically Contingent Process: Structuration and the Time-Geography of Becoming Places," *Annals of the Association of American Geographers* 74 (June 1984): 279–97.

15. Brenda E. Stevenson, *Life in Black and White: Family and Community in the Slave South* (New York: Oxford University Press, 1996), 160, 206–57; Brenda E. Stevenson, "Distress and Discord in Virginia Slave Families, 1830–1860," in *In Joy and In Sorrow: Women, Family and Marriage in the Victorian South*, ed. Carol Bleser (New York: Oxford University Press, 1990), 103–24; Ann Paton Malone, *Sweet Chariot: Slave Family and Household Structure in Nineteenth-Century Louisiana* (Chapel Hill: University of North Carolina Press, 1992), 258–72.

16. Gutman, *Black Family*, 11–18, tables 2–4; John W. Blassingame, *The Slave Community: Plantation Life in the Antebellum South*, rev. ed. (New York: Oxford University Press, 1979), 165; Malone, *Sweet Chariot*, 166–68, tables 5.3–4, 5.7, 6.1; Donald R. Shaffer, *After the Glory: The Struggles of Black Civil War Veterans* (Lawrence: University Press of Kansas, 2004), 103, 109.

17. James C. Scott, *Domination and the Arts of Resistance: Hidden Transcripts* (New Haven: Yale University Press, 1990); Stephanie M. H. Camp, *Closer to Freedom: Enslaved Women and Everyday Resistance in the Plantation South* (Chapel Hill: University of North Carolina Press, 2004).

18. See, for example, Ira Berlin and Philip D. Morgan, eds., *Cultivation and Culture: Labor and the Shaping of Slave Life in the Americas* (Charlottesville: University Press of Virginia, 1993); Larry E. Hudson Jr., ed., *Working Toward Freedom: Slave Society*

and Domestic Economy in the American South (Rochester, N.Y.: University of Rochester Press, 1994; Larry E. Hudson Jr., *To Have and to Hold: Slave Work and Family Life in Antebellum South Carolina* (Athens: University of Georgia Press, 1997); Betty Wood, *Women's Work, Men's Work: The Informal Slave Economies of Lowcountry Georgia* (Athens: University of Georgia Press, 1995); Dylan C. Penningroth, *The Claims of Kinfolk: African American Property and Community in the Nineteenth-Century South* (Chapel Hill: University of North Carolina Press, 2003).

19. Blassingame, *Slave Community*, 105–6, 147–48, 315–17; George P. Rawick, *From Sundown to Sunup: The Making of the Black Community*, ser. 1, vol. 1 of *The American Slave: A Composite Autobiography*, ed. George P. Rawick (Westport, Conn.: Greenwood, 1972), 9–10, 93, 110; Lawrence W. Levine, *Black Culture and Black Consciousness: Afro-American Folk Thought from Slavery to Freedom* (Oxford: Oxford University Press, 1977), 29–30, 33, 37, 81; Thomas L. Webber, *Deep Like the Rivers: Education in the Slave Quarter Community, 1831–1865* (New York: Norton, 1978), 63–70, 150–52, 261–62; Paul D. Escott, *Slavery Remembered: A Record of Twentieth-Century Slave Narratives* (Chapel Hill: University of North Carolina Press, 1979), xiv, 18–22, 114–17; William L. Van Deburg, *The Slave Drivers: Black Agricultural Labor Supervisors in the Antebellum South* (1979; New York: Oxford University Press, 1988), 14, 19–25, 29–30, 86–88, 114–16; Mechal Sobel, *Trabelin' On: The Slave Journey to an Afro-Baptist Faith* (Princeton: Princeton University Press, 1988), 116–18; Deborah Gray White, *Ar'n't I a Woman? Female Slaves in the Plantation South* (New York: Norton, 1985), 131–32, 141, 153–58; Charles Joyner, *Down by the Riverside: A South Carolina Slave Community* (Urbana: University of Illinois Press, 1985), xvi, 80, 85–86; Sterling Stuckey, *Slave Culture: Nationalist Theory and the Foundations of Black America* (New York: Oxford University Press, 1987), vii, 30; Margaret Washington Creel, *"A Peculiar People": Slave Religion and Community-Culture Among the Gullahs* (New York: New York University Press, 1988), 1–2, 4; Roderick A. McDonald, *The Economy and Material Culture of Slaves: Goods and Chattels on the Sugar Plantations of Jamaica and Louisiana* (Baton Rouge: Louisiana State University Press, 1993), 165–67; John M. Vlach, *Back of the Big House: The Architecture of Plantation Slavery* (Chapel Hill: University of North Carolina Press, 1993), 14–16, 231; Lorena S. Walsh, *From Calabar to Carter's Grove: The History of a Virginia Slave Community* (Charlottesville: University Press of Virginia, 1997), 150, 166–67, 169–71, 175, 223–24; Hudson, *To Have and to Hold*; Lisa C. Tolbert, *Constructing Townscapes: Space and Society in Antebellum Tennessee* (Chapel Hill: University of North Carolina Press, 1999), 120, 193–94, 201, 205, 210–14, 220–24; Philip D. Morgan, *Slave Counterpoint: Black Culture in the Eighteenth-Century Chesapeake and Lowcountry* (Chapel Hill: University of North Carolina Press, 1998), xxii–xxiii, 20, 101–4, 121–24, 442–43; Thomas C. Buchanan, *Black Life on the Mississippi: Slaves, Free Blacks, and the Western Steamboat World* (Chapel Hill: University of North Carolina Press, 2004), esp. 5–8, 17–18, 20, 82; David E. Walker, *No More, No More: Slavery and Cultural Resistance in Havana and New Orleans* (Minneapolis:

University of Minnesota Press, 2004), vii–viii; David Brion Davis, *Inhuman Bondage: The Rise and Fall of Slavery in the New World* (New York: Oxford University Press, 2006), 199–204.

20. Emily West, *Chains of Love: Slave Couples in Antebellum South Carolina* (Urbana: University of Illinois Press, 2004), 3, 11, 13, 30, 34, 81, 116, 158; Hudson, *To Have and to Hold*, xiv–xv, xx, 58, 65; Marie J. Schwartz, *Born in Bondage: Growing Up Enslaved in the Antebellum South* (Cambridge: Harvard University Press, 2000), 5, 78; Philip D. Morgan, "The Ownership of Property by Slaves in the Mid-Nineteenth-Century Low Country," *JSH* 49 (August 1983): 402–5, 414–20; Philip D. Morgan, "Work and Culture: The Task System and the World of Lowcountry Blacks, 1700–1880," *WMQ*, 3rd ser., 39 (October 1982): 592–99; Loren Schweninger, "The Underside of Slavery: Internal Economy, Self-Hire, and Quasi-Freedom in Virginia, 1750–1865," *Slavery and Abolition* 12 (September 1991): 2, 16; David S. Cecelski, *The Waterman's Song: Slavery and Freedom in Maritime North Carolina* (Chapel Hill: University of North Carolina Press, 2001), 122–23, 139–40, 143, 149.

21. Eugene D. Genovese, *Roll, Jordan, Roll: The World the Slaves Made* (New York: Pantheon, 1974), 91. Herbert G. Gutman also both asserted and questioned the autonomy of the slave family; see Gutman, *Black Family*; Herbert G. Gutman, "The Black Family in Slavery and Freedom: A Revised Perspective," in *Power and Culture: Essays on the American Working Class*, ed. Ira Berlin (New York: Pantheon, 1987), 361–62.

22. Robert L. Olwell, *Masters, Slaves, and Subjects: The Culture of Power in the South Carolina Low Country, 1740–1790* (Ithaca: Cornell University Press, 1998), 9, 51, 281, 165; Jennifer L. Morgan, *Laboring Women: Reproduction and Gender in New World Slavery* (Philadelphia: University of Pennsylvania Press, 2004), 9–11, 122, 126, 130.

23. Shane White, *Somewhat More Independent: The End of Slavery in New York City, 1777–1810* (Athens: University of Georgia Press, 1991), 182, 190–200; Edward A. Pearson, " 'A Countryside Full of Flames': A Reconsideration of the Stono Rebellion and Slave Rebelliousness in the Early Eighteenth Century South Carolina Lowcountry," in *Stono: Documenting and Interpreting a Southern Slave Revolt*, ed. Mark M. Smith (Columbia: University of South Carolina Press, 2005), 89, 99.

24. Michael A. Gomez, *Exchanging Our Country Marks: The Transformation of African Identities in the Colonial and Antebellum South* (Chapel Hill: University of North Carolina Press, 1998), 6–13, 186–290; James Sidbury, *Plowshares into Swords: Race, Rebellion, and Identity in Gabriel's Virginia, 1730–1810* (Cambridge: Cambridge University Press, 1997), esp. 16–29, 44–46, 252–54.

25. For further discussion of the persistence of community in the historiography of slavery, see Anthony E. Kaye, "Neighbourhoods and Solidarity in the Natchez District of Mississippi: Rethinking the Antebellum Slave Community," *Slavery and Abolition* 23 (April 2002): 1–3, 17–19.

26. Jean-Jacques Rousseau, *The Social Contract*, trans. Maurice Cranston (London: Penguin, 1968), book 1, chaps. 6–8, book 2, chaps. 4, 7; Immanuel Kant, *Groundwork of the Metaphysics of Morals*, trans. Mary Gregor (Cambridge: Cambridge University Press, 1998), 39–47, 52–66; John Rawls, *A Theory of Justice* (Cambridge: Harvard University Press, 1971), chap. 4, sec. 40, chap. 9, sec. 78; Jürgen Habermas, *The Structural Transformation of the Public Sphere: An Inquiry into a Category of Bourgeois Society*, trans. Thomas Burger with Frederick Lawrence (Cambridge: MIT Press, 1991), 43–51, 73–90; Charles Taylor, *Ethics of Authenticity* (Cambridge: Harvard University Press, 2005). See also Michel Foucault, "What Is Enlightenment?" in *The Foucault Reader*, ed. Paul Rabinow (New York: Pantheon, 1984), 32–50.

27. Webber, *Deep Like the Rivers*, 261–62. On the contrary, one scholar has argued that in the early republic, Americans used the concept of autonomy to justify slavery. See François Furstenberg, "Beyond Freedom and Slavery: Autonomy, Virtue, and Resistance in Early American Political Discourse," *JAH* 89 (March 2003): 1295–1330.

28. Stevenson, *Life in Black and White*, 226–57. Dylan Penningroth has called attention to conflict among slaves in general. See, for example, Penningroth, "My People, My People: The Dynamics of Community in Southern Slavery," in *New Studies in the History of American Slavery*, ed. Edward E. Baptist and Stephanie M. H. Camp (Athens: University of Georgia Press, 2006), 166–76.

29. Nell Irvin Painter, "Soul Murder and Slavery: Toward a Fully Loaded Cost Accounting" and "Three Southern Women and Freud: A Non-Exceptionalist Approach to Race, Class, and Gender in the Slave South," both in *Southern History across the Color Line* (Chapel Hill: University of North Carolina Press, 2002), 15–39, 93–111; Stephanie J. Shaw, "Mothering under Slavery in the Antebellum South," in *Mothering: Ideology, Experience, and Agency*, ed. Evelyn N. Glenn, Grace Chang, and Linda R. Forcey (New York: Routledge, 1994), 237–58, esp. 237, 245; Sharla M. Fett, *Working Cures: Healing, Health, and Power on Southern Slave Plantations* (Chapel Hill: University of North Carolina Press, 2002); Jennifer L. Morgan, *Laboring Women*, 9–11, 69–106, 144–65.

30. Camp, *Closer to Freedom*, 7–8, 12–34; Stephanie McCurry, *Masters of Small Worlds: Yeoman Households, Gender Relations, and the Political Culture of the Antebellum South Carolina Low Country* (New York: Oxford University Press, 1995), 19–30, 112–18. See also Kirsten E. Wood, *Masterful Women: Slaveholding Widows from the American Revolution through the Civil War* (Chapel Hill: University of North Carolina Press, 2004), 2–5.

31. Genovese, *Roll, Jordan, Roll*, esp. 3–7, 89–93, 281–84, 661–65; Elizabeth Fox-Genovese, *Within the Plantation Household: Black and White Women of the Old South* (Chapel Hill: University of North Carolina Press, 1988), 24–32, 66–70, 82–99, 131–34, 178–86; Willie Lee Rose, "The Domestication of Domestic Slavery," in *Slavery and Freedom*, ed. William W. Freehling (Oxford: Oxford University Press, 1982), 18–36; Drew Gilpin Faust, *James Henry Hammond and the Old South: A*

Design for Mastery (Baton Rouge: Louisiana State University Press, 1982), 69–104; Peter Kolchin, "Reevaluating the Antebellum Slave Community: A Comparative Perspective," *JAH* 70 (December 1983): 579–601; Peter Kolchin, *Unfree Labor: American Slavery and Russian Serfdom* (Cambridge: Harvard University Press, 1987), 195–241; Peter Kolchin, *American Slavery, 1619–1877*, rev. ed. (New York: Hill and Wang, 2003), 148–53. For a probing critique of paternalism that also challenges the concept of autonomy, see Saidiya V. Hartman, *Scenes of Subjection: Terror, Slavery, and Self-Making in Nineteenth-Century America* (New York: Oxford University Press, 1997), esp. 53.

32. Scholars have long noticed a difference in tone in the master-slave relation between the Atlantic seaboard and the Old Southwest. For recent elaborations on this theme, see James Oakes, *The Ruling Race: A History of American Slaveholders* (New York: Knopf, 1982), 76–95; Joan E. Cashin, *A Family Venture: Men and Women on the Southern Frontier* (New York: Oxford University Press, 1991). For varied attempts to reconcile paternalism and bourgeois liberalism in the ideology of planters, see James Oakes, *Slavery and Freedom: An Interpretation of the Old South* (New York: Knopf, 1990); Douglas R. Egerton, "Markets without a Market Revolution: Southern Planters and Capitalism," *Journal of the Early Republic* 16 (Summer 1996): 207–21; Mark M. Smith, *Mastered by the Clock: Time, Slavery, and Freedom in the American South* (Chapel Hill: University of North Carolina Press, 1997); Christopher Morris, "The Articulation of Two Worlds: The Master-Slave Relationship Reconsidered," *JAH* 85 (December 1998): 982–1007; Walter Johnson, *Soul by Soul: Life Inside the Antebellum Slave Market* (Cambridge: Harvard University Press, 1999), 24–41, 102–15; Jeffrey R. Young, *Domesticating Slavery: The Master Class in Georgia and South Carolina, 1670–1837* (Chapel Hill: University of North Carolina Press, 1999); Ariela J. Gross, *Double Character: Slavery and Mastery in the Antebellum Southern Courtroom* (Princeton: Princeton University Press, 2000).

33. Genovese, *Roll, Jordan, Roll*, 148–49.

34. Ranajit Guha, *Elementary Aspects of Peasant Insurgency in Colonial India* (Delhi, India: Oxford University Press, 1983); James C. Scott, *Weapons of the Weak: Everyday Forms of Peasant Resistance* (New Haven: Yale University Press, 1985); Scott, *Domination and the Arts of Resistance*; Florencia Mallon, *Peasant and Nation: The Making of Postcolonial Mexico and Peru* (Berkeley: University of California Press, 1995); Steven Hahn, *A Nation Under Our Feet: Black Political Struggles in the Rural South from Slavery to the Great Migration* (Cambridge: Harvard University Press, 2003).

35. C. Vann Woodward, "The Search for Southern Identity," in *The Burden of Southern History*, 3rd ed. (Baton Rouge: Louisiana State University Press, 1993), 3–25, esp. 22–24; Carl N. Degler, *Place over Time: The Continuity of Southern Distinctiveness* (Baton Rouge: Louisiana State University Press, 1977); Michael O'Brien, *The Idea of the American South, 1920–1941* (Baltimore: Johns Hopkins University Press, 1979); Jimmie Franklin, "Black Southerners, Shared Experience, and Place: A Reflection," *JSH* 60 (February 1994): 3–18.

36. For a fine recent synthesis of this literature, see Ira Berlin, *Generations of Captivity: A History of African American Slaves* (Cambridge: Harvard University Press, 2003).

37. Dell Upton, "Black and White Landscapes in Eighteenth Century Virginia," *Places: A Quarterly Journal of Environmental Design* 2 (Winter 1985): 59–72; Dell Upton, "New Views of the Virginia Landscape," *Virginia Magazine of History and Biography* 96 (October 1988): 403–70; Vlach, *Back of the Big House*; Elsa Barkley Brown, "Negotiating and Transforming the Public Sphere: African American Political Life in the Transition from Slavery to Freedom," *Public Culture* 7 (Fall 1994): 107–46; Elsa Barkley Brown and Gregg D. Kimball, "Mapping the Terrain of Black Richmond, 1852–1915," *Journal of Urban History* 21 (March 1995): 296–346; Mary P. Ryan, *Civic Wars: Democracy and Public Life in the American City during the Nineteenth Century* (Berkeley: University of California Press, 1997); McCurry, *Masters of Small Worlds*; Camp, *Closer to Freedom*; Walker, *No More, No More*, 19–58; Rebecca J. Griffin, " 'Goin' Back over to See That Girl': Competing Social Spaces in the Lives of the Enslaved in Antebellum North Carolina," *Slavery and Abolition* 25 (April 2004): 94–113.

38. On the Southern Claims Commission records, see Penningroth, *Claims of Kinfolk*, 1–12; Frank W. Klingberg, *The Southern Claims Commission* (Berkeley: University of California Press, 1955), vii, 85, 124, 170–73. The commission disallowed nearly 60 percent of all cases on which it ruled, frequently on the basis of testimony by former slaves. As a result, disallowed claims appealed to the U.S. Court of Claims often contain valuable testimony from former slaves. Files include original testimony taken by the Southern Claims Commission as well as subsequent testimony submitted by claimants exclusively to the court. See USCC.

39. See CWPF.

40. Anthony Giddens, *The Constitution of Society: Outline of the Theory of Structuration* (Berkeley: University of California Press, 1984). For a useful critical introduction, see Stephen Loyal, *The Sociology of Anthony Giddens* (London: Pluto, 2003). For recent discussions of the problem of agency in American social history, see Barbara J. Fields, "Whiteness, Racism, and Identity," *International Labor and Working-Class History* 60 (Fall 2001): 48–56; Walter Johnson, "On Agency," *Journal of Social History* 37 (Fall 2003): 113–24.

41. Noralee Frankel, *Freedom's Women: Black Women and Families in Civil War Era Mississippi* (Bloomington: Indiana University Press, 1999); Nancy D. Bercaw, *Gendered Freedoms: Race, Rights, and the Politics of Household in the Delta, 1861–1875* (Gainesville: University Press of Florida, 2003); Laura F. Edwards, *Gendered Strife and Confusion: The Political Culture of Reconstruction* (Urbana: University of Illinois Press, 1997); Leslie A. Schwalm, *A Hard Fight for We: Women's Transition from Slavery to Freedom in South Carolina* (Urbana: University of Illinois Press, 1997); Elizabeth Regosin, *Freedom's Promise: Ex-Slave Families and Citizenship in the Age of Emancipation* (Charlottesville: University Press of Virginia, 2002); Shaffer, *After the*

Glory. Work on the welfare state includes Theda Skocpol, *Protecting Soldiers and Mothers: The Political Origins of Social Policy in the United States* (Cambridge: Harvard University Press, 1992); Ann S. Orloff, *The Politics of Pensions: A Comparative Analysis of Britain, Canada, and the United States, 1880–1940* (Madison: University of Wisconsin Press, 1993); on demographic change, see Robert W. Fogel, "New Sources and New Techniques for the Study of Secular Trends in Nutritional Status, Health, Mortality, and the Process of Aging," *Historical Methods* 26 (Winter 1993): 5–6, 21–29; Dora L. Costa, "Height, Weight, Wartime Stress, and Older Age Mortality: Evidence from the Union Army Records," *Explorations in Economic History* 30 (October 1993): 424–49; Dora L. Costa, *The Evolution of Retirement: An American Economic History, 1880–1990* (Chicago: University of Chicago Press, 1998).

42. For some cogent observations about slaves' intimate relations and families based on the pension files, see Gutman, *Black Family*, 238, 585–86 n. 9; Schwalm, *Hard Fight for We*, 51–53, 288 n. 33; Frankel, *Freedom's Women*, 8–13. For quantitative analysis of pension files, see Richard H. Steckel, "Slave Marriage and the Family," *Journal of Family History* 5 (Winter 1980): 406–21.

43. To get some sense of the dimensions of the testimony by former slaves in the pension records, consider that nearly 179,000 African Americans served in the Civil War, more than 135,000 of them from slave states. One study suggests that about half of all African American soldiers had pension files. In Donald R. Shaffer's random sample of 1,044 black soldiers, pension applications were filed under the name of 534 soldiers, or 51.1 percent. See Ira Berlin, Joseph P. Reidy, and Leslie Rowland, eds., *The Black Military Experience*, ser. 2 of *Freedom: A Documentary History of Emancipation, 1861–1867* (Cambridge: Cambridge University Press, 1982), 12, table 1; Shaffer, *After the Glory*, appendix, 203.

44. John W. Oliver, "History of the Civil War Military Pensions, 1861–1865," *Bulletin of the University of Wisconsin: History Series* 4 (1917): 10, 15–21, 27.

45. Ibid., 36–37, 61–71, 87–89; Skocpol, *Protecting Soldiers and Mothers*, 110, 115–21; Orloff, *Politics of Pensions*, 136, table 4.1.

46. William H. Glasson, *History of Military Pension Legislation in the United States* (New York: Columbia University Press, 1900), 114–16; Skocpol, *Protecting Soldiers and Mothers*, 111; Dora L. Costa, *Evolution of Retirement*, 36–37, 197–98, 212.

47. Eligible pensioners were obliged to connect ailments to military service under the Arrears Act, merely to prove they had served under the Dependent Pension Act. Oliver, "History of the Civil War Military Pensions," 10, 15–21, 27.

48. Dora L. Costa, *Evolution of Retirement*, 33–35, 197–98.

49. Skocpol, *Protecting Soldiers and Mothers*, 116.

50. Oliver, "History of the Civil War Military Pensions," 11, 16, 33, 49–50, 98–101; Skocpol, *Protecting Soldiers and Mothers*, 116.

51. John H. Wager to Sir, 23 March 1875, Thomas Scott File, Widow's Certificate

129600; W. A. Pless to Hon. Commissioner of Pensions, 9 January 1899, Henry Brown File, Widow's Applications 167916, 572357, CWPF.

52. Will Press to Hon. Commissioner of Pensions, 9 January 1899, Fountain Ballard, Deposition, 5 January 1899, James Wright, General Affidavit, 8 December 1893, Daniel Robinson File, Invalid's Certificate 580256, CWPF.

53. Charity Smith and Israel Taylor, Depositions, 13 January 1886, James Dickson and William Jefferson, Depositions, 14 January 1886, John Smith File, Widow's Application 194940; Mahala Knox, Deposition, 27 September 1886, James H. Clements to Hon. John C. Black, 27 September 1886, William Knox File, Widow's Certificate 197339, CWPF.

54. Delila Clasby, Deposition, 3 October 1884, Elisha Clasby File, Widow's Certificate 232233, CWPF. For Clasby's testimony about her enduring bond to her first husband, hanged for his part in killing an overseer, see chap. 2.

55. Most affidavits were filed with the Pension Bureau on forms labeled "Additional Evidence," "Claimant's Affidavit," or "General Affidavit." For witnesses who denied statements that appeared over their name in affidavits, see Frank Yates, Deposition, 21 December 1896, Ransom Brantley, Deposition, 24 December 1896, Robert Lloyd File, Invalid's Certificate 557039; Julius Simmons, Deposition, 6 June 1885, Adam Butler File (alias Adam Phillips), Minor's Certificate 216035; Charles Harvey, Deposition, 23 June 1906, Burris Mitchell File, Widow's Application 768436; William A. House, Deposition, 4 May 1895, Alice Dorsey, Deposition, 23 April 1895, Nelson Grooms File, Minor's Certificate 413156, CWPF. Citations to "Affidavits" refer to handwritten testimony, sworn to before a court clerk, sometimes to correct errors in previous affidavits submitted on bureau forms.

56. The bureau employed nearly 400 special examiners in 1884 (Oliver, "History of the Civil War Military Pensions," 83–85). When examiners neglected to label a document, they are identified in the notes in brackets: for example, [Exhibit].

57. Widow's Claim for Pension, 30 August 1879, William Madison File, Widow's Certificate 232198, CWPF.

58. Mary Ann Madison, Deposition, 24 January 1887, ibid.

59. Ibid.

60. Frank Humphrey, Deposition, 28 January 1887, Rose Ballard, Deposition, 13 February 1887, ibid.

61. Mary Ann Madison, Deposition, 18 February 1887, ibid.

62. Edwin M. Clarke to Hon. John C. Clark, 22 February 1887, ibid.

63. On the necessity of comparing evidence from different types of sources, see John W. Blassingame, "Using the Testimony of Ex-Slaves: Approaches and Problems," *JSH* 41 (November 1965): 473–92.

64. Degler, *Place over Time*, 67–69; Edward E. Baptist, *Creating an Old South: Middle Florida's Plantation Frontier before the Civil War* (Chapel Hill: University of North Carolina Press, 2002), 2–7, 247–56.

Chapter One

1. Thomas R. Gray, "The Confessions of Nat Turner," in *The Southampton Slave Revolt of 1831: A Compilation of Source Material*, ed. Henry Irving Tragle (Amherst: University of Massachusetts Press, 1971), 307.
2. Matthew 6:33.
3. Thomas R. Gray, "Confessions of Nat Turner," 308.
4. Patrick H. Breen, "A Prophet in His Own Land: Support for Nat Turner and His Rebellion within Southampton's Black Community," in *Nat Turner: A Slave Rebellion in History and Memory*, ed. Kenneth S. Greenberg (New York: Oxford University Press, 2003), 109–10; David F. Allmendinger Jr., "The Construction of *The Confessions of Nat Turner*," in *Nat Turner: A Slave Rebellion in History and Memory*, ed. Kenneth S. Greenberg (New York: Oxford University Press, 2003), 39.
5. Turner's quotation of the Spirit also paraphrased Luke 12:47.
6. Thomas R. Gray, "Confessions of Nat Turner," 308; Exodus 15:24, 16:2, 17:3.
7. Thomas C. Parramore, *Southampton County, Virginia* (Charlottesville: University Press of Virginia, 1978), 78–79, 85, 247 n. 42; Thomas C. Parramore, "Covenant in Jerusalem," in *Nat Turner: A Slave Rebellion in History and Memory*, ed. Kenneth S. Greenberg (New York: Oxford University Press, 2003), 63. Turner obliquely identified these four men with the neighborhood, counting them among those from whom he had kept aloof "years before" (Thomas R. Gray, "Confessions of Nat Turner," 309–10).
8. Allan Kulikoff, *Tobacco and Slaves: The Development of Southern Cultures in the Chesapeake, 1680–1800* (Chapel Hill: University of North Carolina Press, 1986), 330–32; Allan Kulikoff, "The Origins of Afro-American Society in Tidewater Maryland and Virginia, 1700–1790," *WMQ*, 3rd ser., 35 (April 1978): 242, 246, 250; Philip D. Morgan, *Slave Counterpoint: Black Culture in the Eighteenth-Century Chesapeake and Lowcountry* (Chapel Hill: University of North Carolina Press, 1998), 524–30; Lorena S. Walsh, *From Calabar to Carter's Grove: The History of a Virginia Slave Community* (Charlottesville: University Press of Virginia, 1997), xix, 42–50, 223.
9. The proportion of slaves living on plantations with more than twenty slaves also increased from 10 percent to 29 percent between the 1700s and the 1770s. Philip D. Morgan, *Slave Counterpoint*, 41, table 2; Allan Kulikoff, *The Agrarian Roots of American Capitalism* (Charlottesville: University Press of Virginia, 1992), 229–31, 244–45.
10. Kulikoff, "Origins of Afro-American Society," 251–54. John T. Schlotterbeck has observed that in Virginia after 1750, the "unit of the slave community" was the neighborhood, which comprised adjoining plantations ("The Internal Economy of Slavery in Rural Piedmont Virginia," in *The Slaves' Economy: Independent Production by Slaves in the Americas*, ed. Ira Berlin and Philip D. Morgan [London: Cass, 1991], 172). For further evidence on cross-plantation ties, see Philip D. Morgan, *Slave Counterpoint*, 473, 475–76, 522; Ira Berlin, *Many Thousands Gone: The First Two*

Centuries of Slavery in North America (Cambridge: Harvard University Press, 1998), 316; Marvin L. M. Kay and Lorin L. Cary, *Slavery in North Carolina, 1748–1775* (Chapel Hill: University of North Carolina Press, 1995), 163–64. One scholar has argued that by 1730, slaves had made a habit of planning insurrections under the cover of ostensibly social occasions that convened bondmen from different plantations. The evidence adduced, however, is inconclusive. See Anthony S. Parent Jr., *Foul Means: The Formation of a Slave Society in Virginia, 1660–1740* (Chapel Hill: University of North Carolina Press, 2003), 147–62.

11. John W. Blassingame, ed., *Slave Testimony: Two Centuries of Letters, Speeches, Interviews, and Autobiographies* (Baton Rouge: Louisiana State University Press, 1977), 130, 128.

12. Ibid., 138–39, 141.

13. Ibid., 134. Slaveholders were aware that the terms of discipline on other plantations impacted the terms of struggle on their own places. See Elizabeth Fox-Genovese and Eugene D. Genovese, *The Mind of the Master Class: History and Faith in the Southern Slaveholders' Worldview* (Cambridge: Cambridge University Press, 2005), 373.

14. Blassingame, *Slave Testimony*, 136.

15. Ibid., 155, 151, 158, 163–64.

16. Ibid., 160–61.

17. Ibid., 158, 161–62. Planters made much of instances in which they disciplined cruel masters in their vicinity, but such instances were, in fact, exceedingly rare. See Fox-Genovese and Genovese, *Mind of the Master Class*, 374–79.

18. Elizabeth Green, Deposition, 16 May 1895, G. E. Brown to Commissioner of Pensions Hon. William Lochren, 12 July 1895, Widow's Certificate 417873, CWPF, #P-72, FSSP.

19. Frederick Douglass, *My Bondage and My Freedom* (1855; reprint, Urbana: University of Illinois Press, 1987), 27–28.

20. Blassingame, *Slave Testimony*, 216.

21. According to the most widely accepted estimate of the volume of the slave migration, with owners and via the interregional trade combined, 287,831 went to the Deep South during the 1830s; 188,863 during the 1840s; 250,637 during the 1850s (Michael Tadman, *Speculators and Slaves: Masters, Traders, and Slaves in the Old South* [Madison: University of Wisconsin Press, 1989], 5–12, table 2.1). For the formulation of the migration to the Old Southwest as a second middle passage, see Ira Berlin, *Generations of Captivity: A History of African-American Slaves* (Cambridge: Harvard University Press, 2003), 161–63; Don H. Doyle, *Faulkner's County: The Historical Roots of Yoknapatawpha* (Chapel Hill: University of North Carolina Press, 2001), 127–31.

22. Robert W. Fogel and Stanley L. Engerman, *Time on the Cross: The Economics of American Negro Slavery* (1974; reprint, New York: Norton, 1989), 47; Tadman, *Speculators and Slaves*, 21.

23. Steven Deyle, *Carry Me Back: The Domestic Slave Trade in American Life* (New York: Oxford University Press, 2005), 99, 103–5, 147–48; Frederic Bancroft, *Slave Trading in the Old South* (1931; New York: Ungar, 1959), 300–305; Jim Barnett and H. Clark Burkett, "The Forks of the Road Slave Market at Natchez," *JMH* 63 (2001): 169–87.

24. Herbert Gutman and Richard Sutch, "The Slave Family: Protected Agent of Capitalist Masters or Victim of the Slave Trade?" in *Reckoning with Slavery: A Critical Study in the Quantitative History Of American Negro Slavery* (New York: Oxford University Press, 1976), 101–4, 110–32; Herbert G. Gutman, *The Black Family in Slavery and Freedom, 1750–1925* (New York: Vintage, 1976), 129–55; Tadman, *Speculators and Slaves*, 141–60; Brenda E. Stevenson, "Distress and Discord in Virginia Slave Families, 1830–1860," in *In Joy and In Sorrow: Women, Family, and Marriage in the Victorian South*, ed. Carol Bleser (New York: Oxford University Press, 1990), 104–10; Brenda E. Stevenson, *Life in Black and White: Family and Community in the Slave South* (New York: Oxford University Press, 1996), 172–76, 181–82, 204–8, 223–25, 233–35, 256–57; Anne Patton Malone, *Sweet Chariot: Slave Family and Household Structure in Nineteenth-Century Louisiana* (Chapel Hill: University of North Carolina Press, 1992), 207–17.

25. For the argument that slave traders and migrating planters took a similar toll on slave families, see Edward E. Baptist, *Creating an Old South: Middle Florida's Plantation Frontier before the Civil War* (Chapel Hill: University of North Carolina Press, 2002), 66–67.

26. Tadman, *Speculators and Slaves*, 136, 141–43, 147–51.

27. Joan E. Cashin, *A Family Venture: Men and Women on the Southern Frontier* (Baltimore: Johns Hopkins University Press, 1994), 50.

28. These percentages combine Tadman's estimate that slave traders conveyed 60–70 percent of migrants to the Deep South and Pritchett's estimate, based on a regression analysis of Tadman's data, that the traders' share was about half (Tadman, *Speculators and Slaves*, 31; Jonathan B. Pritchett, "Quantitative Estimates of the United States Interregional Slave Trade, 1820–1860," *Journal of Economic History* 61 [June 2001]: 467–75).

29. After the Civil War, Rachel Tilden sought a pension as the widow of a Union soldier, Jerry Moore (Rachel Moore, Exhibit, 18 March 1875, Samuel Wilkins and Burrel [Burl] Lewis, "Additional Evidence," 19 March 1869, Jerry Moore File, Widow's Certificate 127426, CWPF).

30. After the Hartwells returned to Tennessee in 1888, Hartwell told the story to their employer, B. F. Johnson, who related it to the Pension Bureau. However, the bureau failed to decide the claim of Hartwell's widow before her death (B. F. Johnson, General Affidavit, 13 March 1890, Warrick Hartwell File, Widow's Application 417332, CWPF). On slaves' ability to influence the terms of sale in the domestic slave trade, see Walter Johnson, *Soul by Soul: Life Inside the Antebellum Slave Market* (Cambridge: Harvard University Press, 1999), 59, 162–88.

31. Deyle, *Carry Me Back*, 98–107, 110–11, 145–49.

32. Expenses of Traveling with Negroes from VA to Miss, 24 October–26 December 1834, James A. Mitchell Papers, ser. E, RASP; map of Virginia, Maryland, and Delaware and map of Kentucky and Tennessee, both in David H. Burr, *The American Atlas* (London: Arrowsmith, 1839).

33. Slave Rental Contract, 21 January 1836, Joseph T. Hicks to Samuel Smith Downey, 27 February 1836, Samuel Smith Downey Papers, ser. F, RASP.

34. In addition to the examples that appear in this chapter, see Jno. R. Gwyn, Deposition, 5 April 1842; Quitman and McMurran, Memorandum, 23 September 1842, Correspondence and Financial and Legal Items, Quitman Family Papers, ser. J, RASP; Henry Watson, *Narrative of Henry Watson, a Fugitive Slave* (Boston: Marsh, 1848), 10, EE. On the effects of yellow fever on migrants during the early republic, see Adam Rothman, *Slave Country: American Expansion and the Origins of the Deep South* (Cambridge: Harvard University Press, 2005), 184, 188–90.

35. Joseph T. Hicks to Samuel Smith Downey, 27 February 1836, 28 March 1836, 27 July 1836, Downey Papers, RASP.

36. Joseph T. Hicks to Samuel Smith Downey, 14 May 1836, 14 July 1836, ibid.

37. Joseph T. Hicks to Samuel Smith Downey, 25 August 1836, ibid. A yellow fever epidemic struck Natchez the following year, when 207 people died (D. Clayton James, *Antebellum Natchez* [Baton Rouge: Louisiana State University Press, 1968], 257).

38. Joseph T. Hicks to Samuel Smith Downey, 27 February 1836, 14 July 1836, Downey Papers, RASP.

39. Joseph T. Hicks to Samuel Smith Downey, 14 May 1836, 14 July 1836, ibid.

40. For a discussion of Knight and a racist discourse of "acclimation," see Walter Johnson, *Soul by Soul*, 139–40.

41. Jno. Knight to Wm. M. Beall, 30 June 1844, John Knight Papers, ser. F, RASP.

42. Deyle, *Carry Me Back*, 56–57, 103, 130, 135–36, 159.

43. Jno. Knight to William M. Beal, 12 August 1844, 22 May 1845, Knight Papers, RASP.

44. Deyle, *Carry Me Back*, 145, 157–73, 291–96, appendix B.

45. Mary Ann Madison, Depositions, 24 January 1887, 18 February 1887, Rose Ballard, Deposition, 13 February 1887, Eugenia Mullins, Deposition, 16 February 1887, William Madison File, Widow's Certificate 232198, CWPF.

46. Jno. Knight to Wm. M. Beall, 16 February 1835, 7 October 1837, Knight Papers, RASP.

47. Randolph B. Campbell, "Slavery in the Natchez Trace Collection," in *Inside the Natchez Trace Collection*, ed. Katherine J. Adams and Lewis L. Gould (Baton Rouge: Louisiana State University Press, 1999), 38; Richard Holcombe Jr., *Debt, Investment, Slaves: Credit Relations in East Feliciana Parish, Louisiana, 1825–1885* (Tuscaloosa: University of Alabama Press, 1995), 20, 25, 39, 49–74; Deyle, *Carry Me Back*, 160–61.

48. John Nevitt Diary, 6–7 January 1831, 21 January 1832, ser. J, RASP.

49. By then, Turner was managing Palmyra plantation for his brother in-law, John A. Quitman (Sold to Charles L. Longcope by Ballard Franklin, 24 November 1836, Receipt of Jno. R. George, 10 December 1842, Quitman Family Papers, RASP). For a discussion of this transaction from the standpoint of Turner, Quitman, and slave trader Rice Ballard, see Ariela J. Gross, *Double Character: Slavery and Mastery in the Antebellum Southern Courtroom* (Princeton: Princeton University Press, 2000), 57–61.

50. See appendix, table A.1.

51. James D. Douglass Estate to James Derrah[?], 2 November 1838, James D. Douglass Papers; Estate of Joseph Devenport to Sid Hawkins, 3 March 1861, Joseph Devenport Papers; Benjamin Roach to Warren County Jails, 14 May 1855, Ben Roach to the Jail of Claiborne County, 21 June 1855, Benjamin Roach Family Papers, NTC.

52. 20 Slaves Sold, Public Notice Enclosed in Doctor A. P. Merrill to John Henderson, 1 February 1833, Robert Moore Papers; John C. Jenkins to Dear Sir, 4 January 1836, John Carmichael Jenkins Family Papers; Henry S. Allen Jr. Papers, NTC.

53. For examples of planters on adjoining plantations appointed as commissioners to settle estates, see Estate of Simeon Gibson, 6 August 1841, Estates of William and Sarah Rowan, 9 March 1841, Estate of C. Stephen Smith, 18 December 1841, ACPRER, 1:81–84, 85, 91, 99–103.

54. Benjamin Roach to Warren County Jails, 14 May 1855, Benjamin Roach Bought of Daniel Swett, 18 June 1855, Ben Roach to the Jail of Claiborne County, 21 June 1855, Estate B. Roach to Steamer P. C. Wallis, 28 July 1855, Estate of Benj. Roach to Daniel Swett, 15 December 1855, Sale of 25 Negroes, 29 December 1855, Probate Records, Roach Family Papers, NTC; William K. Scarborough, *Masters of the Big House: Elite Slaveholders of the Mid-Nineteenth-Century South* (Baton Rouge: Louisiana State University Press, 2003), 445, 468, appendixes C, D.

55. On the slave trade as a definitive feature of antebellum slavery, see Tadman, *Speculators and Slaves*, xv, 9–10; Norrece T. Jones Jr., *Born a Child of Freedom, Yet a Slave: Mechanisms of Control and Strategies of Resistance in Antebellum South Carolina* (Hanover, N.H.: University Press of New England, 1990), 3, 37–63; Walter Johnson, *Soul by Soul*; Berlin, *Generations of Captivity*, 159–244; Deyle, *Carry Me Back*.

56. A Pension Bureau investigator recorded Mrs. Perryman's name as "Payriman," using a phonetic spelling of her pronunciation. Lettie P[erry]man and Mitchell Howard, Depositions, 25 May 1900, Zachariah Thomas and Silas Burt, Depositions, 1 June 1900, Robert Johnson File, Widow's Certificate 207202, CWPF.

57. Lettie P[erry]man, Deposition, 25 May 1900, ibid.; Robert Johnson File, Widow's Certificate 207202; John Wilkes, Deposition, 18 January 1897, Robert Banks File, Invalid's Certificate 872427; Sancho L[l]oyd and Robert L[l]oyd, General Affidavit, 21 December 1895, Sunday Gardner File, Sister's Application 359652; Severn Woods, Deposition, 26 December 1896, Robert Lloyd File, Invalid's Certificate

557039; Sancho Lloyd, Deposition, 21 December 1889, Sancho Lloyd File, Invalid's Application 541771; Eliza Harris, Deposition, 1 October 1884, Elisha Clasby File, Widow's Certificate 232233, CWPF.

58. James C. Cobb, *The Most Southern Place on Earth: The Mississippi Delta and the Roots of Regional Identity* (New York: Oxford University Press, 1992), 3; Sam Bowers Hilliard, *Atlas of Antebellum Southern Agriculture* (Baton Rouge: Louisiana State University Press, 1984), maps 32−38.

59. Charles Lyell, *A Second Visit to the United States of North America* (London: Murray, 1849), 2:205−6, 214; Eugene W. Hilgard, *Report on the Geology and Agriculture of the State of Mississippi* (Jackson, Miss.: Barksdale, 1860), 313−17, 323; Benjamin L. C. Wailes, *Report on the Agriculture and Geology of Mississippi: Embracing a Sketch of the Social and Natural History of the State* (Jackson, Miss.: Barksdale, 1854), 352−53.

60. Wailes, *Report on Agriculture and Geology*, 312−13, 315−21, 325−28; Mark M. Smith, *Listening to Nineteenth-Century America* (Chapel Hill: University of North Carolina Press, 2001), 19.

61. John James Audubon, *Writings and Drawings*, ed. Christopher Irmscher (New York: Library of America, 1999), 231−32, 739−40; Wailes, *Report on Agriculture and Geology*, 314−15, 318−19, 322−23, 326.

62. See appendix, table A.1.

63. John M. Vlach, *Back of the Big House: The Architecture of Plantation Slavery* (Chapel Hill: University of North Carolina Press, 1993), 33−122.

64. Estate of Peter Bisland, Map of Oakland, April 1839, Estate of Simeon Gibson, Map, 2 July 1841, Estates of William and Sarah Rowan, Maps of Lands Assigned to J. R. Rowan, Mary Rowan, Thos Rowan, February 1837, Estate of C. Stephen Smith, Allotment of Dower, 18 December 1841, ACPRER, 1:3−4, 81−82, 85−89, 102; Land Survey of Adams County, Township 7, Range 1 West, 13 May 1846, MA A2 1800 d4, Real Property Map of Jefferson County, 9 March 1832, MA B2 JE, Cartographic Collection, MDAH.

65. Some archaeologists analyze the organization of plantation space in terms of "social control." See Charles E. Oser Jr., "Toward a Theory of Power for Historical Archaeology: Plantations and Space," in *The Recovery of Meaning: Historical Archaeology in the Eastern United States*, ed. Mark P. Leone and Parker B. Potter Jr. (Washington, D.C.: Smithsonian Institution Press, 1988), 313−43; Brian W. Thomas, "Power and Community: The Archaeology of Slavery at the Hermitage Plantation," *American Antiquity* 63 (October 1998): 531−51. My analysis of neighborhood suggests, however, that the organization of space is less important than how it is used and interpreted. Furthermore, in the Natchez District, the plantation was only part of the social terrain, which slaves extended to adjoining plantations and conceptualized in terms of neighborhood. From this point of view, scholars of the colonial Chesapeake who have emphasized how different classes interpreted the same landscape in different ways have made a signal contribution. See Rhys Isaac,

The Transformation of Virginia, 1740–1790 (Chapel Hill: University of North Carolina Press, 1982); Dell Upton, "Black and White Landscapes in Eighteenth Century Virginia," *Places: A Quarterly Journal of Environmental Design* 2 (Winter 1985): 59–72; Terrence W. Epperson, "Constructing Difference: The Social and Spatial Order of the Chesapeake Plantation," in *"I, Too, Am America": Archaeological Studies of African-American Life*, ed. Theresa A. Singleton (Charlottesville: University Press of Virginia, 1999), 159–72.

66. Nevitt Diary, 25–26 March 1830; Everard Green Baker Diary, 28 June 1854, ser. J, RASP; Diary, 12, 14, 18 April 1859, Benjamin L. C. Wailes Papers; Walter Wade Plantation Diary, 9, 25, 28 January 1854, MDAH.

67. Estate of Peter Bisland, Plan of Fairfield, 18 May 1839, ACPRER, 1:4.

68. Vlach, *Back of the Big House*, 231.

69. Shane White and Graham White, *The Sounds of Slavery: Discovering African American History through Songs, Sermons, and Speech* (Boston: Beacon, 2005), 1–2, 5; Mark M. Smith, *Listening to Nineteenth-Century America*, 34, 38, 77; Vlach, *Back of the Big House*, 124.

70. Isaac, *Transformation of Virginia*, 52–53.

71. Estate of Peter Bisland, Estate of C. Stephen Smith, ACPRER, 1:1–4, 99–102, 134.

72. Estate of William and Sarah Rowan, Estate of Simeon Gibson, Estate of Katherine Minor, 21 December 1846[?], ACPRER, 1:81–89, 507–8. For examples in South Carolina and Virginia, see Joyce E. Chaplin, *An Anxious Pursuit: Agrarian Innovation and Technology in the Lower South, 1730–1815* (Chapel Hill: University of North Carolina Press, 1993), 270–73; Walsh, *Calabar to Carter's Grove*, 10–14.

73. On slaveholders' neighborhoods, see Robert Kenzer, *Kinship and Neighborhood in a Southern Community: Orange County, North Carolina, 1849–1881* (Knoxville: University of Tennessee Press, 1987); Stephanie McCurry, *Masters of Small Worlds: Yeoman Households, Gender Relations, and the Political Culture of the Antebellum South Carolina Low Country* (New York: Oxford University Press, 1995), 24–26, 116–21; Edward E. Baptist, "The Migration of Planters to Antebellum Florida: Kinship and Power," *JSH* 62 (August 1996): 527–54; Carolyn Earle Billingsley, *Communities of Kinship: Antebellum Families and the Settlement of the Cotton Frontier* (Athens: University of Georgia Press, 2004), 4, 47–51.

74. Christopher J. Olsen, *Political Culture and Secession in Mississippi: Masculinity, Honor, and the Antiparty Tradition, 1830–1860* (New York: Oxford University Press, 2000), 6, 71–120, 138–44, 164–67; Daniel W. Crofts, *Old Southampton: Politics and Society in a Virginia County, 1834–1869* (Charlottesville: University Press of Virginia, 1992), 126–31, 154–64; Drew Gilpin Faust, *James Henry Hammond and the Old South: A Design for Mastery* (Baton Rouge: Louisiana State University Press, 1982), 131.

75. Olsen, *Political Culture and Secession*, 118.

76. Christopher Morris, *Becoming Southern: The Evolution of a Way of Life, Warren County and Vicksburg, Mississippi, 1770–1860* (New York: Oxford University Press, 1995), 85–91.

77. Ibid., 143–45, 153–55. On road construction and neighborhoods, see also Warren R. Hofstra, *The Planting of New Virginia: Settlement and Landscape in the Shenandoah Valley* (Baltimore: Johns Hopkins University Press, 2004), 146–60.

78. The process of extending the scale of social relations played out across the South and the United States during the antebellum period. See Richard D. Brown, *Modernization: The Transformation of American Life, 1600–1865* (New York: Hill and Wang, 1976), 97, 122–33, 142–43.

79. In 1842 a newspaper editor lamented the propensity of big planters, the "one-thousand-bale planters," to bypass Natchez in commercial transactions. These planters "sell their cotton in Liverpool; buy their wines in London or Havre; their negro clothing in Boston; their plantation implements and supplies in Cincinnati; and their groceries and fancy articles in New Orleans" (William Banks Taylor, "Southern Yankees: Wealth, High Society, and Political Economy in the Late Antebellum Natchez Region," *JMH* 59 [1997]: 97–121, esp. 115).

80. Cashin, *Family Venture*, 10–22, 85–91; Orville V. Burton, *In My Father's House Are Many Mansions: Family and Community in Edgefield, South Carolina* (Chapel Hill: University of North Carolina Press, 1985), 117–18.

81. On how slaveholders appropriated the law's power over slaves, see Charles S. Sydnor, "The Southerner and the Laws," *JSH* 6 (February 1940): 3–23; David Brion Davis, *The Problem of Slavery in Western Culture* (Ithaca: Cornell University Press, 1969), 31–35; Eugene D. Genovese, *Roll, Jordan, Roll: The World the Slaves Made* (New York: Pantheon, 1974), 3–7, 25–70, 87–97, 661–65; Willie Lee Rose, "The Domestication of Domestic Slavery," in *Slavery and Freedom*, ed. William W. Freehling (New York: Oxford University Press, 1982), 23–25; Peter Kolchin, *American Slavery, 1619–1877*, rev. ed. (New York: Hill and Wang, 2003), 127–32.

82. Gutman, *Black Family*, 123–39; Stevenson, *Life in Black and White*, 213–22.

83. See, for example, Jefferson County Tract Book, Film 1939758, Jefferson County Will Records, Film 1907066, Family History Center, State College, Pennsylvania.

84. On the separation of families in the interregional slave trade, see Gutman and Sutch, "Slave Family"; Tadman, *Speculators and Slaves*, esp. 118–20, 136–51.

85. Bertram Wyatt-Brown, "The Ideal Typology and Ante-Bellum Southern History: A Testing of a New Approach," *Societas* 5 (Winter 1975): 11; Jane Turner Censer, *North Carolina Planters and Their Children, 1800–1860* (Baton Rouge: Louisiana State University Press, 1984), 105–7; Kirsten E. Wood, *Masterful Women: Slaveholding Widows from the American Revolution through the Civil War* (Chapel Hill: University of North Carolina Press, 2004), 29–30.

86. Alice Simpson, Exhibit, 4 February 1875, James Simpson File, Widow's Certificate 168061, CWPF.

87. Manerva Young, Deposition, 24 March 1891, Dennis Douglass File, Widow's Certificate 289245; Joseph Witherspoon, Exhibit, 28 December 1874, Allen Alexander File, Widow's Certificate 97533; Barnett Baily, Deposition, 16 February 1882, John Smith File, Widow's Certificate 199737, CWPF.

88. *Woodville Republican*, 25 December 1830.

89. Lucy Saddler, Deposition, 24 March 1891, Dennis Douglass File, CWPF.

90. Mary Ann Madison, Depositions, 24 January 1887, 18 February 1887, Rose Ballard, Deposition, 13 February 1887, William Madison File, CWPF.

91. Aventine Plantation Diary, 23 January 1854, 6, 20 February 1854, MDAH.

92. On law as both a reflection of the ideology of the planter class and a means of disciplining its members, see Genovese, *Roll, Jordan, Roll*, 25–70; Mark V. Tushnet, *The American Law of Slavery, 1810–1860: Considerations of Humanity and Interest* (Princeton: Princeton University Press, 1981).

93. The fine was $10 for each slave under an 1823 statute, $20 under the code of 1857 (George Poindexter, comp., *The Revised Code of the Laws of Mississippi* [Natchez, Miss.: Baker, 1824], 371, 389; William L. Sharkey, comp., *The Revised Code of the Statute Laws of Mississippi* [Jackson, Miss.: Barksdale, 1857], 244).

94. Frederick Stanton, Exhibit, 24 December 1874, Isaac Sloan Exhibit, 28 December 1874, Allen Alexander File, Widow's Certificate 97553, CWPF.

95. Harriet Willis, Deposition, 18 June 1897, Claiborne Wilson File, Widow's Certificate 449117, CWPF.

96. Harry Alexander, Deposition, 3 October 1884, Elisha Clasby File, Widow's Certificate 232233, CWPF.

97. Emanuel Genifer and James Genifer, [Exhibit], 12 March 1875, Thomas Scott File, Widow's Certificate 129600, CWPF; Testimony of Lewis Johnson, Robert Jones, 29 September 1903, Thomas Y. Berry Claim, Case 11085, USCC.

98. Testimony of Curtis Lockhart, 19 January 1878, John Turner, 18 February 1878, John Alverson Claim, Case 3391, USCC.

99. Winthrop D. Jordan, *Tumult and Silence at Second Creek: An Inquiry into a Civil War Slave Conspiracy* (Baton Rouge: Louisiana State University Press, 1993), 199; George P. Rawick, Jan Hillegas, and Ken Lawrence, eds., *The American Slave: A Composite Autobiography*, supplement ser. 1 (Westport, Conn.: Greenwood, 1977), 9:1490; Eugene D. Genovese, *From Rebellion to Revolution: Afro-American Slave Revolts in the Making of the Modern World* (Baton Rouge: Louisiana State University Press, 1979), 126–28; William K. Scarborough, "Slavery — The White Man's Burden," in *Perspectives and Irony in American Slavery*, ed. Harry P. Owens (Jackson: University Press of Mississippi, 1976), 112.

100. Fonsylvania belonged to Benjamin L. C. Wailes, and adjoining Kensington belonged to his niece (Diary, 26–29 December 1859, Wailes Papers, MDAH; Charles S. Sydnor, *A Gentleman of the Old Natchez Region: Benjamin L. C. Wailes* [Durham, N.C.: Duke University Press, 1938], 92–93). For socializing between

slaves on Dr. James W. Metcalfe's Bourbon and York plantations during the Christmas season, see Bourbon Plantation Journal, 25, 28 December 1847, Metcalfe Family Papers, MDAH.

101. Randy J. Sparks, *On Jordan's Stormy Banks: Evangelicalism in Mississippi, 1773–1876* (Athens: University of Georgia Press, 1994), 68; Mechal Sobel, *Trabelin' On: The Slave Journey to an Afro-Baptist Faith* (Princeton: Princeton University Press, 1988), 187–88; Janet Duitsman Cornelius, *Slave Missions and the Black Church in the Antebellum South* (Columbia: University of South Carolina Press, 1999), 47; Berlin, *Generations of Captivity*, 206–7. On evangelical missions to slaves in the South before 1820, see Sylvia R. Frey and Betty Wood, *Come Shouting to Zion: African American Protestantism in the American South and British Caribbean to 1830* (Chapel Hill: University of North Carolina Press, 1998), 149–81; Christine Leigh Heyrman, *Southern Cross: The Beginnings of the Bible Belt* (New York: Knopf, 1997).

102. Donald G. Mathews, *Religion in the Old South* (Chicago: University of Chicago Press, 1977), 76–78, 150–207; Blake Touchstone, "Planters and Slave Religion in the Deep South," in *Masters and Slaves in the House of the Lord: Race and Religion in the American South*, ed. John B. Boles (Lexington: University Press of Kentucky, 1988), 99–126; Albert J. Raboteau, *Slave Religion: The "Invisible Institution" in the Antebellum South* (Oxford: Oxford University Press, 1978), 144–50, 171–74, 180–204; Cornelius, *Slave Missions*, 31–40, 46–56, 67–68.

103. Rawick, Hillegas, and Lawrence, *American Slave*, 10:2057–59.

104. Mathews, *Religion in the Old South*, 136–84; Cornelius, *Slave Missions*, 35–36, 51–52, 55–56; Frey and Wood, *Come Shouting to Zion*, xiii–xiv.

105. Charles S. Sydnor, *Slavery in Mississippi* (1933; reprint, Baton Rouge: Louisiana State University Press, 1966), 58–59; Touchstone, "Planters and Slave Religion," 103–4, 112–17.

106. Sparks, *On Jordan's Stormy Banks*, 98–104, 116, 127–40; Touchstone, "Planters and Slave Religion," 100; Raboteau, *Slave Religion*, 160–61.

107. A. Hutchinson, comp., *Code of Mississippi* (Jackson, Miss.: Price and Fall, 1848), 534.

108. Cornelius, *Slave Missions*, 62–65.

109. Walter F. Pitts Jr., *Old Ship of Zion: The Afro-Baptist Ritual in the African Diaspora* (New York: Oxford University Press, 1993), 37–38, 47, 50. Cornelius suggests that slaves used the term "hush arbor," while "brush arbor" and "brush harbor" were terms white people used for camp revivals (*Slave Missions*, 9).

110. Rawick, Hillegas, and Lawrence, *American Slave*, 7:623, 1:235; Shane White and White, *Sounds of Slavery*, 62, 108.

111. Cornelius, *Slave Missions*, 8–12.

112. The following discussion on the role of storytelling in the creation of neighborhoods has been informed by J. Nicholas Entrikin, *The Betweenness of Place: Towards a Geography of Modernity* (Baltimore: Johns Hopkins University Press, 1991); Yi-

Fu Tuan, *Space and Place: The Perspective of Experience* (Minneapolis: University Press of Minnesota, 1977), esp. 33, 71–85, 136–40.

113. Lewis Griffin, Deposition, 20 February 1904, Archie Powell (alias Archie Coal) File, Minor's Certificate 576366; Mary Johnson, Deposition, 6 May 1912, Charles Cooper File, Invalid's Certificate 464874, CWPF.

114. Thomas Davis, Exhibit, 22 December 1874, Henry Sellers File, Widow's Certificate 131103, CWPF.

115. Eliza Harris, Missouri Porterfield, Depositions, 1 October 1884, Elisha Clasby File; Iseral Mitchel, Exhibit, 6 February 1875, James Simpson File, CWPF.

116. Joseph Witherspoon, Exhibit, 28 December 1874, Allen Alexander File, CWPF.

117. Land Survey of Adams County, Township 7, Range 1 West, MDAH; Testimony of James A. Fox, 10 December 1873, James A. Fox Claim, Case 10663, SCC; Testimony of Elisha Fox, 6 August 1874, Elisha Fox Claim, Case 3668, USCC.

118. Estate of Peter Bisland, ACPRER, 1:1–2, 44, 134.

119. Jordan, *Tumult and Silence*, 107 n. 16.

120. Sancho L[l]oyd and Robert L[l]oyd, General Affidavit, 21 December 1895, Sunday Gardner File, CWPF.

121. On attempts by slaves, including men on Grove and Palatine, to form alliances beyond neighborhood boundaries, see chaps. 4 and 6.

122. On the multiplicity of collective identities among slaves, see James Sidbury, *Ploughshares into Swords: Race, Rebellion, and Identity in Gabriel's Virginia, 1730–1810* (Cambridge: Cambridge University Press, 1997), 3–6, 38–49.

123. W. E. Thompson to Hon. William Lochren, 3 March 1894, Lucy Waller, Deposition, 20 February 1894, Robert Waller File, Widow's Certificate 394324, CWPF.

124. Henry Clay Bruce, *The New Man: Twenty-nine Years a Slave, Twenty-nine Years a Free Man* (1895; reprint, Lincoln: University of Nebraska Press, 1996), 11; Bancroft, *Slave Trading in the Old South*, 292.

125. Mary Ann Madison, Deposition, 24 January 1887, William Madison File, CWPF.

126. Zadrick Bowie, Deposition, 8 April 1890, John Posey File, Widow's Application 374485, CWPF.

127. Testimony of Wallace Tuner, 5 July 1873, Thomas Turner Claim, Case 4330, Adams County, SCC.

128. Moses Fletcher, Deposition, 26 September 1898, Samuel Davis File, Widow's Certificate 523708, CWPF.

129. Caroline Ramsay, Exhibit, 26 May 1884, Eliza Purviance, Deposition, 23 August 1884, inside page of Bible enclosed in Dennis Ramsay File, Mother's Certificate 209614; Mary Jane Foster, [Exhibit], 23 January 1883, Dr. Thomas A. Phillips, [Exhibit], 6 December 1876, Adam Butler File (alias Adam Phillips), Minor's Certificate 216035; Adaline Tester, Exhibit, 20 May 1884, Moses Tester File, Widow's Application 417482, CWPF.

130. Isaac Gaines and Felow Gaines, Affidavit, 3 July 1869, Adaline Tester, Exhibit, 20 May 1884, Moses Tester File, Widow's Application 417482, CWPF.

244 Notes to Pages 46–49

131. Jane Douglass Reynold, Deposition, 24 March 1891, Dennis Douglass File, Widow's Certificate 289245, CWPF.

132. Patsy Payton, [Exhibit], 19 January 1875, Beverly Payton (alias Dudley Payton) File, Widow's Certificate 168060; Phil[ander] Perry, Deposition, 2 February 1899, Burl Lewis File, Invalid's Certificate 606008, CWPF.

133. Mary Williams, Deposition, 11 January 1875, James Williams File, Widow's Certificate 98159, CWPF.

134. Jack Goody, "Time: Social Organisation," in *International Encyclopedia of the Social Sciences*, ed. D. L. Sills (New York: Macmillan, 1968), 16:30–41, esp. 31; Nancy D. Munn, "The Cultural Anthropology of Time," *Annual Review of Anthropology* 21 (1992): 93–123, esp. 94.

135. Washington Gray, Deposition, 22 July 1899, Burl Lewis File, CWPF. Burl Lewis was bought by Andrew Brown in 1854 (John Hebron Moore, *Andrew Brown and Cypress Lumbering in the Old Southwest* [Baton Rouge: Louisiana State University Press, 1967], 135). For a discussion of the markers Lewis used to establish the time of his arrival in Natchez, see chap. 5.

136. The starting point on the creation of collective memory remains Maurice Halbwachs, *The Collective Memory*, trans. Francis J. Ditter Jr. and Vida Yazdi Ditter (New York: Harper and Row, 1980). See also Jacques Le Goff, *History and Memory*, trans. Steven Rendell and Elizabeth Claman (New York: Columbia University Press, 1992); Alon Confino, "Collective Memory and Cultural History: Problems of Method," *AHR* 102 (December 1997): 1386–1403.

137. For the population in Adams County, see appendix, table A.1. The total population in the six counties of the Yazoo-Mississippi Delta was 17,183 in 1850. In Washington County that year, the average slaveholding was 81.7, and the ratio of slaves to white people was 14.5 to 1 (Cobb, *Most Southern Place*, 8, 30, table 1).

138. Nancy Bercaw, *Gendered Freedoms: Race, Rights, and the Politics of Household in the Delta, 1861–1875* (Gainesville: University Press of Florida, 2003), 19–22.

139. Depositions by Dick Richards and Dearmas Thibodeaux, n.d., both enclosed in Lt. W. H. Cornelius to Col. W. A. Reno, 21 April 1866, Unregistered Letters Received, Assistant Subassistant Commissioner, New Iberia, La., Bureau of Refugees, Freedmen, and Abandoned Lands, #A-8735, FSSP.

140. Israel Campbell, *An Autobiography Bond and Free; or, Yearnings for Freedom, from My Green Brier House* (Philadelphia:. Brinckloe, 1861), 76–94, 105–9, EE.

141. Virginia Pounds Brown, *Toting the Lead Row: Ruby Pickens Tartt, Alabama Folklorist* (University: University of Alabama Press, 1981), 94–95, 121, 134, 143, 148 n. 24; Harold Courlander, *Negro Folk Music U.S.A.* (1963; reprint, New York: Dover, 1991), 80–85; Marie J. Schwartz, *Born in Bondage: Growing Up Enslaved in the Antebellum South* (Cambridge: Harvard University Press, 2000), 186.

142. Randall M. Miller, ed., *Dear Master: Letters of a Slave Family* (1978; reprint, Athens: University of Georgia Press, 1990), 142, 160.

143. Ibid., 155, 260.

144. On slaveholdings in Florida and the trans-Mississippi West, see Hilliard, *Atlas of Antebellum Southern Agriculture*, maps 36–38, 42; Baptist, *Creating an Old South*, 69–70, 73–74, 290, tables A.7–8; Randolph B. Campbell, *An Empire for Slavery: The Peculiar Institution in Texas, 1821–1865* (Baton Rouge: Louisiana State University Press, 1989), 55–60.

145. Stephen Crawford, "The Slave Family: A View from the Slave Narratives," in *Strategic Factors in Nineteenth Century American Economic History: Essays to Honor Robert W. Fogel*, ed. Claudia Goldin and Hugh Rockoff (Chicago: University of Chicago Press, 1992), 347, table 11.12; Emily West, "The Debate on the Strength of Slave Families: South Carolina and the Importance of Cross-Plantation Marriages," *Journal of American Studies* 33 (August 1999): 225–28.

Chapter Two

1. Mary Ann Madison, Deposition, 24 January 1887, William Madison File, Widow's Certificate 232198, CWPF. On Helam's attempt to conceal two prior husbands and her use of the surname "Helam" during her marriage to Madison, see introduction.

2. Mary Ann Madison, Deposition, 18 February 1887, Rose Ballard, Deposition, 13 February 1887, Charles Ace, Deposition, 17 February 1887, ibid. I am grateful to Anna Clark of the University of Minnesota for calling my attention to the wifely service entailed in bathing. See also Marli F. Weiner, *Mistresses and Slaves: Plantation Women in South Carolina, 1830–80* (Urbana: University of Illinois Press, 1998), 133.

3. For another interpretation, based on the pension files, of intimate relations among slaves in Mississippi, see Noralee Frankel, *Freedom's Women: Black Women and Families in Civil War Era Mississippi* (Bloomington: Indiana University Press, 1999), 8–13.

4. For accounts of intimate relations that treat living together and marriage as synonymous, see Herbert G. Gutman, *The Black Family in Slavery and Freedom* (New York: Vintage, 1976), 11–18, tables 2–4; John W. Blassingame, ed., *The Slave Community: Plantation Life in the Antebellum South*, rev. ed. (New York: Oxford University Press, 1979), 165; Jo Ann Manfra and Robert Dykstra, "Serial Marriage and the Origins of the Black Stepfamily: The Rowanty Evidence," *JAH* 72 (June 1985): 18–44; Ann Paton Malone, *Sweet Chariot: Slave Family and Household Structure in Nineteenth-Century Louisiana* (Chapel Hill: University of North Carolina Press, 1992), 166–68, tables 5.3–4, 5.7, 6.1.

5. Robert W. Fogel and Stanley L. Engerman, *Time on the Cross: The Economics of American Negro Slavery* (1974; reprint, New York: Norton, 1989), 142; Marie J. Schwartz, *Born in Bondage: Growing Up Enslaved in the Antebellum South* (Cambridge: Harvard University Press, 2000), 184–85; Emily West, "The Debate on the Strength of Slave Families: South Carolina and the Importance of Cross-Plantation Marriages," *Journal of American Studies* 33 (August 1999): 223, 238; Rebecca J. Griffin, " 'Goin' Back over to See That Girl': Competing Social

Spaces in the Lives of the Enslaved in Antebellum North Carolina," *Slavery and Abolition* 25 (April 2004): 108.

6. Harry Alexander, Deposition, 3 October 1884, Elisha Clasby File, Widow's Certificate 232233, CWPF.

7. Children could leave home without passes because they were too young to produce children or work in the fields (Marie J. Schwartz, *Born in Bondage*, 184–85, 200; Emily West, *Chains of Love: Slave Couples in Antebellum South Carolina* [Urbana: University of Illinois Press, 2004], 26–27).

8. Delila Clasby, Opening Statements, 1 October 1884, 5 January 1885, Delila Clasby, Deposition, 3 October 1884, Harry Alexander, Deposition, 3 October 1884, Elisha Clasby File, CWPF.

9. Delila Clasby, Opening Statement, 1 October 1884, Delila Clasby, Deposition, 3 October 1884, Eliza Harris, Deposition, 1 October 1884, ibid.

10. Gutman, *Black Family*, 123–39; Brenda E. Stevenson, *Life in Black and White: Family and Community in the Slave South* (New York: Oxford University Press, 1996), 213–22.

11. The register includes 4,627 marriages of men and women enslaved in Adams and Warren Counties as well as Concordia Parish, Louisiana (Gutman, *Black Family*, 18–24, 145–51, 569–70 nn. 4, 7, 9). Although Gutman discussed separations in terms of "marriage" and cohabitation interchangeably, Union officers evidently asked registrants whether they had previously "lived with another." See column headings in "Page from a Marriage Register," in Ira Berlin, Joseph P. Reidy, Leslie S. Rowland, eds., *The Black Military Experience*, ser. 2 of *Freedom: A Documentary History of Emancipation* (New York: Cambridge University Press, 1982), doc. 309. For an analysis of the registers from Adams County in conjunction with those from Tennessee and Louisiana, see Blassingame, *Slave Community*, 175–77.

12. On owners requiring slaves to take spouses, see Deborah Gray White, *Ar'n't I A Woman? Female Slaves in the Plantation South* (New York: Norton, 1985), 85–88, 102–3; Marie J. Schwartz, *Born in Bondage*, 189–94.

13. Peter Laslett, "Household and Family on the Slave Plantations of the U.S.A.," in *Family Life and Illicit Love in Earlier Generations: Essays in Historical Sociology* (Cambridge: Cambridge University Press, 1977), 233–60; Gutman, *Black Family*; Manfra and Dykstra, "Serial Marriage"; Stevenson, *Life in Black and White*, 160, 206–57; Brenda E. Stevenson, "Distress and Discord in Virginia Slave Families, 1830–1860," in *In Joy and In Sorrow: Women, Family, and Marriage in the Victorian South*, ed. Carol Bleser (New York: Oxford University Press, 1990), 103–24; Malone, *Sweet Chariot*, 258–72; West, *Chains of Love*, 43–79.

14. Blassingame, *Slave Community*, 157–91; Eugene D. Genovese, *Roll, Jordan Roll: The World the Slaves Made* (New York: Pantheon, 1974), 443–501; Gutman, *Black Family*; Thomas L. Webber, *Deep Like the Rivers: Education in the Slave Quarter Community, 1831–1865* (New York: Norton, 1978), 111–17, 157–79; Drew Gilpin Faust, *James Henry Hammond and the Old South: A Design for Mastery* (Baton Rouge:

Louisiana State University Press, 1982), 83–85; Deborah Gray White, *Ar'n't I a Woman?* 105–10, 146–50; Jacqueline Jones, *Labor of Love, Labor of Sorrow: Black Women, Work, and Family from Slavery to the Present* (New York: Vintage, 1986), 31–38, 43; Stephen Crawford, "The Slave Family: A View from the Slave Narratives," in *Strategic Factors in Nineteenth Century American Economic History: Essays to Honor Robert W. Fogel*, ed. Claudia Goldin and Hugh Rockoff (Chicago: University of Chicago Press, 1992), 349, tables 11.1, 11.13.

15. Stevenson, *Life in Black and White*, 256.

16. Scholars emphasizing the importance of serial monogamy to the durability of slave families have made an important contribution. See Christie Farnham, "Saphire? The Issue of Dominance in the Slave Family, 1830–1865," in *"To Toil the Livelong Day": America's Women at Work, 1789–1980*, ed. Carol Groneman and Mary Beth Norton (Ithaca: Cornell University Press, 1987), 73–75; Manfra and Dykstra, "Serial Marriage." In the Natchez District, however, one of the intimate relations that contributed to serial partners, sweethearting, was not monogamous, as will be discussed later in this chapter.

17. U.S. Pension Bureau, *Regulations Relating to Army and Navy Pensions, with Statutes* (Washington, D.C.: Government Printing Office, 1881), 37.

18. The Pension Bureau undertook an extensive investigation of what appeared to be rival claims of Eliza Hutson and Lucinda Hudson to the pension of John Hutson, who had served in Company A of the 58th U.S. Colored Infantry. The bureau determined that Eliza Hutson was the widow of the soldier John Hutson, who died in 1866, four years before Lucinda Hudson married one John Hudson in Louisiana. Eliza Hutson, Deposition, 28 October 1901, M. W. Cuddy to Chief of the Criminal Section, 11 January 1902, John Hutson File, Widow's Application 696256, CWPF.

19. James Trussell and Richard Steckel, "The Age of Slaves at Menarche and Their First Birth," *Journal of Interdisciplinary History* 8 (Winter 1978): 477–505; Marie J. Schwartz, *Born in Bondage*, 173–74, 188–89; Stevenson, *Life in Black and White*, 238.

20. Thomas Green enlisted under his owner's surname, Scott. His relationship to Charity Dunbar turned up in an investigation of Martha Dudley's claim to be Thomas Green's widow. A special examiner concluded that she was not because Green already had a wife at the time of his relationship with Dudley (John H. Wager to Hon. J. H. Baker, 23 March 1875, Thomas Scott File, Widow's Certificate 129600, CWPF; U.S. Pension Bureau, *Regulations Relating to Army and Navy Pensions*, 36).

21. Martha Dudley testified as Martha Scott; Charity Dunbar as Charity Creighton, the surname of David Creighton, her husband since 1865. Martha Scott, Exhibit, 22 March 1875, Charity Creighton, [Exhibit], 13 March 1875, Thomas Scott File, CWPF.

22. Winthrop D. Jordan, *Tumult and Silence at Second Creek: An Inquiry into a Civil War Slave Conspiracy* (Baton Rouge: Louisiana State University Press, 1993), 176, 271.

Orange lived on Brighton plantation, which was near but did not adjoin either Forest or Palatine. See map 3.

23. Michael Wayne, *Death of an Overseer: Reopening a Murder Investigation from the Plantation South* (New York: Oxford University Press, 2001), 46, 67–71, 154.

24. George Washington, [Exhibit], 12 March 1875, Charity Creighton, [Exhibit], 13 March 1875, Thomas Scott File, CWPF.

25. Charity Creighton, [Exhibit], 13 March 1875, ibid. Sweethearting reminds us that not all slave families headed by women were matrifocal, defined as a family either dominated by a woman or "centered" around the relationship between mother and child. Women who had children as sweethearts had a more tenuous hold on their children than did parents who lived together or married. On the matrifocal character of slave families, see Deborah Gray White, "Female Slaves: Sex Roles and Status in the Antebellum Plantation South," *Journal of Family History* 3 (Fall 1983): 256–58; Stevenson, *Life in Black and White*, 209–12, 220–38, 256–57, 325–26, 396 n. 15; Claire Robertson, "Africa into the Americas? Slavery and Women, the Family, and the Gender Division of Labor," in *More than Chattel: Black Women and Slavery in the Americas*, ed. David Barry Gaspar and Darlene Clark Hine (Bloomington: Indiana University Press, 1996), 9–20.

26. Patsy Clayborne went by that name before the war and testified before the Pension Bureau under the name of Patsy Payton. John H. Wager to Hon. J. H. Baker, 30 January 1875, Patsy Payton, Exhibit, 19 January 1875, Grandisson Barton and Robert West, [Exhibits], 20 January 1875, Timothy Green, [Exhibit], 22 January 1875, Beverly Payton (alias Dudley Payton) File, Widow's Certificate 168060, CWPF.

27. Deborah Gray White, *Ar'n't I a Woman?* 112–17; Jacqueline Jones, *Labor of Love, Labor of Sorrow*, 29–32, 36–39; Marie J. Schwartz, *Born in Bondage*, 3.

28. Crawford, "Slave Family," 349–50.

29. Susan Alexander, Exhibit, 26 December 1874, Joseph Witherspoon, Exhibit, 28 December 1874, Allen Alexander File, Widow's Certificate 97533, CWPF.

30. On taking up among former slaves in Mississippi, see Frankel, *Freedom's Women*, 90–91.

31. The special examiner for the Pension Bureau, Dow McClain, concluded that Bettie Wood and Daniel Robinson had, in fact, married during the Civil War. Robinson was in the unenviable position of a man alone in old age, looking back on two relationships that ended badly—to Wood and to the woman over whom they parted around 1880—which could explain his resolve to prevent either of them from obtaining his pension after his death. "I have no wife at all and No living woman Can claim to be my wife," he told the pension examiner, "and I never will have one for the time is out." Daniel Robinson, Deposition, 16 December 1898, Bettie Robinson, Deposition, 1 October 1904, Dow McClain to Hon. Commissioner of Pensions, 14 October 1904, Daniel Robinson File, Widow's Certificate 581335, CWPF. On Wood and Robinson's wartime marriage, see chap. 6.

32. Bettie Robinson, Deposition, 1 October 1904, Martha Johnson, Deposition, 6 October 1904, ibid.

33. James H. Clements to Commissioner of Pensions, 10 March 1882, Commissioner William W. Dudley to the Hon. Secretary of the Interior, 17 July 1882, Emma Smith, Exhibit, 9 January 1882, John Smith File, Widow's Application 165592, CWPF.

34. Emma Smith, Exhibit, 9 January 1882, Barnett Baily, Deposition, 16 February 1882, Granville Cox, Deposition, 9 January 1882, John Smith File, CWPF.

35. Mrs. E. M. Williams, Deposition, 27 May 1895, Jno. H. Phillips to Hon. Commissioner of Pensions, 9 July 1895, Fanny McKinney, Deposition, 11 April 1895, Anderson White, Deposition, 17 May 1895, Nelson Grooms File, Minor's Certificate 413156, CWPF.

36. An extensive literature has documented slaves' use of names to mark ties of kinship, including those between spouses, parents and children, the generations, and fictive kin. See, for example, Gutman, *Black Family*, 185–201; Paul D. Escott, *Slavery Remembered: A Record of Twentieth-Century Slave Narratives* (Chapel Hill: University of North Carolina Press, 1979), 50–51, table 2.7; Charles Joyner, *Down by the Riverside: A South Carolina Slave Community* (Urbana: University of Illinois Press, 1984), 217–22; Cheryll Ann Cody, "There Was No 'Absalom' on the Ball Plantations: Slave-Naming Practices in the South Carolina Low Country, 1720–1865," *AHR* 92 (June 1987): 563–96.

37. Eugene D. Genovese, *A Consuming Fire: The Fall of the Confederacy in the Mind of the White Christian South* (Athens: University of Georgia Press, 1998), 5–23, 32–33.

38. Henry Hughes, "Treatise on Sociology," in *The Ideology of Slavery: Proslavery Thought in the Antebellum South, 1830–1860*, ed. Drew Gilpin Faust (Baton Rouge: Louisiana State University Press, 1981), 268.

39. Fogel and Engerman, *Time on the Cross*, 84–85; Willie Lee Rose, "The Domestication of Domestic Slavery," in *Slavery and Freedom*, ed. William W. Freehling (Oxford: Oxford University Press, 1982), 19–20; Crawford, "Slave Family," 338–39, 347–49, tables 11.4, 11.12–14.

40. Blassingame, *Slave Community*, 151–52.

41. Mary Ann Madison, Deposition, 24 January 1887, William Madison File; Lucy Saddler, Deposition, 24 March 1891, Dennis Douglass File, Widow's Certificate 289245, CWPF; Jno. Knight to Wm. M. Beall, 1 February [1846], John Knight Papers, ser. F., RASP.

42. Joseph Anderson, Harwood Shaw, Depositions, 28 May 1904, Susan Brown, Deposition, 5 March 1904, Lewis Griffin, Deposition, 20 February 1904, Archie Powell (alias Archie Coal) File, Minor's Certificate 576366, CWPF.

43. Genovese, *Roll, Jordan, Roll*, 473; Richard H. Steckel, *The Economics of U.S. Slave and Southern White Fertility* (New York: Garland, 1985), 229.

44. Winthrop D. Jordan, *White over Black: American Attitudes Toward the Negro, 1550–1812* (1968; reprint, New York: Norton, 1977), 150–64, 457–64; Rose, "Domes-

tication of Domestic Slavery," 18–19; Deborah Gray White, *Ar'n't I a Woman?* 27–47.

45. Jacqueline Jones, *Labor of Love, Labor of Sorrow*, 29–43; Elizabeth Fox-Genovese, *Within the Plantation Household: Black and White Women of the Old South* (Chapel Hill: University of North Carolina Press, 1988), 290–98, 325–27, 348–59, 372–74.

46. William H. Williams, Deposition, 28 October 1901, John Hudson File, CWPF.

47. Marie J. Schwartz, *Born in Bondage*, 48–52.

48. Eliza Hutson, Deposition, 28 October 1901, Thomas Scott File, CWPF.

49. Deborah Gray White, *Ar'n't I a Woman?* 41–42; Wilma King, *Stolen Childhood: Slave Youth in Nineteenth-Century America* (Bloomington: Indiana University Press, 1995), 113; Marie J. Schwartz, *Born in Bondage*, 45; Weiner, *Mistresses and Slaves*, 141; William Dusinberre, *Them Dark Days: Slavery in the American Rice Swamps* (New York: Oxford University Press, 1996), 248–49.

50. George Washington and Susan B[are]field, [Exhibits], 12 March 1875, Thomas Scott File, CWPF.

51. Emanuel Genifer and James Genifer, [Exhibit], 12 March 1875, ibid.

52. Mahala Knox's testimony convinced special examiner James H. Clements that she had been the wife of William Knox and then subsequently of Spencer Ball. Clements concluded, therefore, that she was neither Knox's widow nor any longer entitled to a pension. Clements still had his doubts about her attorney, James L. Dickinson, however, and recommended that another special examiner continue to inquire whether Dickinson had embezzled from her. James H. Clements to Hon. John C. Black, 27 September 27, 1886, Mahala Knox, Merritt Morton, and Ambrose Blue, Depositions, 27 September 1886, William Knox File, Widow's Certificate 197339, CWPF.

53. Mahala Knox, Deposition, 27 September 1886, ibid.

54. On common surnames among slave spouses, see Gutman, *Black Family*, 230–56. For other examples in the Natchez District, see Henry Cole, Exhibit, 5 February 1875, James Simpson File, Widow's Certificate 168061; William A. House, Deposition, 4 May 1895, Nelson Grooms File, Minor's Certificate 413156, CWPF.

55. Grim's application was denied on the grounds that her husband's name did not appear in regimental records. Caroline Grim, Harry Henry, and George Randall, Affidavit, 21 December 1867, Benjamin Grim File, Widow's Application 156440, CWPF. See also Joseph Witherspoon, Exhibit, 28 December 1874, Allen Alexander File, CWPF.

56. Lucinda Brazil and Mary Carter, [Exhibit], 12 February 1875, Susan Swanson, [Exhibit], 12 February 1875, Nelson Davis File, Widow's Certificate 92460; James H. McCoy, Affidavit, 8 March 1876, George Carter File, Widow's Certificate 173491, CWPF.

57. Rachel Meguire and Isaac French, Exhibits, 28 December 1874, Jackson Meguire File, Widow's Certificate 90188, CWPF.

58. Louisa Woods, Exhibit, 30 December 1874, Susan Alexander, Exhibit, 26 December 1874, Allen Alexander File, CWPF.

59. For additional examples of slaves seeking their owners' consent to marry, see Rebecca Mitchel[l], [Exhibit], 9 March 1875, Other Mitchell File, Widow's Certificate 98273; Amy Davis, Claimant's Affidavit, 22 March 1892, Henry Brown File, Widows' Applications 167916, 572357, CWPF.

60. Susan Sillers Darden Diary, 12 December 1853, 7 February 1854, 10 January 1856, 3 January 1858, Darden Family Papers, MDAH. On the unsettling effects of steady purchases on previously resident families, see Malone, *Sweet Chariot*, 108–9, 179–80.

61. Eliza Jones's mother may have had a child by Jerry Bingaman. Eliza Jones said her father's name was Harry Jones, but her sister was Betsy Bingaman. Eliza Jones had three children by Elijah Hall, who replaced Bingaman as driver. She had the first of these children after her husband, Elisha Grayson, enlisted but before he died. She testified before the Pension Bureau under her late husband's surname, Grayson. Eliza Grayson, Depositions, 28 April 1882, 28 October 1893, Willis Latham and Elijah Hall, Depositions, 28 April 1882, Elisha Grayson File, Widow's Certificate 389530, CWPF.

62. William Fountain and Jane Clay, Depositions, 30 October 1893, Prosper K. Montgomery and Willis Latham, Depositions, 28 April 1882, Eliza Grayson, Deposition, 28 October 1893, ibid.

63. Henry Watson, *Narrative of Henry Watson, a Fugitive Slave* (Boston: Marsh, 1848), 18, EE; John B. Cade, "Out of the Mouths of Ex-Slaves," *Journal of Negro History* 20 (July 1935): 304–5.

64. Testimony of Samuel Chase, 14 September 1872, Lewis Jackson, 23 September 1887, Samuel Chase Claim, Case 1990, USCC; Easter Wilson, Deposition, 11 June 1897, Claiborne Wilson File, Widow's Certificate 449117, CWPF; Blassingame, *Slave Community*, 168–69; Genovese, *Roll, Jordan, Roll*, 475–81; Leslie H. Owens, *This Species of Property: Slave Life and Culture in the Old South* (New York: Oxford University Press, 1976), 193; Mechal Sobel, *Trabelin' On: The Slave Journey to an Afro-Baptist Faith* (Princeton: Princeton University Press, 1988), 176–78.

65. Blassingame, *Slave Community*, 168–70; Genovese, *Roll, Jordan, Roll*, 481; Gutman, *Black Family*, 270–76, 282–84; Milly Sims, [Exhibit], 12 January 1875, Henry Jones File, Minor Application 230880; Chaney Sellers, Exhibit, 21 December 1874, Henry Sellers File, Widow's Certificate 131103, CWPF. For an owner who used the Methodist vow of the 1850s, see Walter Wade Plantation Diary, 14 January 1854, MDAH.

66. A. B. Archer to Dear Edward, 7 January 1855, Richard Thompson Archer Family Papers, NTC; Marie J. Schwartz, *Born in Bondage*, 200–205; Weiner, *Mistresses and Slaves*, 74, 82.

67. Tishne Price testified under the name Tishne Lewis. Her application for a widow's pension was denied because she lived with another man shortly after the death of

her husband, Henry Lewis. Tishne Lewis, Deposition, 24 November 1884, Henry Lewis File, Widow's Application 216342, CWPF.

68. Basil Kiger to My Dear Wife, 1 January 1852, Kiger Family Papers, NTC.

69. Jordan, *Tumult and Silence*, 13 n. 9.

70. Margaret Dupee Young married Dalton Reid three years after John Young's death in 1864 and testified under the name Margaret Reid. Her remarriage disqualified her from receiving a pension as Young's widow. Margaret Reid, Affidavit, 11 December 1889, John Young File, Widow's Application 41055, CWPF.

71. Moses Reed and Catherine Wright, Affidavit, 13 April 1869, Mary Jane Green and Amelia Morton, Affidavit, 27 July 1870, James Reed File, Minor's Certificate, 198010; Moses Reed, Deposition, 9 January 1889, James Doddin (alias Daniel Reed) File, Widow's Certificate 252874, CWPF.

72. Samuel Darden, Deposition, 23 January 1889, Moses Reed, Deposition, 9 January 1889, Phillis Reed, Deposition, 12 January 1888, James Doddin (alias Daniel Reed) File, CWPF.

73. Susan Sillers Darden Diary, 23 June 1854, 28 March 1857, Darden Family Papers, MDAH.

74. Ibid.; Blassingame, *Slave Community*, 165; Genovese, *Roll, Jordan, Roll*, 475–81; Gutman, *Black Family*, 273–74.

75. Chaney Sellers, Exhibit, 21 December 1874, Major Minor and Thomas Davis, Exhibit, 22 December 1874, Henry Sellers File, CWPF. See also Diary, 13, 15 July 1858, Benjamin L. C. Wailes Papers, MDAH; J. Carlyle Sitterson, "The William J. Minor Plantations: A Study in Ante-Bellum Absentee Ownership," *JSH* 9 (February 1943): 69.

76. Tishne Lewis, Deposition, 24 November 1884, Henry Lewis File; Rachel Moore, Exhibit, 18 March 1875, Jerry Moore File, Widow's Certificate 127426, CWPF.

77. John G. Jones Journal, 7 April 1835, MDAH.

78. Ibid.

79. On antebellum understandings of legal marriage, see Margaret A. Burnham, "An Impossible Marriage: Slave Law and Family Law," *Law and Inequality* 5 (July 1987): 187–225; Hendrik Hartog, *Man and Wife in America: A History* (Cambridge: Harvard University Press, 2000), 1, 23–26, 91–93, 103–5, 193–96; Peter W. Bardaglio, *Reconstructing the Household: Families, Sex, and the Law in the Nineteenth-Century South* (Chapel Hill: University of North Carolina Press, 1995), 79–112, esp. 96–101; Victoria E. Bynum, *Unruly Women: The Politics of Social and Sexual Control in the Old South* (Chapel Hill: University of North Carolina Press, 1992), 59–63.

80. Fox-Genovese, *Within the Plantation Household*, 296–97.

81. David I. Kertzer, *Ritual, Politics, and Power* (New Haven: Yale University Press, 1988), 1–4, 8–12, 37–46, 99–101. For a different view, see Charles Joyner, "History as Ritual: Rites of Power and Resistance on the Slave Plantation," in *Shared Traditions: Southern History and Folk Culture* (Urbana: University of Illinois Press, 1999), 93–96; Roger D. Abrahams, *Singing the Master: The Emergence of African-*

American Culture in the Plantation South (New York: Penguin, 1993). Rhys Isaac used the master-slave relation brilliantly in an essay on theory and method in his study of public ritual among colonial planters, but slaves are most conspicuous in the body of the work by their absence (*The Transformation of Virginia, 1740–1790* [Chapel Hill: University of North Carolina Press, 1982], 323–57, appendix: "A Discourse on the Method: Action, Structure, and Meaning"). Witnesses before the Pension Bureau made no mention of the practice of jumping the broomstick. Other scholars have pointed out that this practice was never part of the wedding ceremony but one of the games that sometimes followed it (Blassingame, *Slave Community*, 166–67; King, *Stolen Childhood*, 64).

82. Rose Ballard, Deposition, 13 February 1887, William Madison File; Chaney Sellers, Exhibit, 21 December 1874, Henry Sellers File; inside page of Bible, enclosed in Dennis Ramsay File, Mother's Certificate 209614, CWPF; Richard H. Steckel, "Slave Marriage and the Family," *Journal of Family History* 5 (Winter 1980): 411–13, table 4.

83. Susan Alexander, Exhibit, 26 December 1874, Allen Alexander File, CWPF.

84. King, *Stolen Childhood*, 63; Marie J. Schwartz, *Born in Bondage*, 202.

85. Genovese, *Roll, Jordan, Roll*, 475–81; Emily Ellis and Thos. F. Baker, Depositions, 13 May 1890, Edmond Elliott (alias Ellis) File, Widow's Certificate 270308, CWPF.

86. *Woodville Republican*, 28 January 1845.

87. Ibid.

88. Ibid.

89. Patsy Payton, [Exhibit], 19 January 1875, Beverly Payton (alias Dudley Payton) File; Lucy Saddler, Deposition, 24 March 1891, Dennis Douglass File; Sandy McGinnis, Deposition, 23 January 1907, Willis Latham File, Invalid's Certificate 833129, CWPF.

90. Ronald L. F. Davis, *The Black Experience in Natchez, 1720–1880* (Natchez Historical Park, Miss.: Eastern National Park and Monument Association, 1994), 115–16.

91. Marie J. Schwartz, *Born in Bondage*, 200–205.

92. Ibid., 192–94. Schwartz argues that owners' willingness to respect spouses who were joined in weddings diminished as the South expanded and the slave trade progressed. This argument may well be correct, at least insofar as it applies to the Upper South.

93. Basil Kiger to My Dear Wife, 29 October 1851, Kiger Family Papers, NTC.

94. Walter Johnson, *Soul by Soul: Life Inside the Antebellum Slave Market* (Cambridge: Harvard University Press, 1999), 34–35.

95. Willis Hartwell and Jamie Holloway, General Affidavit, 16 May 1890, James C. Farmer and B. F. Johnson, General Affidavits, 13 March 1890, Warrick Hartwell File, Widow's Application 417332, CWPF. For an account of the Hartwells' sale together by the trader, see chap. 1.

96. Monmouth was John A. Quitman's home place in the suburbs of Natchez (Ronald L. F. Davis, *Black Experience in Natchez*, 115–16).

97. Annie Rosalie Quitman Journal, vol. 13, 14 May 1857, Quitman Family Papers, ser. J, RASP; Randolph Delehanty and Van Jones Martin, *Classic Natchez* (Savannah, Ga.: Martin–St. Martin, 1996), 128.

98. Louis Murray and Alice Murray, Additional Evidence, 24 February 1869, Ben Lewis, [Exhibit], 1 March 1875, Stephen Jones, [Exhibit], 2 March 1875, Harris Stewart File, Widow's Certificate 132717, CWPF.

99. Escott found that 27.5 percent of all married couples belonged to different owners; Stephen C. Crawford, 10.4 percent. Emily West has extrapolated a higher estimate (19 percent) from Crawford's figures and concluded that cross-plantation marriages accounted for 33.5 percent of the total in South Carolina. See Escott, *Slavery Remembered*, 50–52; Crawford, "Slave Family," 345–47; West, *Chains of Love*, 47–48.

100. Gutman, *Black Family*, 131–42; West, "Debate on the Strength of Slave Families," 237; Stevenson, *Life in Black and White*, 208–12, 217, 229–32.

101. Crawford, "Slave Family," 334, 347–49, tables 11.12–11.14; West, *Chains of Love*, 46–47, 86.

102. For other examples of neighborhood marriages in addition to those mentioned, see Testimony of Nelson Ashby, 31 July 1873, Belfield Hicks Claim, Case 12941, Warren County, SCC.

103. Karen F. Olwig, *Cultural Adaptation and Resistance on St. John: Three Centuries of Afro-Caribbean Life* (Gainesville: University of Florida Press, 1987), 55–68; Karen F. Olwig, "Women, 'Matrifocality' and Systems of Exchange," *Ethnohistory* 28 (Winter 1981): 66; Karen F. Olwig, "Finding a Place for the Slave Family: Historical Anthropological Perspectives," *Folk* 23 (1981): 350.

104. Bernard Moitt, *Women and Slavery in the French Antilles, 1635–1848* (Bloomington: University of Indiana Press, 2001), 80–100; Alida C. Metcalf, "Searching for the Slave Family in Colonial Brazil: A Reconstruction from São Paulo," *Journal of Family History* 16 (July 1991): 284, 290–93; Manolo Garcia Florentino and José Roberto Góes, "Slavery, Marriage, and Kinship in Rural Rio de Janeiro, 1790–1830," in *Identity in the Shadow of Slavery*, ed. Paul E. Lovejoy (London: Continuum, 2000), 151–61; Linda Wimmer, "Ethnicity and Family Formation among Slaves on Tobacco Farms in the Bahian Recôncavo, 1698–1820," in *Enslaving Connections: Changing Cultures of Africa and Brazil during the Era of Slavery*, ed. José C. Curto and Paul E. Lovejoy (New York: Humanity, 2004), 152–53.

105. Emilia Viotti da Costa, *The Brazilian Empire: Myths and Histories*, rev. ed. (Chapel Hill: University of North Carolina Press, 2000), 135–36; Stuart B. Schwartz, *Sugar Plantations in the Formation of Brazilian Society: Bahia, 1550–1835* (Cambridge: Cambridge University Press, 1985), 389; Metcalf, "Searching for the Slave Family," 286; Florentino and Góes, "Slavery, Marriage, and Kinship," 151–55.

106. James H. Sweet, *Recreating Africa: Culture, Kinship, and Religion in the African-*

Portuguese World, 1441–1770 (Chapel Hill: University of North Carolina Press, 2003), 34–50.

107. Stuart B. Schwartz, *Sugar Plantations*, 358, 385–94, 411–12; Mary C. Karasch, *Slave Life in Rio de Janeiro, 1808–1850* (Princeton: Princeton University Press, 1987), 287–91; Wimmer, "Ethnicity and Family Formation," 154.

108. A. J. R. Russell-Wood, *Slavery and Freedom in Colonial Brazil*, rev. ed. (Oxford: Oneworld, 2002), 179.

109. Elizabeth A. Kuznesof, "Sexual Politics, Race, and Bastard-Bearing in Nineteenth Century Brazil: A Question of Culture or Power?" *Journal of Family History* 16 (July 1991): 241–49; Kátia M. de Queirós Mattoso, *To Be a Slave in Brazil, 1550–1888*, trans. Arthur Goldhammer (New Brunswick, N.J.: Rutgers University Press, 1991), 108–10.

110. Karasch, *Slave Life in Rio de Janeiro*, 294–96; Metcalf, "Searching for the Slave Family," 290.

111. Stanley Stein, *Vassouras: A Brazilian Coffee County, 1850–1900* (1957; reprint, Princeton: Princeton University Press, 1985), 155.

112. Orlando Patterson, *The Sociology of Slavery: An Analysis of the Origins, Development, and Structure of Negro Slave Society in Jamaica* (London: MacGibbon and Kee, 1967), 163; Barbara Bush, *Slave Women in Caribbean Society, 1650–1838* (Kingston, Jamaica: Randle, 1990), 86–87, 97–98; Marietta Morrissey, *Slave Women in the New World: Gender Stratification in the Caribbean* (Lawrence: University Press of Kansas, 1989), 89–90; Stanley L. Engerman and B. W. Higman, "The Demographic Structure of the Caribbean Slave Societies in the Eighteenth and Nineteenth Centuries," in *The Slave Societies of the Caribbean*, vol. 3 of *General History of the Caribbean*, ed. Franklin W. Knight (London: UNESCO, 1997), 87.

113. Moitt, *Women and Slavery*, 17–18, 82–89; Arlette Gautier, *Les Soeurs de Solitude: La Condition Féminine dans l'Esclavage aux Antilles du XVIIe au XIXe Siècle* (Paris: Éditions Caribéennes, 1985), 99–106.

114. Bush, *Slave Women in Caribbean Society*, 85–87, 97–103.

115. Jean Besson, "The Creolization of African-American Slave Kinship in Jamaican Free Villages and Maroon Communities," in *Slave Cultures and the Cultures of Slavery*, ed. Stephan Palmié (Knoxville: University of Tennessee Press, 1995), 188–91; Patterson, *Sociology of Slavery*, 162–66.

116. Herman L. Bennett, *Africans in Colonial Mexico: Absolutism, Christianity, and Afro-Creole Consciousness, 1570–1640* (Bloomington: Indiana University Press, 2003), 79–110. Proceedings before an ecclesiastical magistrate to obtain a marriage license in Colonial Mexico between 1584 and 1810 bore several striking similarities to those before a special examiner of the U.S. Pension Bureau after the Civil War. The church's requirement of proof of single status put prior relationships of both parties at issue, as did the pension statute. Witnesses also provided some of the same information to magistrates that witnesses provided to the Pension Bureau, including their age, owner, place of residence, how long they had known the

couple, and the circumstances of their relationship. The legal rights that were accorded married couples in Spanish America included a prohibition against owners selling either spouse beyond a certain distance. See Bennett, *Africans in Colonial Mexico.*

117. Harry Alexander, Deposition, 2 October 1884, Elisha Clasby File; Rachel Meguire, Exhibit, 28 December 1874, Jackson Meguire File, CWPF. Weekday visits by husbands were relatively rare in the South as a whole. See Crawford, "Slave Family," 333.

118. Testimony of Edward Hicks, 13 May 1875, Absalom Grant Claim, Case 5516, USCC.

119. Testimony of Henry Hunt, 6 May 1873, Henry Hunt Claim, Case 10840, Warren County, SCC.

120. Gutman, *Black Family,* 220–28.

121. Jones Journal, 7 April 1835, MDAH; Marie J. Schwartz, *Born in Bondage,* 51–52.

122. Tishne Lewis, Deposition, 24 November 1884, Henry Lewis File, CWPF.

123. Marie J. Schwartz, *Born in Bondage,* 184–85; Deborah Gray White, *Ar'n't I a Woman?* 76; Stephanie M. H. Camp, "The Pleasures of Resistance: Enslaved Women and Body Politics in the Plantation South, 1830–1861," *JSH* 68 (August 2002): 545.

124. Stevenson, *Life in Black and White,* 231.

125. West, *Chains of Love,* 11, 27, 45, 57–60, 55.

126. Marie J. Schwartz, *Born in Bondage,* 161.

127. Delila Clasby, Opening Statement, 1 October 1884, Elisha Clasby File, CWPF.

128. William Banks Taylor, "Southern Yankees: Wealth, High Society, and Political Economy in the Late Antebellum Natchez Region," *JMH* 59 (1997): 109.

129. During the Civil War, Hager Johnson and George Washington were married by an army chaplain (Hager Washington, Deposition, 29 December 1894, Henry Carter, 1 February 1895, William Gr[a]y and William Henderson, Depositions, 19 January 1895, George Washington File, Widow's Certificate 408157, CWPF).

130. Daniel returned to Walnut Hills in early May and killed his owner, Joel Cameron. According to one attorney involved in the case, Daniel killed Cameron for prohibiting him from keeping one of his wives (Henry S. Foote, *Casket of Reminiscences* [1874; reprint, New York: Negro Universities Press, 1968], 201–10).

131. Eliza Grayson, Deposition, 28 April 1882, Elisha Grayson File; Emma Smith, Exhibit, 9 January 1882, John Smith File, CWPF.

132. Annette Gordon-Reed, *Thomas Jefferson and Sally Hemings: An American Controversy* (Charlottesville: University Press of Virginia, 1997), esp. 158–209; Joshua D. Rothman, *Notorious in the Neighborhood: Sex and Families across the Color Line in Virginia, 1787–1861* (Chapel Hill: University of North Carolina Press, 2003), 1–4, 12–56, 133–68; Trevor Burnard, *Mastery, Tyranny, and Desire: Thomas Thistlewood and His Slaves in the Anglo-Jamaican World* (Chapel Hill: University of North Carolina Press, 2004). Scholars, applying a wide range of interpretive methods to

varied sources, have extensively documented the prevalence of rape. For recent discussions, see Norrece T. Jones Jr., "Rape in Black and White: Sexual Violence in the Testimony of Enslaved and Free Americans," in *Slavery and the American South*, ed. Winthrop D. Jordan (Jackson: University Press of Mississippi, 2003), 93–108; Nell Irvin Painter, "Three Southern Women and Freud: A Non-Exceptionalist Approach to Race, Class, and Gender in the Slave South," in *Southern History across the Color Line* (Chapel Hill: University of North Carolina Press, 2002), 15–39, 93–111; Edward E. Baptist, " 'Cuffy,' 'Fancy Maids,' and 'One-Eyed Men': Rape, Commodification, and the Domestic Slave Trade in the United States," *AHR* 107 (December 2001): 1619–50; West, *Chains of Love*, 163–64, appendix 2; Stevenson, *Life in Black and White*, 236–41; Crawford, "Slave Family," 336–38, tables 11.2–3; Catherine Clinton, " 'Southern Dishonor': Flesh, Blood, Race, and Bondage," in *In Joy and In Sorrow: Women, Family, and Marriage in the Victorian South, 1830–1900*, ed. Carol Bleser (New York: Oxford University Press, 1991), 58, 61–66. For early discussions, see Cade, "Out of the Mouths of Ex-Slaves," 302–3, 307–8; Blassingame, *Slave Community*, 154–56, 172–77; Escott, *Slavery Remembered*, 43–46, table 2.1–2; Catherine Clinton, *Plantation Mistress: Woman's World in the Old South* (New York: Pantheon, 1982), 200–205, 212–13, 221; Faust, *James Henry Hammond*, 86–88.

133. Marie J. Schwartz, *Born in Bondage*, 174.

134. William H. Williams, Deposition, 28 October 1901, John Hutson File, CWPF.

135. Eveline Perano lost her pension because the bureau determined that she had taken another husband after she was separated from James Perano and therefore was not his wife at the time he enlisted, as required by statute. Sallie Bright, Deposition, 5 October 1894, Aurilla Ross, Deposition, 27 October 1894, Assistant Secretary Jno. N. Reynolds to Commissioner of Pensions, 4 May 1895, James Perano File, Widow's Certificate 160774, CWPF.

136. Ellen Shields, Deposition, 5 December 1894, ibid.

137. Christopher Morris, *Becoming Southern: The Evolution of a Way of Life, Warren County and Vicksburg, Mississippi, 1770–1860* (New York: Oxford University Press, 1995), 63, 77–79; Christopher Morris, "Within the Slave Cabin: Violence in Mississippi Slave Families," in *Over the Threshold: Intimate Violence in Early America*, ed. Christine Daniels and Michael V. Kennedy (New York: Routledge, 1999), 272–73.

138. Darlene Clark Hine, "Rape and the Inner Lives of Southern Black Women: Thoughts on the Culture of Dissemblance," in *Southern Women: Histories and Identities*, ed. Virginia Bernhard, Betty Brandon, Elizabeth Fox-Genovese, and Theda Perdue (Columbia: University of Missouri Press, 1992), 177–89; Stevenson, *Life in Black and White*, 239–40.

139. Eveline Perano, now Miller, Deposition, 4 October 1894, James Perano File, CWPF.

140. Aurilla Ross testified under her married name. The special examiner implied par-

enthetically that her given name, Aurilla, sounded like Gabrielle, the feminine form of her father's name. Aurilla (or Gabrielle) Ross, Deposition, 27 October 1894, ibid.

141. Diana Falkner, Deposition, 14 October 1918, John Jones (alias Jonas Falkner) File, Widow's Certificate 856509, CWPF.

142. Eliza Grayson, Elijah Hall, and Willis Latham, Depositions, 28 April 1882, Elisha Grayson File, CWPF.

143. Marie J. Schwartz, *Born in Bondage*, 44–46.

Chapter Three

1. Plantation Book, Endpapers, Memo of Negroes, 1 January 1860, 18 April 1860, 16, 18 May 1860, James Allen and Family Papers, MDAH.

2. Ibid., 5, 14 April 1860, 20, 29 May 1860, 8 June 1860.

3. Ibid., 1 January 1861.

4. Ibid., 7 April 1860, 6, 21 April 1861, 27, 29 July, 1861, 29 March 1862, 9 November 1862.

5. Testimony of Richard Eastman, 25 January 1873, Richard Eastman Claim, Case 8244, USCC.

6. Plantation Book, 24 October 1860, 17 May 1862, Allen and Family Papers, MDAH.

7. W. E. B. Du Bois, *Black Reconstruction in America* (1935; reprint, New York: Atheneum, 1962), 3–16; Kenneth M. Stampp, *The Peculiar Institution: Slavery in the Ante-Bellum South* (1956; reprint, New York: Vintage, 1989), 34.

8. Adaline Tester, Exhibit, 20 May 1884, Moses Tester File, Widow's Application 417482; Lucy Saddler, Deposition, 24 March 1891, Dennis Douglass File, Widow's Certificate 289245, CWPF.

9. Sam Davis, Deposition, 29 April 1898, Henry Brown File, Widow's Applications 167916, 572357, CWPF. See also Henry Watson, *Narrative of Henry Watson, a Fugitive Slave* (Boston: Marsh, 1848), 5, EE.

10. Testimony of Jerry Rainey, 20 January 1873, Oliver B. Flowers Claim, Case 6960, Warren County, SCC.

11. Amos Wright, Deposition, 5 February 1912, William Wright File, Widow's Application 856421, CWPF.

12. According to one study of the Works Progress Administration narratives, 79 percent of daughters of house servants held a domestic position as their first employment (Stephen Crawford, "Quantified Memory: A Study of the W.P.A. and Fisk University Slave Narrative Collections" [Ph.D. diss., University of Chicago, 1980], 63, cited in Emily West, *Chains of Love: Slave Couples in Antebellum South Carolina* [Urbana: University of Illinois Press, 2004], 104).

13. Testimony of Eliza Green, 9 June 1875, Mrs. Nettie M. Fletcher, 3 August 1877, Matilda Anderson Claim, Case 6935; Testimony of William Green, n.d., Dick

Green Claim, Case 6963, Warren County, SCC; Testimony of Matilda Anderson, 1 June 1872, William Green, 21 November 1891, Eliza Green Claim, Case 2557, USCC.

14. Bertram Wyatt-Brown, "The Ideal Typology and Ante-Bellum Southern History: A Testing of a New Approach," *Societas* 5 (Winter 1975): 11; Jane Turner Censer, *North Carolina Planters and Their Children, 1800–1860* (Baton Rouge: Louisiana State University Press, 1984), 105–7; Kirsten E. Wood, *Masterful Women: Slaveholding Widows from the American Revolution through the Civil War* (Chapel Hill: University of North Carolina Press, 2004), 29–30.

15. Charles S. Sydnor, *A Gentleman of the Old Natchez Region: Benjamin L. C. Wailes* (Durham, N.C.: Duke University Press, 1938), 92–93; D. Clayton James, *Antebellum Natchez* (Baton Rouge: Louisiana State University Press, 1968), 138; Morton Rothstein, "The Changing Social Networks and Investment Behavior of a Slaveholding Elite in the Antebellum South: Some Natchez 'Nabobs,' 1800–1860," in *Entrepreneurs in Cultural Context*, ed. Sidney M. Greenfield, Arnold Strickon, and Robert T. Aubey (Albuquerque: University of New Mexico Press, 1979), 73–74, 79; Robert E. May, *John A. Quitman: Old South Crusader* (Baton Rouge: Louisiana State University Press, 1985), 19–29; Randolph B. Campbell, "Slavery in the Natchez Trace Collection," in *Inside the Natchez Trace Collection*, ed. Katherine J. Adams and Lewis L. Gould (Baton Rouge: Louisiana State University Press, 1999), 46; Michael Wayne, *Death of an Overseer: Reopening a Murder Investigation from the Plantation South* (New York: Oxford University Press, 2001), 70.

16. Henry Turner to Dear Sir, 2 May 1845, Quitman Family Papers, ser. J, RASP.

17. A. B. Archer to Dear Edward, 4 April 1855, Richard Thompson Archer Family Papers, NTC.

18. The Mississippi Supreme Court also recognized owners' binding ties to a "family slave" in *McRae v. Walker* (1840). The court ruled that such ties made a slave unique for the purposes of recovering damages and constituted an exception to the rule that the value of slaves was generally commensurate (Mark V. Tushnet, *The American Law of Slavery, 1810–1860* [Princeton: Princeton University Press, 1981], 165; Thomas D. Morris, *Southern Slavery and the Law, 1619–1860* [Chapel Hill: University of North Carolina Press, 1996], 119–20).

19. Eliza Purviance, Deposition, 23 August 1884, Sarah Preston, Deposition, 10 June 1884, Anthony Stafford and Nancy Robert, Depositions, 17 June 1884, Dennis Ramsay File, Mother's Certificate 209614, CWPF.

20. Mrs. Lotta Miller, Deposition, 31 May 1884, William F. Ogden, Deposition, 4 June 1884, Dennis Ramsay File, ibid. For another example of house servants whose children became house servants, see Philander Perry, Declaration for Pension, 19 February 1910, M. Whitehead to Hon. Commissioner of Pensions, 16 February 1911, Philander Perry File, Invalid's Certificate 854744, CWPF.

21. Wilma King, *Stolen Childhood: Slave Youth in Nineteenth-Century America* (Bloomington: Indiana University Press, 1995), 27–29.

22. Catherine Clinton, *Plantation Mistress: Woman's World in the Old South* (New York: Pantheon, 1982), 18.

23. Marli F. Weiner, *Mistresses and Slaves: Plantation Women in South Carolina, 1830–1880* (Urbana: University of Illinois Press, 1998), 32, 43–44.

24. Ibid., 125–29; Elizabeth Fox-Genovese, *Within the Plantation Household: Black and White Women of the Old South* (Chapel Hill: University of North Carolina Press, 1988), 22–24, 34–35, 81–88, 92–95; King, *Stolen Childhood*, 29.

25. Eliza Quitman to My Dearest John, 21 February 1836, Quitman Family Papers, RASP.

26. Fox-Genovese, *Within the Plantation Household*, 24, 309.

27. U.S. Census Office, *Population of the United States in 1860: Compiled from the Original Returns of the Eighth Census* (Washington, D.C.: Government Printing Office, 1964), 270.

28. Will Book A, Last Will of Elizabeth Green, 29 October 1833, Film 1939756; Will Book B-4, Everard Green, 8 March 1813, Jefferson County Will Records, Film 1907066, Family History Center, State College, Pennsylvania.

29. Marie J. Schwartz, *Born in Bondage: Growing Up Enslaved in the Antebellum South* (Cambridge: Harvard University Press, 2000), 109–11.

30. Eveline Perano, now Miller, Deposition, 4 October 1894, Ellen Shields, Deposition, 5 December 1894, Aurilla Ross, Deposition, 27 October 1894, James Perano File, Widow's Certificate 160774, CWPF.

31. John Hutson File, Widow's Application 696256, CWPF; West, *Chains of Love*, 84, 130, 163–64, appendix 2; Stephen C. Crawford, "The Slave Family: A View from the Slave Narratives," in *Strategic Factors in Nineteenth Century American History: Essays to Honor Robert W. Fogel*, ed. Claudia Goldin and Hugh Rockoff (Chicago: University of Chicago Press, 1992), 336–37, 343–44, tables 11.2–3.

32. Fox-Genovese, *Within the Plantation Household*, 34–35, 92–95.

33. Marie J. Schwartz, *Born in Bondage*, 66–67, 116–19. According to one estimate, about 20 percent of planter women employed wet nurses (Sally G. McMillen, *Motherhood in the Old South: Pregnancy, Childbirth, and Infant Rearing* [Baton Rouge: Louisiana State University Press, 1990], 118, table 4, appendix 1).

34. Deborah Gray White, *Ar'n't I A Woman? Female Slaves in the Plantation South* (New York: Norton, 1985), 129; King, *Stolen Childhood*, 13.

35. *Woodville Republican*, 24 January 1846.

36. Testimony of Lewis Jackson, 23 September 1887, Samuel Chase Claim, Case 1990, USCC.

37. Jacqueline Jones, *Labor of Love, Labor of Sorrow: Black Women, Work, and Family from Slavery to the Present* (New York: Vintage, 1986), 29; Jean E. Friedman, *The Enclosed Garden: Women and Community in the Evangelical South, 1830–1900* (Chapel Hill: University of North Carolina Press, 1985), 71; Stephanie J. Shaw, "Mothering under Slavery in the Antebellum South," in *Mothering: Ideology, Experience, and*

Agency, ed. Evelyn N. Glenn, Grace Chang, and Linda R. Forcey (New York: Routledge, 1994), 242–44; Marie J. Schwartz, *Born in Bondage*, 69–70, 74.

38. Jno. Knight to William M. Beall, 22 May 1845, John Knight Papers, ser. F, RASP.

39. Helam's namesake was Mary Hakes, who had married Jefferson Hakes by the time of her testimony. Mary Hakes and Jefferson Hakes, Depositions, 11 February 1887, Charles Ace, Deposition, 17 February 1887, William Madison File, Widow's Certificate 232198, CWPF.

40. On the language of fictive kinship, see Herbert G. Gutman, *The Black Family in Slavery and Freedom* (New York: Vintage, 1976), 45, 93–97, 186–90, 216–27; Ira Berlin, *Generations of Captivity: A History of African-American Slaves* (Cambridge: Harvard University Press, 2003), 190–93.

41. Testimony of Henry Shaifer, n.d., Rebecca Foster Claim, Case 5724, USCC.

42. Diary, 1 March 1843, James Wistar Metcalfe Papers, ser. J, RASP; Bourbon Plantation Journal, 27 October 1847, 1–6, 15–21 November 1847, 29–31 December 1847, 5–10 April 1848, Metcalfe Family Papers, MDAH.

43. Grandisson Barton, [Exhibit], 20 January 1875, Robert West, [Exhibit], 20 January 1875, Beverly Payton (alias Dudley Payton) File, Widow's Certificate 168060, CWPF.

44. Testimony of Curtis Lockhart, 19 January 1878, John Turner, 18 February 1878, John Alverson Claim, Case 3391, USCC.

45. Warren County Board of Police Minutes, 42–50, 88–97, County Records, MDAH. On the construction and maintenance of public roads, see Bradley G. Bond, *Political Culture in the Nineteenth Century South: Mississippi, 1830–1900* (Baton Rouge: Louisiana State University Press, 1995), 13, 28–31; Christopher Morris, *Becoming Southern: The Evolution of a Way of Life, Warren County and Vicksburg, Mississippi, 1770–1860* (New York: Oxford University Press, 1995), 133–40.

46. Slaves Subject to Road Duty, Adams County, Mississippi, 1850–57, Slaves and Slavery Collection, NTC. For examples of slaves sent on road duty, see B. G. Commission to Overseer of Roads, 20 May 1856, Kiger Family Papers; A List of Hands on Pine Woods in 1848, Archer Family Papers, NTC; Aventine Plantation Diary, 11 January 1859, 1 September 1859; Susan Sillers Darden Diary, 23 March 1854, 5, 9 April 1855, 13 April 1859, Darden Family Papers, MDAH.

47. Overseer Report, [July 1833], Joseph E. Davis Papers, NTC; Walter Wade Plantation Diary, 9 April 1852; Diary, 9, 11 June 1857, 12 April 1860, typescript, Benjamin L. C. Wailes Papers, MDAH.

48. John Nevitt Diary, 27 July 1830, 28 October 1830, ser. J, RASP.

49. Claimant's Request for Findings of Fact and Brief on the Merits, n.d., Naomi Fowler Claim, Case 13189, USCC.

50. John Hebron Moore, *Agriculture in Ante-Bellum Mississippi* (New York: Bookman, 1958), 43; William K. Scarborough, "Heartland of the Cotton Kingdom," in *A History of Mississippi*, ed. Richard A. McLemore (Hattiesburg: University and Col-

lege Press of Mississippi, 1973), 1:312; Robert W. Fogel and Stanley L. Engerman, *Time on the Cross: The Economics of American Negro Slavery* (1974; reprint, New York: Norton, 1989), 203–5.

51. Franklee G. Whartenby, *Land and Labor Productivity in United States Cotton Production, 1800–1840* (New York: Arno, 1977), 177, appendix D.

52. Studies of sugar production in the Caribbean are illuminating on the coordination of labor on cotton plantations and its cohesive effects, although the coordination of work was especially intense on sugar plantations, which combined agricultural and industrial production. See Sydney W. Mintz, *Sweetness and Power: The Place of Sugar in Modern History* (New York: Viking, 1985), 46–52; Dale Tomich, *Slavery in the Circuit of Sugar: Martinique and the World Economy, 1830–1848* (Baltimore: Johns Hopkins University Press, 1990), 217–37; Dale Tomich, "White Days, Black Days: The Working Day and the Crisis of Slavery in the French Caribbean," in *Through the Prism of Slavery: Labor, Capital, and World Economy* (Lanham, Md.: Rowman and Littlefield, 2004), 139–51.

53. Charles S. Sydnor, *Slavery in Mississippi* (1933; reprint, Baton Rouge: Louisiana State University Press, 1966), 67–69; William K. Scarborough, *The Overseer: Plantation Management in the Old South* (1966; reprint, Athens: University of Georgia Press, 1984), 8–10, table 1; Eugene D. Genovese, *Roll, Jordan, Roll: The World the Slaves Made* (New York: Pantheon, 1974), 11–13, 365–66.

54. William K. Scarborough, *Masters of the Big House: Elite Slaveholders of the Mid-Nineteenth-Century South* (Baton Rouge: Louisiana State University Press, 2003), 12, 125, 134–36, 143–45, 444–47, 467–73, appendixes C, D; Winthrop D. Jordan, *Tumult and Silence at Second Creek: An Inquiry into a Civil War Slave Conspiracy* (Baton Rouge: Louisiana State University Press, 1993), 13 n. 9, 47–49; D. Clayton James, *Antebellum Natchez*, 148–49; James C. Cobb, *The Most Southern Place on Earth: The Mississippi Delta and the Roots of Southern Identity* (New York: Oxford University Press, 1992), 9–10; Ariela J. Gross, *Double Character: Slavery and Mastery in the Antebellum Southern Courtroom* (Princeton: Princeton University Press, 2000), 29, 36–37; Herbert Weaver, *Mississippi Farmers, 1850–1860* (Nashville: Vanderbilt University Press, 1945), 22.

55. Seventy-five planters owning at least 250 slaves resided in South Carolina, forty-nine in Louisiana, and forty-five in the Natchez District of Mississippi (Adams, Claiborne, Jefferson, Warren, and Wilkinson Counties). Those forty-five planters owned at least 9,054 slaves in the Natchez District, 7,672 in Louisiana, and 1,822 in the Delta (calculated from Scarborough, *Masters of the Big House*, appendix D). For the total number of slaves in the Natchez District, see appendix, table A.1.

56. Morton Rothstein, "The Antebellum Plantation as a Business Enterprise: A Review of Scarborough's *The Overseer*," *Explorations in Entrepreneurial History* 6 (Fall 1968): 131; Scarborough, *Masters of the Big House*, 155–57, 225–26.

57. Sydnor, *Slavery in Mississippi*, 67; Stampp, *Peculiar Institution*, 36–38, 40.

58. Lewis C. Gray calculated a combined median slaveholding of seventy for Wilkinson, Adams, Jefferson, and Claiborne Counties and of fifty-six for Warren County and adjacent Yazoo County (*History of Agriculture in the Southern United States to 1860* [New York: Smith, 1941], 1:531, table 12).

59. In the Black Belt, absenteeism and large slaveholdings also prevailed in the low country, the southern piedmont in central Georgia, and southern Louisiana (Lewis C. Gray, *History of Agriculture*, 1:531–36, 545, tables 12, 13; Julia Floyd Smith, *Slavery and Rice Culture in Low Country Georgia, 1750–1860* [Knoxville: University of Tennessee Press, 1985], 43–44, table A-1; William Dusinberre, *Them Dark Days: Slavery in the American Rice Swamps* [New York: Oxford University Press, 1996], 78, 310–12; J. Carlyle Sitterson, *Sugar Country: The Cane Sugar Industry in the South, 1753–1950* [Lexington: University of Kentucky Press, 1953], 54–56, 63, 67; Berlin, *Generations of Captivity*, 177, 187, 200–201).

60. *Woodville Republican*, 8 February 1840; Sydnor, *Slavery in Mississippi*, 87; Scarborough, *Overseer*, 67–70, 82, 88, 93–94, 105.

61. Testimony of Lewis Pinkney, 7 October 1872, Russell S. Sessions Claim, Case 8532; Testimony of Squire Myers, 21 July 1873, John M. and Wm. B. Johnson Claim, Case 18061; Testimony of William Eaglin, 23 May 1873, Thomas Bradshaw Claim, Case 11363, Warren County, SCC; Testimony of Balor Hill, 6 November 1871, Estate of C. D. Hamilton Claim, Case 9648; Testimony of Benjamin Jones, 22 June 1874, Daniel A. Cameron Claim, Case 3510; Testimony of John Wooley, 1 June 1874, Martha Crane Claim, Case 8313, USCC; Genovese, *Roll, Jordan, Roll*, 365–66; Fogel and Engerman, *Time on the Cross*, 210–12.

62. James H. Stone, "Black Leadership in the Old South: The Slave Drivers of the Rice Kingdom" (Ph.D. diss., Florida State University, 1976), 17–38; James M. Clifton, "The Rice Driver: His Role in Slave Management," *South Carolina Historical Magazine* 82 (October 1981): 331, 339–44.

63. Philip D. Morgan, "Work and Culture: The Task System and the World of Lowcountry Blacks, 1700–1880," *WMQ*, 3rd ser., 39 (October 1982): 563–99.

64. Ibid., 581–82; John Scott Strickland, "Traditional Culture and Moral Economy: Social and Economic Change in the South Carolina Low Country, 1865–1910," in *The Countryside in the Age of Capitalist Transformation: Essays in the Social History of Rural America*, ed. Steven Hahn and Jonathan Prude (Chapel Hill: University of North Carolina Press, 1985), 145; Larry E. Hudson Jr., *To Have and to Hold: Slave Work and Family Life in Antebellum South Carolina* (Athens: University of Georgia Press, 1997), 2–3, 12.

65. Joyce E. Chaplin, *An Anxious Pursuit: Agricultural Innovation and Modernity in the Lower South, 1730–1815* (Chapel Hill: University of North Carolina Press, 1993): 268–70; Stone, "Black Leadership in the Old South," 17–38; Clifton, "Rice Driver," 336–39, 342.

66. Wade Plantation Diary, 7, 25–26 May 1851, 9–10 March 1854, 16, 23, 28, 30 June 1855, MDAH.

67. Diary, 10–13 May 1857, 15 July 1858, 11–13, 15 April 1859, Wailes Papers, MDAH; Genovese, *Roll, Jordan, Roll*, 16–17.

68. Eugene D. Genovese, *The Political Economy of Slavery: Studies in the Economy and Society of the Slave South* (New York: Vintage, 1967), 44; Sydnor, *Slavery in Mississippi*, 16.

69. Dugal G. McCall Plantation Journal, 1–10 July 1852, 23–25 December 1852, ser. F, RASP; Wade Plantation Diary, 7 August 1850, 20 January 1854, MDAH; Steven F. Miller, "Plantation Labor Organization and Slave Life on the Cotton Frontier: The Alabama-Mississippi Black Belt, 1815–1840," in *Cultivation and Culture: Labor and the Shaping of Slave Life in the Americas*, ed. Ira Berlin and Philip D. Morgan (Charlottesville: University Press of Virginia, 1993), 161–62; Lewis C. Gray, *History of Agriculture*, 1:548; Jacqueline Jones, *Labor of Love, Labor of Sorrow*, 17.

70. Nevitt Diary, 1–19 January 1830; Diary, 21, 24, 27 January 1843, 8–21, 26 February 1843, 7 March 1843, Metcalfe Papers, RASP; 5 Trips to Pine Woods in April, n.d., Archer Family Papers, NTC; John Hebron Moore, *Andrew Brown and Cypress Lumbering in the Old Southwest* (Baton Rouge: Louisiana State University Press, 1967), 67.

71. Henry Turner to My Dear Sir, 11, 26 June 1842, Quitman Family Papers, RASP.

72. Robert W. Fogel, *Without Consent or Contract: The Rise and Fall of American Slavery* (New York: Norton, 1989), 45–47; John F. Olson, "The Occupational Structure of Southern Plantations during the Late Antebellum Era," in *Markets and Production*, vol. 1 of *Without Consent or Contract (Technical Papers)*, ed. Robert W. Fogel and Stanley L. Engerman (New York: Norton, 1992), 137–56; Jacqueline Jones, *Labor of Love, Labor of Sorrow*, 13–25.

73. For further discussion of mobile trades and travels outside the neighborhood, see chap. 5.

74. On women's relative difficulty in leaving plantations, see Deborah Gray White, *Ar'n't I a Woman?* 70–77; Stephanie M. H. Camp, "The Pleasures of Resistance: Enslaved Women and Body Politics in the Plantation South, 1830–1861," *JSH* 68 (August 2002): 545.

75. Aventine Plantation Diary, 2, 15, 19–22, 31 January 1859, 6 April 1859, MDAH; George P. Rawick, Jan Hillegas, and Ken Lawrence, eds., *The American Slave: A Composite Autobiography*, supplement ser. 1. (Westport, Conn.: Greenwood, 1977), 7:342; Steven F. Miller, "Plantation Labor Organization," 159–69; Lewis C. Gray, *History of Agriculture*, 1:549–55, 2:701–2.

76. Aventine Plantation Diary, 11 March 1859; Wade Plantation Diary, 19 April 1851, MDAH; Fogel, *Without Consent or Contract*, 75; Jacob Metzer, "Rational Management, Modern Business Practices, and Economies of Scale in Antebellum Southern Plantations," in *Markets and Production*, ed. Fogel and Engerman, 201, table 10.2.

77. Norman R. Yetman, ed., *Life under the "Peculiar Institution": Selections from the Slave Narrative Collection* (New York: Holt, Rinehart, and Winston, 1970), 73.

78. Testimony of Anthony Cooper, Katie Brenton, Leana Jones, 1 June 1873, Louisa S. Bobo Claim, Case 2142, USCC.

79. John Hebron Moore, *The Emergence of the Cotton Kingdom in the Old Southwest: Mississippi, 1770–1860* (Baton Rouge: Louisiana State University Press, 1988), 37, 51–52, table 1; Lewis C. Gray, *History of Agriculture*, 2:852; Genovese, *Political Economy of Slavery*, 112–13; Olson, "Occupational Structure," 146–47, 167 n. 15.

80. Robert H. Crist to Dear Father, 1 April 1860, typescript, Old Courthouse Museum, Vicksburg, Mississippi; Sydnor, *Slavery in Mississippi*, 10 n. 47; Jacqueline Jones, *Labor of Love, Labor of Sorrow*, 16; Fox-Genovese, *Within the Plantation Household*, 172–73.

81. Frederick Law Olmsted, *A Journey in the Back Country* (1860; reprint, New York: Schocken, 1970), 72, 81.

82. Bourbon Plantation Journal, 21 March 1848, York Plantation Journal, 12 May 1852, Metcalfe Family Papers, MDAH.

83. Genovese, *Political Economy of Slavery*, 124–53; William M. Mathew, *Edmund Ruffin and the Crisis of Slavery in the Old South: The Failure of Agricultural Reform* (Athens: University of Georgia Press, 1988), 56–66, 110–25, 196–212; James C. Bonner, "Genesis of Agricultural Reform in the Cotton Belt," *JSH* 9 (November 1943): 485–87; Theodore Rosengarten, "*The Southern Agriculturalist* in an Age of Reform," in *Intellectual Life in Antebellum Charleston*, ed. Michael O'Brien and David Moltke-Hansen (Knoxville: University of Tennessee Press, 1986), 280–85.

84. Steven Stoll, *Larding the Lean Earth: Soil and Society in Nineteenth-Century America* (New York: Hill and Wang, 2002), 120–69.

85. Genovese, *Political Economy of Slavery*, 90–91, 136–41.

86. Sydnor, *Gentleman of the Old Natchez Region*, 152–69; Scarborough, "Heartland of the Cotton Kingdom," 315–20; Franklin L. Riley, ed., "Diary of a Mississippi Planter, January 1, 1840, to April, 1863," *Mississippi Historical Society Publications* 10 (1909): 305–9.

87. Joseph Holt Ingraham, *The South-West, by a Yankee* (1835; reprint, Ann Arbor: University Microfilms, 1966), 2:86–88. See also Frederick Law Olmsted, *The Cotton Kingdom: A Traveller's Observations on Cotton and Slavery in the American Slave States*, ed. Arthur M. Schlesinger (New York: Knopf, 1953), 410.

88. Moore, *Emergence of the Cotton Kingdom*, 7–8; Christopher Morris, *Becoming Southern*, 156–57; Genovese, *Political Economy of Slavery*, 98; Stoll, *Larding the Lean Earth*, 15–16, 134–37.

89. Everard Green Baker Diary, 4, 9 April 1850, ser. J, RASP.

90. Peter Temin, *The Jacksonian Economy* (New York: Norton, 1969), 131, 133 n. 36, table 4.4.

91. Scarborough, "Heartland of the Cotton Kingdom," 312–25; Moore, *Emergence of the Cotton Kingdom*, 14–22; Lewis C. Gray, *History of Agriculture*, 2:691–700, 898–90; Gavin Wright, "Slavery and the Cotton Boom," *Explorations in Economic History* 12 (October 1975): 439–51. For the argument that the stimulus agricultural inno-

vation received from economic depression during the 1840s was typical of the entire history of capitalism, see Carville Earle, "Myth of the Southern Soil Miner: Macrohistory, Agricultural Innovation, and Environmental Change," in *The Ends of the Earth: Perspectives on Modern Environmental History*, ed. Donald Worster (New York: Cambridge University Press, 1988), 178–86. For an interesting discussion of how southern thinkers construed the intellectual and moral implications of this economic crisis, see Drew Gilpin Faust, *A Sacred Circle: The Dilemma of the Intellectual in the Old South, 1840–1860* (1977; reprint, Philadelphia: University of Pennsylvania Press, 1986), 11–14.

92. Scarborough, *Masters of the Big House*, 14, 444–47, 467–73; Jordan, *Tumult and Silence*, 47–49.

93. Baker Diary, 36–37, RASP; Clement Eaton, *Jefferson Davis* (New York: Free Press, 1977), 38.

94. Moore, *Emergence of the Cotton Kingdom*, 18–36.

95. Ann Barnes Archer to Dear Edward, 25 March 1855, Archer Family Papers, NTC; Sydnor, *Gentleman of the Old Natchez Region*, 157; Scarborough, "Heartland of the Cotton Kingdom," 310–11, 315–25.

96. For examples of plantations in the Natchez District where slaves planted peas as well as corn and cotton, see Wade Plantation Diary, 2 June 1851; Diary, 20 October 1859, Wailes Papers; Aventine Plantation Diary, 5 February 1859, 9 April 1859, Receipt for Supplies, MDAH; Mack Swearingen, "Thirty Years of a Mississippi Plantation: Charles Whitmore of Montpelier," *JSH* 1 (May 1935): 198–211. On the shift toward mixed agriculture in Mississippi and the Deep South generally, see Moore, *Agriculture in Ante-Bellum Mississippi*, 69–92, 109–27, 175–78; Moore, *Emergence of the Cotton Kingdom*, 24–27, 54; Paul W. Gates, *The Farmer's Age: Agriculture, 1816–1860* (1960; reprint, New York: Harper Torchbooks, 1968), 99–100, 169–71; Mathew, *Edmund Ruffin and the Crisis of Slavery*, esp. 131–39; Genovese, *Political Economy of Slavery*, 41–153; Earle, "Myth of the Southern Soil Miner," 191–92, 201–4.

97. Baker Diary, 29–30, 36–37, 70, RASP; Diary, 16 February 1855, Darden Family Papers, MDAH; Plantation Book, 18 April 1860, 16–18 May 1860, Allen and Family Papers, MDAH; Swearingen, "Thirty Years of a Mississippi Plantation," 204–5; Sydnor, *Gentleman of the Old Natchez Region*, 161; Jordan, *Tumult and Silence*, 42; Genovese, *Political Economy of Slavery*, 90.

98. Robert E. Gallman and Gavin Wright pointed out that cotton and corn could be harvested in succession rather than at the same time. As Carville Earle has noted, however, the crops had to be tilled simultaneously in the spring. Whether corn and cotton were complementary or competed for labor has important implications for the stance of southern farmers and planters toward the market, as these and other historians have explained. See Robert E. Gallman, "Self-Sufficiency in the Cotton Economy of the Antebellum South," *Agricultural History* 44 (January 1970): 5–23;

Gavin Wright, *The Political Economy of the Cotton South: Households, Markets, and Wealth in the Nineteenth Century* (New York: Norton, 1978), 55–74; Carville Earle, "The Price of Precocity: Technical Choice and Ecological Constraint in the Cotton South, 1840–1890," *Agricultural History* 66 (Summer 1992): 25–60, esp. 30 n. 7. From the slaves' standpoint, cultivating corn in addition to cotton increased the pace of work in different ways, depending on whether the crops were complementary or competitors. Field laborers had to cultivate both crops in spring before lay-by and harvest corn before cotton in summer during an interval when all field work had formerly slacked off.

99. Charles Whitmore Diaries, SHC; Nevitt Diary, 1829–30; Diary, 22 January 1843, 6 February 1843, Metcalfe Papers, RASP; Scarborough, "Heartland of the Cotton Kingdom," 311–13; Sydnor, *Gentleman of the Old Natchez Region*, 110; King, *Stolen Childhood*, 5, 30, 73; Marie J. Schwartz, *Born in Bondage*, 61–62, 135.

100. Ralph V. Anderson and Robert E. Gallman, "Slaves as Fixed Capital: Slave Labor and Southern Economic Development," *JAH* 44 (June 1977): 24–39; Drew Gilpin Faust, *James Henry Hammond and the Old South: A Design for Mastery* (Baton Rouge: Louisiana State University Press, 1982), 126, 128; Mathew, *Edmund Ruffin and the Crisis of Slavery*, 137, 147–48; Chaplin, *Anxious Pursuit*, 299, 305. For the increased demands on slave labor on the cotton frontier, see Steven F. Miller, "Plantation Labor Organization," 155–69; Berlin, *Generations of Captivity*, 175–79.

101. Moore, *Emergence of the Cotton Kingdom*, 29–30, 36; Scarborough, *Masters of the Big House*, 157; Swearingen, "Thirty Years of a Mississippi Plantation," 204–5.

102. Baker Diary, 14, 27, 28 March 1850, 3–4 June 1850, RASP. Slaves on Richland planted two crops of corn again in 1852 (Baker Diary, 26 March 1852, 23 May 1852, RASP). See also Plantation Book, 2, 12 February 1861, 13, 25 May 1861, 27 June 1861, Allen and Family Papers, MDAH.

103. Diary, 10 April 1856, 24 February 1857, 13, 17 April 1857, Darden Family Papers, MDAH.

104. Jno. Knight to William M. Beall, 22 May 1845, 7 May [1846], Knight Papers, RASP.

105. Bourbon Plantation Journal, 26 January 1843, 6–21, 28 February 1843, 1–5 March 1848, Metcalfe Family Papers, MDAH; Sydnor, *Gentleman of Old Natchez*, 155; Moore, *Emergence of Cotton Kingdom*, 32–41; Lewis C. Gray, *History of Agriculture*, 2:701–2, 797; Earle, "Price of Precocity," 35–37.

106. Bourbon Plantation Journal, 19–26 August 1847, 15, 22 September 1847, Metcalfe Family Papers, MDAH; Moore, *Agriculture in Ante-Bellum Mississippi*, 59–60; Earle, "Myth of the Southern Soil Miner," 202.

107. Nevitt Diary, 31 July 1830, 3–7 August 1830, RASP; Aventine Plantation Diary, 23 July–8 August 1859, MDAH; Swearingen, "Thirty Years of a Mississippi Plantation," 209; Moore, *Emergence of the Cotton Kingdom*, 53–54.

108. McCall Plantation Journal, 28 May–25 June 1850, 30 December 1850, RASP; Bourbon Plantation Journal, July 1860, Metcalfe Family Papers, MDAH; Sydnor, *Gentleman of the Old Natchez Region*, 115.

109. Lewis C. Gray, *History of Agriculture*, 2:708.

110. For land cleared, see figures on increased improved acres, 1850–60, in appendix, table A.2.

111. Estimates in this paragraph are based on figures compiled in appendix, table A.2. For an estimate of the increased acreage cultivated by slaves statewide, attributed to increased mechanization rather than increased exploitation, see Scarborough, "Heartland of the Cotton Kingdom," 321–22.

112. Leak reckoned the tasks for hoe gangs in yards: 5,300 yards for women weeding cotton and 6,600 for men; between 8,000 and 10,000 for women thinning cotton plants to one or two sturdy stalks and 10,000–12,000 for men. Diary, vol. 2, 3 June 1846, 29 March 1847, 6, 23 May 1848, 5, 19 June 1848, Francis Terry Leak Papers, ser. J, RASP. For an account of the transition to task labor on the Leak plantation, see Moore, *Emergence of the Cotton Kingdom*, 95–96.

113. Aventine Plantation Diary, 8 March 1859, 9, 11–16 April 1859, 4, 18, 23 July 1859, 8 August 1859, Record of Cotton Picked on Aventine in 1859, MDAH; Jordan, *Tumult and Silence*, 38–45.

114. Stephanie M. H. Camp, "'I Could Not Stay There': Enslaved Women, Truancy, and the Geography of Everyday Forms of Resistance in the Antebellum Plantation South," *Slavery and Abolition* 23 (December 2002): 5–7.

115. Nevitt Diary, 2, 10, 24 January 1830, 14 February 1830, 2–3 May 1830, 19 September 1830, 7 November 1830, 3 December 1830, RASP. For other examples of Sunday labor in the Natchez District, see Diary, 5 February 1843, Metcalfe Papers, RASP; Aventine Plantation Diary, 1, 8 May 1859, 18 September 1859, MDAH.

116. Nevitt Diary, 13, 27 May 1832, 3 June 1832, 1 July 1832, 9, 16, 23 September 1832, RASP.

117. Henry Turner to My Dear Sir, 7 January 1842, Quitman Family Papers, RASP. See also Betty Wood, "'Never on a Sunday?' Slavery and the Sabbath in Low-country Georgia, 1750–1830," in *From Chattel Slaves to Wage Slaves: The Dynamics of Labour Bargaining in the Americas*, ed. Mary Turner (Kingston, Jamaica: Randle, 1995), 79–96.

118. Nigel O. Bolland, "Proto-Proletarians? Slave Wages in the Americas: Between Slave Labour and Free Labour," in *From Chattel Slaves to Wage Slaves: The Dynamics of Labour Bargaining in the Americas*, ed. Mary Turner (Kingston, Jamaica: Randle, 1995), 132–35.

119. Ira Berlin and Philip D. Morgan, "Introduction," in *Cultivation and Culture: Labor and the Shaping of Slave Life in the Americas*, ed. Berlin and Morgan (Charlottesville: University Press of Virginia, 1993), 20–22; Dylan C. Penningroth, *The*

Claims of Kinfolk: African American Property and Community in the Nineteenth-Century South (Chapel Hill: University of North Carolina Press, 2003), 55–57.

120. Claire Robertson, "Africa into the Americas? Slavery and Women, the Family, and the Gender Division of Labor," in *More Than Chattel: Black Women and Slavery in the Americas*, ed. David Barry Gaspar and Darlene Clark Hine (Bloomington: Indiana University Press, 1996), 17–20; Hudson, *To Have and to Hold*, 32–78; Penningroth, *Claims of Kinship*, esp. 82–85, 104. The records of the Southern Claims Commission obscure the fact that auxiliary production was family labor. Men filed most freedpeople's claims and generally counted all property as their own, but a few claimants let on how they had collaborated with their women and children.

121. Testimony of Samuel Chase, 14 September 1872, Samuel Chase Claim, USCC.

122. Ted Ownby, *American Dreams in Mississippi: Consumers, Poverty, and Culture* (Chapel Hill: University of North Carolina Press, 1999), 50–60; Penningroth, *Claims of Kinfolk*, 45–78.

123. On the integral connections between staple and independent production, see Tomich, *Slavery in the Circuit of Sugar*, 259–80; Berlin and Morgan, "Introduction," 1–45; Mary Turner, "Introduction," in *From Chattel Slaves to Wage Slaves: The Dynamics of Labour Bargaining in the Americas*, ed. Turner (Kingston, Jamaica: Randle, 1995), 9–12.

124. Lewis C. Gray, *History of Agriculture*, 1:564; Philip D. Morgan, "Work and Culture," 563–99; Betty Wood, *Women's Work, Men's Work: The Informal Economies of Lowcountry Georgia* (Athens: University of Georgia Press, 1995), 12–100; Hudson, *To Have and to Hold*, 17, 66–69; Penningroth, *Claims of Kinfolk*, 45–109.

125. Philip D. Morgan, "The Ownership of Property by Slaves in the Mid-Nineteenth-Century Low Country," *JSH* 49 (August 1983): 408, table 3; Lawrence T. McDonnell, "Money Knows No Master: Market Relations and the American Slave Community," in *Developing Dixie: Modernization in a Traditional Society*, ed. Winfred B. Moore Jr., Joseph F. Tripp, and Lyon G. Tyler Jr. (Westport, Conn.: Greenwood, 1988), 33.

126. Charles Joyner, *Down by the Riverside: A South Carolina Slave Community* (Urbana: University of Illinois Press, 1985), 52; Loren Schweninger, "Slave Independence and Enterprise in South Carolina, 1780–1865," *South Carolina Historical Magazine* 93 (April 1992): 110–11; Robert L. Olwell, "'A Reckoning of Accounts': Patriarchy, Market Relations, and Control on Henry Laurens's Lowcountry Plantations, 1762–1785," in *Working Toward Freedom: Slave Society and Domestic Economy in the American South*, ed. Larry E. Hudson Jr. (Rochester, N.Y.: University of Rochester Press, 1994), 37–38; Hudson, *To Have and to Hold*, 10–11, 18–20; Betty Wood, "'Never on a Sunday?'" 83–84.

127. On the predominance of slave women in Charleston markets during the colonial period, see Philip D. Morgan, *Slave Counterpoint: Black Culture in the Eighteenth-Century Chesapeake and Lowcountry* (Chapel Hill: University of North Carolina

Press, 1998), 250–52; Robert L. Olwell, "'Loose, Idle, and Disorderly': Slave Women in the Eighteenth-Century Charleston Marketplace," in *More Than Chattel: Black Women and Slavery in the Americas*, ed. David Barry Gaspar and Darlene Clark Hine (Bloomington: Indiana University Press, 1996), 97–110. On Savannah in the early republic, see Betty Wood, *Women's Work, Men's Work*, 86–87.

128. Philip D. Morgan, "Ownership of Property by Slaves," 399–420; Loren Schweninger, *Black Property Owners in the South, 1790–1915* (Urbana: University of Illinois Press, 1990), 33–34, 57–59; Dylan Penningroth, "Slavery, Freedom, and Social Claims to Property among African Americans in Liberty County, Georgia, 1850–1880," *JAH* 84 (September 1997): 1–28.

129. Philip D. Morgan, "Ownership of Property by Slaves," 408, table 3.

130. Barbara J. Fields, "The Nineteenth-Century South: History and Theory," *Plantation Society in the Americas* 2 (April 1983): 7–27, esp. 9 n. 9; Michael Mullin, *Africa in America: Slave Acculturation and Resistance in the American South and the British Caribbean, 1736–1831* (Urbana: University of Illinois Press, 1992), 126–27; Joseph P. Reidy, "Obligation and Right: Patterns of Labor, Subsistence, and Exchange in the Cotton Belt of Georgia, 1790–1860," in *Cultivation and Culture: Labor and the Shaping of Slave Life in the Americas*, ed. Ira Berlin and Philip D. Morgan (Charlottesville: University Press of Virginia, 1993), 152–54; John Campbell, "As 'A Kind of Freeman'? Slaves' Market-Related Activities in the South Carolina Up Country, 1800–1860," in ibid., 243–74.

131. Philip D. Morgan, "Work and Culture," 565–66, 575–79, 586–87.

132. Nevitt Diary, 2, 9 January 1830, 20 February 1830, 12, 26 June 1830, 3 July 1830, 7, 28 August 1830, 18 September 1830, RASP; Aventine Plantation Diary, 12–13 April 1859, 2, 9 July 1859, 3 May 1859; Diary, 23 May 1857, Wailes Papers, MDAH.

133. Diary, 21 January 1843, 4 February 1843, Metcalfe Papers, RASP.

134. McCall Plantation Journal, 8 June 1850, RASP.

135. Wade Plantation Diary, List of Negro Corn 1852, Account for Negroes' Corn for 1856; Diary, Account of Poultry, 16 October 1854, Darden Family Papers; Diary, 31 December 1858, 29 October 1860, Wailes Papers; Aventine Plantation Diary, 13 November 1859, Items Sent to Mrs. Lizzy Shields to Natchez, Record of the Corn Crop of Aventine People, MDAH; Sydnor, *Slavery in Mississippi*, 96, 98; Janet Sharp Hermann, *The Pursuit of a Dream* (New York: Vintage, 1983), 14.

136. Christopher Morris, *Becoming Southern*, 12–14.

137. See, for example, Testimony of Thomas Bradshaw, Allen B. Richardson, 23 May 1873, Thomas Bradshaw Claim, Case 11363; Testimony of Dick Green, 14 October 1871, Dick Green Claim, Case 6963, Warren County, SCC; Testimony of Samuel Chase, 14 September 1872, Samuel Chase Claim, USCC.

138. Testimony of David Cook, Andrew Downs, D. H. Alverson, 27 February 1872,

David Cook Claim, Case 3531, USCC; Sydnor, *Slavery in Mississippi*, 96–98; U. B. Phillips, *American Negro Slavery: A Survey of the Supply, Employment, and Control of Negro Labor as Determined by the Plantation Regime* (1918; reprint, Baton Rouge: Louisiana State University Press, 1990), 268, 305; Stampp, *Peculiar Institution*, 164–65.

139. Testimony of Waller Wade, Jerry Smithson, 10 May 1873, Waller Wade Claim, Case 13746, Yazoo County, SCC; Moore, *Emergence of the Cotton Kingdom*, 103.

140. Wade Plantation Diary, 19, 26 April 1851, MDAH.

141. Sidney W. Mintz, *Caribbean Transformations* (1974; reprint, New York: Columbia University Press, 1989), 180–83, 186–88, 193–94; Michael Mullin, "Slave Economic Strategies: Food, Markets and Property," in *From Chattel Slaves to Wage Slaves: The Dynamics of Labour Bargaining in the Americas*, ed. Mary Turner (Kingston, Jamaica: Randle, 1995), 72; Hudson, *To Have and to Hold*, 41–42; Woodville K. Marshall, "Provision Ground and Plantation Labor in Four Windward Islands: Competition for Resources during Slavery," in *Cultivation and Culture: Labor and the Shaping of Slave Life in the Americas*, ed. Ira Berlin and Philip D. Morgan (Charlottesville: University Press of Virginia, 1993), 205–10. Supervision of slave labor in the provision grounds was not unknown in other parts of the Caribbean, however. See Dale Tomich, "*Une Petite Guinée*: Provision Ground and Plantation in Martinique, 1830–1848," in *Cultivation and Culture: Labor and the Shaping of Slave Life in the Americas*, ed. Ira Berlin and Philip D. Morgan (Charlottesville: University Press of Virginia, 1993), 230–31.

142. I erred in counting trade among the social relations binding neighborhoods together in Anthony E. Kaye, "Neighbourhoods and Solidarity in the Natchez District of Mississippi: Rethinking the Antebellum Slave Community," *Slavery and Abolition* 23 (April 2002): 1–24; Anthony E. Kaye, "The Personality of Power: The Ideology of Slaves in the Natchez District and the Delta of Mississippi, 1830–1865" (Ph.D. diss., Columbia University, 1999). Neighborhood trade in the low country may not have been much more extensive than in the Natchez District. Although authors have hinted at trade between plantations, examples and evidence are scant. See Schweninger, "Slave Independence and Enterprise," 122; Larry E. Hudson Jr., " 'All That Cash': Work and Status in the Slave Quarters," in *Working Toward Freedom*, ed. Hudson (Athens: University of Georgia Press, 1997), 77, 79, 86. The most careful student of independent production in the low country, Philip D. Morgan, did not count neighboring slaves among slaves' trading partners, who included passing traders, neighboring whites, and fellow slaves ("Work and Culture," 573).

143. Henry Hughes, "Treatise on Sociology," in *The Ideology of Slavery: Proslavery Thought in the Antebellum South, 1830–1860*, ed. Drew Gilpin Faust (Baton Rouge: Louisiana State University Press, 1981), 245, 254.

144. Alex Lichtenstein, " 'That Disposition to Theft, with Which They Have Been

Branded': Moral Economy, Slave Management, and the Law," *Journal of Social History* 21 (Spring 1988): 424–32; Gross, *Double Character*, 145–46; McDonnell, "Money Knows No Master," 36–37; Hudson, *To Have and to Hold*, 10–11, 17; Olwell, " 'Reckoning of Accounts,' " 38–39.

145. Lewis C. Gray, *History of Agriculture*, 565; Sydnor, *Gentleman of the Old Natchez Region*, 103; Ownby, *American Dreams*, 59–60.

146. Sydnor, *Slavery in Mississippi*, 97. Slaves faced a similar dilemma and developed a similar solution to the problem of marriage in the absence of legal sanction. See chap. 2.

147. Ownby, *American Dreams*, 50; Sydnor, *Gentleman of the Old Natchez Region*, 103–4; Robert L. Olwell, *Masters, Slaves, and Subjects: The Culture of Power in the South Carolina Low Country, 1740–1790* (Ithaca: Cornell University Press, 1998), 152–56.

148. Forest Plantation in Account with Mrs. Mary F. Dunbar, 25 December 1859, Mary F. Dunbar Papers; Est. B. H. Jennison, 25 December 1839, Financial Records, William L. Sharkey Papers, NTC; Cash Book, 23 December 1859, Surget Family Papers; Diary, 31 December 1858, Wailes Papers, MDAH; William K. Scarborough, "Slavery—The White Man's Burden," in *Perspectives and Irony in American Slavery*, ed. Harry P. Owens (Jackson: University Press of Mississippi, 1976), 114; Stampp, *Peculiar Institution*, 165; Sydnor, *Gentleman of the Old Natchez Region*, 103.

149. Plantation Book, Tobacco Sold to the Negroes, 9 July 1849–April 1850, Tobacco Sold the Negroes in 1857, Kiger Family Papers, NTC; Hermann, *Pursuit of a Dream*, 14, 18–19; Genovese, *Roll, Jordan, Roll*, 535.

150. Buena Vista Plantation Book, List of Money and Articles Paid the Negroes for Wood in 1852, Kiger Family Papers, NTC.

151. Nevitt Diary, 27 July 1830, RASP; Diary, 22 October–2 November 1855, 10 January 1858, 15 July 1858, Wailes Papers, MDAH.

152. Nevitt Diary, 25 December 1830, 25 December 1831, RASP; Scarborough, "Slavery," 112; Ownby, *American Dreams*, 57–58.

153. Forest Plantation in Account with Mrs. Mary F. Dunbar, 25 December 1859, Mary F. Dunbar Papers; Buena Vista Plantation Book, December 1851, Kiger Family Papers, NTC; Diary, 25 December 1855, Darden Family Papers; Diary, 31 December 1858, Wailes Papers, MDAH.

154. Aventine Plantation Diary, 17 May 1859, MDAH.

155. Roderick A. McDonald, *The Economy and Material Culture of Slaves: Goods and Chattels on the Sugar Plantations of Jamaica and Louisiana* (Baton Rouge: Louisiana State University Press, 1994), 55, 59; John Campbell, "As 'A Kind of Freeman'?" 259–63; Hudson, *To Have and to Hold*, 19.

156. Diary, Account of Poultry, n.d., Darden Family Papers, MDAH.

157. Wade Plantation Diary, 7–8, 14 May 1851, Negroes' Crop for 1855, Account for

Negroes' Corn for 1856 and 1857; Aventine Plantation Diary, Record of the Corn Crop of Aventine People, 13 November 1859, MDAH.

158. Penningroth, *Claims of Kinfolk*, 61–63, 67–68; Moore, *Emergence of the Cotton Kingdom*, 279–81.

159. *Woodville Republican*, 12 October 1839, 16 November 1839; Sydnor, *Slavery in Mississippi*, 99.

160. Testimony of Reuben Cunningham and Stephen Johnson, 31 May 1873, Alexander Hutchinson Claim, Case 11562, USCG.

161. Testimony of Samuel Chase, 14 September 1872, Lewis Jackson, 23 September 1877, Samuel Chase Claim, USCC.

162. Diary, 9 October 1854, 26 December 1855, 14 December 1856, Darden Family Papers, MDAH; Testimony of Henry Hunt, 6 May 1873, Henry Hunt Claim, Case 10840, Warren County, SCC; Testimony of Henry Banks, 24 June 1873, Henry Banks Claim, Case 14443, Warren County, SCC; Christopher Morris, *Becoming Southern*, 226 n. 28.

163. Leslie H. Owens, *This Species of Property: Slave Life and Culture in the Old South* (New York: Oxford University Press, 1976), 54; Hermann, *Pursuit of a Dream*, 14; McDonald, *Economy and Material Culture of Slaves*, 70.

164. Jno. Knight to Wm. M. Beall, 27 January 1844, Knight Papers, RASP; Palatine Day Book, Rules and Regulations, 18 January 1854, Surget Family Papers, MDAH.

165. Testimony of Thomas Bradshaw, 23 May 1873, Thomas Bradshaw Claim, SCC; Testimony of James Smith, 6 November 1871, Estate of C. D. Hamilton Claim, Case 9648, USCC; Hermann, *Pursuit of a Dream*, 18; Christopher Morris, *Becoming Southern*, 75.

166. Plantation Book, 28 December 1851, Your Attached Husband to My Dear Wife, 29 October 1852, Kiger Family Papers, NTC; Diary, 21, 24, 27 January 1843, Metcalfe Papers; Henry Turner to My Dear Sir, 7 January 1842, 26 June 1842, Quitman Family Papers; Baker Diary, 13 February 1849, 11 November 1849, 6 December 1849, RASP.

167. The commission stipulated those terms on the form that all claimants used to petition for compensation. See SCC.

168. Testimony of James Smith, 6 November 1871, Estate of C. D. Hamilton Claim, USCC.

169. Testimony of William Johnson, 11 March 1873, Henry Daniels Claim, Case 1939, USCC.

170. Testimony of Cyrus Lee, 6 November 1876, Mary A. Brooks Claim, Case 3480, USCC. For other examples of former slaves who professed no knowledge of prices during slavery, see Testimony of William Anderson, 20 January 1872, L. D. Aldrich Claim, Case 5848; Testimony of John Turner, 18 February 1878, John Alverson Claim, USCC.

171. Wade Plantation Diary, List of Negro Corn, MDAH; Number of Barrels of Corn the Negros Made for Themselves, Kiger Family Papers, NTC.

172. Lotta Miller, Deposition, 31 May 1884, Dennis Ramsay File, Mother's Certificate 209614, CWPF.

173. Aventine Plantation Diary, 3, 10, 17 May 1859, 13 November 1859, Record of the Corn Crop of Aventine People, MDAH.

174. Diary, Account of Poultry, 25 December 1855, Darden Family Papers, MDAH.

175. Ibid., 26 December 1855.

176. Christopher Morris, *Becoming Southern*, 75, 226 n. 28. Among slaveholders, stores were a male preserve and shopping was largely men's business (Ownby, *American Dreams*, 11, 25–26).

177. Emphasis added. Aventine Plantation Diary, 9 July 1859, MDAH; Fogel and Engerman, *Time on the Cross*, 142.

178. Wade Plantation Diary, 19 April 1851, MDAH.

179. Diary, 10 January 1858, 15 July 1858, Wailes Papers, MDAH.

180. Elvira Anderson explained that her husband did not join her in her claim for two calves and cows because "I owned the property claimed as mine before we were married" (Testimony of Elvira Anderson, 5 May 1873, Elvira Anderson Claim, Case 14172, Warren County, SCC; Penningroth, *Claims of Kinfolk*, 103–7).

181. Testimony of Henry Hunt, 6 May 1873, Henry Hunt Claim, SCC; Alexander Smith, Deposition, 28 March 1893, Henry Hunt File, Invalid's Certificate 956385, CWPF; Hudson, *To Have and to Hold*, 63.

182. Penningroth, *Claims of Kinfolk*, 91–97.

183. Testimony of Louisa Lattimer, 3 July 1873, Andrew Black Claim, Case 10361, Warren County, SCC.

184. In October 1863, Emory Anderson married Elvira Holly (Testimony of Emory Anderson and Elvira Anderson, 5 May 1873, Elvira Anderson Claim, SCC).

185. Testimony of Benjamin Stinyard, Charles Burnam, 26 July 1872, Benjamin Stinyard Claim, Case 6999, Warren County, SCC.

186. Sydnor, *Slavery in Mississippi*, 97–98.

187. Buena Vista Plantation Book, Tobacco Sold to the Negroes, July 1849–April 1850, Tobacco Sold the Negros in 1857, Kiger Family Papers, NTC; Christopher Morris, *Becoming Southern*, 75; Ownby, *American Dreams*, 55–56; Marie J. Schwartz, *Born in Bondage*, 142.

188. Testimony of Russell Giles, 16 May 1877, Russell Giles Claim, Case 11583; Testimony of J. S. Acuff, 15 October 1872[?], Peter Jackson Claim, Case 14295, Warren County, SCC.

189. Testimony of Elijah Sharkey, 31 July 1873, Belfield Hicks Claim, Case 12941, Warren County, SCC. On the vagaries of Hicks's testimony in various claims, see Kaye, "Personality of Power," 21.

190. Testimony of William Scott, 29 October 1871, William Scott Claim, Case 7001,

Warren County; Testimony of Anthony Lewis, 20 July 1872, Anthony Lewis Claim, Case 15293, Claiborne County; Testimony of Nelson Finley, 30 January 1874, Nelson Finley Claim, Case 16219, Wilkinson County, SCC.

191. Peter Jackson, Henry Watson, and Alfred Swan acquired draft animals during the war. Andrew Black and Henry Morris hired their time during the 1850s. See Testimony of Andrew Black, 13 July 1873, Andrew Black Claim; Testimony of Peter Jackson, 15 October 1872, Peter Jackson Claim; Testimony of Henry Morris, 9 August 1873, Henry Morris Claim, Case 8142; Testimony of Henry Watson, 11 October 1873, Henry Watson Claim, Case 16555, Warren County; Testimony of Alfred Swan, 14 January 1878, Alfred Swan Claim, Case 19740, Adams County, SCC. For other examples of how slaves obtained horses, mules, and cows before the Civil War, see Testimony of Jesse Williams, Mary Griffin, 25 May 1877, Jesse Williams Claim, Case 10839; Testimony of John L. Green, n.d., Andrew Downs Claim, Case 12105; Testimony of William Green, 6 March 1875, William Green Claim, Case 6962, Warren County, SCC. For examples of slaves who acquired draft animals during the war, see chap. 6.

192. Philip D. Morgan, "Ownership of Property by Slaves," 412–15; Hudson, *To Have and to Hold*, 23–25.

193. Testimony of Henry Watson, 11 October 1873, Henry Watson Claim, SCC.

194. Richard C. Wade, *Slavery in the Cities: The South, 1820–1860* (London: Oxford University Press, 1964), 38–55; Robert S. Starobin, *Industrial Slavery in the Old South* (London: Oxford University Press, 1970), 128–37.

195. Southern jurists recognized hiring out as a rental arrangement and drew analogies to renting other forms of property instead of reasoning within the law of master and servant. Jurists were mainly concerned, however, with the arrangement between slaveholders who rented out slaves to employers rather than with slaves who rented their time from their owners and hired themselves out to employers (Thomas D. Morris, *Southern Slavery and Law*, 132–58).

196. Testimony of Amos Cooper, 22 December 1873, Amos Cooper Claim, Case 21867, Yazoo County, SCC.

197. David R. Goldfield, "Pursuing the American Urban Dream: Cities in the Old South," in *The City in Southern History: The Growth of Urban Civilization in the South*, ed. Blaine A. Brownell and Goldfield (Port Washington, N.Y.: Kennikat, 1977), 53, 56–59, 64–67; Claudia D. Goldin, *Urban Slavery in the American South, 1820–1860: A Quantitative History* (Chicago: University of Chicago Press, 1976), 55, 69–89, 123–25, table 14; Barbara J. Fields, *Slavery and Freedom on the Middle Ground* (New Haven: Yale University Press, 1985), 18–22, 27–28, 48–49; Kate C. Larson, *Bound for the Promised Land: Harriet Tubman, Portrait of an American Hero* (New York: Random House, 2004), 21–42; Charles B. Dew, "Disciplining Slave Ironworkers in the Antebellum South: Coercion, Conciliation, and Accommodation," *AHR* 79 (April 1974): 393–418; Keith C. Barton, "'Good Cooks and

Washers': Slave Hiring, Domestic Labor, and the Market in Bourbon County, Kentucky," *JAH* 84 (September 1997): 436–60.

198. Richard B. Morris, "The Measure of Bondage in the Slave States," *Mississippi Valley Historical Review* 41 (September 1954): 230; Clement Eaton, "Slave-Hiring in the Upper South: A Step toward Freedom," *Mississippi Valley Historical Review* 46 (March 1960): 663–78; Wade, *Slavery in the Cities*, 33–36; Goldin, *Urban Slavery*, 25–26, 35–37, 114–15, tables 6–7; Sarah S. Hughes, "Slaves for Hire: The Allocation of Black Labor in Elizabeth City County, Virginia, 1782–1810," *WMQ*, 3rd ser., 35 (April 1978): 260–86.

199. Starobin, *Industrial Slavery*, 13, 66–67, 120, 181; Randolph B. Campbell, "Research Note: Slave Hiring in Texas," *AHR* 93 (February 1988): 107–14, esp. 108; John E. Gonzales, "Flush Times, Depression, War, and Compromise," in *History of Mississippi*, ed. Richard A. McLemore (Hattiesburg: University and College Press of Mississippi, 1973), 290–91.

200. For other examples of witnesses who said they hired their time from their owner or who talked about others who hired their time without mentioning owners, see Testimony of George W. Boyd, 7 October 1871, Minerva Boyd Claim, Case 6942, Warren County; Testimony of James K. Hyman, Richard Dorsey, 8 July 1873, Richard Dorsey Claim, Cases 4337, 20298, Adams County, SCC; Ben Lewis, [Exhibit], 1 March 1875, Harris Stewart File, Widow's Certificate 132717, CWPF.

201. Testimony of Robert Johnson, William Bailey, 11 April 1874, William A. Bailey Claim, Case 16217, Wilkinson County, SCC.

202. J[o]hn All[e]n, Affidavit, 27 April 1843, *State v. Jehn Allen alias John Allen*, Natchez Trace Crime and Punishment Collection, NTC.

203. A. Hutchinson, comp., *Code of Mississippi* (Jackson, Miss.: Price and Fall, 1848), 519; Sydnor, *Slavery in Mississippi*, 172–80; Goldin, *Urban Slavery*, 133–38.

204. The Southern Claims Commission rejected Edwards's petition on grounds that it was unclear whether Union soldiers had seized his horse and mule for army purposes. Testimony of Benjamin Edwards, Albert Johnson, 14 September 1877, Summary Report, n.d., Benjamin Edwards Claim, Case 9546, USCC.

205. Testimony of Amos Cooper, 22 December 1873, Amos Cooper Claim, SCC.

206. Testimony of Matilda Anderson, 20 May 1873, Matilda Anderson Claim; Testimony of Matilda Anderson, 22 May 1873, Testimony of Minerva Jones, 9 [May] 1873, Minerva Jones Claim, Case 6974, Warren County, SCC.

207. Marie J. Schwartz, *Born in Bondage*, 34–42; Jacqueline Jones, *Labor of Love, Labor of Sorrow*, 17–18.

208. Testimony of Dick Green, 22 May 1873, Minerva Jones Claim, SCC; McMillen, *Motherhood in the Old South*, 70.

209. Testimony of Jack Hyland, 2 April 1872, Jack Hyland Claim, Case 19956; Testimony of Daniel Murfee, 21 July 1873, Daniel Murfee Claim, Case 18062; Testimony of Lewis Parker, 21 May 1873, Lewis Parker Claim, Case 12710, Warren

County; Testimony of Henry Morris, 9 August 1873, Henry Morris Claim; Testimony of William Hitch, 28 February 1877, William Hitch Claim; Testimony of Richard Dorsey, 8 July 1873, Richard Dorsey Claim, Adams County, SCC.

210. Mary Beth Corrigan, "'It's a Family Affair': Buying Freedom in the District of Columbia, 1850–1860," in *Working Toward Freedom: Slave Society and Domestic Economy in the American South*, ed. Larry E. Hudson Jr. (Rochester, N.Y.: University of Rochester Press, 1994), 163–91.

211. Testimony of Daniel Murfee, 21 July 1873, Daniel Murfee Claim, SCC.

212. Testimony of Jackson French, 1 April 1873, Summary Report, [?] December 1874, Jackson French Claim, Case 17047, Claiborne County; Testimony of Isham Lewis, 20 May 1873, Isham Lewis Claim, Case 6981, Warren County; Testimony of Richard Dorsey, 8 July 1873, Richard Dorsey Claim, Adams County, SCC.

213. Testimony of Jackson French, 1 April 1873, Jackson French Claim, Case 17047, Claiborne County, SCC.

Chapter Four

1. Diary, 5 June 1855, 18 April 1859, 30 January 1862, Benjamin L. C. Wailes Papers, MDAH.

2. Ibid., 4–6 June 1859.

3. For an excerpt from Wailes's diary recounting the episode, see Michael Wayne, *Death of an Overseer: Reopening a Murder Investigation from the Plantation South* (New York: Oxford University Press, 2001), 89–90.

4. Diary, 4–6 June 1859, Wailes Papers, MDAH.

5. *State v. Bill*, May Term 1853, Indictment, 8 May 1852, Affidavit, 13 May 1852, Instructions for Defendant Given by the Court and Instructions for the State Given by the Court, n.d. November 1852, Drawer 345, ACCCR. Testimony that other slaves wanted Lassley dead and may have conspired to kill him is evident in the judge's instructions to the jury on how to consider evidence of these scenarios in Bill's first trial. The judge ordered Bill tried a third time, but the outcome of that proceeding is unknown. For a discussion of these trials, see chap. 5. Scholars have yet to connect the killing of Lassley to the two subsequent incidents nearby. For an instructive discussion of the latter — the killings of overseers Y. W. McBride and Duncan Skinner — see Wayne, *Death of an Overseer*.

6. The Lassley place appears as the "Lessley tract" in the "Map of Cedar Grove and Surrounding Plantations" in Wayne, *Death of an Overseer*, 15. The tract is identified as Matthew Lassley's plantation in Estate of C. Stephen Smith, 18 December 1841, ACPRER, 1:99–103.

7. The account in this and the following two paragraphs follows Wayne, *Death of an Overseer*, 9–18, 34.

8. Ibid., 47, 98.

9. A third slave, Reuben, was indicted and convicted but received a new trial based on

evidence that he did not directly participate in the crime. *State v. Reuben, John, and Tom*, November Term 1857, Drawer 352; *State v. Reuben*, May Term 1859, Drawer 355, ACCCR. Testimony at trial revealed that Reuben was with his children at the time of the killing (Wayne, *Death of an Overseer*, 64–65).

10. William L. Sharkey, comp., *The Revised Code of the Statute Laws of Mississippi* (Jackson, Miss.: Barksdale, 1857), 625.

11. Farrar's letter, written to William B. Foules, is printed in Wayne, *Death of an Overseer*, 35–36. Although Foules was the owner of Parker, Baker, and Mandamus plantation, Farrar wrote to Foules in his capacity as a member of the Adams County Board of Police, which was responsible for carrying out executions.

12. Ibid., 35–37, 175, 211.

13. Ibid., 214. Farrar was evidently satisfied with the final arrangements for the execution; he served on the committee that performed the odious task of fixing the value of Parker and Baker for the purposes of compensating Foules (*State v. Reuben, John, and Tom*, November Term 1857, Certificate of Execution, 29 January 1858, Drawer 352, ACCCR).

14. Harry Alexander, Deposition, 3 October 1884, Elisha Clasby File, Widow's Certificate 232233, CWPF.

15. Wayne, *Death of an Overseer*, 102, 212, appendix 3.

16. Some scholars have questioned whether the plot existed except in planters' imaginations. See Drew Gilpin Faust, "The Inquisition in Mississippi: A Review of *Tumult and Silence at Second Creek*," *New York Times Book Review*, 9 May 1993, 29; Wayne, *Death of an Overseer*, 101–2.

17. Winthrop D. Jordan, *Tumult and Silence at Second Creek: An Inquiry into a Civil War Slave Conspiracy* (Baton Rouge: Louisiana State University Press, 1993, 119). Some of the men on Brighton might have felt a particular urgency for a showdown if they were aware of the impending sale of their kinfolk by their owner, John S. Mosby, a small planter prone to drunkenness whose school for planter children was falling on hard times (Jordan, *Tumult and Silence*, 105–6).

18. Ibid., 100–101, 114, 123–24.

19. Ibid., 100.

20. Ibid., 107–8; John Carmichael Jenkins Family Papers, NTC. The absence of men in the white family may have made Forest a convenient location for discussing the business. The plantation was owned by Mary Dunbar, a widow. John C. Jenkins, her brother-in-law on adjoining Elgin, had also died in 1856.

21. Jordan, *Tumult and Silence*, 271–72, doc. A.

22. Ibid., 125–26, 168, 282. According to the record of George's testimony, he named the rebels' target as "Mr. Marshall." It is possible, as Winthrop Jordan asserts, that George was referring to George Marshall, but his father, Levin Marshall, seems the more likely candidate, given his proximity to Forest. On Marshall's holdings, see William K. Scarborough, *Masters of the Big House: Elite Slaveholders of the Mid-*

Nineteenth-Century South (Baton Rouge: Louisiana State University Press, 2003), 3–4, 14–15, 467, appendix D.

23. Jordan, *Tumult and Silence*, 125.

24. Ibid., 121.

25. Runaways' use of aliases is discussed later in this chapter.

26. Jordan, *Tumult and Silence*, 124.

27. Ibid., 163.

28. Ibid., 117, 123–24, 142, 169.

29. Ibid., 162–63, 166, 168, 271–72, doc. A.

30. Norman R. Yetman, "The Background of the Slave Narrative Collection," *American Quarterly* 19 (Autumn 1967): 534–53; C. Vann Woodward, "History from Slave Sources: A Review Essay," *AHR* 79 (April 1974): 470–81.

31. Jordan, *Tumult and Silence*, 127–35.

32. On Aventine plantation, see chap. 3.

33. Jordan, *Tumult and Silence*, 131.

34. Ibid., 88–90, 115–16, 278–79, appendix.

35. Eugene D. Genovese, *From Rebellion to Revolution: Afro-American Slave Revolts in the Making of the Modern World* (Baton Rouge: Louisiana State University Press, 1979), 11–12; Steven Hahn, *A Nation Under Our Feet: Black Political Struggles in the Rural South from Slavery to the Great Migration* (Cambridge: Harvard University Press, 2003), 60; Douglas R. Egerton, *Gabriel's Rebellion: The Virginia Slave Conspiracies of 1800 and 1802* (Chapel Hill: University of North Carolina Press, 1993), 34–49.

36. John Nevitt Diary, 11 December 1830, 13 December 1832, ser. J, RASP.

37. Diary, 11 April 1859, 20 December 1859, Wailes Papers, MDAH.

38. John Hope Franklin and Loren Schweninger, *Runaway Slaves: Rebels on the Plantation* (Oxford: Oxford University Press, 1999), 101–9; Margaret Washington Creel, *"A Peculiar People": Slave Religion and Community-Culture Among the Gullahs* (New York: New York University Press, 1988), 239–40. On slaves who ran away to old neighborhoods after a westward migration within Virginia during the 1760s and 1770s, see Lorena S. Walsh, *From Calabar to Carter's Grove: The History of a Virginia Slave Community* (Charlottesville: University Press of Virginia, 1997), 213–14.

39. *Mississippi Free Trader*, 16 October 1850; Thomas C. Buchanan, *Black Life on the Mississippi: Slaves, Free Blacks, and the Western Steamboat World* (Chapel Hill: University of North Carolina Press, 2004), 101–21, esp. 105, 108–9, 112, 115.

40. *Woodville Republican*, 19 February 1842, 21 November 1848.

41. Thomas D. Morris, *Free Men All: The Personal Liberty Laws of the North, 1780–1861* (Baltimore: Johns Hopkins University Press, 1975); Stanley W. Campbell, *The Slave Catchers: Enforcement of the Fugitive Slave Law, 1850–1860* (Chapel Hill: University of North Carolina Press, 1970). For other fugitives from the Natchez District expected by owners to head for the North, see *Woodville Republican*, 11 September 1830; *Mississippi Free Trader*, 5 November 1845, 16 June 1847.

42. On the obstacles in the path of escape from the Lower South to the North, see Franklin and Schweninger, *Runaway Slaves*, 116–20.

43. For other examples of slaves who ran away soon after they were purchased, see *Peter Lapice v. John W. Monett*, *John A. Miller v. Frederick Stanton*, February Term 1831, Drawer 167; *Isaac Foster v. John McKinley*, May Term 1831, Drawer 171, ACCCR; Nevitt Diary, 5 January 1832, 16, 19 March 1832, RASP; Christopher Morris, *Becoming Southern: The Evolution of a Way of Life, Warren County and Vicksburg, Mississippi, 1770–1860* (New York: Oxford University Press, 1995), 67; Kenneth M. Stampp, *The Peculiar Institution: Slavery in the Ante-Bellum South* (1956; reprint, New York: Vintage, 1989), 112–13; Franklin and Schweninger, *Runaway Slaves*, 55–57.

44. *Woodville Republican*, 5 September 1840.

45. *Mississippi Free Trader*, 25 January 1843, 16 June 1847.

46. See, for example, Dempsey Jackson's notice for Ennis in Wayne, *Death of an Overseer*, 99.

47. *Mississippi Free Trader*, 10 December 1845.

48. George Poindexter, comp., *The Revised Code of the Laws of Mississippi* (Natchez, Miss.: Baker, 1824), 377.

49. *Woodville Republican*, 23 July 1836, 18 February 1837.

50. Ibid., 31 August 1830.

51. Ibid., 24 October 1840.

52. *Mississippi Free Trader*, 2 January 1847.

53. Franklin and Schweninger, *Runaway Slaves*, 100–103, 109.

54. Jno. Knight to Wm. M. Beall, 7 May 1845 [1846], John Knight Papers, ser. F, RASP; *Mississippi Free Trader*, 26 July 1848.

55. William K. Scarborough, *The Overseer: Plantation Management in the Old South* (1966; reprint, Athens: University of Georgia Press, 1984), 91–92. See also Henry Watson, *Narrative of Henry Watson, a Fugitive Slave* (Boston: Marsh, 1848), 15, EE.

56. Henry Turner to My Dear Sir, 12 October 1843, Quitman Family Papers, ser. J, RASP.

57. Nevitt Diary, 31 May 1830, RASP.

58. Ibid., 14 January 1829, 1 September 1829, 1–4 February 1830, 2, 4, 29 May 1830.

59. Ibid., 8 January 1829, 8 April 1831.

60. Ibid., 3–4 May 1832, 28 July 1832, 3 August 1832, 23 November 1832, 13 December 1832.

61. Francis Burchett, hearing the shot that killed Young, gave chase and captured Henry and Bob, though not before the latter shot Burchett in the stomach. Judge Stanhope Posey's notes on Bob's trial indicate that Henry testified that he saw Bob for the first time at Port Gibson. But Henry also testified that he was owned by a Mr. Ferguson, presumably the same Elbert Ferguson who owned Bob. See *State v. Bob (a Negro Slave)*, October Term 1847, Brief of Testimony, 19 November 1847, vol. 26, Correspondence and Papers, Governor Albert G. Brown, RG 27, MDAH.

62. On slaves' distinction between "taking" and "stealing," see Herbert Aptheker, *American Negro Slave Revolts* (1943; reprint, New York: International, 1974), 141–42; Stampp, *Peculiar Institution*, 125–27; Eugene D. Genovese, *Roll, Jordan, Roll: The World the Slaves Made* (New York: Pantheon, 1974), 607–8.

63. *Woodville Republican*, 4 October 1845, 10 January 1846.

64. Hanes's reprieve was brief. He was found guilty of first-degree murder and executed on 9 January 1846 (ibid., 10 January 1846).

65. Bourbon Plantation Journal, 17 September 1847, 5 November 1847, Metcalfe Family Papers, MDAH.

66. Genovese, *From Rebellion to Revolution*, 77–78.

67. Everard Green Baker Diary, 15 March 1849, ser. J, RASP.

68. Susan Sillers Darden Diary, 23 June 1857, Darden Family Papers, MDAH.

69. Ibid., 13, 17–18, 23, 27 May 1859, 20 June 1859; see also 7 January 1856, 8 June 1856.

70. *Mississippi Free Trader*, 18 July 1848. The items Sol carried were standard paraphernalia for conjurers (Walter C. Rucker, *The River Flows On: Black Resistance, Culture, and Identity Formation in Early America* [Baton Rouge: Louisiana State University Press, 2005], 184).

71. On runaways' resort to theft and violence in general, see Franklin and Schweninger, *Runaway Slaves*, 77–86.

72. Joseph Holt Ingraham, *The South-West, by a Yankee* (1835; reprint, Ann Arbor: University Microfilms, 1966), 2:261–63.

73. Sam Bowers Hilliard, *Atlas of Antebellum Southern Agriculture* (Baton Rouge: Louisiana State University Press, 1984), maps 76–81, 85–90, 97–100; Ira Berlin, *Generations of Captivity: A History of African-American Slaves* (Cambridge: Harvard University Press, 2003), 149–50, 176–78.

74. Jno. Knight to Wm. M. Beall, 7 May 1845 [1846], Knight Papers, RASP.

75. Steven F. Miller, "Plantation Labor Organization and Slave Life on the Cotton Frontier: The Alabama-Mississippi Black Belt, 1815–1840," in *Cultivation and Culture: Labor and the Shaping of Slave Life in the Americas*, ed. Ira Berlin and Philip D. Morgan (Charlottesville: University Press of Virginia, 1993), 166.

76. Stampp, *Peculiar Institution*, 114; Scarborough, *Masters of the Big House*, 427, appendix A.

77. Aventine Plantation Diary, 30–31 January 1859, MDAH. On the increased intensity and coordination of work at Aventine in 1859, see chap. 3.

78. Ibid., 15–21 August 1859. See also, U. B. Phillips, *Life and Labor in the Old South* (New York: Grosset and Dunlap, 1929), 208.

79. William R. Hogan and Edwin A. Davis, eds., *William Johnson's Natchez: The Antebellum Diary of a Free Negro* (1951; reprint, Baton Rouge: Louisiana State University Press, 1993), 93, 133, 447; *Mississippi Free Trader*, 17 May 1843; Petition for Habeas Corpus, 3 May 1845, WCCCP; *State v. Bill*, May Term 1853, ACCCR; *State v. George*, April Term 1845, Criminal Court Cases, Warren County, Slaves

and Slavery Collection, NTC; Christopher Waldrep, *Roots of Disorder: Race and Criminal Justice in the American South, 1817–80* (Urbana: University of Illinois Press, 1998), 26; Christopher Morris, *Becoming Southern*, 80–82.

80. *State v. David*, May Term 1846, Indictment, 18 May 1846, Drawer 331, ACCCR.

81. *State v. Tarleton and Spencer, Slaves*, April Term 1847, Indictment, 4 May 1847, WCCCP.

82. Randolph B. Campbell, "Slavery in the Natchez Trace Collection," in *Inside the Natchez Trace Collection*, ed. Katherine J. Adams and Lewis L. Gould (Baton Rouge: Louisiana State University Press, 1999), 37–38.

83. Plantation Book, 16–17 January 1861, 29 December 1861, James Allen and Family Papers, MDAH.

84. Ann Barnes Archer to My Dear Abram, 17 December 1854, Richard Thompson Archer Family Papers, NTC; Randolph B. Campbell, "Slavery in the Natchez Trace Collection," 47–48, 51–53.

85. Diary, 29 September 1853, 13 April 1859, 15 June 1862, Wailes Papers, MDAH.

86. Ibid., 10, 22 May 1857; Charles S. Sydnor, *A Gentleman of the Old Natchez Region: Benjamin L. C. Wailes* (Durham, N.C.: Duke University Press, 1938), 179–81. It was not unusual for slaves and owners with strong ties to mediate them by way of animals (Diary, 4 March 1855, 26 January 1856, Darden Family Papers, MDAH).

87. Diary, 7 October 1853, 26 February 1858, 1 October 1858, 31 July 1861, Wailes Papers, MDAH.

88. Ibid., 10–13 May 1857, 2–3 December 1857, 15 July 1858, 11–13 April 1859.

89. Ibid., 27 January 1857, 9–10 September 1857.

90. Benjamin L. C. Wailes, *Report on the Agriculture and Geology of Mississippi: Embracing a Sketch of the Social and Natural History of the State* (Jackson, Miss.: Barksdale, 1854); Sydnor, *Gentleman of the Old Natchez Region*, 143–69, 239–58; Michael O'Brien, *Conjectures of Order: Intellectual Life in the American South, 1810–1860* (Chapel Hill: University of North Carolina Press, 2005), 1:15, 20, 513–514, 517, table 1; Morton Rothstein, "The Changing Social Networks and Investment Behavior of a Slaveholding Elite in the Antebellum South: Some Natchez 'Nabobs,' 1800–1860," in *Entrepreneurs in Cultural Context*, ed. Sidney M. Greenfield, Arnold Strickon, and Robert T. Aubey (Albuquerque: University of New Mexico Press, 1979), 65–88; William K. Scarborough, "Lords or Capitalists? The Natchez Nabobs in Comparative Perspective," *JMH* 54 (August 1992): 239–67.

91. James Oakes, *The Ruling Race: A History of American Slaveholders* (New York: Knopf, 1982), 156; Scarborough, *Overseer*, 70.

92. U. B. Phillips, *American Negro Slavery: A Survey of the Supply, Employment, and Control of Negro Labor as Determined by the Plantation Regime* (1918; reprint, Baton Rouge: Louisiana State University Press, 1990), 273–74; Charles S. Sydnor, *Slavery in Mississippi* (1933; reprint, Baton Rouge: Louisiana State University Press, 1966), 71–72, 117–18; Stampp, *Peculiar Institution*, 51, 77–78, 82–83, 172–75, 178,

184; Genovese, *Roll, Jordan, Roll*, 14–15; Drew Gilpin Faust, *James Henry Hammond and the Old South: A Design for Mastery* (Baton Rouge: Louisiana State University Press, 1982), 117; Oakes, *Ruling Race*, 153–60.

93. Scarborough, *Overseer*, 6–7, 68–71.

94. For Affleck's instructions, with a planter's amendments in the margins, see "The Duties of an Overseer," Doro Plantation Record Book, vol. 9, Charles Clark and Family Papers, MDAH.

95. Your Attached Husband to My Dear Wife, 29 October 1852, Kiger Family Papers, NTC; David Brion Davis, *The Problem of Slavery in Western Culture* (Ithaca: Cornell University Press, 1966), 58–70; Genovese, *Roll, Jordan, Roll*, 87–89.

96. Jordan, *Tumult and Silence*, 303, doc. C.

97. Diary, 13 June 1856, 13, 17 April 1857, Darden Family Papers, MDAH.

98. James M. Baird, "Between Slavery and Independence: Power Relations between Dependent White Men and Their Superiors in Late Colonial and Early National Virginia with Particular Reference to the Overseer-Employer Relationship" (Ph.D. diss., Johns Hopkins University, 1999), 106–49. See also Faust, *James Henry Hammond*, 124–25; Oakes, *Ruling Race*, 154–55.

99. Testimony of Squire Myers, 21 July 1873, John M. Johnson Claim, Case 18061, Warren County, SCC; Albert Brooks, Deposition, 28 July 1891, Aaron Barefield File, Widow's Certificate 305104, CWPF; William L. Van Deburg, *The Slave Drivers: Black Agricultural Labor Supervisors in the Antebellum South* (1979; reprint, New York: Oxford University Press, 1988), 50–51, 96.

100. Testimony of Richard Eastman, 25 January 1873, Richard Eastman Claim, Case 8244, USCC.

101. Six weeks later, their owner, James Allen, whipped both Eastman and Elias, though it is unclear whether it was for their altercation in June or for a subsequent transgression (Plantation Book, 17 June 1862, 31 July 1862, Allen and Family Papers, MDAH).

102. Copy of the Pardon of Sam, 9 June 1832, vol. 15, Correspondence and Papers, Governor A. M. Scott, RG 27, MDAH.

103. Testimony of Edward Howard, 1 June 1874, Martha Crane Claim, Case 8313, USCC; Sydnor, *Slavery in Mississippi*, 73; William K. Scarborough, "Heartland of the Cotton Kingdom," in *History of Mississippi*, ed. Richard A. McLemore (Hattiesburg: University and College Press of Mississippi, 1973), 337; Genovese, *Roll, Jordan, Roll*, 370.

104. Testimony of Balor Hill, November 6, 1871, Estate of C. D. Hamilton Claim, Case 9648, USCC.

105. William Fountain, Deposition, 30 October 1893, Eliza Grayson, Deposition, 28 October 1893, Elisha Grayson File, Widow's Certificate 389530, CWPF.

106. Genovese, *Roll, Jordan, Roll*, 358.

107. Stampp, *Peculiar Institution*, 130–32.

108. Harold Courlander, *Negro Folk Music, U.S.A.* (1963; reprint, New York: Dover, 1991), 28–29, 85–92, 115–19.

109. Katherine J. Adams, "Natchez District Women: Voices of Southern Women in the Natchez Trace Collection," in *Inside the Natchez Trace Collection*, ed. Adams and Lewis L. Gould (Baton Rouge: Louisiana State University Press, 1999), 59.

110. On slaves' ability to play drivers, overseers, and owners off against one another, see Sydnor, *Slavery in Mississippi*, 71; Phillips, *American Negro Slavery*, 281, 304; Stampp, *Peculiar Institution*, 105–9; Genovese, *Roll, Jordan, Roll*, 14–22, 372–73, 381; Scarborough, *Overseer*, x, 97, 102, 120.

111. Walter Wade Plantation Diary, 6, 10 February 1854, 14, 18, 21–23 March 1854, MDAH.

112. Sydnor, *Gentleman of the Old Natchez Region*, 93.

113. Diary, 9 October 1857, 31 December 1857, Wailes Papers, MDAH.

114. Ibid., 21 October 1857, 1 December 1859.

115. Sydnor, *Slavery in Mississippi*, 29, 39; John W. Blassingame, *The Slave Community: Plantation Life in the Antebellum South*, rev. ed. (New York: Oxford University Press, 1979), 151–53; Genovese, *Roll, Jordan, Roll*, 451–58; Herbert G. Gutman, *The Black Family in Slavery and Freedom, 1750–1925* (New York: Vintage, 1976), 264–69.

116. Deborah Gray White, *Ar'n't I A Woman? Female Slaves in the Plantation South* (New York: Norton, 1985), 76.

117. Jean E. Friedman, *The Enclosed Garden: Women and Community in the Evangelical South, 1830–1900* (Chapel Hill: University of North Carolina Press, 1985), 30–31; Brenda E. Stevenson, *Life in Black and White: Family and Community in the Slave South* (New York: Oxford University Press, 1996), 60, 227.

118. Kirsten E. Wood, *Masterful Women: Slaveholding Widows from the American Revolution through the Civil War* (Chapel Hill: University of North Carolina Press, 2004), 35–60, 79, 83–90; Catherine Clinton, *Plantation Mistress: Woman's World in the Old South* (New York: Pantheon, 1982), 32–35; Cynthia A. Kierner, *Beyond the Household: Women's Place in the Early South, 1700–1835* (Ithaca: Cornell University Press, 1998), 2, 172–74.

119. Genovese, *Roll, Jordan, Roll*, 500.

120. For a brilliant discussion of the subversive potential of such appropriations, see Jean Besson, *Martha Brae's Two Histories: European Expansion and Caribbean Culture-Building in Jamaica* (Chapel Hill: University of North Carolina Press, 2002), esp. 20–26. Also revealing is James Sidbury, *Plowshares into Swords: Race, Rebellion, and Identity in Gabriel's Virginia, 1730–1810* (Cambridge: Cambridge University Press, 1997), 55–94.

121. Henry Turner to Dear Sir, 15 September 1843, 12, 17, 26 October 1843, Quitman Family Papers, RASP; Leslie H. Owens, *This Species of Property: Slave Life and Culture in the Old South* (New York: Oxford University Press, 1976), 160–61.

122. Waldrep, *Roots of Disorder*, 22–24.

123. Ira Berlin, *Many Thousands Gone: The First Two Centuries of Slavery in North America* (Cambridge: Harvard University Press, 1998), 113; Stephanie M. H. Camp, *Closer to Freedom: Enslaved Women and Everyday Resistance in the Plantation South* (Chapel Hill: University of North Carolina Press, 2004), 13–16.

124. Poindexter, *Revised Code*, 371–72, 374, 381–82.

125. A. Hutchinson, comp., *Code of Mississippi* (Jackson, Miss.: Price and Fall, 1848), 539.

126. Poindexter, *Revised Code*, 376–78.

127. George P. Rawick, Jan Hillegas, and Ken Lawrence, eds., *The American Slave: A Composite Autobiography*, supp. ser. 1 (Westport, Conn.: Greenwood, 1977), 7:595.

128. Poindexter, *Revised Code*, 377–79, 440; Sydnor, *Slavery in Mississippi*, 78–79.

129. Christopher J. Olsen, *Political Culture and Secession in Mississippi: Masculinity, Honor, and the Antiparty Tradition, 1830–1860* (Oxford: Oxford University Press, 2000), 118.

130. Rawick, Hillegas, and Lawrence, *American Slave*, 8:833–34, 1244–45, 9:1769, 10:2411; J. Michael Crane, "Controlling the Night: Perceptions of the Slave Patrol System in Mississippi," *JMH* 61 (Summer 1999): 129–32; Sally E. Hadden, *Slave Patrols: Law and Violence in Virginia and the Carolinas* (Cambridge: Harvard University Press, 2001), 62–63, 84–90, 105–9, 124–29.

Chapter Five

1. Anthony Stafford, Deposition, 17 June 1884, Dennis Ramsay File, Mother's Certificate 209614, CWPF.

2. Clifton H. Johnson, ed., *God Struck Me Dead: Religious Conversion Experiences and Autobiographies of Ex-Slaves* (1945; Philadelphia: Pilgrim, 1969), 15–18.

3. Ibid.

4. Ibid., 13; Walter F. Pitts Jr., *Old Ship of Zion: The Afro-Baptist Ritual in the African Diaspora* (New York: Oxford University Press, 1993), 66–69, 155, 175.

5. Randy J. Sparks, *On Jordan's Stormy Banks: Evangelism in Mississippi, 1773–1876* (Athens: University of Georgia Press, 1994), 129–30; Albert J. Raboteau, *Slave Religion: The "Invisible Institution" in the Antebellum South* (New York: Oxford University Press, 1978), 239–43; Janet Duitsman Cornelius, *"When I Can Read My Title Clear": Literacy, Slavery, and Religion in the Antebellum South* (Columbia: University of South Carolina Press, 1991), 3, 59–60, 85–88, 91–93.

6. Erskine Clarke, *Dwelling Place: A Plantation Epic* (New Haven: Yale University Press, 2005), 103–6, 125–61; Blake Touchstone, "Planters and Slave Religion in the Deep South," in *Masters and Slaves in the House of the Lord: Race and Religion in the American South*, ed. John B. Boles (Lexington: University Press of Kentucky, 1988), 114–17, 122.

7. John A. B. Jones Text Book, 15 October 1854, John G. and John A. B. Jones Journals, MDAH.

8. Ibid., 13 August 1854; Matthew 11:28–30.

9. Ibid., 5 February 1854, 5 March 1854, 2, 23 April 1854, 14 June 1854, 17 February 1857; Romans 14:17; John 3:3, 18:36; Matthew 6:33, 18:3.

10. Eugene D. Genovese, *Roll, Jordan, Roll: The World the Slaves Made* (New York: Pantheon, 1974), 251.

11. Testimony of Harrison Winfield, 23 September 1887, Samuel Chase Claim, Case 1990; Testimony of George Dyson, 23 September 1889, James A. Fox, 28 May 1875, Elisha Fox Claim, Case 3668, USCC. Winfield described his work on the Fox place as part of his work for the "neighboring planters." But he was slightly out of his neighborhood when he worked for Mrs. Fox. The plantation of his owner, George Messenger, adjoined land belonging to the Fox family, but not Mrs. Fox's. The plantation of Winfield's owner is identified as "Baconham," Sophia Fox's as "E. & G. Queen" in Warren County Plantation Map (H. M. Marshall and T. K. Foster, 1888), pt. 10, Old Courthouse Museum, Vicksburg, Mississippi.

12. Larry M. James, "Biracial Fellowship in Antebellum Baptist Churches," in *Masters and Slaves in the House of the Lord: Race and Religion in the American South*, ed. John B. Boles (Lexington: University Press of Kentucky, 1988), 45–47.

13. Dugal G. McCall Plantation Journal, 18 July 1852, ser. J, RASP.

14. Nancy Roberts, Deposition, 17 June 1884, Dennis Ramsay File, CWPF; Testimony of William Scott, Joseph Howe, 29 October 1871, William Scott Claim, Case 7001, Warren County, SCC.

15. Testimony of Henry A. Leach, 21 November 1874, Elisha Fox Claim, Case 3668, USCC.

16. Charles Whitmore Diaries, 3–8 June 1839, 12 August 1839, 17–22 January 1842, SHC; Ariela J. Gross, *Double Character: Slavery and Mastery in the Antebellum Southern Courtroom* (Princeton: Princeton University Press, 2000), 10–11, illustrations 1A–C.

17. Winthrop D. Jordan, *Tumult and Silence at Second Creek: An Inquiry into a Civil War Slave Conspiracy* (Baton Rouge: Louisiana State University Press, 1993), 9–11; Ronald L. F. Davis, *The Black Experience in Natchez, 1720–1880* (Natchez Historical Park, Miss.: Eastern National Park and Monument Association, 1994), 3, illustration B; Ann Paton Malone, *Sweet Chariot: Slave Family and Household Structure in Nineteenth-Century Louisiana* (Chapel Hill: University of North Carolina Press, 1992), 78, map 4.1; Lisa C. Tolbert, *Constructing Townscapes: Space and Society in Antebellum Tennessee* (Chapel Hill: University of North Carolina Press, 1999), 59–63.

18. Thomas C. Buchanan, *Black Life on the Mississippi: Slaves, Free Blacks, and the Western Steamboat World* (Chapel Hill: University of North Carolina Press, 2004), 19–51, 101–47.

19. Aventine Plantation Diary, 3 January 1859, 6 February 1859, 19 June 1859, 11 September 1859, MDAH. Montebello was on the outskirts of Natchez, Aventine

was across Second Creek at the south end of the county, and Highland was north of the creek between Fatherland and Elgin (Jordan, *Tumult and Silence*, 122–23).

20. Easter Wilson and Eliza Warren went by those names at the time of their testimony. Wilson went by the name of her owner in Tennessee (Stockard) and of her father (Cross) before her marriage, as Warren may have before hers. Eliza Warren, Deposition, 17 June 1897, Easter Wilson, Deposition, 10 February 1896, Claiborne Wilson File, Widow's Certificate 449117, CWPF.

21. John Nevitt Diary, 6–8 January 1831, 4, 20 February 1831, 2 May 1831, ser. J, RASP.

22. Ibid., 12 June 1831, 11 October 1831.

23. Ben Lewis, [Exhibit], 1 March 1875, Harris Stewart File, Widow's Certificate 132717, CWPF; Michael P. Johnson, "Work, Culture, and the Slave Community: Slave Occupations in the Cotton Belt in 1860," *Labor History* 27 (Summer 1986): 325–55.

24. Henry Turner to Dear Sir, 11 June 1842, 26 September 1842, Quitman Family Papers, ser. J, RASP. See also Accounts for Karnac Plantation, 23 March 1846, Rice C. Ballard Papers, NTC.

25. Everard Green Baker Diary, 2, 21, 30 May 1849, 2 June 1849, 21, 30 October 1849, ser. J; McCall Plantation Journal, 30 June 1852, 21 September 1852, 20 October 1852, 23–24 December 1852, RASP; Walter Wade Plantation Diary, 21 February 1850, MDAH.

26. Ann to My Dear Husband, 3 June 1849, Richard Thompson Archer Family Papers, NTC.

27. Robert E. May, *John A. Quitman: Old South Crusader* (Baton Rouge: Louisiana State University Press, 1985), 78–89.

28. Nichols was one of three servants in Quitman's retinue, including a free black man hired in Pittsburgh and a slave purchased in New Orleans during a layover en route to Mexico. Ibid., 147–99.

29. J. A. Quitman to My Beloved Wife, 22 November 1846, Quitman Family Papers, RASP.

30. Louisa to My Dearest Father, 29 December 1846, ibid.; Clement Eaton, *Jefferson Davis* (New York: Free Press, 1977), 134–35, 140.

31. J. A. Quitman to My Beloved Wife, 20 February 1847, Quitman Family Papers, RASP; May, *John A. Quitman*, 145–46.

32. Eveline Perano, now Miller, 4 October 1894, James Perano File, Widow's Certificate 160774, CWPF.

33. Expenses of Wilkins and Eugene to Virginia, 1 July 1853, Receipt from Barnum's City Hotel, 19 July 1853, Benjamin Roach Family Papers, NTC.

34. Receipts from Tontline, 11 June 1853, New York Hotel, 5 July 1853, Tremont House, 8 September 1853, Robert C. and Sarah W. Dunbar Papers, NTC.

35. Quoted in May, *John A. Quitman*, 144–45. See also J. A. Quitman to My Beloved

Wife, 20 February 1847, Annie Rosalie Quitman Journal, 25 December 1857, 25 April 1858, vol. 13, Quitman Family Papers, RASP.

36. Morton Rothstein, "The Changing Social Networks and Investment Behavior of a Slaveholding Elite in the Antebellum South: Some Natchez 'Nabobs,' 1800–1860," in *Entrepreneurs in Cultural Context*, ed. Sidney M. Greenfield, Arnold Strickon, and Robert T. Aubey (Albuquerque: University of New Mexico Press, 1979), 84.

37. John Hebron Moore, *Andrew Brown and Cypress Lumbering in the Old Southwest* (Baton Rouge: Louisiana State University Press, 1967), 37–59, 73–111; Francine Gray, Affidavit, 26 August 1918, Washington Gray File, Invalid's Certificate 855925, CWPF.

38. Henry Frederick Shugart Diary, 1–4 May 1839, 29 September 1839, 10 October 1839, 3 November 1839; Diary, 10–12 May 1857, Benjamin L. C. Wailes Papers, MDAH; May, *John A. Quitman*, 143.

39. Shugart Diary, 15, 19 February 1839, 14, 16, 19, 23 September 1839, 12, 18, 22, 30 November 1839, 9, 13, 17, 23 December 1839, MDAH.

40. Springfield Plantation Book, 1 June 1846, List of Slaves, 1 December 1853, John A. Quitman and Family Papers, MDAH; May, *John A. Quitman*, 44, 131–33.

41. Aventine Plantation Diary, 16, 23, 30 January 1859, 6 February 1859, Receipt for Supplies upon Aventine Plantation during 1859, MDAH.

42. Susan Sillers Darden Diary, 11–12, 16, 26 January 1855, 31 October 1855, 1, 2, 21, 26, 29, 30 November 1855, Darden Family Papers, MDAH. For a comparable seasonal mobility among slaves sent from tidewater plantations to fish in the estuaries and surf of coastal North Carolina, see David S. Cecelski, *The Waterman's Song: Slavery and Freedom in Maritime North Carolina* (Chapel Hill: University of North Carolina Press, 2001), 63–76.

43. D. Clayton James, *Antebellum Natchez* (Baton Rouge: Louisiana State University Press 1968), 168–70, 239–41, 259–61; Christopher Waldrep, *Roots of Disorder: Race and Criminal Justice in the American South, 1817–80* (Urbana: University of Illinois Press, 1998), 25; Tolbert, *Constructing Townscapes*, 20–32, 40–59, 95–116, 187–224. See also Richard C. Wade, *Urban Frontier: The Rise of Western Cities* (Cambridge: Harvard University Press, 1959), 39–71; Richard C. Wade, *Slavery in the Cities: The South, 1820–1860* (London: Oxford University Press, 1964), 142–79; Joshua D. Rothman, *Notorious in the Neighborhood: Sex and Families across the Color Line in Virginia, 1787–1861* (Chapel Hill: University of North Carolina Press, 2003), 92–99, 111–29.

44. *State v. John Botto*, April Term 1849, WCCCP; *State v. Manuel and Gabriel*, May Term 1855, Drawer 341, ACCCR; Waldrep, *Roots of Disorder*, 33–34.

45. D. Clayton James, *Antebellum Natchez*, 261.

46. Nevitt Diary, 19 July 1829, 13 March 1831, RASP; Whitmore Diaries, 7 June 1849, SHC.

47. Walker may have been engaged in clandestine trade with the grocer, Daniel Dexter. Although Dexter had accused Walker of beating him and Jane attested to Walker's threat, a jury found Walker not guilty of assault with intent to murder. The jurors may have thought that there was more than Dexter admitted to his story that $23 and a piece of calico had gone missing from his store. *State v. Henry*, March Term 1837, Testimony of Jane and Daniel Dexter, 31 January 1837, Indictment, n.d., Drawer [?], ACCCR.

48. *State v. Charles Dollar*, April Term 1837, Indictment, n.d.; *State v. Henry Swaps*, April Term 1837, Warrant, 20 April 1837, WCCCP. See also *State v. McCombs*, April Term 1839, Civil and Criminal Court Cases, Warren County, Slaves and Slavery Collection, NTC.

49. *Woodville Republican*, 12 October 1839, 16 November 1839.

50. *Adams Co. v. Pascal Andrew*, *Adams Co. v. Louis Zinger*, *Adams Co. v. Frederick Sullivan*, Drawer 331, ACCCR; Timothy R. Buckner, "Vicksburg's Civil War on Vice: Drinking, Gambling, and Race in the Antebellum South," *JMH* 67 (2005): 311–30.

51. Diary, 15 August 1857, Darden Family Papers, MDAH.

52. Gant spent more time with his relatives at Seltzertown when he was hired there in 1853. David Gant, Exhibit, 28 May 1878, Daniel Hubbard File, Widow's Certificate 181456, CWPF.

53. Anderson Watson, Deposition, 25 January 1887, William Madison File, Widow's Certificate 232198, CWPF. For other examples of friendships that slaves made working outside the neighborhood, see Burrl [Burl] Lewis, Deposition, 23 May 1890, Peter Yeager, Deposition, 31 May 1890, John Bruce File, Invalid's Certificate 488630; Robert Jones, Deposition, 14 May 1910, Andrew January File, Widow's Certificate 703093, CWPF.

54. Waldrep, *Roots of Disorder*, 21–24, 45–46.

55. Charles S. Sydnor, "The Southerner and the Laws," *JSH* 6 (February 1940): 3–23; David Brion Davis, *The Problem of Slavery in Western Culture* (Ithaca: Cornell University Press, 1969), 31–35; Genovese, *Roll, Jordan, Roll*, 3–7, 25–37, 87–97, 661–65. During the antebellum period, slaveholders, to a limited yet increasing extent, used the state to police one another as well as slaves. Law reflected a dual attempt to impose order on slaves where owners failed to effect it and to enforce certain obligations to slaves that owners often failed to meet. Scholars, therefore, have had good reason to examine the state's intrusion into the master-slave relation to understand slaveholders' ideology. See Genovese, *Roll, Jordan, Roll*, 37–70; Mark V. Tushnet, *The American Law of Slavery, 1810–1860: Considerations of Humanity and Interest* (Princeton: Princeton University Press, 1981); Willie Lee Rose, "The Domestication of Domestic Slavery," in *Slavery and Freedom*, ed. William W. Freehling (Oxford: Oxford University Press, 1982), 23–25; Peter Kolchin, *American Slavery, 1619–1817*, rev. ed. (New York: Hill and Wang, 2003), 127–32.

56. For an insightful discussion of how slaves influenced civil court proceedings in absentia, see Gross, *Double Character*, esp. 34, 37, 72–121.

57. George Poindexter, comp., *The Revised Code of the Laws of Mississippi* (Natchez, Miss.: Baker, 1824), 130, 373; Diary, 9–10 September 1857, Wailes Papers, MDAH.

58. Although Mississippi slaves had a statutory right to sue for freedom, in practice, there as in other states in the Deep South, such proceedings rarely made it to court. A study of legal proceedings before state supreme courts in the South found a total of just five freedom suits in Mississippi (Marion J. Russell, "American Slave Discontent in the Records of the High Courts," *Journal of Negro History* 31 [October 1946]: 415, 418, tables II-B, III).

59. Burl Lewis, Deposition, 24 July 1899, Burl Lewis File, Invalid's Certificate 606008, CWPF.

60. Caroline Christian and Rachel Meguire, Exhibits, 28 December 1874, Jackson Meguire File, Widow's Certificate 90188, CWPF. See also Ben Lewis, [Exhibit], 1 March 1875, Harris Stewart File, Widow's Certificate 132717, CWPF.

61. Diary, 6 April 1857, Darden Family Papers, MDAH; Bradley G. Bond, *Political Culture in the Nineteenth Century South: Mississippi, 1830–1900* (Baton Rouge: Louisiana State University Press, 1995), 13, 28–31; Christopher Morris, *Becoming Southern: The Evolution of a Way of Life, Warren County and Vicksburg, Mississippi, 1770–1860* (New York: Oxford University Press, 1995), 133–40.

62. Wade Plantation Diary, 9 April 1852, MDAH.

63. Poindexter, *Revised Code*, 377–79, 440; Charles S. Sydnor, *Slavery in Mississippi* (1933; reprint, Baton Rouge: Louisiana State University Press, 1966), 78–79.

64. Diary, 29–30 December 1856, Darden Family Papers, MDAH.

65. Poindexter, *Revised Code*, 371.

66. On the appointment of slave patrols by neighborhood, see Christopher J. Olsen, *Political Culture and Secession in Mississippi: Masculinity, Honor, and the Antiparty Tradition, 1830–1860* (Oxford: Oxford University Press, 2000), 118.

67. Harry Alexander, Deposition, 3 October 1884; Elisha Clasby File, Widow's Certificate 232233, CWPF; Waldrep, *Roots of Disorder*, 16.

68. Foules was the recipient, however, of Alexander K. Farrar's letter warning against making a spectacle of hanging Henderson, Reuben, and Anderson for the other killing of an overseer in that neighborhood. See chap. 4. For cases in which Foules took an official part in his capacity as justice of the peace, see *State v. Ellis*, May Term 1840, Testimony of Peter and Tim, 25 October 1837, Drawer 239; *State v. David*, May Term 1846, Certificate of David's Monetary Value, 15 June 1846, Drawer 331, ACCCR.

69. Rachel Meguire, Exhibit, 28 December 1874, Jackson Meguire File, CWPF.

70. Testimony of Benjamin Stinyard, n.d., Benjamin Stinyard Claim, Case 6999; Testimony of Henry Banks, 24 June 1873, Henry Banks Claim, Case 14443, Warren County, SCC.

71. Poindexter, *Revised Code*, 19–27; Thomas D. Morris, *Southern Slavery and the Law, 1619–1860* (Chapel Hill: University of North Carolina Press, 1996), 210–15;

Arthur F. Howington, *What Sayeth the Law: The Treatment of Slaves and Free Blacks in the State and Local Courts of Tennessee* (New York: Garland, 1986), 138–40.

72. County courts, composed of three justices of the peace, shared jurisdiction over crimes by slaves with circuit courts until 1833, when the county courts were abolished and circuit courts acquired sole jurisdiction over felony trials of slaves (Poindexter, *Revised Code*, 371–76, 379–82; A. Hutchinson, comp., *Code of Mississippi* [Jackson, Miss.: Price and Fall, 1848], 704, 710; Waldrep, *Roots of Disorder*, 24).

73. Nevitt Diary, 11 December 1830, RASP.

74. After 1854, noncapital offenses were tried by two justices of the peace and five slave owners, and the defendant lost any right to appeal to the circuit court and state supreme court (Waldrep, *Roots of Disorder*, 16–17, 24; *Bob Minor, a Slave v. the State, Mississippi Reports* (1859), 36:630.

75. Thomas D. Morris, *Southern Slavery and Law*, 230–37.

76. *State v. Henry*, March Term 1837, Testimony of Jane, 31 January 1837, Costs in Magistrates Court, 28 March 1837, ACCCR. Fees were a main attraction of the office of justice of the peace (Olsen, *Political Culture and Secession*, 139).

77. Poindexter, *Revised Code*, 382–83; Hutchinson, *Code of Mississippi*, 515; William L. Sharkey, comp., *The Revised Code of the Statute Laws of Mississippi* (Jackson, Miss.: Barksdale, 1857), 249. The charge was adapted from a statute enacted in Virginia in 1723, but its origins were biblical (Deuteronomy 15:17). See Thomas D. Morris, *Southern Slavery and Law*, 229–33; Sydnor, *Slavery in Mississippi*, 84.

78. According to the justice's warrant for David's arrest, he "acknowledged to me and others" that he murdered overseer James Ward (*State v. David*, May Term 1846, Warrant, 12 May 1846, ACCCR).

79. Waldrep, *Roots of Disorder*, 32, 50.

80. Eight slaves testified in *State v. Granville*, April Term 1849, WCCCP. Lewis testified for the state, but Dicy, Cynthia, and her son, Reuben, testified for the defense in *State v. David*, May Term 1846, ACCCR. Three slave men testified for the defense in *State v. Lewis*, May Term 1850, Drawer 331; six slaves testified in *State v. Ned*, November Term 1852, Drawer 339; eight slaves testified in *State v. Bill*, November Term 1852, Drawer 345; three slave women testified in *State v. Little Jordan*, May Term 1855, Drawer 348, ACCCR; Poindexter, *Revised Code*, 127–28, 384.

81. Poindexter, *Revised Code*, 381.

82. Hutchinson, *Code of Mississippi*, 522, 738–39; Sydnor, *Slavery in Mississippi*, 83–85.

83. Brown got a reprieve when the state supreme court agreed to hear an appeal of his conviction for rape, but he hanged in January 1851. See *State v. Wash*, October Term 1849, Chief Justice William L. Sharkey to the Clerk of the Circuit Court of Warren County, 28 November 1849, True Copy of the Judgment of the High Court of Errors and Appeals, 30 November 1850, endorsement, 17 January 1851; *State v. Granville*, Judge George W. L. Smith to Sheriff, 27 October 1849, Endorse-

ment, 30 November 1849; *State v. Frank*, April Term 1849, Judge Geo. W. L. Smith to the Sheriff, 1 November 1849, WCCCP.

84. A. E. K. Nash, "A More Equitable Past? Southern Supreme Courts and the Protection of the Antebellum Negro," *North Carolina Law Review* 48 (February 1970): 197–242; A. E. K. Nash, "Fairness and Formalism in the Trials of Blacks in the State Supreme Courts of the Old South," *Virginia Law Review* 56 (February 1970): 64–100; Daniel J. Flanigan, "Criminal Procedure in Slave Trials in the Antebellum South," *JSH* 40 (November 1974): 537–64; Edward L. Ayers, *Vengeance and Justice: Crime and Punishment in the Nineteenth-Century South* (New York: Oxford University Press, 1984), 134–37; Diane M. Sommerville, *Rape and Race in the Nineteenth-Century South* (Chapel Hill: University of North Carolina Press, 2004), 19–41, 86–101; Thomas D. Morris, *Southern Slavery and Law*, 223–27; Howington, *What Sayeth the Law*, 71–216.

85. Waldrep, *Roots of Disorder*, 44–58; Kenneth M. Stampp, *The Peculiar Institution: Slavery in the Ante-Bellum South* (1956; reprint, New York: Vintage, 1989), 224–28; Genovese, *Roll, Jordan, Roll*, 39–43; Thomas D. Morris, *Southern Slavery and Law*, esp. 51, 382–83, 434–39. Under the state Constitution of 1832, the Supreme Court was renamed the High Court of Error and Appeals (Hutchinson, *Code of Mississippi*, 382–83).

86. Although the court could proceed against slaves without indictments, it routinely presented them. See *State v. David*, May Term 1846, Indictment with Endorsement, 18 May 1846; *State v. Lewis*, May Term 1850, Indictment with Endorsement, 13 May 1850; *State v. Bill*, May Term 1853, Indictment with Endorsement, 8 May 1852, ACCCR; *State v. Frank*, October Term 1849, Indictment with Endorsement, 23 October 1849; *State v. Granville*, October Term 1849, Indictment with Endorsement, 22 October 1849; *State v. Wash*, October Term 1849, Indictment with Endorsement, 16 October 1849, WCCCP.

87. Gross, *Double Character*, 35; Poindexter, *Revised Code*, 306, 382–83, 891; Hutchinson, *Code of Mississippi*, 385; *Woodville Republican*, 6 December 1845. Compare the hierarchical design of courthouses in colonial Virginia and the relatively egalitarian layout of the antebellum courthouse in Union County, North Carolina (A. G. Roeber, "Authority, Law, and Custom: The Rituals of Court Day in Tidewater, Virginia, 1720–1750," *WMQ*, 3rd ser., 37 [January 1980]: 29–32, 36–38; Wayne Durrill, "A Tale of Two Courthouses: Civic Space, Political Power, and Capitalist Development in a New South Community, 1843–1890," *Journal of Social History* 35 [Spring 2002]: 659–81).

88. Evidence from 177 civil trials in Adams County involving slave property suggests that most people in court would have appeared less wealthy than the typical slave owner in the Natchez District. Although defendants were wealthier than the general population (22 percent of the defendants owned more than fifty slaves compared to 12 percent in the population at large), the median defendant owned just

ten slaves; 81 percent of jurors and 80 percent of witnesses owned ten or fewer slaves (Gross, *Double Character*, 34, 163, appendix, table 4).

89. Poindexter, *Revised Code*, 382; Hutchinson, *Code of Mississippi*, 515, 522.

90. The governor nonetheless declined to prevent Stephen's hanging. R. M. Gaines to His Excellency A. M. Scott, 27 October 1832, vol. 15, Correspondence and Papers, Governor A. M. Scott, RG 27, MDAH.

91. Criminal Court Minutes, *State v. Eliza*, 28, 31 March 1837, 11–12 December 1837, 25, 29 June 1838, 2, 5, 7 July 1838, vol. 245, Historic Natchez Foundation, Natchez, Mississippi.

92. Criminal Court Minutes, *State v. Peter*, 13–14 December 1837, 27 June 1838, vol. 245, Historic Natchez Foundation; *State v. Peter*, February and May Term 1840, Drawer 239, Historic Natchez Foundation.

93. Waldrep, *Roots of Disorder*, 2, 15–16, 43–44; Michael S. Hindus, *Prison and Plantation: Crime, Justice, and Authority in Massachusetts and South Carolina, 1767–1878* (Chapel Hill: University of North Carolina Press, 1980), 129–61; Andrew Fede, "Legitimized Violent Slave Abuse in the American South, 1619–1865: A Case Study of Law and Social Change in Six Southern States," *American Journal of Legal History* 29 (April 1985): 93–150; Philip J. Schwarz, *Twice Condemned: Slaves and the Criminal Laws of Virginia* (Baton Rouge: Louisiana State University Press, 1988).

94. Poindexter, *Revised Code*, 306, 382–83, 891; Hutchinson, *Code of Mississippi*, 385, 522, 535.

95. Sydnor, *Slavery in Mississippi*, 84–85; Carl N. Degler, "The Irony of American Negro Slavery," in *Perspectives and Irony in American Slavery*, ed. Harry P. Owens (Jackson: University Press of Mississippi, 1976), 13.

96. *State v. Bill*, May Term 1853, Pleas, 8 May 1852, Affidavi[t] of Bill, 13 May 1852, ACCCR; Poindexter, *Revised Code*, 382–83. Mississippi's supreme court had never ruled on a slave's right to self-defense, although Tennessee and North Carolina recognized that right (Thomas D. Morris, *Southern Slavery and Law*, 278–80).

97. *State v. Bill*, May Term 1853, Affidavi[t] of Bill, 13 May 1852, ACCCR. Perhaps scholars' distinction between procedural due process and substantive due process manifested itself to slave defendants as a court's willingness to hear a slave's side of the story. Some historians have argued that the prosecution of slaves in court adhered to legal rules but denied legal protections to slaves' property and persons. See Nash, "A More Equitable Past?"; Nash, "Fairness and Formalism"; Flanigan, "Criminal Procedure in Slave Trials"; Ayers, *Vengeance and Justice*, 134–37; Sommerville, *Rape and Race in the Nineteenth-Century South*, 19–41, 86–101; Thomas D. Morris, *Southern Slavery and Law*, 223–27; Howington, *What Sayeth the Law*, 71–216.

98. Joseph G. Baldwin, *The Flush Times of Alabama and Mississippi* (1853; reprint, New York: Sagamore, 1957), 36, 144, 148–50.

99. Ibid., 151, 176–78; Henry S. Foote, *Casket of Reminiscences* (1874; reprint, New York: Negro Universities Press, 1968), 431.

100. *State v. Bill*, May Term 1853, Summonses, 21 October 1852, Instructions for the Defendant Given by the Court, n.d. November 1852, ACCCR; Tushnet, *American Law of Slavery*, 78; Thomas D. Morris, *Southern Slavery and Law*, 280–84.

101. Hutchinson, *Code of Mississippi*, 885.

102. *State v. Bill*, May Term 1853, Instructions for the Defendant Given by the Court, November 1852, Instructions for the State Given by the Court, November 1852, ACCCR.

103. The third trial was continued at the May 1853 term of the district court (*State v. Bill*, May Term 1853, Indictment, 8 May 1852, with Endorsement, n.d., ACCCR).

104. Criminal Court Minutes, *State v. Henry*, 30 March 1837, *State v. Phil*, *State v. Harriet*, 5–6 October 1838, *State v. Harriet*, 29 January 1840, vol. 245, Historic Natchez Foundation.

105. Criminal Court Minutes, *State v. Ellis*, 13–14 December 1837, Historic Natchez Foundation; *State v. Harrison*, November Term 1865, WCCCP; Waldrep, *Roots of Disorder*, 48–58; Tushnet, *American Law of Slavery*, 77–92; Sommerville, *Rape and Race*, 86–101.

106. Henry S. Foote, *The Bench and Bar of the South and Southwest* (St. Louis: Soule, Thomas, and Wentworth, 1876), 98–100.

107. Gross, *Double Character*, 22–26; Orville V. Burton, *In My Father's House Are Many Mansions: Family and Community in Edgefield, South Carolina* (Chapel Hill: University of North Carolina Press, 1985), 29; Thomas D. Russell, "Slave Auctions on the Courthouse Steps: Court Sales of Slaves in Antebellum South Carolina," in *Slavery and the Law*, ed. Paul Finkelman (Madison, Wis.: Madison House, 1997), 329–64. Although the only empirical study to date of the proportion of local sales made at courthouses is of South Carolina, one student of the slave trade across the South suggests that the proportion in other states was comparable (Steven Deyle, *Carry Me Back: The Domestic Slave Trade in American Life* [Oxford: Oxford University Press, 2005], 166–67).

108. William R. Hogan and Edwin A. Davis, eds., *William Johnson's Natchez: The Antebellum Diary of a Free Negro* (1951; reprint, Baton Rouge: Louisiana State University Press, 1993), 500. For examples of slaves on offer at sheriff's sales, see *Woodville Republican*, 30 November 1839, 6 January 1841, 27 March 1841.

109. Hogan and Davis, *William Johnson's Natchez*, 745–46; James T. McIntosh, ed., *The Papers of Jefferson Davis: June 1841–July 1846* (Baton Rouge: Louisiana State University Press, 1974), 228; William C. Davis, *Jefferson Davis: The Man and His Hour* (New York: Harper Collins, 1991), 94–95; Edwin A. Miles, *Jacksonian Democracy in Mississippi* (Chapel Hill: University of North Carolina Press, 1960), 13–14; May, *John A. Quitman*, 88; Tolbert, *Constructing Townscapes*, 72, 80, 112.

110. Hogan and Davis, *William Johnson's Natchez*, 672–73; Ralph A. Wooster, *The People in Power: Courthouse and Statehouse in the Lower South, 1850–1860* (Knoxville: University of Tennessee Press, 1969), 76–79, 90–93; Richard P. McCor-

mick, *The Second American Party System: Party Formation in the Jacksonian Era* (1966; reprint, New York: Norton, 1973), 295–303; Miles, *Jacksonian Democracy*, 27–29, 32, 42–43, 162; D. Clayton James, *Antebellum Natchez*, 97–98, 112–19, 123–24.

111. Christopher Morris, *Becoming Southern*, 148–50; Olsen, *Political Culture and Secession*, 97–119.

112. Rose Ballard, Deposition, 13 February 1887, William Madison File, Widow's Certificate 232198, CWPF. I am grateful to Timothy L. Wesley for calling this evidence to my attention.

113. Ibid.; Hogan and Davis, *William Johnson's Natchez*, 286–87, 290–300, 304, 352–55, 454, 459, 498–508; Jordan, *Tumult and Silence*, 35–36; Miles, *Jacksonian Democracy*, 78–81, 155; Arthur M. Schlesinger Jr., *The Age of Jackson* (1945; reprint, Boston: Little, Brown, 1953), 207–8.

114. Reuben Davis, *Recollections of Mississippi and Mississippians* (Boston: Houghton Mifflin, 1890), 197–98; Clement Eaton, *Jefferson Davis*, 49.

115. William J. Cooper, *The South and the Politics of Slavery, 1828–1856* (Baton Rouge: Louisiana State University Press, 1978), 186–219; Michael F. Holt, *The Rise and Fall of the American Whig Party: Jacksonian Politics and the Onset of the Civil War* (New York: Oxford University Press, 1999), 162–83; May, *John A. Quitman*, 117–22.

116. McIntosh, *Papers of Jefferson Davis*, 2:103 n. 102, 165–77; Cooper, *South and the Politics of Slavery*, 214–16.

117. Burl Lewis, Deposition, 24 July 1899, Burl Lewis File, CWPF.

118. William H. Williams, who served in the Union army under the name of Wesley Lord, began to keep his age in 1853, when he was twenty-five years old. Wesley Lord to Mr. V. Warner Pension Commishner, 6 May 1907, Wesley Lord File, Invalid's Certificate 532771, CWPF.

119. Miles, *Jacksonian Democracy*, 52; William C. Davis, *Jefferson Davis*, 94–95, 103–5, 213–14. On Clay's visits to Natchez and his antislavery reputation, see Robert V. Remini, "Henry Clay and the Natchez Connection," *JMH* 54 (1992): 269–78; Merrill D. Peterson, *The Great Triumvirate: Webster, Clay, and Calhoun* (New York: Oxford University Press, 1987), 284–87, 376.

120. Charles S. Sydnor, ed., "A Description of Seargent S. Prentiss in 1838," *JSH* 10 (November 1944): 475–79; Reuben Davis, *Recollections of Mississippi*, 195; Olsen, *Political Culture and Secession*, 39–54, 67–68, 152–55.

121. George Bright, Deposition, 5 October 1894, James Perano File, CWPF.

122. *Lewis v. the State, Mississippi Reports* (1847), 17:115.

123. M. Howard to Major Genl. Howard, 7 April 1866, Registered Letters Received, H-14 1866, Assistant Commissioner for Mississippi, Bureau of Refugees, Freedmen, and Abandoned Lands, #A-9113, FSSP. It would be anachronistic to categorize slaves' conception of "a people" as nationalism. To be sure, that conception rested on foundations similar to those of nationalism. Slaves' collective identities

of peoplehood as well as neighborhood were grounded in kinship and attachments to land, for example. And kinship is often pressed into service when nationalist claims or loyalties are invoked, and ideologues have often seized on attachments to land to whip up such sentiments. (Benedict R. O'G. Anderson, *Imagined Communities: Reflections on the Origin and Spread of Nationalism*, rev. ed. [London: Verso, 1991], 9–12, 19–22, 76–77; E. J. Hobsbawm, *Nations and Nationalism since 1780: Programme, Myth, Reality*, 2nd ed. [Cambridge: Cambridge University Press, 1992], 63–71; Elie Kedourie, *Nationalism*, 4th ed. [Oxford: Blackwell, 1993], 113–20). After the Civil War, freedpeople confronted conditions such as the rise of capitalism and print culture that proved conducive to the spread of nationalism from Europe to Southeast Asia during the nineteenth century (Anderson, *Imagined Communities*). Freedpeople also pursued a variety of arguably nationalist projects. They founded independent towns, such as Mound Bayou in the Mississippi Delta; mass movements to migrate to the North, such as the Exodusters to Kansas; and mass movements to emigrate to Liberia and other points in West Africa. These endeavors harnessed ties of kinship and aspirations for control over social space that had long gone into the making of neighborhoods during slavery (Steven Hahn, *A Nation Under Our Feet: Black Political Struggles in the Rural South from Slavery to the Great Migration* [Cambridge: Harvard University Press, 2003]). Yet none of these developments — the spread of nationalism in modern history, the freedpeople's nationalist endeavors, or their development from the social relations that had undergirded slaves' conceptions of peoplehood and neighborhood — were inevitable. The achievement of recent scholarship on nationalism is the recognition that nationalisms are not discovered but made. This broad consensus prevails among scholars despite many differences in interpretation, disciplinary orientation, and analytic approach (Ernest Gellner, *Encounters with Nationalism* [Oxford: Blackwell, 1994], 34–46, 59–73; Florencia E. Mallon, *Peasant and Nation: The Making of Postcolonial Mexico and Peru* [Berkeley: University of California Press, 1995], esp. 1–20; Kedourie, *Nationalism*, xiii–xviii, 1, 136–44; Anderson, *Imagined Communities*; Hobsbawm, *Nations and Nationalism*). Slaves' collective identities of neighborhood and peoplehood rested on social foundations that were bulwarks of nationalism at other times and in other places. But it would be a mistake to equate those antebellum identities with nationalism itself.

Chapter Six

1. Testimony of Richard Sullivan, n.d., Randall Pollard, 28 January 1874, Anderson Thomas, 21 July 1875, Andrew Brown Claim, Case 1233, USCC.
2. Testimony of Jacob Robinson, 24 July 1875, ibid.
3. Testimony of Bur[l] Lewis, n.d., ibid. The testimony of Brown's former slaves underscored his disloyalty and undermined his heirs' claim for compensation

by the Southern Claims Commission (Ariela J. Gross, *Double Character: Slavery and Mastery in the Antebellum Southern Courtroom* [Princeton: Princeton University Press, 2000], 157–58).

4. Burl Lewis, Deposition, 24 July 1899, Washington Gray, Deposition, 22 July 1899, Burl Lewis File, Invalid's Certificate 606008; Mack Burnett, Deposition, 21 June 1892, Benjamin Parker, Deposition, 28 June 1892, Mack Burnett File, Invalid's Certificate 804062, CWPF.

5. The commission's "standing interrogatories" are reprinted in Frank W. Klingberg, *The Southern Claims Commission* (Berkeley: University of California Press, 1955), appendix.

6. Percy L. Rainwater, *Mississippi: Storm Center of Secession, 1856–1861* (1938; reprint, New York: Da Capo, 1969), 196–99; William L. Barney, *The Secessionist Impulse: Alabama and Mississippi in 1860* (Princeton: Princeton University Press, 1974), 132, 145–50, 197–99, 231–38, 265–72.

7. Testimony of Dick Green, 14 October 1871, Dick Green Claim, Case 6963, Warren County, SCC; Bell I. Wiley, *Southern Negroes, 1861–1865* (1938; reprint, Baton Rouge: Louisiana State University Press, 1965), 16–19; Leon F. Litwack, *Been in the Storm So Long: The Aftermath of Slavery* (New York: Vintage, 1980), 3–8, 21–27, 115–16; Ira Berlin, Barbara J. Fields, Thavolia Glymph, Joseph P. Reidy, and Leslie S. Rowland, eds., *The Destruction of Slavery*, ser. 1, vol. 1 of *Freedom: A Documentary History of Emancipation, 1861–1867* (Cambridge: Cambridge University Press, 1985), 8–9, 25; Paul D. Escott, "The Context of Freedom: Georgia's Slaves during the Civil War," *Georgia Historical Quarterly* 58 (Spring 1974): 81–83; Lynda J. Morgan, *Emancipation in Virginia's Tobacco Belt, 1850–1870* (Athens: University of Georgia Press, 1992), 106–8; Leslie A. Schwalm, *A Hard Fight for We: Women's Transition from Slavery to Freedom in South Carolina* (Urbana: University of Illinois Press, 1997), 126.

8. Testimony of James K. Hyman, 8 July 1873, Richard Dorsey Claim, Cases 4337, 20298, Adams County, SCC.

9. Winthrop D. Jordan, *Tumult and Silence at Second Creek: An Inquiry into a Civil War Slave Conspiracy* (Baton Rouge: Louisiana State University Press, 1993), 17–18, 75–83; John K. Bettersworth, *Confederate Mississippi: The People and Policies of a Cotton State in Wartime* (Baton Rouge: Louisiana State University Press, 1943), 25; Sally E. Hadden, *Slave Patrols: Law and Violence in Virginia and the Carolinas* (Cambridge: Harvard University Press, 2001), 167–87.

10. Testimony of Charles Burnam, 26 July 1872, Benjamin Stinyard Claim, Case 6999, SCC.

11. Testimony of Anthony Lewis, Clem Hardeman, Lloyd Wigenton, 20 July 1872, Anthony Lewis Claim, Case 15293, Claiborne County, SCC.

12. Testimony of Samuel Chase, 14 September 1872, Lewis Jackson, 23 September 1887, Samuel Chase Claim, Case 1990, USCC; Testimony of Amos Cooper,

22 December 1873, Amos Cooper Claim, Case 21867, Yazoo County, SCC; Jordan, *Tumult and Silence*, 18, 52–53.

13. Testimony of Harrison Winfield, 23 September 1887, Samuel Chase Claim, USCC.

14. On ministers and literacy, see Janet Duitsman Cornelius, *"When I Can Read My Title Clear": Literacy, Slavery, and Religion in the Antebellum South* (Columbia: University of South Carolina Press, 1991), 3, 59–60, 85–94.

15. For a provocative account of African American soldiers' similarly unifying effect in low country South Carolina, see Julie Saville, *The Work of Reconstruction: From Slave to Wage Laborer in South Carolina, 1860–1870* (Cambridge: Cambridge University Press, 1994), 143–51.

16. Testimony of George Braxton, 5 July 1873, Thomas Turner Claim, Case 4330, Adams County, SCC. Witnesses did not identify which members of the Surget or Shields families Turner and Braxton belonged to. Gabriel B. Shields, however, married Catherine Surget in 1838, and Turner probably visited Braxton on Montebello, the Shields home place (Irene S. Gillis and Norman E. Gillis, *Adams County Mississippi Marriages, 1802–1859* [Shreveport, La.: Gill, 1976]). For examples of other slaves who picked up military intelligence from owners or owners' kin, see Testimony of Russell Giles, 16 May 1877, Russell Giles Claim, Case 11583, Warren County, SCC; Testimony of Charles Anderson and Cato Rux, 15 January 1873, Estate of Hal W. Green Claim, Case 7864, USCC.

17. Testimony of Louisa Lattimer, 3 July 1873, Andrew Black Claim, Case 10361, Warren County, SCC.

18. Testimony of Edward Howard, 1 June 1874, Martha Crane Claim, Case 8313, USCC.

19. Two of the carriage drivers hanged were from Prosper K. Montgomery's and Samuel Darden's plantations. Slaves belonging to Jessie Darden and Samuel Scott were also implicated (Jordan, *Tumult and Silence*, 9–19, 304, doc. C). On intimate relations at the Montgomery, Scott, and Darden plantations, see chap. 2.

20. Testimony of Henry Banks, 24 June 1873, Henry Banks Claim, Case 14443, Warren County, SCC. For similar concerns among other slaves in Natchez and Vicksburg, see Testimony of George W. Walton, 4 October 1871, Ambrose Holmes Claim, Case 6971, Warren County; Testimony of David Combs, 2 July 1873, David Combs Claim, Case 20299, Adams County, SCC.

21. Testimony of Lewis Jackson, 23 September 1887, Samuel Chase Claim; Testimony of Lewis Baker, Henry Moore, 7 March 1872, Lewis Baker Claim, Case 8475, USCC.

22. Testimony of Minerva Boyd, 7 October 1871, Minerva Boyd Claim, Case 6942, Warren County, SCC.

23. Benjamin Quarles, *The Negro in the Civil War* (Boston: Little, Brown, 1953), 51–53; Litwack, *Been in the Storm So Long*, 27; Berlin et al., *Destruction of Slavery*, 9–10; Barbara J. Fields, *Slavery and Freedom on the Middle Ground: Maryland during the*

Nineteenth Century (New Haven: Yale University Press, 1985), 92; Willie Lee Rose, *Rehearsal for Reconstruction: The Port Royal Experiment* (1964; reprint, London: Oxford University Press, 1976), 4, 12–13; Edmund L. Drago, "How Sherman's March Through Georgia Affected the Slaves," *Georgia Historical Quarterly* 57 (Fall 1973): 362–63; Carl Moneyhon, *The Impact of the Civil War and Reconstruction on Arkansas: Persistence in the Midst of Ruin* (Baton Rouge: Louisiana State University Press, 1994), 135–36.

24. Don E. Fehrenbacher, ed., *Abraham Lincoln: Speeches and Writings* (New York: Library of America, 1989), 2:215–24, 279–97.

25. Jordan, *Tumult and Silence*, 5, 212–15.

26. Although my argument here suggests that the main trajectory of the slaves' debates did not cross the line into insurrection, this analysis has benefited from an engagement with Steven Hahn's argument that they did (*A Nation Under Our Feet: Black Political Struggles in the Rural South from Slavery to the Great Migration* [Cambridge: Harvard University Press, 2003], 62–115). On the geography of the conspiracy, see chap. 4.

27. Jordan, *Tumult and Silence*, 100, 170–72, 175–76.

28. Ibid., 107, 116–17, 122–23.

29. Ibid., 212, 216–17, 221–25.

30. Ibid., 111–13, 141, 203.

31. Ibid., 5; the testimony of Pleasant Scott and James Carter before the Southern Claims Commission appears on 325–29, docs. M, N.

32. Ibid., 247–49, 257–58; Testimony of George Braxton, 5 July 1873, Thomas Turner Claim, Case 4330, Adams County, SCC. Braxton's informant, Thomas Turner, presumably knew the seven executed slaves who also belonged to the Surget clan. Turner, in his capacity as messenger servant, would have stopped occasionally at the Surgets' Cherry Grove plantation, the most likely site of ten hangings. For another ex-slave who feared Farrar as a hangman, see Gross, *Double Character*, 156. For Farrar's role in the investigation of the murder of overseer Duncan Skinner, see chap. 4.

33. Testimony of James K. Hyman, George W. Carter, 8 July 1873, Richard Dorsey Claim, SCC.

34. Testimony of Nelson Finley and William Harris, 30 January 1874, Nelson Finley Claim, Case 16219, Wilkinson County; Testimony of David Combs, 2 July 1873, David Combs Claim, SCC.

35. Jordan, *Tumult and Silence*, 88.

36. Testimony of Henry Banks, 24 June 1873, Henry Banks Claim, SCC.

37. Testimony of Lewis Jackson, 23 September 1887, Samuel Chase Claim, USCC.

38. Testimony of Nelson Finley, William Harris, Mack Washington, 30 January 1874, Nelson Finley Claim, SCC; James M. McPherson, *The Negro's Civil War: How American Blacks Felt and Acted During the War for the Union* (1965; reprint, New York: Ballantine, 1991), 57–59, 62–63, 67–68, 210; Vincent Harding, *There Is a*

River: The Black Struggle for Freedom in America (1981; reprint, New York: Harcourt, Brace, Jovanovich, 1992), 220, 226–28; John Cimprich, *Slavery's End in Tennessee, 1861–1865* (University: University of Alabama Press, 1985), 21–22, 60, 84–85; Litwack, *Been in the Storm So Long*, 24–25, 108–9, 121–22, 169–72, 217–18; Drago, "How Sherman's March Through Georgia Affected the Slaves," 364–65.

39. Testimony of David Combs, 2 July 1873, David Combs Claim; Testimony of Louisa Latimer, 3 July 1873, Andrew Black Claim; Testimony of James K. Hyman, 8 July 1873, Richard Dorsey Claim, SCC.

40. Testimony of William Harris, Mack Washington, 30 January 1874, Nelson Finley Claim, SCC.

41. Drew Gilpin Faust, *The Creation of Confederate Nationalism: Ideology and Identity in the Civil War South* (Baton Rouge: Louisiana State University Press, 1989), 14, 16–19; Jordan, *Tumult and Silence*, 64.

42. Testimony of Richard Sullivan, n.d., Andrew Brown Claim, USCC.

43. Testimony of Cato Rux, 15 January 1873, Estate of Hal W. Green Claim, USCC.

44. Armstead L. Robinson, *Bitter Fruits of Bondage: The Demise of Slavery and the Collapse of the Confederacy, 1861–1865* (Charlottesville: University of Virginia Press, 2005), 180–88; James L. Roark, *Masters Without Slaves: Southern Planters in the Civil War and Reconstruction* (New York: Norton, 1977), 46–50; Drew Gilpin Faust, *Mothers of Invention: Women of the Slaveholding South and the American Civil War* (Chapel Hill: University of North Carolina Press, 1996), 30–35, 53–79.

45. Bettersworth, *Confederate Mississippi*, 64–65, 190–91; William K. Scarborough, *The Overseer: Plantation Management in the Old South* (1966; reprint, Athens: University of Georgia Press, 1984), 139–43.

46. Plantation Book, 20 March 1862, 16, 21 April 1862, 11 May 1862, 1, 2, 12 September 1862, 2, 6, 19, 27–28 October 1862, James Allen and Family Papers, MDAH.

47. Ibid., 17 May 1862, 21 April 1862, 5 August 1862.

48. Testimony of Jerry Smithson, 10 May 1873, Jerry Smithson Claim, Case 13747, Yazoo County, SCC; Testimony of John Williams, A. W. Br[ie]n, 8 October 1872, A. W. Brien Claim, Case 1398, USCC; Bettersworth, *Confederate Mississippi*, 147–52.

49. Plantation Book, 6, 7, 9, 14 June 1862, Allen and Family Papers, MDAH.

50. Testimony of Richard Dorsey, 5 July 1873, Thomas Turner Claim, SCC. Samuel Chase also acquired a mule during this period (Testimony of Samuel Chase, 14 September 1872, Samuel Chase Claim, USCC).

51. Testimony of Henry Banks, Albert Webster, 24 June 1873, Henry Banks Claim, SCC.

52. Testimony of Minerva Boyd, Moses W. White, George W. Boyd, 7 October 1871, Minerva Boyd Claim, SCC.

53. Testimony of Richard Dorsey, 8 July 1873, Richard Dorsey Claim, SCC.

54. Testimony of Jeff Claiborne, 2 November 1891, London Mitchell, James Craw-

ford, 11 May 1875, H. F. Kriger, 29 October 1891, Martha R. Blanton Claim, Case 3307, USCC; Lawrence N. Powell and Michael Wayne, "Self-Interest and the Decline of Confederate Nationalism," in *The Old South in the Crucible of War*, ed. Harry P. Owens and James J. Cooke (Jackson: University Press of Mississippi, 1983), 31–32; Robinson, *Bitter Fruits*, 106–9, 190–95; Berlin et al., *Destruction of Slavery*, 40–42; Roark, *Masters Without Slaves*, 80; Schwalm, *Hard Fight for We*, 82–85; Moneyhon, *Impact of the Civil War and Reconstruction*, 115–16.

55. Testimony of Nelson Ashby, 11 October 1872, Mary E. Acuff Claim, Case 6934, Warren County, SCC.

56. Testimony of Benjamin Jones, 22 June 1874, Daniel A. Cameron Claim, Case 3510, USCC.

57. James M. McPherson, *Battle Cry of Freedom: The Civil War Era* (New York: Oxford University Press, 1988), 405–21.

58. Plantation Book, 25–27 May 1862, Allen and Family Papers, MDAH.

59. Testimony of Balor Hill, 6 November 1871, Estate of C. D. Hamilton Claim, Case 9648; Testimony of Reuben Cunningham, Stephen Johnson, 31 May 1873, Alexander Hutchinson, 30 May 1873, Alexander Hutchinson Claim, Case 11562, USCC.

60. Testimony of Lewis Jackson, 23 September 1887, Samuel Chase Claim, USCC.

61. Testimony of Thomas C. Drummond, Martha Bradshaw, 28 May 1875, Thomas Brown, 22 June 1875, Alexander Brown, 2 July 1875, Thomas C. Drummond Claim, Case 16294; Testimony of Allen Harris, 10 March 1875, Allen Harris Claim, Case 16557, Warren County, SCC; William Wells Brown, *The Negro in the American Rebellion: His Heroism and His Fidelity* (Boston: Lee and Shepard, 1867), 308.

62. Testimony of George W. Walton, Ambrose Holmes, 4 October 1871, Ambrose Holmes Claim, SCC; Clarence L. Mohr, *On the Threshold of Freedom: Masters and Slaves in Civil War Georgia* (Athens: University of Georgia Press, 1986), 72; Litwack, *Been in the Storm So Long*, 20.

63. Michael B. Ballard, *Vicksburg: The Campaign That Opened the Mississippi* (Chapel Hill: University of North Carolina Press, 2004); Robinson, *Bitter Fruits*, 189–219; McPherson, *Battle Cry of Freedom*, 578–88, 626–32; Mark Grimsley, *The Hard Hand of War: Union Military Policy Toward Southern Civilians, 1861–1865* (Cambridge: Cambridge University Press, 1995), 151–57.

64. Testimony of Edward Hicks, 13 May 1875, Absalom Grant Claim, Case 5516; Testimony of Thomas Green, 25 July 1873, Estate of Francis Hyland Claim, Case 12121, USCC.

65. Testimony of Esther Cameron, Benjamin Jones, Cyrus Lee, 22 June 1874, Daniel A. Cameron Claim; Testimony of Hal Brooks, 6 November 1876, Uriah G. Flowers, 19 October 1876, Mary A. Brooks Claim, Case 3480, USCC.

66. Testimony of Squire Myers, 21 July 1873, John M. Johnson Claim, Case 18061, Warren County, SCC.

67. Testimony of Edward Hicks, 13 May 1875, Absalom Grant Claim, Case 5516,

USCC; John Cimprich, "Slave Behavior during the Federal Occupation of Tennessee, 1862–1865," *Historian* 44 (May 1982): 335, 342; LeeAnn Whites, *The Civil War as a Crisis in Gender: Augusta, Georgia, 1860–1890* (Athens: University of Georgia Press, 1995), 122–24.

68. Testimony of Charles Anderson, 15 January 1873, Estate of Hal W. Green Claim; Testimony of Curtis Lockhart, 19 January 1878, John Alverson Claim, Case 3391, USCC.

69. Testimony of Henry A. Leach, 21 November 1874, Elisha Fox Claim, Case 3668, USCC; Testimony of William Green, 6 March 1875, Mary G. Wright, 5 March 1875, William Green Claim, Case 6962, Warren County, SCC; James T. Currie, *Enclave: Vicksburg and Her Plantations, 1863–1870* (Jackson: University Press of Mississippi, 1980), xxi–xxiii.

70. Hahn, *Nation Under Our Feet*, 68–82.

71. Testimony of Charles Anderson, 15 January 1873, Estate of Hal W. Green Claim, USCC.

72. Testimony of Cyrus Lee, 6 November 1876, Mary A. Brooks Claim, USCC.

73. Testimony of Samuel Chase, Henry Watson, 14 September 1872, Samuel Chase Claim, USCC.

74. Testimony of Henry Banks, Albert Webster, 24 June 1873, Henry Banks Claim; Testimony of John Cole, 20 May 1873, John Cole Claim, Case 16558, Warren County, SCC.

75. Mary Carter and Lucinda Braziel, Susan Swanson, [Exhibits], 12 February 1875, Nelson Davis File, Widow's Certificate 92460; Em[ily] Stewart, [Exhibit], 20 February 1875, Thomas Swanson, [Exhibit], 1 March 1875, Stephen Jones, [Exhibit], 2 March 1875, Harris Stewart File, Widow's Certificate 132717; Mary Carter, Affidavit, 8 March 1876, George Carter File, Widow's Certificate 173491, CWPF.

76. Testimony of Olive Lee, 1 March 1875, Olive Lee Claim, Case 10664; Testimony of Peter Jackson, 15 October 1872, Peter Jackson Claim, Case 14295, Warren County; Testimony of William Green, n.d. [1871], Dick Green Claim; Testimony of Henry Banks, Deposition, 24 June 1873, Henry Banks Claim; Testimony of John Smith, 2 July 1873, David Combs Claim, SCC; Litwack, *Been in the Storm So Long*, 106–7.

77. York Plantation Journal, 11 July 1863, Metcalfe Family Papers, MDAH; Mahalia Dorris, General Affidavit, 25 February 1888, Roley Washington, General Affidavit, 4 February 1889, Foster Dorris File, Mother's Certificate 271888, CWPF. See also Wesley Lord, Deposition, 23 June 1899, Wesley Lord File, Invalid's Certificate 532771, CWPF.

78. Testimony of Wallace Turner, 5 July 1873, Thomas Turner Claim; Testimony of Henry Anderson, 15 January 1873, Henry Anderson Claim, Case 17480; Testimony of Joseph Johnson, 4 January 1878, Alfred Swann Claim, Case 19740, Adams County, SCC; Ira Berlin, Thavolia Glymph, Steven F. Miller, Joseph P. Reidy, Leslie S. Rowland, and Julie Saville, eds., *The Wartime Genesis of Free Labor: The*

Lower South, ser. 1, vol. 3 of *Freedom: A Documentary History of Emancipation* (Cambridge: Cambridge University Press, 1990), 628–29, doc. 174.

79. Mary Ann Madison, Deposition, 24 January 1887, George Hamlin and Alexander White, Depositions, 12 February 1887, William Madison File, Widow's Certificate 232198; Frances Taylor, Deposition, 25 August 1893, Samuel McDowell File, Father's Certificate 384066, CWPF; John Eaton, *Grant, Lincoln, and the Freedmen* (New York: Longmans, Green, 1907), 105; Ronald L. F. Davis, *The Black Experience in Natchez, 1720–1880* (Natchez Historical Park, Miss.: Eastern National Park and Monument Association, 1994), 133–34; Bell I. Wiley, *The Plain People of the Confederacy* (1943; reprint, Chicago: Quadrangle, 1963), 70–72.

80. Testimony of Henry Hunt, 6 May 1873, Henry Hunt Claim, Case 10840, Warren County; Testimony of Nelson Finley, 30 January 1874, Nelson Finley Claim, SCC.

81. Ronald L. F. Davis, *Black Experience in Natchez*, 133–34; Berlin et al., *Destruction of Slavery*, 15–16, 33–34, 60–61.

82. Testimony of Anthony Lewis, 20 July 1872, Anthony Lewis Claim, SCC; Eugene D. Genovese, *Roll, Jordan, Roll: The World the Slaves Made* (New York: Pantheon, 1974), 97; Litwack, *Been in the Storm So Long*, 154.

83. Ira Berlin, Joseph P. Reidy, and Leslie S. Rowland, eds., *The Black Military Experience*, ser. 2 of *Freedom: A Documentary History of Emancipation* (Cambridge: Cambridge University Press, 1982), 532–34, docs. 52–53; Noah A. Trudeau, *Like Men of War: Black Troops in the Civil War, 1862–1865* (Boston: Little, Brown, 1998), 46–59.

84. Circular from the Adjutant General's Office, 3 February 1887, Louis Dixon File, Widow's Certificate 247698, CWPF.

85. Tobias Orey, Deposition, 26 December 1891, Circular from the Adjutant General's Office, 14 January 1869, George Dorsey File, Widow's Certificate 363630, CWPF.

86. Willis Latham, Deposition, 28 April 1882, Elisha Grayson File; Bureau of Pensions to Record and Pension Division of the War Department, 22 March 1892, Willis Latham and William Hall, Affidavit, 18 July 1868, James Jones File, Widow's Certificate 179592, CWPF.

87. In March 1864, the Union army changed the state designations of black regiments. The Ninth Louisiana was redesignated the 63rd U.S. Colored Infantry. The Third Mississippi, organized at Warrenton in Warren County on 19 May 1863, was redesignated the 53rd U.S. Colored Infantry. See Frederick H. Dyer, comp., *A Compendium of the War of the Rebellion: Regimental Histories* (1908; reprint, New York: Yoseloff, 1959), 3:1214, 1344.

88. Burl Lewis, Deposition, 24 July 1899, Burl Lewis File; Phillis Reed, Deposition, 12 January 1888, James Doddin (alias Daniel Reed) File, Widow's Certificate 252874; Rachel Moore, Exhibit, 18 March 1875, Jerry Moore File, Widow's Certificate 127426, CWPF.

89. The units raised in the Natchez District, in addition to the 58th U.S. Colored Infantry, 63rd U.S. Colored Infantry, 6th U.S. Colored Heavy Artillery, and 3rd

U.S. Colored Cavalry, were the 51st U.S. Colored Infantry, 52nd U.S. Colored Infantry, 53rd U.S. Colored Infantry, 66th U.S. Colored Infantry, 70th U.S. Colored Infantry, 71st U.S. Colored Infantry, 5th U.S. Colored Heavy Artillery, and Battery C and Battery D of the 2nd U.S. Colored Light Artillery.

90. Wesley Lord, Deposition, 23 June 1899, Wesley Lord File, CWPF.

91. Harrison Willis, Deposition, 23 July 1900, Harrison Barnes File, Invalid's Certificate 987018; Jesse Branson, Deposition, 22 March 1899, Jesse Branson File, Invalid's Certificate 766387; Lewis Griffin, Deposition, 20 February 1904, Gabe Phillips, Deposition, 21 January 1904, Archie Powell (alias Archie Coal) File, Minor's Application 576366, CWPF.

92. Patsy Payton, [Exhibit], 19 January 1875, Beverly Payton (alias Dudley Payton) File, Widow's Certificate 168060, CWPF.

93. Berlin, Reidy, and Rowland, *Black Military Experience*, 433–42.

94. U.S. War Department, *Revised United States Army Regulations* (Philadelphia: Childs, 1863), 131, 486–87, 501–2; Caesar Gordon alias Kearney, Deposition, 28 January 1902, Caesar Kearney (alias Caesar Gordon) File, Invalid's Application 967953, CWPF; Berlin, Reidy, and Rowland, *Black Military Experience*, 28–29, doc. 179; Joseph T. Glatthaar, *Forged in Battle: The Civil War Alliance of Black Soldiers and White Officers* (New York: Free Press, 1990), 111–20.

95. Berlin et al., *Wartime Genesis*, 73, 649, 810, docs. 188, 201, 202A–B; Berlin, Reidy, and Rowland, *Black Military Experience*, 660, docs. 276A, 286, 309; Herbert G. Gutman, *The Black Family in Slavery and Freedom, 1750–1925* (New York: Vintage, 1976), 18–24, 412–18; Noralee Frankel, *Freedom's Women: Black Women and Families in Civil War Era Mississippi* (Bloomington: Indiana University Press, 1999), 40–45; Louis S. Gerteis, *From Contraband to Freedman: Federal Policy Toward Southern Blacks, 1861–1865* (Westport, Conn.: Greenwood, 1973), 85–86; C. Peter Ripley, "The Black Family in Transition: Louisiana, 1860–1865," *JSH* 41 (August 1975): 379–80; Cimprich, *Slavery's End*, 74–75.

96. Hager Washington, Deposition, 29 December 1894, George Washington File, Widow's Application 129861, CWPF.

97. Fanny Sloan, General Affidavit, 4 October 1897, Wrapper with Endorsement by Chief of Record and Pension Office, War Department, 27 September 1897, Isaac Sloan File, Invalid's Certificate 695975, CWPF.

98. Harry Nichols, Deposition, 25 May 1918, Adjutant General's Office to U.S. Bureau of Pensions, 9 July 1923, Harry Nichols File, Invalid's Certificate 1074493; Henry Brown, Deposition, 22 October 1917, Benjamin Fort File, Invalid's Certificate 989519, CWPF; Frankel, *Freedom's Women*, 41; Donald R. Shaffer, *After the Glory: The Struggles of Black Civil War Veterans* (Lawrence: University Press of Kansas, 2004), 102.

99. William Carter to Bureau of Pensions, 19 May 1899, 6 April 1915, William Carter File, Invalid's Certificate 1005623, CWPF.

100. Jennie Williams, Deposition, 5 October 1904, Daniel Robinson File, Widow's

Certificate 581335, CWPF. On Bettie Wood and Daniel Robinson's intimate relations prior to the war, see chap. 2.

101. Patsy Payton, [Exhibit], 19 January 1875, Beverly Payton (alias Dudley Payton) File; William Carter to Bureau of Pensions, 19 May 1899, 6 April 1915, William Carter File, CWPF.

102. Moses Fletcher, General Affidavit, 14 June 1889, Samuel McDowell File; Willis Latham, Deposition, 28 April 1882, Elisha Grayson File, Widow's Certificate 389530; Willis Latham, Affidavit, 18 July 1868, James Jones File, Widow's Certificate 179592; Moses Reed, Deposition, 9 January 1889, James Doddin (alias Daniel Reed) File; Isham Falkner, Deposition, 30 August 1904, John Jones (alias Jonas Falkner) File, Invalid's Certificate 746277; Em[ily] Stewart, [Exhibit], 20 February 1875, Thomas Swanson, [Exhibit], 1 March 1875, Harris Stewart File, CWPF.

103. Thomas Green was known by his neighbors and comrades by that name, but he was identified in pension records as Thomas Scott (Winston Lee, Emanuel Genifer, James Genifer, [Exhibits], 12 March 1875, Thomas Scott File, Widow's Certificate 129600, CWPF). For other examples of regimental comrades who had lived on adjoining plantations, see Frank Yates, Deposition, 21 December 1896, Robert Lloyd File, Invalid's Certificate 557039; Moses Harrison and Horace Allen, General Affidavit, [8 July 1897], Robert Harrison and Henry Brown, General Affidavit, [16 March] 1903, Charles Pratt File, Invalid's Certificate 965519; Silas Burt, Zachariah Thomas, Depositions, 1 June 1900, Lettie P[erry]man, Deposition, 25 May 1900, Robert Johnson File, Widow's Certificate 207202; Sancho L[l]oyd and Robert L[l]oyd, General Affidavit, 21 December 1895, Sunday Gardner File, Sister's Application 359657, CWPF; C. W. Babbit, *Map of Adams County, Mississippi (1891)* (Chancery Clerk's Office, Adams County Courthouse, Natchez, Miss., n.d.).

104. Moses Fletcher, General Affidavit, 14 June 1889, Samuel McDowell File, CWPF.

105. Noah A. Trudeau, "Proven Themselves in Every Respect to Be Men: Black Cavalry in the Civil War," in *Black Soldiers in Blue: African American Troops in the Civil War Era*, ed. John David Smith (Chapel Hill: University of North Carolina Press, 2002), 283; Berlin, Reidy, and Rowland, *Black Military Experience*, doc. 210. The other units, besides the 58th U.S. Colored Infantry, to serve mainly in Natchez and Vicksburg were the 71st U.S. Colored Infantry and the 5th and 6th U.S. Colored Heavy Artillery (Dyer, *Compendium of the War*, 3:1344, 1721, 1733, 1734).

106. Berlin, Reidy, and Rowland, *Black Military Experience*, 483–516.

107. Ibid., 204.

108. Dyer, *Compendium of the War*, 2:786, 3:1334, 1720–21; Trudeau, *Like Men of War*, 46–59, 396–408.

109. Trudeau, "Black Cavalry," 276–77, 287, 291–94; Dyer, *Compendium of the War*, 3:1720–21.

110. McPherson, *Negro's Civil War*, 225–28; Berlin, Reidy, and Rowland, *Black Military Experience*, docs. 210, 213; Trudeau, "Black Cavalry," 281, 284, 292–94.

111. Moses Reed and Joseph Thornton, Depositions, 9 January 1889, Phillis Reed, Deposition, 12 January 1888, James Doddin (alias Daniel Reed) File, CWPF; Berlin, Reidy, and Rowland, *Black Military Experience*, 17–18, 20–22, 30, 362–68, doc. 50; Berlin et al., *Wartime Genesis*, 20–24, 40–41, 45–46, 50–51, 629, 650; Berlin et al., *Destruction of Slavery*, 32–34, 250, 254–56, 258. Others toiled for varied rates off the payroll as personal servants, washing clothes, cutting cordwood, barbering, and driving hacks.

112. John Eaton, *Grant, Lincoln, and the Freedmen*, 116, 122, 207; Berlin et al., *Wartime Genesis*, 49, 633–34, doc. 198; Lawrence N. Powell, *New Masters: Northern Planters during the Civil War and Reconstruction* (New Haven: Yale University Press, 1980), 82–86, 102; Gerteis, *From Contraband to Freedman*, 85, 92–97, 102–6; C. Peter Ripley, *Slaves and Freedmen in Civil War Louisiana* (Baton Rouge: Louisiana State University Press, 1976), 44–49, 56–59, 74–75, 88–91; Cimprich, *Slavery's End*, 68, 71–72.

113. Testimony of Philip Hart, 6 September 1871, Gabriel Boger Claim, Case 6940; Testimony of Philip Hart, Ellen Anderson, 9 May 1871, Julia Ann McCaskill, 9 September 1871, Julia Ann McCaskill Claim, Case 1946, Warren County; Testimony of Wallace Turner, 5 July 1873, Thomas Turner Claim, SCC; Berlin et al., *Wartime Genesis*, 24, 41–42, 47, 64–65, 635–36, 643–46, doc. 209; Frankel, *Freedom's Women*, 20–21, 28, 45–55; Powell, *New Masters*, 45–48, 109.

114. Army regulations for Davis Bend are reprinted in Berlin et al., *Wartime Genesis*, docs. 182, 205, 216, 220; Janet Sharp Hermann, *The Pursuit of a Dream* (New York: Vintage, 1983), 3–9, 12–14, 37–60; Thavolia Glymph, "The Second Middle Passage: The Transition from Slavery to Freedom at Davis Bend, Mississippi" (Ph.D. diss., Purdue University, 1994), 17–24, 47–51, 102–5.

115. William Wells Brown, *Negro in the American Rebellion*, 306; John Eaton, *Grant, Lincoln, and the Freedmen*, 85–86; Steven J. Ross, "Freed Soil, Freed Labor, Freed Men: John Eaton and the Davis Bend Experiment," *JSH* 44 (May 1978): 220–21.

116. Berlin et al., *Wartime Genesis*, doc. 220; Glymph, "Second Middle Passage," 117–23; Ross, "Freed Soil, Freed Labor, Freed Men," 222–26; Currie, *Enclave*, 101–7.

117. On the advent of the market in labor after the war, see Michael Wayne, *The Reshaping of Plantation Society: The Natchez District, 1860–1880* (Baton Rouge: Louisiana State University Press, 1983).

118. John Eaton, *Grant, Lincoln, and the Freedmen*, 218–19; Wayne, *Reshaping of Plantation Society*, 42–46, 50–51, 200–202; Ripley, *Slaves and Freedmen*, 76–83, table 1; Berlin et al., *Wartime Genesis*, 24–26, 43–44, 70–72.

119. Testimony of George Washington, Millie Washington, Morris Gearry, 26 July 1872, George Washington Claim, Case 13910; Testimony of Henry Watson, Emma Watson, 11 October 1863, Henry Watson Claim, Case 16555, Warren County, SCC.

120. Testimony of Martha Bradshaw, Thomas C. Drummond, 28 May 1875, Thomas C. Drummond Claim, SCC.

121. Testimony of Sarah Burton, 24 March 1875, Summary Report, 4 December 1876, Sarah Burton Claim, Case 8009, USCC.

122. Ibid.

123. Testimony of Edward Hicks, 13 May 1875, Absalom Grant Claim, USCC; Testimony of Henry Anderson, 15 January 1873, Henry Anderson Claim; Testimony of John Mann, 4 January 1878, Alfred Swan Claim; Testimony of Thomas C. Drummond, 28 May 1875, Thomas C. Drummond Claim; Testimony of Russell Giles, 16 May 1877, Russell Giles Claim, SCC; Bettersworth, *Confederate Mississippi*, 104–6, 108–11; Stephen V. Ash, *When the Yankees Came: Conflict and Chaos in the Occupied South, 1861–1865* (Chapel Hill: University of North Carolina Press, 1995), 80.

124. Testimony of Henry Banks, 24 June 1873, Henry Banks Claim, SCC. On objectification, see Karl Marx, *A Critical Analysis of Capitalist Production*, vol. 1 of *Capital: A Critique of Political Economy*, ed. Friedrich Engels, trans. Samuel Moore and Edward Aveling (1887; reprint, New York: International Publishers, 1967), 76–89; Georg Lukács, *History and Class Consciousness: Studies in Marxist Dialectics*, trans. Rodney Livingstone (Cambridge: MIT Press, 1971), 83–87.

125. Testimony of Henry Hunt, 6 May 1873, Henry Hunt Claim, SCC.

126. Testimony of Henry Watson, James Puckett, 11 October 1873, Henry Watson Claim, Case 16555, Warren County, SCC; James E. Yeatman, *A Report on the Condition of the Freedmen of the Mississippi* (St. Louis: Western Sanitary Commission, 1864), 8; Mohr, *Threshold of Freedom*, 90–91. For more on the Union army's failure to pay freedpeople for military labor and confiscation of draft animals in the fall of 1863, see Anthony E. Kaye, "Slaves, Emancipation, and the Powers of War: Views from the Natchez District of Mississippi," in *The War Was You and Me: Civilians in the American Civil War*, ed. Joan E. Cashin (Princeton: Princeton University Press, 2002), 69–70.

127. Patsy Payton, [Exhibit], 19 January 1875, Beverly Payton (alias Dudley Payton) File, CWPF.

128. Testimony of Nelson Finley, 30 January 1874, Nelson Finley Claim, SCC.

129. Testimony of Gabriel Boger, Philip Hart, 9 September 1871, Philip Hart Claim, Case 1945, Warren County, SCC; Caesar Gordon alias Kearney, Deposition, 28 January 1902, Caesar Kearney (alias Caesar Gordon) File, CWPF; John Eaton, *Grant, Lincoln, and the Freedmen*, 157–58; Berlin et al., *Wartime Genesis*, docs. 137, 168, 209, 213; Berlin et al., *Destruction of Slavery*, 35–36, 260; Currie, *Enclave*, 62–66; Ash, *When the Yankees Came*, 76–77, 99–107, 165–69.

130. Testimony of Richard Eastman, 25 September 1873, Richard Eastman Claim, Case 8244, USCC; Plantation Book, 16 May 1865, Allen and Family Papers, MDAH.

131. Testimony of Anthony Lewis, 20 July 1872, Anthony Lewis Claim, SCC.

132. Testimony of Elvira Anderson, 5 May 1873, Elvira Anderson Claim, Case 14172; Testimony of William Green, 6 March 1875, William Green Claim; Testimony of Peter Jackson, n.d., Peter Jackson Claim; Testimony of Matilda Anderson, 20 May 1873, Matilda Anderson Claim, SCC; Litwack, *Been in the Storm So Long*, 177.

Epilogue

1. M. Howard to Coll. Thomas, 25 January 1866, Registered Letters Received, H-14 1866, Assistant Commissioner for Mississippi, Bureau of Refugees, Freedmen, and Abandoned Lands, #A-9113, FSSP.

2. M. Howard to Major Genl. Howard, 7 April 1866, Registered Letters Received, H-104 1866, ibid.

3. John Wilkes, Deposition, 18 January 1897, Robert Banks File, Invalid's Certificate 872427, CWPF.

4. Vernon L. Wharton, *The Negro in Mississippi, 1865–1890* (1947; reprint, New York: Harper and Row, 1965), 106.

5. Susan Alexander, Exhibit, 26 December 1874, Isaac Sloan, Exhibit, 28 December 1874, George Jefferson, [Exhibit], 29 December 1874, Allen Alexander File, Widow's Certificate 97533; Isaac Sloan and Frank Brown, Affidavit, 24 August 1878, Thornton Buckner File, Widow's Certificate 189265, CWPF.

6. Charlotte Grant, Exhibit, 7 May 1879, Grant Peyton File, Widow's Certificate 357835, CWPF. Under the pension laws, if Charlotte Grant had married Richard Lewis, she would have ceased to be Peyton Grant's widow and would no longer have received his pension.

7. Henry Brooks, George Chaney, and Richard Lewis, Exhibits, 6 May 1879, Anderson Watson and George Chaney, General Affidavit, 29 August 1876, ibid.

8. U.S. Congress, Senate, *Reports of the Freedmen's Bureau Assistant Commissioners and Laws in Relation to Freedmen*, 39th Cong., 2nd sess., Sen. Exec. Doc. 6 (Washington, D.C.: Government Printing Office, 1867), 192–95.

9. On the struggle over freedpeople's mobility in the black codes and during Reconstruction generally, see William Cohen, *At Freedom's Edge: Black Mobility and the Southern White Quest for Racial Control, 1861–1915* (Baton Rouge: Louisiana State University Press, 1991), 3–167, esp. 28–37. For overviews of the black codes in Mississippi and more broadly throughout the South, see Wharton, *Negro in Mississippi*, 80–96; Eric Foner, *Reconstruction: America's Unfinished Revolution* (New York: Harper and Row, 1988), 198–216.

10. Michael Wayne, *The Reshaping of Plantation Society: The Natchez District, 1860–1880* (Baton Rouge: Louisiana State University Press, 1983), 44–52.

11. John Hope Franklin, ed., *Reminiscences of an Active Life: The Autobiography of John Roy Lynch* (Chicago: University of Chicago Press, 1970), 21.

12. Noralee Frankel, *Freedom's Women: Black Women and Families in Civil War Era Mississippi* (Bloomington: University of Indiana Press, 1999), 79–122.

13. Ibid., 100–103.

14. Emma Hunt, Deposition, 24 March 1893, Henry Hunt File, Widow's Certificate 370999; Elvira Mitchell, Depositions, 13 June 1906, 11 August 1906, Burris Mitchell File, Widow's Application 768436, CWPF.

15. Joe M. Richardson, *Christian Reconstruction: The American Missionary Association and Southern Blacks, 1861–1890* (Athens: University of Georgia Press, 1986); William E. Montgomery, *Under Their Own Vine and Fig Tree: The African-American Church in the South, 1865–1900* (Baton Rouge: Louisiana State University Press, 1993); Reginald F. Hildebrand, *The Times Were Strange and Stirring: Methodist Preachers and the Crisis of Emancipation* (Durham, N.C.: Duke University Press, 1995).

16. Rena Turner, Deposition, 4 November 1904, Wilson Turner File, Widow's Certificate 582915, CWPF; Donald R. Shaffer, *After the Glory: The Struggles of Black Civil War Veterans* (Lawrence: University Press of Kansas, 2004), 108–9.

17. U.S. Congress, Senate, *Denial of the Franchise in Mississippi, 1875 and 1876*, 44th Cong., 2nd sess., Sen. Misc. Doc. 45 (Washington, D.C.: Government Printing Office, 1877), 188.

18. Ibid., 165; John Hope Franklin, *Reminiscences*, 101–3.

19. U.S. Congress, Senate, *Denial of the Franchise*, 165–70, 185.

20. Ibid., 180–81, 187.

21. Steven Hahn, *A Nation Under Our Feet: Black Political Struggles in the Rural South from Slavery to the Great Migration* (Cambridge: Harvard University Press, 2003), 241–45, 260; Foner, *Reconstruction*, 355–56, 362–64; Wharton, *Negro in Mississippi*, 164–72. The Natchez District did not succumb to the intimidation and fraud that reduced the Republican vote and defeated the Republican state constitution the first time it was submitted for the voters' approval in 1868 (Lawrence N. Powell, "Correcting for Fraud: A Quantitative Reassessment of the Mississippi Ratification Election of 1868," *JSH* 55 [November 1989]: 633–58; Wharton, *Negro in Mississippi*, 153).

22. Eric Foner, *Freedom's Lawmakers: A Directory of Black Officeholders during Reconstruction*, rev. ed. (Baton Rouge: Louisiana State University Press, 1996), 54; Frederick H. Dyer, comp., *A Compendium of the War of the Rebellion: Regimental Histories* (1908; reprint, New York: Yosseloff, 1959), 3:1721.

23. Foner, *Freedom's Lawmakers*, 116, 180–81; Joseph H. Borome, ed., "The Autobiography of Hiram Rhoades Revels Together with Some Letters by and about Him," *Midwest Journal* 5 (Winter 1952–53): 8; John Hope Franklin, *Reminiscences*, 54–56, 73–80.

24. U.S. Congress, Senate, *Denial of the Franchise*, 156.

25. John Hope Franklin, *Reminiscences*, 59–65.

26. For an argument that a different set of urban-based cleavages — divisions over offices and patronage — undermined Republicans' hold on power, see Michael W. Fitzgerald, "Republican Factionalism and Black Empowerment: The Spencer-

Warner Controversy and Alabama Reconstruction, 1868–1880," *JSH* 64 (August 1998): 473–94.

27. Christopher J. Olsen, *Political Culture and Secession in Mississippi: Masculinity, Honor, and the Antiparty Tradition, 1830–1860* (New York: Oxford University Press, 2000).

28. On violence between Democrats and Republicans as a struggle over public space, see Stephen Kantrowitz, *Ben Tillman and the Reconstruction of White Supremacy* (Chapel Hill: University of North Carolina Press, 2000), 64–66.

29. U.S. Congress, Senate, *Mississippi in 1875*, 44th Cong., 1st sess., Sen. Rep. 527 (Washington, D.C.: Government Printing Office, 1876), 2:1742–44.

30. Julie Saville, *The Work of Reconstruction: From Slave to Wage Laborer in South Carolina, 1860–1870* (New York: Cambridge University Press, 1994), 143–51, 172–78; Hahn, *Nation Under Our Feet*, 265–313.

31. U.S. Congress, Senate, *Affairs in the Late Insurrectionary States*, 42nd Cong., 2nd sess., Sen. Rep. 41 (Washington, D.C.: Government Printing Office, 1870–71), *South Carolina*, 3:1757–61.

32. Ibid., 3:1985–86. The confessions were made as guilty pleas before the U.S. Circuit Court at Columbia, South Carolina. The court sentenced the witnesses to six months in prison and two years in prison plus a $50 fine, respectively. On the court proceedings, see Lou F. Williams, *The Great South Carolina Ku Klux Klan Trials, 1871–1872* (Athens: University of Georgia Press, 1996).

33. U.S. Congress, Senate, *Affairs in the Late Insurrectionary States*, *Georgia*, 1:321, 430, 2:690.

34. Ibid., *North Carolina*, 100–101.

35. Ibid., *Georgia*, 2:651–52.

36. U.S. Congress, Senate, *The Removal of the Negroes from the Southern States to the Northern States*, 46th Cong, 2nd sess., Sen. Rep. 693 (Washington, D.C.: Government Printing Office, 1880), 3:517–21.

Bibliography

Primary Sources

Manuscript Collections

Austin, Texas
  Center for American History, University of Texas
    Natchez Trace Collection
      Henry S. Allen Jr. Papers
      Richard Thompson Archer Family Papers
      Rice C. Ballard Papers
      Barnes-Willis Family Papers
      Sarah Billingslea Papers
      Joel Cameron Papers
      Chamberlain-Hyland-Gould Family Papers
      Robert Cochran Papers
      Civil War Collection
      F. L. Claiborne Papers
      Crime and Punishment Collection
      Joseph E. Davis Papers
      Joseph Devenport Papers
      James S. Douglass Papers
      Mary F. Dunbar Papers
      Robert C. and Sarah W. Dunbar Papers
      Duncan Family Papers
      Everard M. Eggleston Notebook
      F. H. and Thomas P. Farrar Papers
      John Carmichael Jenkins Family Papers
      Kiger Family Papers
      John and John A. Lane Papers
      Map Collection
      Minor Family Papers
      Robert Moore Papers

Thomas W. and Lucy A. Newman Papers
Pearce Noland Family Papers
Robert Ogden Papers
Benjamin Roach Family Papers
William L. Sharkey Papers
Slaves and Slavery Collection
Levin Wailes Papers
James Campbell Wilkins Papers
Winchester Family Papers
Chapel Hill, North Carolina
University of North Carolina
Southern Historical Collection
Charles Whitmore Diaries
Frederick, Maryland
University Publications of America
Records of Ante-Bellum Southern Plantations, edited by Kenneth M. Stampp
Series E, Selections from the University of Virginia Library
James A. Mitchell Papers
Series F, Selections from the Manuscript Department, Duke University Library
Samuel Smith Downey Papers
John Knight Papers
Dugal G. McCall Plantation Journal
Haller Nutt Papers
Series J, Selections from the Southern Historical Collection, University of North Carolina, Chapel Hill
Everard Green Baker Diary
Mary Bateman Diary
Francis Terry Leak Papers
James Fontaine Maury Diary
James Wistar Metcalfe Papers
John Nevitt Diary
Quitman Family Papers
Frank R. Steel Letters
Jackson, Mississippi
Mississippi Department of Archives and History
Cartographic Collection
County Records
Adams County
Board of Police, Minutes
Chancery Clerk, Land Deed Records
Chancery Court, Probate Records
List of Slaves Liable for Public Road Work

Claiborne County
  Board of Police, Minutes
  Chancery Clerk, Land Deed Records
Jefferson County
  Chancery Clerk, Land Deed Records
  Chancery Court, Probate Packets
Warren County
  Board of Police, Minutes
  Chancery Court, Probate Packets
Governor's Office, Record Group 27
  Albert G. Brown
  Alexander G. McNutt
  Hiram G. Runnels
  A. M. Scott
Legislative Records, Record Group 47
  Bills, Memorials, and Petitions
Private Manuscripts
  James Allen and Family Papers
  Aventine Plantation Diary
  Charles Clark and Family Papers
  Darden Family Papers
  Fonsylvania Plantation Diary
  John G. and John A. B. Jones Journals
  Metcalfe Family Papers
  Panther Burn Plantation Account Books
  John A. Quitman and Family Papers
  Ross-Wade Family Papers
  Henry Frederick Shugart Diary
  Horatio Nelson Spencer Papers
  Surget Family Papers
  Walter Wade Plantation Diary
  Benjamin L. C. Wailes Papers
Subject Files
Natchez, Mississippi
  Historic Natchez Foundation
    Adams County Circuit Court Records
    Criminal Court Minutes
State College, Pennsylvania
  Family History Center
    Adams County Real Estate Records
      Probate Real Estate Record, Film 0886340

Jefferson County
  Tract Book, Film 1939758
  Will Records, Films 1907066, 1939756
Vicksburg, Mississippi
  Old Courthouse Museum
    Warren County Circuit Court Papers
    Warren County Plantation Map, H. M. Marshall and T. K. Foster, 1888
Washington, D.C.
  National Archives
    Records of the Veterans Administration, Record Group 15
      Civil War and Later Pension Files, 1861–1942
        3rd U.S. Colored Cavalry, Companies A, K, L
        5th U.S. Colored Heavy Artillery, Companies A–D, K
        6th U.S. Colored Heavy Artillery, Companies A–B, F, K
        41st U.S. Colored Infantry, Company G
        48th U.S. Colored Infantry, Companies H, K
        50th U.S. Colored Infantry, Company I
        51st U.S. Colored Infantry, Companies A–B
        52nd U.S. Colored Infantry, Company A
        58th U.S. Colored Infantry, Companies A–K
        63rd U.S. Colored Infantry, Company C
        66th U.S. Colored Infantry, Companies A, D, K
    U.S. Court of Claims, Record Group 123
    Congressional Jurisdiction Case Files
    General Accounting Office, Third Auditor, Record Group 217
    Southern Claims Commission, Settled Case Files for Approved Claims

Published Primary Sources

Audubon, John James. *Writings and Drawings*. Edited by Christopher Irmscher. New York: Library of America, 1999.

Babbit, C. W. *Map of Adams County, Mississippi (1891)*. Chancery Clerk's Office, Adams County Courthouse, Natchez, Miss., n.d.

Baldwin, Joseph G. *The Flush Times of Alabama and Mississippi*. 1853. New York: Sagamore, 1957.

Berlin, Ira, Joseph P. Reidy, and Leslie S. Rowland, eds. *The Black Military Experience*. Ser. 2 of *Freedom: A Documentary History of Emancipation*. Cambridge: Cambridge University Press, 1982.

Berlin, Ira, Barbara J. Fields, Thavolia Glymph, Joseph P. Reidy, and Leslie S. Rowland, eds. *The Destruction of Slavery*. Ser. 1, vol. 1 of *Freedom: A Documentary History of Emancipation*. Cambridge: Cambridge University Press, 1985.

Berlin, Ira, Thavolia Glymph, Steven F. Miller, Joseph P. Reidy, Leslie S. Rowland, and

Julie Saville, eds. *The Wartime Genesis of Free Labor: The Lower South.* Ser. 1, vol. 3 of *Freedom: A Documentary History of Emancipation.* Cambridge: Cambridge University Press, 1990.

Blassingame, John W., ed. *Slave Testimony: Two Centuries of Letters, Speeches, Interviews, and Autobiographies.* Baton Rouge: Louisiana State University Press, 1977.

Borome, Joseph A., ed. "The Autobiography of Hiram Rhoades Revels Together with Some Letters by and about Him." *Midwest Journal* 5 (Winter 1952–53): 79–92.

Breeden, James O., ed. *Advice Among Masters: The Ideal in Slave Management in the Old South.* Westport, Conn.: Greenwood, 1980.

Brown, William Wells. *The Negro in the American Rebellion: His Heroism and His Fidelity.* Boston: Lee and Shepard, 1867.

Bruce, Henry Clay. *The New Man: Twenty-nine Years a Slave, Twenty-nine Years a Free Man.* 1895. Reprint, Lincoln: University of Nebraska Press, 1996.

Burr, David H. *The American Atlas.* London: Arrowsmith, 1839.

Campbell, Israel. *An Autobiography Bond and Free; or, Yearnings for Freedom, from My Green Brier House.* Philadelphia: Brinckloe, 1861. Electronic Edition, Documenting the American South, University Library, University of North Carolina at Chapel Hill <http://docsouth.unc.edu>.

Cashin, Joan E., ed. *Our Common Affairs: Texts from Women in the Old South.* Baltimore: Johns Hopkins University Press, 1996.

Davis, Reuben. *Recollections of Mississippi and Mississippians.* Boston: Houghton, Mifflin, 1890.

Douglass, Frederick. *My Bondage and My Freedom.* 1855. Edited by William L. Andrews. Urbana: University of Illinois Press, 1987.

Eaton, John. *Grant, Lincoln, and the Freedmen.* New York: Longmans, Green, 1907.

Faust, Drew Gilpin, ed. *The Ideology of Slavery: Proslavery Thought in the Antebellum South, 1830–1860.* Baton Rouge: Louisiana State University Press, 1981.

Foote, Henry S. *The Bench and Bar of the South and Southwest.* St. Louis: Soule, Thomas, and Wentworth, 1876.

——. *Casket of Reminiscences.* 1874. Reprint, New York: Negro Universities Press, 1968.

Franklin, John Hope, ed. *Reminiscences of an Active Life: The Autobiography of John Roy Lynch.* Chicago: University of Chicago Press, 1970.

Hilgard, Eugene W. *Report on the Geology and Agriculture of the State of Mississippi.* Jackson, Miss.: Barksdale, 1860.

Hogan, William R., and Edwin A. Davis, eds. *William Johnson's Natchez: The Ante-Bellum Diary of a Free Negro.* 1951. Reprint, Baton Rouge: Louisiana State University Press, 1993.

Hutchinson, A., comp. *Code of Mississippi.* Jackson, Miss.: Price and Fall, 1848.

Ingraham, Joseph Holt. *The South-West, by a Yankee.* 2 vols. 1835. Reprint, Ann Arbor: University Microfilms, 1966.

Johnson, Clifton H., ed. *God Struck Me Dead: Religious Conversion Experiences and Auto-biographies of Ex-Slaves*. 1945. Philadelphia: Pilgrim, 1969.

Lyell, Charles. *A Second Visit to the United States of North America*. 2 vols. London: Murray, 1849.

McIntosh, James T., ed. *The Papers of Jefferson Davis: June 1841–July 1846*. Baton Rouge: Louisiana State University Press, 1974.

Miller, Randall M., ed. *Dear Master: Letters of a Slave Family*. 1978. Reprint, Athens: University of Georgia Press, 1990.

Mississippi Reports. Columbia, Miss.: Stephens, 1834–60.

Olmsted, Frederick Law. *The Cotton Kingdom: A Traveller's Observations on Cotton and Slavery in the American Slave States*. Edited by Arthur M. Schlesinger. New York: Knopf, 1953.

———. *A Journey in the Back Country*. 1860. Reprint, New York: Schocken, 1970.

Poindexter, George, comp. *The Revised Code of the Laws of Mississippi*. Natchez, Miss.: Baker, 1824.

Rawick, George P., Jan Hillegas, and Ken Lawrence, eds. *The American Slave: A Composite Autobiography*. Supplement ser. 1. 12 vols. Westport, Conn.: Greenwood, 1977.

Riley, Franklin L., ed. "Diary of a Mississippi Planter, January 1, 1840, to April, 1863." *Mississippi Historical Society Publications* 10 (1909): 305–481.

Sharkey, William L., comp. *The Revised Code of the Statute Laws of Mississippi*. Jackson, Miss.: Barksdale, 1857.

Sydnor, Charles S., ed. "A Description of Seargent S. Prentiss in 1838." *Journal of Southern History* 10 (November 1944): 475–79.

Thompson, Charles. *Biography of a Slave*. Dayton: United Brethren Publishing House, 1875. Electronic Edition, Documenting the American South, University Library, University of North Carolina at Chapel Hill <http://docsouth.unc.edu>.

Tragle, Henry Irving, ed. *The Southampton Slave Revolt of 1831: A Compilation of Source Material*. Amherst: University of Massachusetts Press, 1971.

U.S. Bureau of the Census. *Negro Population in the United States, 1790–1915*. Washington, D.C.: Government Printing Office, 1918.

U.S. Congress. Senate. *Affairs in the Late Insurrectionary States*. 42nd Cong., 2nd sess., Report 41. Washington, D.C.: Government Printing Office, 1870–71.

———. *Denial of the Franchise in Mississippi, 1875 and 1876*. 44th Cong., 2nd sess., Miscellaneous Document 45. Washington, D.C.: Government Printing Office, 1877.

———. *Mississippi in 1875*. 44th Cong., 1st sess., Report 527. Washington, D.C.: Government Printing Office, 1876.

———. *The Removal of the Negroes from the Southern States to the Northern States*. 46th Cong, 2nd sess., Report 693. Washington, D.C.: Government Printing Office, 1880.

———. *Reports of the Freedmen's Bureau Assistant Commissioners and Laws in Relation to Freedmen*. 39th Cong., 2nd sess., Executive Document 6. Washington, D.C.: Government Printing Office, 1867.

U.S. Pension Bureau. *Regulations Relating to Army and Navy Pensions, with Statutes.* Washington, D.C.: Government Printing Office, 1881.

U.S. War Department. *Revised United States Army Regulations.* Philadelphia: Childs, 1863.

Wailes, Benjamin L. C. *Report on the Agriculture and Geology of Mississippi: Embracing a Sketch of the Social and Natural History of the State.* Jackson, Miss.: Barksdale, 1854.

Watson, Henry. *Narrative of Henry Watson, a Fugitive Slave.* Boston: Marsh, 1848. Electronic Edition, Documenting the American South, University Library, University of North Carolina at Chapel Hill <http://docsouth.unc.edu>.

Yeatman, James E. *A Report on the Condition of the Freedmen of the Mississippi.* St. Louis: Western Sanitary Commission, 1864.

Yetman, Norman R., ed. *Life under the "Peculiar Institution": Selections from the Slave Narrative Collection.* New York: Holt, Rinehart, and Winston, 1970.

Newspapers

Mississippi Free Trader
Woodville Republican

Secondary Sources

Abrahams, Roger D. *Singing the Master: The Emergence of African-American Culture in the Plantation South.* New York: Penguin, 1993.

Adams, Katherine J. "Natchez District Women: Voices of Southern Women in the Natchez Trace Collection." In *Inside the Natchez Trace Collection*, edited by Katherine J. Adams and Lewis L. Gould, 58–92. Baton Rouge: Louisiana State University Press, 1999.

Adams, Katherine J., and Lewis L. Gould, eds. *Inside the Natchez Trace Collection.* Baton Rouge: Louisiana State University Press, 1999.

Alford, Terry. *Prince Among Slaves: The True Story of an African Prince Sold into Slavery in the American South.* New York: Oxford University Press, 1977.

Allmendinger, David F., Jr. "The Construction of *The Confessions of Nat Turner.*" In *Nat Turner: A Slave Rebellion in History and Memory*, edited by Kenneth S. Greenberg, 24–42. New York: Oxford University Press, 2003.

Anderson, Benedict R. O'G. *Imagined Communities: Reflections on the Origin and Spread of Nationalism.* Rev. ed. London: Verso, 1991.

Anderson, Ralph V., and Robert E. Gallman. "Slaves as Fixed Capital: Slave Labor and Southern Economic Development." *Journal of American History* 44 (June 1977): 24–46.

Aptheker, Herbert. *American Negro Slave Revolts.* 1943. Reprint, New York: International Publishers, 1974.

Armstrong, Thomas F. "From Task Labor to Free Labor: The Transition along Georgia's Rice Coast, 1820–1880." *Georgia Historical Quarterly* 64 (Winter 1980): 432–47.

Ash, Stephen V. *When the Yankees Came: Conflict and Chaos in the Occupied South, 1861–1865*. Chapel Hill: University of North Carolina Press, 1995.

Ayers, Edward L. *Vengeance and Justice: Crime and Punishment in the Nineteenth-Century South*. New York: Oxford University Press, 1984.

Baird, James M. "Between Slavery and Independence: Power Relations between Dependent White Men and Their Superiors in Late Colonial and Early National Virginia with Particular Reference to the Overseer-Employer Relationship." Ph.D. diss., Johns Hopkins University, 1999.

Ballard, Michael B. *Vicksburg: The Campaign That Opened the Mississippi*. Chapel Hill: University of North Carolina Press, 2004.

Bancroft, Frederic. *Slave Trading in the Old South*. 1931. Reprint, New York: Ungar, 1959.

Baptist, Edward E. *Creating an Old South: Middle Florida's Plantation Frontier before the Civil War*. Chapel Hill: University of North Carolina Press, 2002.

———. " 'Cuffy,' 'Fancy Maids,' and 'One-Eyed Men': Rape, Commodification, and the Domestic Slave Trade in the United States." *American Historical Review* 107 (December 2001): 1619–50.

———. "The Migration of Planters to Antebellum Florida: Kinship and Power." *Journal of Southern History* 62 (August 1996): 527–54.

Bardaglio, Peter W. *Reconstructing the Household: Families, Sex, and the Law in the Nineteenth-Century South*. Chapel Hill: University of North Carolina Press, 1995.

Barnes, Kenneth C. *Who Killed John Clayton? Political Violence and the Emergence of the New South, 1861–1893*. Durham, N.C.: Duke University Press, 1998.

Barnett, Jim, and H. Clark Burkett. "The Forks of the Road Slave Market at Natchez." *Journal of Mississippi History* 63 (2001): 169–87.

Barney, William L. *The Secessionist Impulse: Alabama and Mississippi in 1860*. Princeton: Princeton University Press, 1974.

Barton, Keith C. " 'Good Cooks and Washers': Slave Hiring, Domestic Labor, and the Market in Bourbon County, Kentucky." *Journal of American History* 84 (September 1997): 436–60.

Bennett, Herman L. *Africans in Colonial Mexico: Absolutism, Christianity, and Afro-Creole Consciousness, 1570–1640*. Bloomington: Indiana University Press, 2003.

Bercaw, Nancy D. *Gendered Freedoms: Race, Rights, and the Politics of Household in the Delta, 1861–1875*. Gainesville: University Press of Florida, 2003.

Berlin, Ira. *Generations of Captivity: A History of African American Slaves*. Cambridge: Harvard University Press, 2003.

———. *Many Thousands Gone: The First Two Centuries of Slavery in North America*. Cambridge: Harvard University Press, 1998.

Berlin, Ira, and Philip D. Morgan, eds. *Cultivation and Culture: Labor and the Shaping of Slave Life in the Americas*. Charlottesville: University Press of Virginia, 1993.

Besson, Jean. "The Creolization of African-American Slave Kinship in Jamaican Free

Villages and Maroon Communities." In *Slave Cultures and the Cultures of Slavery*, edited by Stephan Palmié, 187–209. Knoxville: University of Tennessee Press, 1995.

———. *Martha Brae's Two Histories: European Expansion and Caribbean Culture-Building in Jamaica*. Chapel Hill: University of North Carolina Press, 2002.

Bettersworth, John K. *Confederate Mississippi: The People and Policies of a Cotton State in Wartime*. Baton Rouge: Louisiana State University Press, 1943.

Billingsley, Carolyn Earle. *Communities of Kinship: Antebellum Families and the Settlement of the Cotton Frontier*. Athens: University of Georgia Press, 2004.

Blassingame, John W. *The Slave Community: Plantation Life in the Antebellum South*. Rev. ed. New York: Oxford University Press, 1979.

———. "Using the Testimony of Ex-Slaves: Approaches and Problems." *Journal of Southern History* 41 (November 1965): 473–92.

Boles, John B., ed. *Masters and Slaves in the House of the Lord: Race and Religion in the American South*. Lexington: University Press of Kentucky, 1988.

Bolland, Nigel O. "Proto-Proletarians? Slave Wages in the Americas: Between Slave Labour and Free Labour." *From Chattel Slaves to Wage Slaves: The Dynamics of Labour Bargaining in the Americas*, edited by Mary Turner, 123–47. Kingston, Jamaica: Randle, 1995.

Bond, Bradley G. *Political Culture in the Nineteenth Century South: Mississippi, 1830–1900*. Baton Rouge: Louisiana State University Press, 1995.

Bonner, James C. "Genesis of Agricultural Reform in the Cotton Belt." *Journal of Southern History* 9 (November 1943): 475–500.

Breen, Patrick H. "A Prophet in His Own Land: Support for Nat Turner and His Rebellion within Southampton's Black Community." In *Nat Turner: A Slave Rebellion in History and Memory*, edited by Kenneth S. Greenberg, 103–18. New York: Oxford University Press, 2003.

Brooks, James F. *Captives and Cousins: Slavery, Kinship, and Community in the Southwest Borderlands*. Chapel Hill: University of North Carolina Press, 2002.

Brown, Elsa Barkley. "Negotiating and Transforming the Public Sphere: African American Political Life in the Transition from Slavery to Freedom." *Public Culture* 7 (Fall 1994): 107–46.

Brown, Elsa Barkley, and Gregg D. Kimball. "Mapping the Terrain of Black Richmond, 1852–1915." *Journal of Urban History* 21 (March 1995): 296–346.

Brown, Richard D. *Modernization: The Transformation of American Life, 1600–1865*. New York: Hill and Wang, 1976.

Brown, Virginia Pounds. *Toting the Lead Row: Ruby Pickens Tartt, Alabama Folklorist*. University: University of Alabama Press, 1981.

Buchanan, Thomas C. *Black Life on the Mississippi: Slaves, Free Blacks, and the Western Steamboat World*. Chapel Hill: University of North Carolina Press, 2004.

Buckner, Timothy R. "Vicksburg's Civil War on Vice: Drinking, Gambling and Race in the Antebellum South." *Journal of Mississippi History* 67 (2005): 311–30.

Burnard, Trevor. *Mastery, Tyranny, and Desire: Thomas Thistlewood and His Slaves in the Anglo-Jamaican World*. Chapel Hill: University of North Carolina Press, 2004.

Burnham, Margaret A. "An Impossible Marriage: Slave Law and Family Law." *Law and Inequality* 5 (July 1987): 187–225.

Burton, Orville V. *In My Father's House Are Many Mansions: Family and Community in Edgefield, South Carolina*. Chapel Hill: University of North Carolina Press, 1985.

Bush, Barbara. *Slave Women in Caribbean Society, 1650–1838*. Kingston, Jamaica: Randle, 1990.

Bynum, Victoria E. *Unruly Women: The Politics of Social and Sexual Control in the Old South*. Chapel Hill: University of North Carolina Press, 1992.

Cade, John B. "Out of the Mouths of Ex-Slaves." *Journal of Negro History* 20 (July 1935): 294–337.

Camp, Stephanie M. H. *Closer to Freedom: Enslaved Women and Everyday Resistance in the Plantation South*. Chapel Hill: University of North Carolina Press, 2004.

———. " 'I Could Not Stay There': Enslaved Women, Truancy, and the Geography of Everyday Forms of Resistance in the Antebellum Plantation South," *Slavery and Abolition* 23 (December 2002): 1–20.

———. "The Pleasures of Resistance: Enslaved Women and Body Politics in the Plantation South, 1830–1861." *Journal of Southern History* 68 (August 2002): 533–72.

Campbell, John. "As 'A Kind of Freeman'? Slaves' Market-Related Activities in the South Carolina Up Country, 1800–1860." In *Cultivation and Culture: Labor and the Shaping of Slave Life in the Americas*, edited by Ira Berlin and Philip D. Morgan, 243–74. Charlottesville: University Press of Virginia, 1993.

Campbell, Randolph B. *An Empire for Slavery: The Peculiar Institution in Texas, 1821–1865*. Baton Rouge: Louisiana State University Press, 1989.

———. "Research Note: Slave Hiring in Texas." *American Historical Review* 93 (February 1988): 107–14.

———. "Slavery in the Natchez Trace Collection." In *Inside the Natchez Trace Collection*, edited by Katherine J. Adams and Lewis L. Gould, 34–57. Baton Rouge: Louisiana State University Press, 1999.

Campbell, Stanley W. *The Slave Catchers: Enforcement of the Fugitive Slave Law, 1850–1860*. Chapel Hill: University of North Carolina Press, 1970.

Carney, Judith A. *Black Rice: The African Origins of Rice Cultivation in the Americas*. Cambridge: Harvard University Press, 2001.

Cashin, Joan E. *A Family Venture: Men and Women on the Southern Frontier*. New York: Oxford University Press, 1991.

Cecelski, David S. *The Waterman's Song: Slavery and Freedom in Maritime North Carolina*. Chapel Hill: University of North Carolina Press, 2001.

Censer, Jane Turner. *North Carolina Planters and Their Children, 1800–1860*. Baton Rouge: Louisiana State University Press, 1984.

Chaplin, Joyce E. *An Anxious Pursuit: Agrarian Innovation and Technology in the Lower South, 1730–1815*. Chapel Hill: University of North Carolina Press, 1993.

Cimprich, John. "Slave Behavior during the Federal Occupation of Tennessee, 1862–1865." *Historian* 44 (May 1982): 335–46.

——. *Slavery's End in Tennessee, 1861–1865*. University: University of Alabama Press, 1985.

Clarke, Erskine. *Dwelling Place: A Plantation Epic*. New Haven: Yale University Press, 2005.

Clifton, James M. "The Rice Driver: His Role in Slave Management." *South Carolina Historical Magazine* 82 (October 1981): 331–53.

Clinton, Catherine. *Plantation Mistress: Woman's World in the Old South*. New York: Pantheon, 1982.

——. "'Southern Dishonor': Flesh, Blood, Race, and Bondage." In *In Joy and In Sorrow: Women, Family, and Marriage in the Victorian South, 1830–1900*, edited by Carol Bleser, 52–68. New York: Oxford University Press, 1991.

Close, Stacy K. *Elderly Slaves of the Plantation South*. New York: Garland, 1997.

Cobb, James C. *The Most Southern Place on Earth: The Mississippi Delta and the Roots of Regional Identity*. New York: Oxford University Press, 1992.

Coclanis, Peter. "How the Low Country Was Taken to Task: Slave-Labor Organization in Coastal South Carolina and Georgia." In *Slavery, Secession, and Southern History*, edited by Robert L. Paquette and Louis A. Ferleger, 59–78. Charlottesville: University Press of Virginia, 2000.

——. "Thickening Description: William Washington's Queries on Rice." *Agricultural History* 64 (Summer 1990): 9–16.

Cody, Cheryll Ann. "There Was No 'Absalom' on the Ball Plantations: Slave-Naming Practices in the South Carolina Low Country, 1720–1865." *American Historical Review* 92 (June 1987): 563–96.

Cohen, William. *At Freedom's Edge: Black Mobility and the Southern White Quest for Racial Control, 1861–1915*. Baton Rouge: Louisiana State University Press, 1991.

Confino, Alon. "Collective Memory and Cultural History: Problems of Method." *American Historical Review* 102 (December 1997): 1386–1403.

Cooper, William J. *The South and the Politics of Slavery, 1828–1856*. Baton Rouge: Louisiana State University Press, 1978.

Cornelius, Janet Duitsman. *Slave Missions and the Black Church in the Antebellum South*. Columbia: University of South Carolina Press, 1999.

——. *"When I Can Read My Title Clear": Literacy, Slavery, and Religion in the Antebellum South*. Columbia: University of South Carolina Press, 1991.

Corrigan, Mary Beth. "'It's a Family Affair': Buying Freedom in the District of Columbia, 1850–1860." In *Working Toward Freedom: Slave Society and Domestic Economy in the American South*, edited by Larry E. Hudson Jr., 163–91. Rochester, N.Y.: University of Rochester Press, 1994.

Costa, Dora L. *The Evolution of Retirement: An American Economic History, 1880–1990*. Chicago: University of Chicago Press, 1998.

——. "Height, Weight, Wartime Stress, and Older Age Mortality: Evidence from the Union Army Records." *Explorations in Economic History* 30 (October 1993): 424–49.

Costa, Emilia Viotti da. *The Brazilian Empire: Myths and Histories*. Rev. ed. Chapel Hill: University of North Carolina Press, 2000.

Courlander, Harold. *Negro Folk Music U.S.A.* 1963. Reprint, New York: Dover, 1991.

Crane, J. Michael. "Controlling the Night: Perceptions of the Slave Patrol System in Mississippi." *Journal of Mississippi History* 61 (Summer 1999): 119–36.

Crawford, Stephen. "The Slave Family: A View from the Slave Narratives." In *Strategic Factors in Nineteenth Century American Economic History: Essays to Honor Robert W. Fogel*, edited by Claudia Goldin and Hugh Rockoff, 331–50. Chicago: University of Chicago Press, 1992.

Creel, Margaret Washington. *"A Peculiar People": Slave Religion and Community-Culture Among the Gullahs*. New York: New York University Press, 1988.

Crofts, Daniel W. *Old Southampton: Politics and Society in a Virginia County, 1834–1869*. Charlottesville: University Press of Virginia, 1992.

Currie, James T. *Enclave: Vicksburg and Her Plantations, 1863–1870*. Jackson: University Press of Mississippi, 1980.

Daniels, Christine. "Gresham's Laws: Labor Management on an Early-Eighteenth-Century Chesapeake Plantation." *Journal of Southern History* 62 (May 1996): 205–37.

Davis, Adrienne. " 'Don't Let Nobody Bother Yo' Principle': The Sexual Economy of American Slavery." In *Sister Circle: Black Women and Work*, edited by Sharon Harley and the Black Women and Work Collective, 103–27. New Brunswick, N.J.: Rutgers University Press, 2002.

Davis, Angela. "Reflections on the Black Woman's Role in the Community of Slaves." *Black Scholar* 3 (December 1971): 3–15.

Davis, David Brion. *Inhuman Bondage: The Rise and Fall of Slavery in the New World*. New York: Oxford University Press, 2006.

——. *The Problem of Slavery in Western Culture* Ithaca: Cornell University Press, 1969.

Davis, Ronald L. F. *The Black Experience in Natchez, 1720–1880*. Natchez Historical Park, Miss.: Eastern National Park and Monument Association, 1994.

Davis, William C. *Jefferson Davis: The Man and His Hour*. New York: Harper Collins, 1991.

Degler, Carl N. "The Irony of American Negro Slavery." In *Perspectives and Irony in American Slavery*, edited by Harry P. Owens, 3–28. Jackson: University Press of Mississippi, 1976.

——. *Place over Time: The Continuity of Southern Distinctiveness*. Baton Rouge: Louisiana State University Press, 1977.

Delehanty, Randolph, and Van Jones Martin. *Classic Natchez*. Savannah, Ga.: Martin–St. Martin, 1996.

Dew, Charles B. "Disciplining Slave Ironworkers in the Antebellum South: Coercion, Conciliation, and Accommodation." *American Historical Review* 79 (April 1974): 393–418.

Deyle, Steven. *Carry Me Back: The Domestic Slave Trade in American Life*. New York: Oxford University Press, 2005.

Diedrich, Maria. " 'My Love Is Black as Yours Is Fair': Premarital Love and Sexuality in the Antebellum Slave Narrative." *Phylon* 47 (Fall 1986): 238–47.

Doyle, Don H. *Faulkner's County: The Historical Roots of Yoknapatawpha*. Chapel Hill: University of North Carolina Press, 2001.

Drago, Edmund L. "How Sherman's March Through Georgia Affected the Slaves." *Georgia Historical Quarterly* 57 (Fall 1973): 361–75.

Du Bois, W. E. B. *Black Reconstruction in America*. 1935. Reprint, New York: Atheneum, 1962.

Durrill, Wayne. "A Tale of Two Courthouses: Civic Space, Political Power, and Capitalist Development in a New South Community, 1843–1890." *Journal of Social History* 35 (Spring 2002): 659–81.

Dusinberre, William. *Slavemaster President: The Double Career of James Polk*. Oxford: Oxford University Press, 2003.

———. *Them Dark Days: Slavery in the American Rice Swamps*. New York: Oxford University Press, 1996.

Dyer, Frederick H., comp. *A Compendium of the War of the Rebellion*. 3 vols. 1908. Reprint, New York: Yoseloff, 1959.

Earle, Carville. "Myth of the Southern Soil Miner: Macrohistory, Agricultural Innovation, and Environmental Change." In *The Ends of the Earth: Perspectives on Modern Environmental History*, edited by Donald Worster, 175–210. New York: Cambridge University Press, 1988.

———. "The Price of Precocity: Technical Choice and Ecological Constraint in the Cotton South, 1840–1890." *Agricultural History* 66 (Summer 1992): 25–60.

Eaton, Clement. *Jefferson Davis*. New York: Free Press, 1977.

———. "Slave-Hiring in the Upper South: A Step toward Freedom." *Mississippi Valley Historical Review* 46 (March 1960): 663–78.

Edwards, Laura F. *Gendered Strife and Confusion: The Political Culture of Reconstruction*. Urbana: University of Illinois Press, 1997.

———. " 'The Marriage Covenant Is at the Foundation of all Our Rights': The Politics of Slave Marriages in North Carolina after Emancipation." *Law and History Review* 14 (Spring 1996): 81–124.

Egerton, Douglas R. *Gabriel's Rebellion: The Virginia Slave Conspiracies of 1800 and 1802*. Chapel Hill: University of North Carolina Press, 1993.

———. "Markets without a Market Revolution: Southern Planters and Capitalism." *Journal of the Early Republic* 16 (Summer 1996): 207–21.

Engerman, Stanley L., and B. W. Higman. "The Demographic Structure of the Caribbean Slave Societies in the Eighteenth and Nineteenth Centuries." In *The Slave Societies of the Caribbean*, vol. 3 of *General History of the Caribbean*, edited by Franklin W. Knight, 45–104. London: UNESCO, 1997.

Entrikin, J. Nicholas. *The Betweenness of Place: Towards a Geography of Modernity*. Baltimore: Johns Hopkins University Press, 1991.

Epperson, Terrence W. "Constructing Difference: The Social and Spatial Order of the Chesapeake Plantation." In *"I, Too, Am America": Archaeological Studies of African-American Life*, edited by Theresa A. Singleton, 159–72. Charlottesville: University Press of Virginia, 1999.

Escott, Paul D. "The Context of Freedom: Georgia's Slaves During the Civil War." *Georgia Historical Quarterly* 58 (Spring 1974): 79–104.

———. *Slavery Remembered: A Record of Twentieth-Century Slave Narratives*. Chapel Hill: University of North Carolina Press, 1979.

Farnham, Christie. "Saphire? The Issue of Dominance in the Slave Family, 1830–1865." In *"To Toil the Livelong Day": America's Women at Work, 1789–1980*, edited by Carol Groneman and Mary Beth Norton, 68–83. Ithaca: Cornell University Press, 1987.

Faust, Drew Gilpin. *The Creation of Confederate Nationalism: Ideology and Identity in the Civil War South*. Baton Rouge: Louisiana State University Press, 1989.

———. "The Inquisition in Mississippi: A Review of *Tumult and Silence at Second Creek*." *New York Times Book Review*, 9 May 1993, 29.

———. *James Henry Hammond and the Old South: A Design for Mastery*. Baton Rouge: Louisiana State University Press, 1982.

———. *Mothers of Invention: Women of the Slaveholding South and the American Civil War*. Chapel Hill: University of North Carolina Press, 1996.

———. *A Sacred Circle: The Dilemma of the Intellectual in the Old South, 1840–1860*. 1977. Reprint, Philadelphia: University of Pennsylvania Press, 1986.

Fede, Andrew. "Legitimized Violent Slave Abuse in the American South, 1619–1865: A Case Study of Law and Social Change in Six Southern States." *American Journal of Legal History* 29 (April 1985): 93–150.

Fett, Sharla M. *Working Cures: Healing, Health, and Power on Southern Slave Plantations*. Chapel Hill: University of North Carolina Press, 2002.

Fields, Barbara J. "The Nineteenth-Century South: History and Theory." *Plantation Society in the Americas* 2 (April 1983): 7–27.

———. *Slavery and Freedom on the Middle Ground*. New Haven: Yale University Press, 1985.

———. "Slavery, Race, and Ideology in the United States of America." *New Left Review* 181 (1990): 95–118.

———. "Whiteness, Racism, and Identity." *International Labor and Working-Class History* 60 (Fall 2001): 48–56.

Fitzgerald, Michael W. "Republican Factionalism and Black Empowerment: The Spencer-Warner Controversy and Alabama Reconstruction, 1868–1880." *Journal of Southern History* 64 (August 1998): 473–94.

Flanigan, Daniel J. "Criminal Procedure in Slave Trials in the Antebellum South." *Journal of Southern History* 40 (November 1974): 537–64.

Florentino, Manolo Garcia, and José Roberto Góes. "Slavery, Marriage, and Kinship in Rural Rio de Janeiro, 1790–1830." In *Identity in the Shadow of Slavery*, edited by Paul E. Lovejoy, 137–62. London: Continuum, 2000.

Fogel, Robert W. "New Sources and New Techniques for the Study of Secular Trends in Nutritional Status, Health, Mortality, and the Process of Aging." *Historical Methods* 26 (Winter 1993): 5–43.

———. *Without Consent or Contract: The Rise and Fall of American Slavery*. New York: Norton, 1989.

Fogel, Robert W., and Stanley L. Engerman. *Time on the Cross: The Economics of American Negro Slavery*. 1974. Reprint, New York: Norton, 1989.

———, eds. *Markets and Production*. Vol. 1 of *Without Consent or Contract (Technical Papers)*. New York: Norton, 1992.

Foner, Eric. *Freedom's Lawmakers: A Directory of Black Officeholders during Reconstruction*. Rev. ed. Baton Rouge: Louisiana State University Press, 1996.

———. *Reconstruction: America's Unfinished Revolution*. New York: Harper and Row, 1988.

Foucault, Michel. "What Is Enlightenment?" In *The Foucault Reader*, edited by Paul Rabinow, 32–50. New York: Pantheon, 1984.

Fox-Genovese, Elizabeth. *Within the Plantation Household: Black and White Women of the Old South*. Chapel Hill: University of North Carolina Press, 1988.

Fox-Genovese, Elizabeth, and Eugene D. Genovese. *The Mind of the Master Class: History and Faith in the Southern Slaveholders' Worldview*. New York: Cambridge University Press, 2005.

Franke, Katherine M. "Becoming a Citizen: Reconstruction Era Regulation of African American Marriages." *Yale Journal of Law and the Humanities* 11 (Summer 1999): 251–308.

Frankel, Noralee. *Freedom's Women: Black Women and Families in Civil War Era Mississippi*. Bloomington: Indiana University Press, 1999.

Franklin, Jimmie. "Black Southerners, Shared Experience, and Place: A Reflection." *Journal of Southern History* 60 (February 1994): 3–18.

Franklin, John Hope, and Loren Schweninger. *Runaway Slaves: Rebels on the Plantation*. Oxford: Oxford University Press, 1999.

French, A. Scot. *The Rebellious Slave: Nat Turner in American Memory*. Boston: Houghton Mifflin, 2004.

Frey, Sylvia R., and Betty Wood. *Come Shouting to Zion: African American Protestantism in the American South and British Caribbean to 1830*. Chapel Hill: University of North Carolina Press, 1998.

Friedman, Jean E. *The Enclosed Garden: Women and Community in the Evangelical South, 1830–1900*. Chapel Hill: University of North Carolina Press, 1985.

Furstenberg, François. "Beyond Freedom and Slavery: Autonomy, Virtue, and Resistance in Early American Political Discourse." *Journal of American History* 89 (March 2003): 1295–1330.

Gallman, Robert E. "Self-Sufficiency in the Cotton Economy of the Antebellum South." *Agricultural History* 44 (January 1970): 5–23.

Gates, Paul W. *The Farmer's Age: Agriculture, 1816–1860.* 1960. Reprint, New York: Harper Torchbooks, 1968.

Gautier, Arlette. *Les Soeurs de Solitude: La Condition Féminine dans l'Esclavage aux Antilles du XVIIe au XIXe Siècle.* Paris: Éditions Caribéennes, 1985.

Gellner, Ernest. *Encounters with Nationalism.* Oxford: Blackwell, 1994.

Genovese, Eugene D. *A Consuming Fire: The Fall of the Confederacy in the Mind of the White Christian South.* Athens: University of Georgia Press, 1998.

———. *From Rebellion to Revolution: Afro-American Slave Revolts in the Making of the Modern World.* Baton Rouge: Louisiana State University Press, 1979.

———. *The Political Economy of Slavery: Studies in the Economy and Society of the Slave South.* New York: Vintage, 1967.

———. *Roll, Jordan, Roll: The World the Slaves Made.* New York: Pantheon, 1974.

Gerteis, Louis S. *From Contraband to Freedman: Federal Policy Toward Southern Blacks, 1861–1865.* Westport, Conn.: Greenwood, 1973.

Giddens, Anthony. *The Constitution of Society: Outline of the Theory of Structuration.* Berkeley: University of California Press, 1984.

Gillis, Irene S., and Norman E. Gillis. *Adams County Mississippi Marriages, 1802–1859.* Shreveport, La.: Gill, 1976.

Glasson, William H. *History of Military Pension Legislation in the United States.* New York: Columbia University Press, 1900.

Glatthaar, Joseph T. *Forged in Battle: The Civil War Alliance of Black Soldiers and White Officers.* New York: Free Press, 1990.

Glymph, Thavolia. "The Second Middle Passage: The Transition from Slavery to Freedom at Davis Bend, Mississippi." Ph.D. diss., Purdue University, 1994.

Goldfield, David R. "Pursuing the American Urban Dream: Cities in the Old South." In *The City in Southern History: The Growth of Urban Civilization in the South,* edited by Blaine A. Brownell and David R. Goldfield, 52–91. Port Washington, N.Y.: Kennikat, 1977.

Goldin, Claudia D. *Urban Slavery in the American South, 1820–1860: A Quantitative History.* Chicago: University of Chicago Press, 1976.

Gomez, Michael A. *Exchanging Our Country Marks: The Transformation of African Identities in the Colonial and Antebellum South.* Chapel Hill: University of North Carolina Press, 1998.

Gonzales, John E. "Flush Times, Depression, War, and Compromise." In *History of Mississippi,* edited by Richard A. McLemore, 1:284–309. Hattiesburg: University and College Press of Mississippi, 1973.

Goody, Jack. "Time: Social Organisation." In *International Encyclopedia of the Social Sciences,* edited by D. L. Sills, 16:30–41. New York: Macmillan, 1968.

Gordon-Reed, Annette. *Thomas Jefferson and Sally Hemings: An American Controversy.* Charlottesville: University Press of Virginia, 1997.

Gray, Lewis C. *History of Agriculture in the Southern United States to 1860.* 2 vols. New York: Smith, 1941.

Greenberg, Kenneth S., ed. *Nat Turner: A Slave Rebellion in History and Memory.* New York: Oxford University Press, 2003.

Griffin, Rebecca J. " 'Goin' Back over to See That Girl': Competing Social Spaces in the Lives of the Enslaved in Antebellum North Carolina." *Slavery and Abolition* 25 (April 2004): 94–113.

Grimsley, Mark. *The Hard Hand of War: Union Military Policy Toward Southern Civilians, 1861–1865.* Cambridge: Cambridge University Press, 1995.

Gross, Ariela J. *Double Character: Slavery and Mastery in the Antebellum Southern Courtroom.* Princeton: Princeton University Press, 2000.

Guha, Ranajit. *Elementary Aspects of Peasant Insurgency in Colonial India.* Delhi, India: Oxford University Press, 1983.

Gutman, Herbert G. *The Black Family in Slavery and Freedom, 1750–1925.* New York: Vintage, 1976.

——. "The Black Family in Slavery and Freedom: A Revised Perspective." In *Power and Culture: Essays on the American Working Class,* edited by Ira Berlin, 357–79. New York: Pantheon, 1987.

Gutman, Herbert G., and Richard Sutch. "The Slave Family: Protected Agent of Capitalist Masters or Victim of the Slave Trade?" In *Reckoning with Slavery: A Critical Study in the Quantitative History Of American Negro Slavery,* 94–133. New York: Oxford University Press, 1976.

Habermas, Jürgen. *The Structural Transformation of the Public Sphere: An Inquiry into a Category of Bourgeois Society.* Translated by Thomas Burger with Frederick Lawrence. Cambridge: MIT Press, 1991.

Hadden, Sally E. *Slave Patrols: Law and Violence in Virginia and the Carolinas.* Cambridge: Harvard University Press, 2001.

Hahn, Steven. *A Nation Under Our Feet: Black Political Struggles in the Rural South from Slavery to the Great Migration.* Cambridge: Harvard University Press, 2003.

Halbwachs, Maurice. *The Collective Memory.* Translated by Francis J. Ditter Jr. and Vida Yazdi Ditter. New York: Harper and Row, 1980.

Harding, Vincent. *There Is a River: The Black Struggle for Freedom in America.* 1981. Reprint, New York: Harcourt, Brace, Jovanovich, 1992.

Hartman, Saidiya V. *Scenes of Subjection: Terror, Slavery, and Self-Making in Nineteenth-Century America.* New York: Oxford University Press, 1997.

Hartog, Hendrik. *Man and Wife in America: A History.* Cambridge: Harvard University Press, 2000.

Hermann, Janet Sharp. *The Pursuit of a Dream.* New York: Vintage, 1983.

Heyrman, Christine Leigh. *Southern Cross: The Beginnings of the Bible Belt.* New York: Knopf, 1997.

Hildebrand, Reginald F. *The Times Were Strange and Stirring: Methodist Preachers and the Crisis of Emancipation.* Durham, N.C.: Duke University Press, 1995.

Hilliard, Sam Bowers. *Atlas of Antebellum Southern Agriculture*. Baton Rouge: Louisiana State University Press, 1984.

Hindus, Michael S. *Prison and Plantation: Crime, Justice, and Authority in Massachusetts and South Carolina, 1767–1878*. Chapel Hill: University of North Carolina Press, 1980.

Hine, Darlene Clark. "Rape and the Inner Lives of Southern Black Women: Thoughts on the Culture of Dissemblance." In *Southern Women: Histories and Identities*, edited by Virginia Bernhard, Betty Brandon, Elizabeth Fox-Genovese, and Theda Perdue, 177–89. Columbia: University of Missouri Press, 1992.

Hobsbawm, E. J. *Nations and Nationalism since 1780: Programme, Myth, Reality*. 2nd ed. Cambridge: Cambridge University Press, 1992.

Hofstra, Warren R. *The Planting of New Virginia: Settlement and Landscape in the Shenandoah Valley*. Baltimore: Johns Hopkins University Press, 2004.

Holcombe, Richard, Jr. *Debt, Investment, Slaves: Credit Relations in East Feliciana Parish, Louisiana, 1825–1885*. Tuscaloosa: University of Alabama Press, 1995.

Holt, Michael F. *The Rise and Fall of the American Whig Party: Jacksonian Politics and the Onset of the Civil War*. New York: Oxford University Press, 1999.

Howington, Arthur F. *What Sayeth the Law: The Treatment of Slaves and Free Blacks in the State and Local Courts of Tennessee*. New York: Garland, 1986.

Hudson, Larry E., Jr. " 'All That Cash': Work and Status in the Slave Quarters." In *Working Toward Freedom: Slave Society and Domestic Economy in the American South*, edited by Larry E. Hudson Jr., 77–94. Rochester, N.Y.: University of Rochester Press, 1994.

———. *To Have and to Hold: Slave Work and Family Life in Antebellum South Carolina*. Athens: University of Georgia Press, 1997.

———, ed. *Working Toward Freedom: Slave Society and Domestic Economy in the American South*. Rochester, N.Y.: University of Rochester Press, 1994.

Huggins, Nathan I. *Black Odyssey: The African American Ordeal in Slavery*. 1977. Reprint, New York: Vintage, 1990.

Hughes, Sarah S. "Slaves for Hire: The Allocation of Black Labor in Elizabeth City County, Virginia, 1782–1810." *William and Mary Quarterly*, 3rd ser., 35 (April 1978): 260–86.

Hyde, Samuel C., Jr. *Pistols and Politics: The Dilemma of Democracy in Louisiana's Florida Parishes, 1810–1899*. Baton Rouge: Louisiana State University Press, 1996.

Isaac, Rhys. *The Transformation of Virginia, 1740–1790*. Chapel Hill: University of North Carolina Press, 1982.

James, D. Clayton. *Antebellum Natchez*. Baton Rouge: Louisiana State University Press, 1968.

James, Larry M. "Biracial Fellowship in Antebellum Baptist Churches." In *Masters and Slaves in the House of the Lord: Race and Religion in the American South*, edited by John B. Boles, 37–57. Lexington: University Press of Kentucky, 1988.

Johnson, Michael P. "Denmark Vesey and His Co-Conspirators." *William and Mary Quarterly*, 3rd ser., 58 (October 2001): 915–76.

———. "Runaway Slaves and the Slave Communities in South Carolina, 1799–1820." *William and Mary Quarterly*, 3rd ser., 38 (July 1981): 418–41.

———. "Work, Culture, and the Slave Community: Slave Occupations in the Cotton Belt in 1860." *Labor History* 27 (Summer 1986): 325–55.

Johnson, Walter. "On Agency." *Journal of Social History* 37 (Fall 2003): 113–24.

———. *Soul by Soul: Life Inside the Antebellum Slave Market*. Cambridge: Harvard University Press, 1999.

Jones, Jacqueline. *Labor of Love, Labor of Sorrow: Black Women, Work, and Family from Slavery to the Present*. New York: Vintage, 1986.

Jones, Norrece T., Jr. *Born a Child of Freedom, Yet a Slave: Mechanisms of Control and Strategies of Resistance in Antebellum South Carolina*. Hanover, N.H.: University Press of New England, 1990.

———. "Rape in Black and White: Sexual Violence in the Testimony of Enslaved and Free Americans." In *Slavery and the American South*, edited by Winthrop D. Jordan, 93–108. Jackson: University Press of Mississippi, 2003.

Jordan, Winthrop D. *Tumult and Silence at Second Creek: An Inquiry into a Civil War Slave Conspiracy*. Baton Rouge: Louisiana State University Press, 1993.

———. *White over Black: American Attitudes Toward the Negro, 1550–1812*. 1968. Reprint, New York: Norton, 1977.

Joyner, Charles. *Down by the Riverside: A South Carolina Slave Community*. Urbana: University of Illinois Press, 1985.

———. "History as Ritual: Rites of Power and Resistance on the Slave Plantation." In *Shared Traditions: Southern History and Folk Culture*, 93–102. Urbana: University of Illinois Press, 1999.

Kant, Immanuel. *Groundwork of the Metaphysics of Morals*. Translated by Mary Gregor. Cambridge: Cambridge University Press, 1998.

Kantrowitz, Stephen. *Ben Tillman and the Reconstruction of White Supremacy*. Chapel Hill: University of North Carolina Press, 2000.

Karasch, Mary C. *Slave Life in Rio de Janeiro, 1808–1850*. Princeton: Princeton University Press, 1987.

Kay, Marvin L. M., and Lorin L. Cary. *Slavery in North Carolina, 1748–1775*. Chapel Hill: University of North Carolina Press, 1995.

Kaye, Anthony E. "Neighborhoods and Nat Turner: The Making of a Slave Rebel and the Unmaking of a Slave Rebellion." *Journal of the Early Republic*. Forthcoming.

———. "Neighbourhoods and Solidarity in the Natchez District of Mississippi: Rethinking the Antebellum Slave Community." *Slavery and Abolition* 23 (April 2002): 1–24.

———. "The Personality of Power: The Ideology of Slaves in the Natchez District and the Delta of Mississippi, 1830–1865." Ph.D. diss., Columbia University, 1999.

———. "Slaves, Emancipation, and the Powers of War: Views from the Natchez District of Mississippi." In *The War Was You and Me: Civilians in the American Civil War*, edited by Joan E. Cashin, 60–84. Princeton: Princeton University Press, 2002.

Kedourie, Elie. *Nationalism*. 4th ed. Oxford: Blackwell, 1993.

Kenzer, Robert. *Kinship and Neighborhood in a Southern Community: Orange County, North Carolina, 1849–1881*. Knoxville: University of Tennessee Press, 1987.

Kertzer, David I. *Ritual, Politics, and Power*. New Haven: Yale University Press, 1988.

Kierner, Cynthia A. *Beyond the Household: Women's Place in the Early South, 1700–1835*. Ithaca: Cornell University Press, 1998.

King, Wilma. *Stolen Childhood: Slave Youth in Nineteenth-Century America*. Bloomington: Indiana University Press, 1995.

Klingberg, Frank W. *The Southern Claims Commission*. Berkeley: University of California Press, 1955.

Kolchin, Peter. *American Slavery, 1619–1817*. Rev. ed. New York: Hill and Wang, 2003.

———. "Reevaluating the Antebellum Slave Community: A Comparative Perspective." *Journal of American History* 70 (December 1983): 579–601.

———. *Unfree Labor: American Slavery and Russian Serfdom*. Cambridge: Harvard University Press, 1987.

Kulikoff, Allan. *The Agrarian Roots of American Capitalism*. Charlottesville: University Press of Virginia, 1992.

———. "The Origins of Afro-American Society in Tidewater Maryland and Virginia, 1700–1790." *William and Mary Quarterly*, 3rd ser., 35 (April 1978): 226–59.

———. *Tobacco and Slaves: The Development of Southern Cultures in the Chesapeake, 1680–1800*. Chapel Hill: University of North Carolina Press, 1986.

Kuznesof, Elizabeth A. "Sexual Politics, Race, and Bastard-Bearing in Nineteenth Century Brazil: A Question of Culture or Power?" *Journal of Family History* 16 (July 1991): 241–60.

Larson, Kate C. *Bound for the Promised Land: Harriet Tubman, Portrait of an American Hero*. New York: Random House, 2004.

Laslett, Peter. "Household and Family on the Slave Plantations of the U.S.A." In *Family Life and Illicit Love in Earlier Generations: Essays in Historical Sociology*, 233–60. Cambridge: Cambridge University Press, 1977.

Le Goff, Jacques. *History and Memory*. Translated by Steven Rendell and Elizabeth Claman. New York: Columbia University Press, 1992.

Levine, Lawrence W. *Black Culture and Black Consciousness: Afro-American Folk Thought from Slavery to Freedom*. Oxford: Oxford University Press, 1977.

Lichtenstein, Alex. "'That Disposition to Theft, with Which They Have Been Branded': Moral Economy, Slave Management, and the Law." *Journal of Social History* 21 (Spring 1988): 413–40.

Litwack, Leon F. *Been in the Storm So Long: The Aftermath of Slavery*. New York: Vintage, 1980.

Loyal, Stephen. *The Sociology of Anthony Giddens*. London: Pluto, 2003.

Lukács, Georg. *History and Class Consciousness: Studies in Marxist Dialectics*. Translated by Rodney Livingstone. Cambridge: MIT Press, 1971.

Mallon, Florencia. *Peasant and Nation: The Making of Postcolonial Mexico and Peru*. Berkeley: University of California Press, 1995.

Malone, Ann Paton. *Sweet Chariot: Slave Family and Household Structure in Nineteenth-Century Louisiana*. Chapel Hill: University of North Carolina Press, 1992.

Manfra, Jo Ann, and Robert Dykstra. "Serial Marriage and the Origins of the Black Stepfamily: The Rowanty Evidence." *Journal of American History* 72 (June 1985): 18–44.

Marshall, Woodville K. "Provision Ground and Plantation Labor in Four Windward Islands: Competition for Resources during Slavery." In *Cultivation and Culture: Labor and the Shaping of Slave Life in the Americas*, edited by Ira Berlin and Philip D. Morgan, 203–20. Charlottesville: University Press of Virginia, 1993.

Martin, John D. *Divided Mastery: Slave Hiring in the Antebellum South*. Cambridge: Harvard University Press, 2004.

Marx, Karl. *A Critical Analysis of Capitalist Production*. Vol. 1 of *Capital: A Critique of Political Economy*. Edited by Friedrich Engels. Translated by Samuel Moore and Edward Aveling. 1887. Reprint, New York: International Publishers, 1967.

Mathew, William M. *Edmund Ruffin and the Crisis of Slavery in the Old South: The Failure of Agricultural Reform*. Athens: University of Georgia Press, 1988.

Mathews, Donald G. *Religion in the Old South*. Chicago: University of Chicago Press, 1977.

Mattoso, Kátia M. de Queirós. *To Be a Slave in Brazil, 1550–1888*. Translated by Arthur Goldhammer. New Brunswick, N.J.: Rutgers University Press, 1991.

May, Robert E. *John A. Quitman: Old South Crusader*. Baton Rouge: Louisiana State University Press, 1985.

McCormick, Richard P. *The Second American Party System: Party Formation in the Jacksonian Era*. 1966. Reprint, New York: Norton, 1973.

McCurry, Stephanie. *Masters of Small Worlds: Yeoman Households, Gender Relations, and the Political Culture of the Antebellum South Carolina Low Country*. New York: Oxford University Press, 1995.

McDonald, Roderick A. *The Economy and Material Culture of Slaves: Goods and Chattels on the Sugar Plantations of Jamaica and Louisiana*. Baton Rouge: Louisiana State University Press, 1993.

McDonnell, Lawrence T. "Money Knows No Master: Market Relations and the American Slave Community." In *Developing Dixie: Modernization in a Traditional Society*, edited by Winfred B. Moore Jr., Joseph F. Tripp, and Lyon G. Tyler Jr., 31–44. Westport, Conn.: Greenwood, 1988.

McKibben, Davidson B. "Negro Slave Insurrection in Mississippi, 1800–1865." *Journal of Negro History* 34 (January 1949): 73–90.

McMillen, Sally G. *Motherhood in the Old South: Pregnancy, Childbirth, and Infant Rearing*. Baton Rouge: Louisiana State University Press, 1990.

McPherson, James M. *Battle Cry of Freedom: The Civil War Era*. New York: Oxford University Press, 1988.

———. *The Negro's Civil War: How American Blacks Felt and Acted During the War for the Union*. 1965. Reprint, New York: Ballantine, 1991.

Metcalf, Alida C. "Searching for the Slave Family in Colonial Brazil: A Reconstruction from São Paulo." *Journal of Family History* 16 (July 1991): 283–97.

Metzer, Jacob. "Rational Management, Modern Business Practices, and Economies of Scale in Antebellum Southern Plantations." In *Markets and Production*, edited by Robert W. Fogel and Stanley L. Engerman, 191–215. New York: Norton, 1992.

Miles, Edwin A. *Jacksonian Democracy in Mississippi*. Chapel Hill: University of North Carolina Press, 1960.

———. "The Mississippi State Insurrection Scare of 1835." *Journal of Negro History* 42 (January 1957): 48–60.

Miller, Steven F. "Plantation Labor Organization and Slave Life on the Cotton Frontier: The Alabama-Mississippi Black Belt, 1815–1840." In *Cultivation and Culture: Labor and the Shaping of Slave Life in the Americas*, edited by Ira Berlin and Philip D. Morgan, 155–69. Charlottesville: University Press of Virginia, 1993.

Mintz, Sidney W. *Caribbean Transformations*. 1974. Reprint, New York: Columbia University Press, 1989.

———. *Sweetness and Power: The Place of Sugar in Modern History*. New York: Viking, 1985.

Mohr, Clarence L. *On the Threshold of Freedom: Masters and Slaves in Civil War Georgia*. Athens: University of Georgia Press, 1986.

Moitt, Bernard. *Women and Slavery in the French Antilles, 1635–1848*. Bloomington: University of Indiana Press, 2001.

Montgomery, William E. *Under Their Own Vine and Fig Tree: The African-American Church in the South, 1865–1900*. Baton Rouge: Louisiana State University Press, 1993.

Morgan, Jennifer L. *Laboring Women: Reproduction and Gender in New World Slavery*. Philadelphia: University of Pennsylvania Press, 2004.

Morgan, Lynda J. *Emancipation in Virginia's Tobacco Belt, 1850–1870*. Athens: University of Georgia Press, 1992.

Morgan, Philip D. "The Ownership of Property by Slaves in the Mid-Nineteenth-Century Low Country." *Journal of Southern History* 49 (August 1983): 399–420.

———. *Slave Counterpoint: Black Culture in the Eighteenth-Century Chesapeake and Lowcountry*. Chapel Hill: University of North Carolina Press, 1998.

———. "Work and Culture: The Task System and the World of Lowcountry Blacks, 1700–1880." *William and Mary Quarterly*, 3rd ser., 39 (October 1982): 563–99.

Moore, John Hebron. *Agriculture in Ante-Bellum Mississippi*. New York: Bookman, 1958.

——. *Andrew Brown and Cypress Lumbering in the Old Southwest*. Baton Rouge: Louisiana State University Press, 1967.

——. *The Emergence of the Cotton Kingdom in the Old Southwest: Mississippi, 1770–1860*. Baton Rouge: Louisiana State University Press, 1988.

——. "Simon Gray, Riverman: A Slave Who Was Almost Free." *Mississippi Valley Historical Review* 49 (December 1962): 472–84.

Morris, Christopher. "The Articulation of Two Worlds: The Master-Slave Relationship Reconsidered." *Journal of American History* 85 (December 1998): 982–1007.

——. *Becoming Southern: The Evolution of a Way of Life, Warren County and Vicksburg, Mississippi, 1770–1860*. New York: Oxford University Press, 1995.

——. "An Event in Community Organization: The Mississippi Insurrection Scare of 1835." *Journal of Social History* 22 (Fall 1988): 93–111.

——. "Within the Slave Cabin: Violence in Mississippi Slave Families." In *Over the Threshold: Intimate Violence in Early America*, edited by Christine Daniels and Michael V. Kennedy, 268–86. New York: Routledge, 1999.

Morris, Richard B. "The Measure of Bondage in the Slave States." *Mississippi Valley Historical Review* 41 (September 1954): 219–40.

Morris, Thomas D. *Free Men All: The Personal Liberty Laws of the North, 1780–1861*. Baltimore: Johns Hopkins University Press, 1975.

——. *Southern Slavery and the Law, 1619–1860*. Chapel Hill: University of North Carolina Press, 1996.

Morrissey, Marietta. *Slave Women in the New World: Gender Stratification in the Caribbean*. Lawrence: University Press of Kansas, 1989.

Mullin, Michael. *Africa in America: Slave Acculturation and Resistance in the American South and the British Caribbean, 1736–1831*. Urbana: University of Illinois Press, 1992.

——. "Slave Economic Strategies: Food, Markets and Property." In *From Chattel Slaves to Wage Slaves: The Dynamics of Labour Bargaining in the Americas*, edited by Mary Turner, 68–78. Kingston, Jamaica: Randle, 1995.

Munn, Nancy D. "The Cultural Anthropology of Time." *Annual Review of Anthropology* 21 (1992): 93–123.

Nash, A. E. K. "Fairness and Formalism in the Trials of Blacks in the State Supreme Courts of the Old South." *Virginia Law Review* 56 (February 1970): 64–100.

——. "A More Equitable Past? Southern Supreme Courts and the Protection of the Antebellum Negro." *North Carolina Law Review* 48 (February 1970): 197–242.

Oakes, James. *The Ruling Race: A History of American Slaveholders*. New York: Knopf, 1982.

——. *Slavery and Freedom: An Interpretation of the Old South*. New York: Knopf, 1990.

O'Brien, Michael. *Conjectures of Order: Intellectual Life in the American South, 1810–1860*. 2 vols. Chapel Hill: University of North Carolina Press, 2005.

——. *The Idea of the American South, 1920–1941*. Baltimore: Johns Hopkins University Press, 1979.

Oliver, John W. "History of the Civil War Military Pensions, 1861–1865." *Bulletin of the University of Wisconsin: History Series* 4 (1917): 1–120.

Olsen, Christopher J. *Political Culture and Secession in Mississippi: Masculinity, Honor, and the Antiparty Tradition, 1830–1860.* New York: Oxford University Press, 2000.

Olson, John F. "The Occupational Structure of Southern Plantations during the Late Antebellum Era." In *Markets and Production*, edited by Robert W. Fogel and Stanley L. Engerman, 137–69. New York: Norton, 1992.

Olwell, Robert L. " 'Loose, Idle, and Disorderly': Slave Women in the Eighteenth-Century Charleston Marketplace." In *More Than Chattel: Black Women and Slavery in the Americas*, edited by David Barry Gaspar and Darlene Clark Hine, 97–110. Bloomington: Indiana University Press, 1996.

——. *Masters, Slaves, and Subjects: The Culture of Power in the South Carolina Low Country, 1740–1790.* Ithaca: Cornell University Press, 1998.

——. " 'A Reckoning of Accounts': Patriarchy, Market Relations, and Control on Henry Laurens's Lowcountry Plantations, 1762–1785." In *Working Toward Freedom: Slave Society and Domestic Economy in the American South*, edited by Larry E. Hudson Jr., 33–52. Rochester, N.Y.: University of Rochester Press, 1994.

Olwig, Karen F. *Cultural Adaptation and Resistance on St. John: Three Centuries of Afro-Caribbean Life.* Gainesville: University of Florida Press, 1987.

——. "Finding a Place for the Slave Family: Historical Anthropological Perspectives." *Folk* 23 (1981): 359–86.

——. "Women, 'Matrifocality,' and Systems of Exchange." *Ethnohistory* 28 (Winter 1981): 59–78.

Orloff, Ann S. *The Politics of Pensions: A Comparative Analysis of Britain, Canada, and the United States, 1880–1940.* Madison: University of Wisconsin Press, 1993.

Oser, Charles E., Jr. "Toward a Theory of Power for Historical Archaeology: Plantations and Space." In *The Recovery of Meaning: Historical Archaeology in the Eastern United States*, edited by Mark P. Leone and Parker B. Potter Jr., 313–43. Washington, D.C.: Smithsonian Institution Press, 1988.

Owens, Harry P., ed. *Perspectives and Irony in American Slavery.* Jackson: University Press of Mississippi, 1976.

Owens, Leslie H. *This Species of Property: Slave Life and Culture in the Old South.* New York: Oxford University Press, 1976.

Ownby, Ted. *American Dreams in Mississippi: Consumers, Poverty, and Culture.* Chapel Hill: University of North Carolina Press, 1999.

Painter, Nell Irvin. *Southern History across the Color Line.* Chapel Hill: University of North Carolina Press, 2002.

Parent, Anthony S., Jr. *Foul Means: The Formation of a Slave Society in Virginia, 1660–1740.* Chapel Hill: University of North Carolina Press, 2003.

Parramore, Thomas C. "Covenant in Jerusalem." In *Nat Turner: A Slave Rebellion in History and Memory*, edited by Kenneth S. Greenberg, 58–76. New York: Oxford University Press, 2003.

——. *Southampton County, Virginia*. Charlottesville: University Press of Virginia, 1978.

Patterson, Orlando. *The Sociology of Slavery: An Analysis of the Origins, Development, and Structure of Negro Slave Society in Jamaica*. London: MacGibbon and Kee, 1967.

Pearson, Edward A. " 'A Countryside Full of Flames': A Reconsideration of the Stono Rebellion and Slave Rebelliousness in the Early Eighteenth Century South Carolina Lowcountry." In *Stono: Documenting and Interpreting a Southern Slave Revolt*, edited by Mark M. Smith, 87–107. Columbia: University of South Carolina Press, 2005.

Penningroth, Dylan C. *The Claims of Kinfolk: African American Property and Community in the Nineteenth-Century South*. Chapel Hill: University of North Carolina Press, 2003.

——. "My People, My People: The Dynamics of Community in Southern Slavery." In *New Studies in the History of American Slavery*, edited by Edward E. Baptist and Stephanie M. H. Camp, 166–76. Athens: University of Georgia Press, 2006.

——. "Slavery, Freedom, and Social Claims to Property among African Americans in Liberty County, Georgia, 1850–1880." *Journal of American History* 84 (September 1997): 1–28.

Peterson, Merrill D. *The Great Triumvirate: Webster, Clay, and Calhoun*. New York: Oxford University Press, 1987.

Phillips, U. B. *American Negro Slavery: A Survey of the Supply, Employment, and Control of Negro Labor as Determined by the Plantation Regime*. 1918. Reprint, Baton Rouge: Louisiana State University Press, 1990.

——. *Life and Labor in the Old South*. New York: Grosset and Dunlap, 1929.

Pitts, Walter F., Jr. *Old Ship of Zion: The Afro-Baptist Ritual in the African Diaspora*. New York: Oxford University Press, 1993.

Powell, Lawrence N. "Correcting for Fraud: A Quantitative Reassessment of the Mississippi Ratification Election of 1868." *Journal of Southern History* 55 (November 1989): 633–58.

——. *New Masters: Northern Planters during the Civil War and Reconstruction*. New Haven: Yale University Press, 1980.

Powell, Lawrence N., and Michael Wayne. "Self-Interest and the Decline of Confederate Nationalism." In *The Old South in the Crucible of War*, edited by Harry P. Owens and James J. Cooke, 29–45. Jackson: University Press of Mississippi, 1983.

Pred, Allan. "Place as Historically Contingent Process: Structuration and the Time-Geography of Becoming Places." *Annals of the Association of American Geographers* 74 (June 1984): 279–97.

Pritchett, Jonathan B. "Quantitative Estimates of the United States Interregional Slave Trade, 1820–1860." *Journal of Economic History* 61 (June 2001): 467–75.

Quarles, Benjamin. *The Negro in the Civil War*. Boston: Little, Brown, 1953.

Raboteau, Albert J. *Slave Religion: The "Invisible Institution" in the Antebellum South*. Oxford: Oxford University Press, 1978.

Rainwater, Percy L. *Mississippi: Storm Center of Secession, 1856–1861*. 1938. Reprint, New York: Da Capo, 1969.

Rawick, George P. *From Sundown to Sunup: The Making of the Black Community*. Ser. 1, vol. 1 of *The American Slave: A Composite Autobiography*, edited by George P. Rawick. Westport, Conn.: Greenwood, 1972.

Rawls, John. *A Theory of Justice*. Cambridge: Harvard University Press, 1971.

Regosin, Elizabeth. *Freedom's Promise: Ex-Slave Families and Citizenship in the Age of Emancipation*. Charlottesville: University Press of Virginia, 2002.

Reidy, Joseph P. "Obligation and Right: Patterns of Labor, Subsistence, and Exchange in the Cotton Belt of Georgia, 1790–1860." In *Cultivation and Culture: Labor and the Shaping of Slave Life in the Americas*, edited by Ira Berlin and Philip D. Morgan, 138–54. Charlottesville: University Press of Virginia, 1993.

Remini, Robert V. "Henry Clay and the Natchez Connection." *Journal of Mississippi History* 54 (August 1992): 269–78.

Richardson, Joe M. *Christian Reconstruction: The American Missionary Association and Southern Blacks, 1861–1890*. Athens: University of Georgia Press, 1986.

Ripley, C. Peter. "The Black Family in Transition: Louisiana, 1860–1865." *Journal of Southern History* 41 (August 1975): 369–80.

———. *Slaves and Freedmen in Civil War Louisiana*. Baton Rouge: Louisiana State University Press, 1976.

Roark, James L. *Masters Without Slaves: Southern Planters in the Civil War and Reconstruction*. New York: Norton, 1977.

Robertson, Claire. "Africa into the Americas? Slavery and Women, the Family, and the Gender Division of Labor." In *More than Chattel: Black Women and Slavery in the Americas*, edited by David Barry Gaspar and Darlene Clark Hine, 9–20. Bloomington: Indiana University Press, 1996.

Robinson, Armstead L. *Bitter Fruits of Bondage: The Demise of Slavery and the Collapse of the Confederacy, 1861–1865*. Charlottesville: University of Virginia Press, 2005.

Roeber, A. G. "Authority, Law, and Custom: The Rituals of Court Day in Tidewater, Virginia, 1720–1750." *William and Mary Quarterly*, 3rd ser., 37 (January 1980): 29–52.

Rose, Willie Lee. *Rehearsal for Reconstruction: The Port Royal Experiment*. 1964. Reprint, London: Oxford University Press, 1976.

———. *Slavery and Freedom*. Edited by William W. Freehling. Oxford: Oxford University Press, 1982.

Rosengarten, Theodore. "*The Southern Agriculturalist* in an Age of Reform." In *Intellectual Life in Antebellum Charleston*, edited by Michael O'Brien and David Moltke-Hansen, 279–94. Knoxville: University of Tennessee Press, 1986.

Ross, Steven J. "Freed Soil, Freed Labor, Freed Men: John Eaton and the Davis Bend Experiment." *Journal of Southern History* 44 (May 1978): 213–32.

Rothman, Adam. *Slave Country: American Expansion and the Origins of the Deep South*. Cambridge: Harvard University Press, 2005.

Rothman, Joshua D. *Notorious in the Neighborhood: Sex and Families across the Color Line in Virginia, 1787–1861*. Chapel Hill: University of North Carolina Press, 2003.

Rothstein, Morton. "The Antebellum Plantation as a Business Enterprise: A Review of Scarborough's *The Overseer*." *Explorations in Entrepreneurial History* 6 (Fall 1968): 128–33.

———. "The Changing Social Networks and Investment Behavior of a Slaveholding Elite in the Antebellum South: Some Natchez 'Nabobs,' 1800–1860." In *Entrepreneurs in Cultural Context*, edited by Sidney M. Greenfield, Arnold Strickon, and Robert T. Aubey, 65–88. Albuquerque: University of New Mexico Press, 1979.

Rousseau, Jean-Jacques. *The Social Contract*. Translated by Maurice Cranston. London: Penguin, 1968.

Rucker, Walter C. *The River Flows On: Black Resistance, Culture, and Identity Formation in Early America*. Baton Rouge: Louisiana State University Press, 2005.

Russell, Marion J. "American Slave Discontent in the Records of the High Courts." *Journal of Negro History* 31 (October 1946): 411–34.

Russell, Thomas D. "Slave Auctions on the Courthouse Steps: Court Sales of Slaves in Antebellum South Carolina." In *Slavery and the Law*, edited by Paul Finkelman, 329–64. Madison, Wis.: Madison House, 1997.

Russell-Wood, A. J. R. *Slavery and Freedom in Colonial Brazil*. Rev. ed. Oxford: Oneworld, 2002.

Saville, Julie. *The Work of Reconstruction: From Slave to Wage Laborer in South Carolina, 1860–1870*. Cambridge: Cambridge University Press, 1994.

Scarborough, William K. "Heartland of the Cotton Kingdom." In *History of Mississippi*, edited by Richard A. McLemore, 1:310–51. Hattiesburg: University and College Press of Mississippi, 1973.

———. "Lords or Capitalists? The Natchez Nabobs in Comparative Perspective." *Journal of Mississippi History* 54 (August 1992): 229–67.

———. *Masters of the Big House: Elite Slaveholders of the Mid-Nineteenth-Century South*. Baton Rouge: Louisiana State University Press, 2003.

———. *The Overseer: Plantation Management in the Old South*. 1966. Reprint, Athens: University of Georgia Press, 1984.

———. "Slavery—The White Man's Burden." In *Perspectives and Irony in American Slavery*, edited by Harry P. Owens, 103–35. Jackson: University Press of Mississippi, 1976.

Schlesinger, Arthur M., Jr. *The Age of Jackson*. 1945. Reprint, Boston: Little, Brown, 1953.

Schlotterbeck, John T. "The Internal Economy of Slavery in Rural Piedmont Virginia." In *The Slaves' Economy: Independent Production by Slaves in the Americas*, edited by Ira Berlin and Philip D. Morgan, 170–81. London: Cass, 1991.

Schwalm, Leslie A. *A Hard Fight for We: Women's Transition from Slavery to Freedom in South Carolina*. Urbana: University of Illinois Press, 1997.

Schwartz, Marie J. *Born in Bondage: Growing Up Enslaved in the Antebellum South.* Cambridge: Harvard University Press, 2000.

Schwartz, Stuart B. *Sugar Plantations in the Formation of Brazilian Society: Bahia, 1550–1835.* Cambridge: Cambridge University Press, 1985.

Schwarz, Philip J. *Twice Condemned: Slaves and the Criminal Laws of Virginia.* Baton Rouge: Louisiana State University Press, 1988.

Schweninger, Loren. *Black Property Owners in the South, 1790–1915.* Urbana: University of Illinois Press, 1990.

———. "Slave Independence and Enterprise in South Carolina, 1780–1865." *South Carolina Historical Magazine* 93 (April 1992): 101–25.

———. "The Underside of Slavery: Internal Economy, Self-Hire, and Quasi-Freedom in Virginia, 1750–1865." *Slavery and Abolition* 12 (September 1991): 1–22.

Scott, James C. *Domination and the Arts of Resistance: Hidden Transcripts.* New Haven: Yale University Press, 1990.

———. *Weapons of the Weak: Everyday Forms of Peasant Resistance.* New Haven: Yale University Press, 1985.

Shaffer, Donald R. *After the Glory: The Struggles of Black Civil War Veterans.* Lawrence: University Press of Kansas, 2004.

Shaw, Stephanie J. "Mothering under Slavery in the Antebellum South." In *Mothering: Ideology, Experience, and Agency,* edited by Evelyn N. Glenn, Grace Chang, and Linda R. Forcey, 237–58. New York: Routledge, 1994.

Shenton, James P. *Robert John Walker: A Politician from Jackson to Lincoln.* New York: Columbia University Press, 1961.

Sidbury, James. *Plowshares into Swords: Race, Rebellion, and Identity in Gabriel's Virginia, 1730–1810.* Cambridge: Cambridge University Press, 1997.

Sitterson, J. Carlyle. *Sugar Country: The Cane Sugar Industry in the South, 1753–1950.* Lexington: University of Kentucky Press, 1953.

———. "The William J. Minor Plantations: A Study in Ante-Bellum Absentee Ownership." *Journal of Southern History* 9 (February 1943): 59–74.

Skocpol, Theda. *Protecting Soldiers and Mothers: The Political Origins of Social Policy in the United States.* Cambridge: Harvard University Press, 1992.

Smith, Julia Floyd. *Slavery and Rice Culture in Low Country Georgia, 1750–1860.* Knoxville: University of Tennessee Press, 1985.

Smith, Mark M. *Listening to Nineteenth-Century America.* Chapel Hill: University of North Carolina Press, 2001.

———. *Mastered by the Clock: Time, Slavery, and Freedom in the American South.* Chapel Hill: University of North Carolina Press, 1997.

Sobel, Mechal. *Trabelin' On: The Slave Journey to an Afro-Baptist Faith.* Princeton: Princeton University Press, 1988.

Soltow, Lee. *Men and Wealth in the United States, 1850–1870.* New Haven: Yale University Press, 1975.

Sommerville, Diane M. *Rape and Race in the Nineteenth-Century South*. Chapel Hill: University of North Carolina Press, 2004.

Sparks, Randy J. *On Jordan's Stormy Banks: Evangelicalism in Mississippi, 1773–1876*. Athens: University of Georgia Press, 1994.

Stampp, Kenneth M. *The Peculiar Institution: Slavery in the Ante-Bellum South*. 1956. Reprint, New York: Vintage, 1989.

Starobin, Robert S. *Industrial Slavery in the Old South*. London: Oxford University Press, 1970.

Steckel, Richard H. *The Economics of U.S. Slave and Southern White Fertility*. New York: Garland, 1985.

———. "Slave Marriage and the Family." *Journal of Family History* 5 (Winter 1980): 406–21.

Stein, Stanley. *Vassouras: A Brazilian Coffee County, 1850–1900*. 1957. Reprint, Princeton: Princeton University Press, 1985.

Stevenson, Brenda E. "Distress and Discord in Virginia Slave Families, 1830–1860." In *In Joy and In Sorrow: Women, Family and Marriage in the Victorian South*, edited by Carol Bleser, 103–24. New York: Oxford University Press, 1990.

———. *Life in Black and White: Family and Community in the Slave South*. New York: Oxford University Press, 1996.

Stoll, Steven. *Larding the Lean Earth: Soil and Society in Nineteenth-Century America*. New York: Hill and Wang, 2002.

Stone, James H. "Black Leadership in the Old South: The Slave Drivers of the Rice Kingdom." Ph.D. diss., Florida State University, 1976.

Strickland, John Scott. "Traditional Culture and Moral Economy: Social and Economic Change in the South Carolina Low Country, 1865–1910." In *The Countryside in the Age of Capitalist Transformation: Essays in the Social History of Rural America*, edited by Steven Hahn and Jonathan Prude, 141–78. Chapel Hill: University of North Carolina Press, 1985.

Stuckey, Sterling. *Slave Culture: Nationalist Theory and the Foundations of Black America*. New York: Oxford University Press, 1987.

Swearingen, Mack. "Thirty Years of a Mississippi Plantation: Charles Whitmore of Montpelier." *Journal of Southern History* 1 (May 1935): 198–211.

Sweet, James H. *Recreating Africa: Culture, Kinship, and Religion in the African-Portuguese World, 1441–1770*. Chapel Hill: University of North Carolina Press, 2003.

Sydnor, Charles S. *A Gentleman of the Old Natchez Region: Benjamin L. C. Wailes*. Durham, N.C.: Duke University Press, 1938.

———. *Slavery in Mississippi*. 1933. Reprint, Baton Rouge: Louisiana State University Press, 1966.

———. "The Southerner and the Laws." *Journal of Southern History* 6 (February 1940): 3–23.

Tadman, Michael. *Speculators and Slaves: Masters, Traders, and Slaves in the Old South*. Madison: University of Wisconsin Press, 1989.

Taylor, Charles. *Ethics of Authenticity*. Cambridge: Harvard University Press, 2005.

Taylor, William Banks. "Southern Yankees: Wealth, High Society, and Political Economy in the Late Antebellum Natchez Region." *Journal of Mississippi History* 59 (1997): 97–121.

Temin, Peter. *The Jacksonian Economy*. New York: Norton, 1969.

Thomas, Brian W. "Power and Community: The Archaeology of Slavery at the Hermitage Plantation." *American Antiquity* 63 (October 1998): 531–51.

Tolbert, Lisa C. *Constructing Townscapes: Space and Society in Antebellum Tennessee*. Chapel Hill: University of North Carolina Press, 1999.

Tomich, Dale. *Slavery in the Circuit of Sugar: Martinique and the World Economy, 1830–1848*. Baltimore: Johns Hopkins University Press, 1990.

———. *Through the Prism of Slavery: Labor, Capital, and World Economy*. Lanham, Md.: Rowman and Littlefield, 2004.

———. "*Une Petite Guinée*: Provision Ground and Plantation in Martinique, 1830–1848." In *Cultivation and Culture: Labor and the Shaping of Slave Life in the Americas*, edited by Ira Berlin and Philip D. Morgan, 221–42. Charlottesville: University Press of Virginia, 1993.

Touchstone, Blake. "Planters and Slave Religion in the Deep South." In *Masters and Slaves in the House of the Lord: Race and Religion in the American South*, edited by John B. Boles, 99–126. Lexington: University Press of Kentucky, 1988.

Trudeau, Noah A. *Like Men of War: Black Troops in the Civil War, 1862–1865*. Boston: Little, Brown, 1998.

———. "Proven Themselves in Every Respect to Be Men: Black Cavalry in the Civil War." In *Black Soldiers in Blue: African American Troops in the Civil War Era*, edited by John David Smith, 276–305. Chapel Hill: University of North Carolina Press, 2002.

Trussell, James, and Richard Steckel. "The Age of Slaves at Menarche and Their First Birth." *Journal of Interdisciplinary History* 8 (Winter 1978): 477–505.

Tuan, Yi-Fu. *Space and Place: The Perspective of Experience*. Minneapolis: University Press of Minnesota, 1977.

Turner, Mary, ed. *From Chattel Slaves to Wage Slaves: The Dynamics of Labour Bargaining in the Americas*. Kingston, Jamaica: Randle, 1995.

Tushnet, Mark V. *The American Law of Slavery, 1810–1860: Considerations of Humanity and Interest*. Princeton: Princeton University Press, 1981.

Upton, Dell. "Black and White Landscapes in Eighteenth Century Virginia." *Places: A Quarterly Journal of Environmental Design* 2 (Winter 1985): 59–72.

———. "New Views of the Virginia Landscape." *Virginia Magazine of History and Biography* 96 (October 1988): 403–70.

Van Deburg, William L. *The Slave Drivers: Black Agricultural Labor Supervisors in the Antebellum South*. 1979. Reprint, New York: Oxford University Press, 1988.

Vlach, John M. *Back of the Big House: The Architecture of Plantation Slavery*. Chapel Hill: University of North Carolina Press, 1993.

Wade, Richard C. *Slavery in the Cities: The South, 1820–1860*. London: Oxford University Press, 1964.

———. *Urban Frontier: The Rise of Western Cities*. Cambridge: Harvard University Press, 1959.

Waldrep, Christopher. *Roots of Disorder: Race and Criminal Justice in the American South, 1817–80*. Urbana: University of Illinois Press, 1998.

———. *Vicksburg's Long Shadow: The Civil War Legacy of Race and Remembrance*. Lanham, Md.: Rowman and Littlefield, 2005.

Walker, David E. *No More, No More: Slavery and Cultural Resistance in Havana and New Orleans*. Minneapolis: University of Minnesota Press, 2004.

Walsh, Lorena S. *From Calabar to Carter's Grove: The History of a Virginia Slave Community*. Charlottesville: University Press of Virginia, 1997.

Wayne, Michael. *Death of an Overseer: Reopening a Murder Investigation from the Plantation South*. New York: Oxford University Press, 2001.

———. *The Reshaping of Plantation Society: The Natchez District, 1860–1880*. Baton Rouge: Louisiana State University Press, 1983.

Weaver, Herbert. *Mississippi Farmers, 1850–1860*. Nashville: Vanderbilt University Press, 1945.

Webber, Thomas L. *Deep Like the Rivers: Education in the Slave Quarter Community, 1831–1865*. New York: Norton, 1978.

Weiner, Marli F. *Mistresses and Slaves: Plantation Women in South Carolina, 1830–1880*. Urbana: University of Illinois Press, 1998.

West, Emily. *Chains of Love: Slave Couples in Antebellum South Carolina*. Urbana: University of Illinois Press, 2004.

———. "The Debate on the Strength of Slave Families: South Carolina and the Importance of Cross-Plantation Marriages." *Journal of American Studies* 33 (August 1999): 221–41.

Whartenby, Franklee G. *Land and Labor Productivity in United States Cotton Production, 1800–1840*. New York: Arno, 1977.

Wharton, Vernon L. *The Negro in Mississippi, 1865–1890*. 1947. Reprint, New York: Harper and Row, 1965.

White, Deborah Gray. *Ar'n't I a Woman? Female Slaves in the Plantation South*. New York: Norton, 1985.

———. "Female Slaves: Sex Roles and Status in the Antebellum Plantation South." *Journal of Family History* 3 (Fall 1983): 248–61.

White, Shane. *Somewhat More Independent: The End of Slavery in New York City, 1777–1810*. Athens: University of Georgia Press, 1991.

White, Shane, and Graham White. *The Sounds of Slavery: Discovering African American History through Songs, Sermons, and Speech*. Boston: Beacon, 2005.

Whites, LeeAnn. *The Civil War as a Crisis in Gender: Augusta, Georgia, 1860–1890*. Athens: University of Georgia Press, 1995.

Wiley, Bell I. *The Plain People of the Confederacy*. 1943. Reprint, Chicago: Quadrangle, 1963.

———. *Southern Negroes, 1861–1865*. 1938. Reprint, Baton Rouge: Louisiana State University Press, 1965.

Williams, Lou F. *The Great South Carolina Ku Klux Klan Trials, 1871–1872*. Athens: University of Georgia Press, 1996.

Wimmer, Linda. "Ethnicity and Family Formation among Slaves on Tobacco Farms in the Bahian Recôncavo, 1698–1820." In *Enslaving Connections: Changing Cultures of Africa and Brazil during the Era of Slavery*, edited by José C. Curto and Paul E. Lovejoy, 149–62. New York: Humanity, 2004.

Wish, Harvey. "The Slave Insurrection Panic of 1856." *Journal of Southern History* 5 (May 1939): 206–22.

Wood, Betty. " 'Never on a Sunday?' Slavery and the Sabbath in Lowcountry Georgia 1750–1830." In *From Chattel Slaves to Wage Slaves: The Dynamics of Labour Bargaining in the Americas*, edited by Mary Turner, 79–96. Kingston, Jamaica: Randle, 1995.

———. *Women's Work, Men's Work: The Informal Slave Economies of Lowcountry Georgia*. Athens: University of Georgia Press, 1995.

Wood, Kirsten E. *Masterful Women: Slaveholding Widows from the American Revolution through the Civil War*. Chapel Hill: University of North Carolina Press, 2004.

Woodward, C. Vann. "History from Slave Sources: A Review Essay." *American Historical Review* 79 (April 1974): 470–81.

———. "The Search for Southern Identity." In *The Burden of Southern History*, 3rd ed., 3–25. Baton Rouge: Louisiana State University Press, 1993.

Wooster, Ralph A. *The People in Power: Courthouse and Statehouse in the Lower South, 1850–1860*. Knoxville: University of Tennessee Press, 1969.

Wright, Gavin. *The Political Economy of the Cotton South: Households, Markets, and Wealth in the Nineteenth Century*. New York: Norton, 1978.

———. "Slavery and the Cotton Boom." *Explorations in Economic History* 12 (October 1975): 439–51.

Wyatt-Brown, Bertram. "The Ideal Typology and Ante-Bellum Southern History: A Testing of a New Approach." *Societas* 5 (Winter 1975): 1–29.

Yetman, Norman R. "The Background of the Slave Narrative Collection." *American Quarterly* 19 (Autumn 1967): 534–53.

Young, Amy L., Michael Tuma, and Cliff Jenkins. "The Role of Hunting to Cope with Risk at Saragossa Plantation, Natchez, Mississippi." *American Anthropologist*, n.s., 103 (September 2001): 692–704.

Young, Jeffrey R. *Domesticating Slavery: The Master Class in Georgia and South Carolina, 1670–1837*. Chapel Hill: University of North Carolina Press, 1999.

Index

Note: In entries for plantations, names of plantation owners appear in parentheses. In modifications, names of plantation owners appear in parentheses only if the plantation is not included in the index as an entry.